The Aging of the American Work Force

LABOR ECONOMICS AND POLICY SERIES

The Aging of the American Work Force

PROBLEMS, PROGRAMS, POLICIES

Edited by Irving Bluestone,
Rhonda J. V. Montgomery,
and John D. Owen

WITH A FOREWORD BY
ANN McLAUGHLIN, SECRETARY OF LABOR

WAYNE STATE UNIVERSITY PRESS
DETROIT 1990

94 93 92 91 90 5 4 3 2 1

Library of Congress Cataloging-in-Publication Data

The Aging of the American work force : problems, programs, policies / edited by Irving Bluestone, Rhonda J. V. Montgomery, and John D. Owen; with a foreword by Ann McLaughlin.
p. cm. — (Labor economics and policy series)
Includes bibliographies and index.
ISBN 0–8143–2174–7 (alk. paper). — ISBN 0–8143–2175–5 (pbk. : alk. paper)
1. Age and employment—United States. I. Bluestone, Irving. II. Montgomery, Rhonda J. V. III. Owen, John D. IV. Series.
HD6280.A447 1990
331.3′94′0973—dc19 89 5572
CIP

The editors wish to thank the U.S. Department of Labor for assisting in the publication of this volume.

Contents

Foreword

During its short lifetime, our country has experienced some quite remarkable changes in the makeup of its population. One of the most consequential of these is what we now often refer to as the aging of our work force. In a relatively few decades the average age of American workers has increased significantly as the "baby boom" generation has matured and the pool of young entry-level workers has been diminished. But while the life span of Americans has been lengthening, there has been a progressive trend toward earlier and earlier departures from the labor force. In other words, people are living longer but spending a shorter period of their lives as active participants in our economy.

These demographic changes, when considered in relation to still other changes in the broad economic and social context in which they have occurred, pose a number of challenges to our employers and unions as well as to our institutions of government. They concern matters of such overriding importance as health care, pension system solvency and retirement security, elder care, education and training for new jobs and new technologies, and the design of jobs and working conditions.

Of special interest to the Department of Labor in this era of global competition and economic restructuring is the imperative need to ensure the full use of *all* the nation's human resources to improve our productive capability and thereby sustain our economic growth and social progress. Without question, older workers constitute a vital part of our human resource potential. Employment policies and practices must be continually adjusted to ensure that older Americans are able to apply their talents, meet their economic and social needs, and make a contribution to our economy and our society. The solutions to these problems will involve all of us, whether as employers, union leaders, public servants, or merely concerned citizens.

The issues growing out of the aging of our population and work force are not without controversy. Differences among us in philosophy, values, and priorities necessarily lead to different prescriptions for dealing with the dilemmas of aging. But these are matters which can be resolved through discussion, debate, and compromise—processes which are the hallmark of our democratic political system. Consequently, one should not expect the views presented throughout this volume to elicit uniform agreement. But they do, at the very least, provide rich food for thought, for deliberation, and for debate, out of which will eventually come the answers which we all seek.

For my own part, I found the issues facing older workers to be so challenging that I created an internal Labor Department Task Force on Older Workers. This task force will study how to ensure full opportunity for all older Americans who wish to work, and how to encourage arrangements that ensure retirement security.

It has been a privilege for the Department of Labor to have contributed to the publication of this book, and it is my personal hope that its messages will be carefully considered by all its readers.

Ann McLaughlin
Secretary of Labor
March 1988

Contributors

Bo Adolfsson, labor counselor at the Swedish Embassy, Washington, D.C., also serves as the government-appointed chairman of the Social Insurance Delegation in Stockholm. Previously, he was the ombudsman in the Department of Negotiation for the Swedish Confederation of Trade Unions, responsible for all insurance programs covering trade union members, including private plans and collective agreements.

Judith K. Barr holds the Sc.D. degree from Johns Hopkins University. At Empire Blue Cross and Blue Shield, she directed a survey of employer attitudes and programs for the employee care-giver. At the New York Business Group on Health, where she is associate director, she is coordinating a study of employer, provider, and community needs for a country-wide central health information program. She is an adjunct assistant professor at New York University Graduate School of Public Administration.

Owen F. Bieber, president of the United Auto Workers Union, has been engaged in union work throughout his adult life. After serving in various capacities in his local union, he was appointed to the UAW Region ID staff and was elected director of the region in 1974. In 1980 he was elected vice president of the UAW and was director of its General Motors Department until his election as president in 1983.

Irving Bluestone, University Professor of Labor Studies and director of the Master of Arts in Industrial Relations program at Wayne State University, served in various capacities with the United Auto Workers Union, first in his local union and then as international representative and administrative assistant to President Walter P. Reuther. He retired from the UAW as vice president and director of its General Motors Department after thirty-eight years of UAW service.

Richard V. Burkhauser has written extensively on labor economics, income support policies, and older worker issues. Among his publications is *A Challenge to Social Security: The Changing Roles of Women and Men in American Society.* Dr. Burkhauser is professor of economics at Vanderbilt University. **Joseph F. Quinn,** chair of the department of economics at Boston College, often collaborates with Richard Burkhauser on studies of older worker behavior. His book on withdrawal patterns from career jobs will be published by the Upjohn Institute this year.

Robert L. Clark has served as principal investigator on numerous research projects examining issues related to an older work force, including age discrimination, early retirement, pension plans, and health care financing. He is the author of several books on these and other issues, including *Cost-Effective Pension Planning* (1982) and *Inflation and the Economic Well-Being of the Elderly* (1984). Dr. Clark is professor of economics at North Carolina State University.

Frank P. Doyle is senior vice president of General Electric's Corporate Relations Staff, with responsibility for employee relations, government relations, public relations, medical operations, and environmental programs. Mr. Doyle holds degrees from Notre Dame University and Rutgers University. He chaired the study on Work and Change for the Committee for Economic Development and served on the Secretary of Labor's Task Force on Worker Dislocation.

Douglas A. Fraser, University Professor of Labor Studies, Wayne State University, and president emeritus of the United Auto Workers Union, became active in his local union and held various elected offices. In 1951, UAW President Walter P. Reuther appointed him administrative assistant. He was elected regional director, vice president, and then president of the UAW. Since his retirement from the UAW in 1983, he has served as Jerry Wurf Fellow and Lecturer at the John F. Kennedy School, Harvard University, and as visiting professor at Columbia University.

David N. Gamse, director of the Worker Equity Department of the American Association of Retired Persons, helped establish the Worker Equity Department, which studies, analyzes, and disseminates information about America's changing work force; offers retirement planning; and, through employer partnerships, education programs, and litigation, works to ensure equal employment opportunity for older persons.

Mary Jablonski is the coauthor, with **Larry Rosenblum,** of "Productivity, Age, and Labor Composition Changes in the U.S.," published in the *Monthly Labor Review.* **Kent Kunze** is the coauthor of a paper, "Recent Changes in the Growth of U.S. Factor Productivity," in that journal. All three contributors are economists at the U.S. Department of Labor Bureau of Labor Statistics.

Ronald E. Kutscher, associate commissioner of the Bureau of Labor Statistics, U.S. Department of Labor, directs the Bureau's program of medium-term projections of the U.S. economy. His recent publications include *Labor Market Projections—Manufacturing Industries in Economic Dislocation and Job Loss* and "Overview and Implications of the Projections to 2000," *Monthly Labor Review* (September 1987). Mr. Kutscher is a member of the National Academy of Science's panel on Secondary School Education for the Changing Workplace. **Howard N. Fullerton, Jr.,** is a demographic statistician at the Bureau of Labor Statistics. He has written several papers on the subject of the aging work force, including a recent article in the *Monthly Labor Review*, "Labor Force Projections: 1986 to 2000."

Leon Lynch, international vice president for human affairs of the United Steelworkers of America, began his union career as a loader in a pipe mill in East Chicago, Indiana. An experienced negotiator for the Steelworkers, he has served on several occasions as a U.S. delegate to International Labor Organization conferences.

Olivia P. Maynard, the director of the Michigan Office of Services to the Aging, chaired the Governor's Task Force on Employment Opportunities for Older Citizens in 1987 and is presently chair of the Older Worker Advisory Committee of the state. She holds a master's degree in social work from the University of Michigan.

Olivia S. Mitchell has made many contributions to the study of the economics of aging, including a recent book, *Retirement, Pensions, and Social Security*, of which she is coauthor. Dr. Mitchell is associate professor of labor economics at the New York State School of Industrial and Labor Relations at Cornell University.

Rhonda J. V. Montgomery is director of the Institute of Gerontology and associate professor of sociology at Wayne State University. Dr. Montgomery has conducted research and published numerous articles on family relations and public policies for the elderly. She is coeditor of the journal *Research on Aging* and coauthor (with Edgar P. Borgatta) of a recent book, *Critical Issues in Aging Policy: Linking Research and Values.* **Edgar P. Borgatta,** professor of sociology at the University of Washington, is past vice president of the American Sociological Association and past president of the International Sociological Association. He has published over 250 books, monographs, and scholarly articles. **Karl D. Kosloski** held both predoctoral and postdoctoral fellowships from the National Institute of Mental Health. He is assistant professor at the Institute of Gerontology, Wayne State University, where he works in the areas of retirement, health care planning, utilization of mental health services, and developmental methodology.

Karen Nussbaum, executive director of 9 to 5, National Association of Working Women, has been organizing women office workers for 15 years. She helped create the first local group of office workers in Boston—"9 to 5"—which today has programs in over a hundred cities. Ms. Nussbaum heads District 925 of the Service Employees International Union and is a member of its executive board. She is coauthor of *9 to 5: The Working Woman's Guide to Office Survival.*

John D. Owen is professor of economics at Wayne State University, where he teaches a course in the economics of aging. Dr. Owen has written widely on the economics of human resources. His book *Working Lives: The American Workforce since 1920* discussed how age patterns of labor supply have changed in the United States over the past seventy years.

Jerome M. Rosow, a former assistant secretary of labor and vice president of Exxon Corporation, is president and founder of Work in America Institute, Inc., a nonprofit research institute devoted to advancing productivity and the quality of working life in America. He coedited, with Clark Kerr, *Work in America: The Decades Ahead* and has directed a number of policy studies, including one entitled "The Future of Older Workers in America."

Anthony P. St. John, vice president for human resources, Chrysler Motors, held several positions at Bethlehem Steel Corporation, including vice president of union relations for the Steel Group, before joining Chrysler. Mr. St. John received an LL.B. degree from the University of Virginia and is a graduate of the Harvard Business School Advanced Management Program.

Steven H. Sandell is a senior staff member in planning and evaluation at the U.S. Department of Health and Human Services, where he analyzes retirement and income security issues. At the National Commission for Employment Policy, he directed the project on National Employment Policy and Older Americans. Dr. Sandell is the editor of *The Problem Isn't Age: Work and Older Americans*, published in 1987.

Stephen E. Baldwin received the doctorate in economics from the University of Washington. He is on the staff of the National Commission for Employment Policy, where he is responsible for policy research on displaced workers and the effects of economic growth on labor markets.

Ernest J. Savoie, director of the Employee Development Office, Ford Motor Company, is responsible for planning, designing, and implementing human resource development programs for Ford hourly and salaried employees worldwide. Mr. Savoie joined Ford in 1960 as a financial analyst and transferred to the Labor Relations staff in 1962. Currently, he is an adjunct associate research scientist at the University of Michigan's Institute of Labor and Industrial Relations. He holds an M.Sc. degree in labor economics and industrial relations from Cornell University.

Stephen I. Schlossberg, director of the Washington branch of the International Labor Office, maintains liaison with the U.S. government, unions, employers, universities, and international organizations. For almost twenty years, Mr. Schlossberg served as general counsel and director of government affairs of the United Auto Workers Union. From 1985 to 1987, he was deputy under secretary for labor-management relations, U.S. Department of Labor. Mr. Schlossberg holds a law degree from the University of Virginia and is the author of *Organizing and the Law*.

Bert Seidman, director, Department of Occupational Safety, Health, and Social Security, AFL-CIO, previously served as an economist in the research department and as an AFL-CIO European Economic Representative. Among the committees and boards on which he serves are the Brookings Institution Advisory Panel on Long Term Care, the Advisory Council on Employee Welfare and Pension Benefit Plans, and the National Council on Aging.

Harold L. Sheppard is director of the International Exchange Center on Gerontology, based at the University of South Florida in Tampa. As director of the Center of Work and Aging of the American Institute for Research, he conducted a number of studies, including *The Graying of Working America*, and a comparative study of retirement policies of five European countries. Currently, he is writing the U.S. report on a multi-country project examining early retirement trends and issues in the United Kingdom, France, West Germany, Sweden, the Netherlands, and the United States.

Robert C. Stempel, president, General Motors Corporation, joined General Motors in 1958 as a senior detailer in the Chassis Design Department. In 1973, he became special assistant to GM's president and in 1978, general manager of Pontiac Motor Division and a vice president of the company. In 1980, he was appointed managing director of Adam Opel AG in the Federal Republic of Germany. Two years later, he was appointed general manager of Chevrolet Motor Division. In 1984, he was made vice president and group executive in charge of the Buick-Oldsmobile-Cadillac Group. In 1986, Mr. Stempel was named executive vice president of General Motors and elected to the board of directors.

John R. Stepp, acting deputy under secretary for labor-management relations, U.S. Department of Labor, directs a bureau which provides technical assistance to employers and unions as they develop and implement cooperative labor-management programs. Prior to his service at the Labor Department, Mr. Stepp was a member of the faculty at Georgia Institute of Technology and national representative and director of Preventive Mediation Activities for the Federal Mediation and Conciliation Service.

Shelby Stewman is professor of demography and sociology at Carnegie Mellon University's School of Urban and Public Affairs. He has written extensively on the relationship of retirement patterns and demographic changes to promotional opportunities within organizational structures.

Alfred S. Warren, Jr., vice president for industrial relations at General Motors Corporation, was involved in the early development of GM's Quality of Work Life program as director of personnel development. He is chairman of the Industrial Relations Policy Committee of the Motor Vehicle Manufacturers Association.

Introduction

The papers in this volume are based on presentations at a conference on the aging of the work force in the United States, held at Wayne State University in Detroit in March 1988. The meeting was sponsored by Wayne State University and the U.S. Department of Labor and organized by the editors.

The presidential campaign of 1988 focused attention on the socioeconomic system of the United States. Little attention, however, was directed to an important issue: the aging of the American work force. Yet this phenomenon will have a significant impact on the national economy and is already being felt today. This issue was the concern of the conference in March. According to our contributors, it will affect the productivity of both public and private sectors: the skill and manpower needs of newly emerging and old-line industries alike; human relations and collective bargaining; the institutions that provide and finance medical care; and our pension system.

Such matters as the obligation of the private sector and/or government to find solutions to the myriad of problems generate strong differences of opinion. National health insurance, portability of pensions, the nature and cost of worker re-education and retraining, productivity of older employees, alternative work arrangements for "senior citizens" such as expanded part-time employment, the question of discriminatory employment practices in older work forces, and the role of the government's Social Security system in national policy intervention—all are public policy matters which must be addressed and on which contributors' views vary.

Though the writers speak from many vantage points—the academic community, labor, management, state and federal government—they are united in the belief that the issue of the aging work force must be recognized and addressed now. As the U.S. Secretary of Labor puts it in the Foreword to this volume, there is an "imperative need to ensure the full use of *all* the nation's human resources to improve our productive capability and thereby sustain our economic growth and social progress," for "older workers constitute a vital part of our human resource potential."

The papers by Irving Bluestone; Olivia Mitchell; Rhonda Montgomery, Edgar Borgatta, and Karl Kosloski; and John Owen were not offered at the conference.

Part I sets forth the theme of the aging of the work force as the baby boom cohort grows older. The challenges faced by government and industry are discussed in papers by John R. Stepp and by Ronald Kutscher and Howard Fullerton, all of the Department of Labor. Rhonda Montgomery, Edgar Borgatta, and Karl Kosloski focus on the importance of societal values to the creation of public policy and practices aimed at demographic changes in the work force.

The aging of the work force has not kept pace with the aging of the population as a whole because of a continuing trend toward earlier retirement. The papers in Part II discuss what might be called a "middle-aging" of the work force, with fewer younger workers but also with fewer people in their sixties or over. The movement toward earlier retirement and the need for adequate pensions for the retiree are discussed in three papers. Douglas Fraser describes the early struggle of the United Auto Workers to obtain pensions for workers who were thought to be "too old to work, too young to die," while Owen Bieber makes the case for adequate pensions for today and for the years ahead. Stephen Schlossberg of the International Labor Organization then looks at the struggle for better pensions from an international viewpoint.

Economists argue that earlier retirements represent the impact of both "pull" and "push" factors: the more attractive retirement packages offered to older workers—the "pull"—and the greater difficulty these workers experience in keeping or finding employment—the "push." John Owen points out that it is often difficult to distinguish between push and pull, since employers frequently design early retirement policies when they wish to trim their work forces. Harold Sheppard describes the contribution of such practices to earlier retirements in a number of European countries he has studied, as well as in the United States. Leon Lynch of the United Steelworkers Union stresses earlier retirement policies, as well as job retraining, as typical of the union's effort to adapt to a rapidly declining industry. In contrast, a Swedish government contributor, Bo Adolfsson, points to the major effort made by Sweden to retain its older workers. While U.S. government efforts to keep older workers employed do not meet the Swedish standard, Steven Sandell and Stephen Baldwin believe that efforts to help those who are displaced are significant and growing.

But the pull factor of attractive pensions also provides an important part of the early retirement story. Robert Clark gives us a detailed description of how private and public pensions have developed to meet the needs of the elderly, so that retirement becomes more attractive than continued employment for many people. Richard Burkhauser and Joseph Quinn provide evidence of an unpredicted effect of pensions: older workers retiring from their principal jobs to collect their pensions, then moving on to a second job, postponing their final retirement from all employment. Meanwhile, pension plan costs increase as the ratio of workers to retirees continues a downward slide, a fact recognized by both union and management contributors.

But the changing population demographics are affecting the workplace, despite the movement toward earlier retirement. Even a simple "middle-aging" of the workplace has profound effects on management, labor, and government. The middle-aging of the work force has been most dramatic in sectors which have stopped growing or are declining, such as the automotive industry, manufacturers of some types of electrical equipment, and steel.

In Part III, which is focused on health issues and costs, Irving Bluestone takes a broad view of the social impact of our aging work force on employment, health care, and income maintenance. He concludes that a greater role for government is indicated. Judith Barr outlines strategies developed in a wide variety of industries to provide health care, including some interesting new methods of cost containment.

The auto industry has been particularly active in addressing health care and other key issues facing older workers and their employers. Robert Stempel describes joint programs between General Motors and the UAW. Improved job security, training for older workers, preretirement counseling, and efforts to control health care costs—which are rising at a rate far exceeding the cost of living, and are higher for an older work force—all are matters of concern at GM. Alfred Warren details the efforts that GM is making to contain these costs without sacrificing quality. Anthony St. John of Chrysler discusses a joint company-union research project on medical care options, which will have practical applications in the near future. Ernest Savoie of Ford sees his company's efforts to deal with what he calls "high age compression" as part of a larger effort to bring about a change in human relations in that company. He identifies key strategic issues as internal cost push (pensions, health care, vacation pay), organizational performance, human values, and teamwork. Frank Doyle describes how global competition and the aging work force now shape collective bargaining at General Electric. He emphasizes that only firms that are competitive can generate the resources required to maintain income and employment. Doyle sees training and retraining of the mature work force as critically important in maintaining competitiveness.

The effects of an aging work force on productivity and related issues are considered in Part IV. Some truisms are challenged here. Olivia Mitchell finds a lack of evidence that job satisfaction or job performance declines with age. Mary Jablonski, Kent Kunze, and Larry

Rosenblum present new evidence that the relative decline in the proportion of young people in the labor force is now contributing to an increased rate of productivity gain in the United States.

Part V focuses on the impact of our aging work force on economic distribution and on barriers to full utilization of the older worker's talents. The adverse effect of women's marginal role in the labor force on their economic position as they age, both as older workers and as retirees, is argued by Karen Nussbaum. To look at the problem from a more positive angle, Shelby Stewman presents new empirical evidence on how early retirement creates a chain of openings and promotions for younger people. Given the dearth of young people available to fill these positions, attractive opportunities may be available for qualified individuals now entering the labor force.

Organizational support from government and the private sector is viewed as an obligation to older citizens by several contributors. David Gamse outlines the broad efforts of the American Association of Retired Persons to obtain more favorable treatment of older workers on the job. Bert Seidman describes the AFL-CIO's support of older workers and retirees and presents a trade union perspective on three major issues as they affect the aging work force: income security, health care, and dependent care. Like Bluestone, he argues for improved benefits and for a more active role by the federal government. In response, Olivia Maynard, director of efforts in behalf of the aging of the State of Michigan, tells of state programs to meet income and other needs of older people and to improve their employment prospects. Speaking for the workers themselves, Jerome Rosow of the Work in America Institute notes the preferences of many older people for continued employment over retirement, and suggests ways of accommodating these preferences, including redesign of work schedules and of jobs, reassignment and relocation opportunities, education and retraining programs, and phased retirement.

It is clear that there is a widespread interest in and concern about the aging of the American work force. Past approaches are being examined critically today, long-held assumptions questioned, and policy agendas appropriate to the needs of the 1990s being developed and even, in some cases, implemented. The correct strategy for the next century is not year clear, but this book offers policymakers, employers, and workers a framework for understanding this new phenomenon in our society.

The editors wish to express their appreciation to the contributors to the book and to those who assisted in its preparation. The cooperation of the U.S. Department of Labor's representative, Richard

Shore, was particularly helpful. Jean Owen's professional touch in editing the papers was indispensable in assuring clarity of subject matter, accuracy of content, and readability. We are grateful for the capable secretarial assistance provided by Lorin Martin, Linda Sioen, Pamela Rodgers, and Camilla Longley in preparing final copy and for the professional management of the conference details by Mary McGlinn Datwyler.

The conference and this publication would not have been possible without the support given by the U.S. Department of Labor, assisted by the Villers Foundation, the United Auto Workers Union, and the Ford Motor Company Fund.

Part I
The Changing Work Force: Fact or Fiction?

Social Policy toward the Older Worker: Assumptions, Values, and Implications

RHONDA J. V. MONTGOMERY,
EDGAR P. BORGATTA,
AND KARL D. KOSLOSKI

The changing demographic makeup of the work force has drawn the attention of employers, unions, and policymakers, some of whom have responded with alarm and advocated revision of current practices. Yet past, present, and future policies and practices reflect societal values both implicit and explicit. The authors explore the underlying assumptions of current employment and retirement practices and raise questions about the desirability of retaining them in future policy and practice. At a minimum, the authors suggest that the values shaping policy be carefully scrutinized before revisions are made. They maintain that future policy should be molded with a conscious recognition of the relationship between desired values and employment and retirement practices.

R. J. V. M.

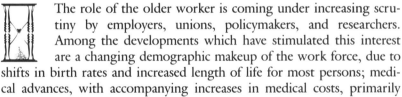

The role of the older worker is coming under increasing scrutiny by employers, unions, policymakers, and researchers. Among the developments which have stimulated this interest are a changing demographic makeup of the work force, due to shifts in birth rates and increased length of life for most persons; medical advances, with accompanying increases in medical costs, primarily associated with older persons; compression in the upper ages among workers in some industries; and the trend toward earlier retirement among certain groups of workers.

Some observers see an increase in the proportion of older workers as cause for alarm, others as a burgeoning resource. Before it is possible to make a pronouncement on whether there is a coming "crisis" in the workplace or whether dramatic shifts in policy are necessary, it is useful to consider not only where we are as a society with respect to a defined role for the older worker but also how we got there. We will look at examples that illustrate the implicit value system that appears to underlie present social policy with respect to older workers. We will then suggest possible policy initiatives that are consistent with both the new demographics and attitudinal changes toward the older worker.

The Present Role of the Older Worker

AN AGING SOCIETY

The American population is changing demographically, with persons generally surviving longer. At the turn of the century, less than one in every ten Americans was 55 years old or older. Presently, the figure is one in five. By the beginning of the next century, the size of this segment of the population will increase yet another 20 percent, from 47 million to roughly 55 million, and by the year 2010, according to the Census Bureau (1983), fully 25 percent of the population will be 55 years old or over.

The aging of the population roughly parallels the aging of the baby boomers, that cohort born from the mid-1940s to the early 1960s. Almost one-third of the current U.S. population (nearly 75 million) was born during this period. Due to their large numbers and increasing life expectancy, the baby boomers are expected to be the dominant age cohort well into the next century.

The effect of the population bulge caused by this cohort is heightened by a smaller than expected succeeding cohort, often referred to as the "baby bust" generation. While the fertility rate soared during the two decades from 1945 to 1964, reaching a high of 3.7 in 1957, it dropped to a low of 1.7, substantially below the replacement rate, in 1976 (U.S. Bureau of the Census, 1982). Partly as the result of these demographic shifts, the average age of the population has been steadily increasing.

The major concern here is the change produced in the dependency ratio (the number of dependents in society supported by each working member). There are various ways of computing this ratio (see, e.g., Adamchak and Friedmann 1983), but no matter how it is conceptualized, two considerations should not be overlooked. First, as the proportion of older adults increases, there is a corresponding reduction in the number of dependent young, which tends to offset, at least in part, the impact of the older group. The exact tradeoff in costs at the individual and societal levels is, as yet, unknown. Second, there are conditions other than changing fertility rates that affect the dependency ratio. These include perturbations in the economy, legislation affecting Social Security and Medicare, and restrictive public and private policies that reduce the ability of older workers to adapt to changing conditions.

In short, demographic shifts in the population structure produce a population with a higher proportion of older persons. Though the implications of this shift for good or ill are not yet apparent, there has been much debate of the merits of alternative solutions to the "problems" created by an aging society.

AN AGING WORK FORCE

Since the composition of the work force is determined, in part, by the composition of the larger population from which it is drawn, the median age of the labor force is slowly increasing. It is important to bear in mind that much of the increase is because the baby boomers are aging, not because older workers are staying in the work force longer. At the beginning of this century, more than two-thirds of American men aged 65 and over were employed. In 1960, the proportion had dropped to roughly one-third (Back 1969); by 1979 the proportion was 19 percent and dropping (Smedley 1979); the figure is expected to fall below 10 percent by the year 2000 (Fullerton 1987).

American workers are opting for retirement at an earlier age. In 1966, 38 percent of workers retired before age 65 under Social Security; by 1976 the number had increased to 66 percent (*U.S. News & World Report* 1978). And even though recent amendments to the Age Discrimination in Employment Act of 1986 remove the age-70 cap in the law and prohibit mandatory retirement based on age for most workers, the trend toward earlier retirement continues (Kutscher and Fullerton, this volume).

Currently, labor force participation begins to decline as early as age 45 for both men and women, as health problems and early retirement options begin to thin the ranks of the employed (Sandell 1987). However, the trend toward earlier retirement is particularly pronounced for males. The parallel for women is not direct, since the labor force participation of women has been changing. Work rates for women below the age of 55 continue to rise, and the work rates of older women remain relatively unchanged (Clark 1988).

As Kutscher and Fullerton point out in their paper, the median age of the post-World War II labor force reached its apex in 1962, at 40.6 years. With the entry of the baby boom generation, the median age dropped dramatically. Since then, it has been increasing steadily. In spite of this increase, however, voluntary decisions by older workers to leave the work force are more than offsetting the effect of the aging of the baby boomers, and the median age of 1962 is unlikely to be matched in the foreseeable future.

Planners wonder whether society will have the ability to finance such a retirement level without a negative impact on the economy and the standard of living. The most frequently invoked scenario, related to the dependency ratio, is that as the average age of workers increases and older workers depart prematurely, fewer workers will be left to support an increasing proportion of retirees. As a result, workers will eventually be unable to afford to retire, and the work force will be inundated with older workers.

Objective data do not support this view. The greatest disparity in the dependency ratio occurred in the early 1960s, when there were over 150 nonworkers for every 100 workers. Since then the ratio has steadily declined, in large part because of increasing labor force participation by women. This trend is expected to continue for the next twenty years before slowly reversing itself. Even when it does, however, the ratio of nonworkers to workers is not expected to exceed 115 nonworkers for every 100 workers. So even when the baby boomers reach retirement age, the dependency ratio is expected to be much more favorable than in the 1960s and 1970s (Sandell 1987). This relatively optimistic view of the future must be tempered somewhat by the expectation that older dependents will be more expensive than younger dependents. High-tech medical advances that increase the length of the dependency period will contribute substantially to health care costs for this group.

Thus the notion of an aging work force is somewhat of a misnomer at present. Although certain sectors have older than average work forces (e.g., the auto industry), this phenomenon largely is caused by union-negotiated work and seniority rules, rather than demographic change. Age compression in industry should not be confused with demographic shifts in the population. Since they have different causes, they are likely to have different solutions. For the most part, aging trends within the general population are being offset by trends toward earlier retirement. The result has been a less rapid aging of the work force. In a similar fashion, increased participation by females in the labor force appears to have forestalled an economically debilitating dependency ratio. Indeed, Adamchak and Friedmann, in their analyses of differing conceptions of the dependency ratio, conclude: "Whatever the reasons for the revolt against the alleged increases in 'dependency' loads resulting from population aging and the institutionalization of retirement, *the argument cannot be justified on the basis of a demonstrable increase in dependency load employing any appropriate measure*" (p. 336).

INTERGENERATIONAL TENSION

A number of analysts have raised the specter of intergenerational conflict as a logical consequence of the present support for older Americans. Groups such as Americans for Generational Equity (AGE), with the ostensible purpose of protecting the economic rights of younger Americans, have been cited as evidence that battle lines are being drawn.

Impetus for such movements is fueled by such inflammatory statements as this: "The baby boomers are paying an unprecedented proportion of their incomes to support the current older generation in retirement, and they will expect today's children to support them in turn. The likely result, unless many fundamental trends are soon reversed, will be a war between young and old" (Longman 1987, p. 2).

In reality, the prospect of such intergenerational conflict seems remote. For example, the tradition of intrafamilial responsibility for informal care-giving appears as strong as ever (Brody 1985; Shanas 1979). In addition, private transfers of money are more likely to proceed from old to young than vice versa (Gibbs 1988). In fact, it has been contended that the whole "intergenerational inequity" argument is based on a series of false assumptions such as the belief that all the elderly are well-off, that allocation of federal monies is a zero-sum game, that conflict is the rule rather than the exception, and that there is no common stake between generations (Kingson et al. 1986).

Other factors that have nothing to do with economic support also promote negative attitudes toward the old by the young. For example, there are prevailing myths that older workers "wear out"; that their knowledge becomes superannuated or even obsolete; that they are accident-prone, forgetful, and so on. One of the achievements of modern social gerontology has been the successful challenging of such myths. Indeed, it might be argued that the heightened awareness of gerontological issues has created a renewed sense of egalitarianism and an advocacy by some policymakers of the view that older workers must be given an opportunity to remain in the workplace. Given their retirement patterns, however, older workers show little sign of wanting or needing such an opportunity.

Implicit Values in Contemporary Social Policy

SOME HISTORICAL NOTES ON RETIREMENT

On the face of it, then, there would seem to be no compelling need for a radical revision of the role of the older worker based solely on demographic trends. This is consistent with Graebner's (1980) observation that the aging of the general population occurs too slowly to account for such historical movements in any more than a general way.

According to Graebner, formal occupational retirement emerged in the American workplace for three main reasons. First, retirement was an assault on the system of permanence that employees attempted to build into their positions, as exemplified by tenure in teaching, seniority on the railroad, and the spoils system in civil service. Retirement served to lessen the "right" of individuals to such occupational permanence.

Second, retirement weakened the effort of "personal influence" and personal relationships in institutions. In other words, a worker's ability came to be more important than his or her family and social connections. Prior to the institutionalization of retirement, public and private corporations were assumed to be providing for the welfare of their older workers, that is, income, status, and activity were to be dispensed to older workers as part of the job. Unfortunately, provision of these gratifications was never uniform. With retirement, these functions were transferred to senior citizens' groups, nursing homes, and retirement communities.

Third, says Graebner, "retirement has historically been sanctioned as a form of unemployment relief; older workers have been retired to create places for younger ones" (p. 266), a policy most blatant in the railroad industry, but applied to other occupations experiencing technological unemployment. To note this function of retirement is not to minimize the discrimination inherent in the process; however, the process is, in large part, implicitly accepted among all age groups.

From Graebner's perspective, certain social and economic values were instrumental in the eventual institutionalization of a retirement role; and, extending this line of reasoning, shifting values will most likely be responsible for any changes in the perceptions or operationalization of this role. In order to explain the renewed interest in the older worker in America, Graebner again points to the economy: "Mandatory retirement was established over the course of the last century because it served real and perceived needs; it is now being dismantled because it is increasingly seen as economically counterproductive for the firm and the nation; because the proposed alternatives seem to offer substantial benefits; and because it is generally accepted that mandatory retirement can be eliminated without significant social dislocation" (p. 250).

From this perspective, the role of the older worker can be seen as being influenced by social values that are based, at least in part, on economic considerations. According to Graebner, it would be a distinct mistake to interpret recent legislation removing mandatory retirement ages as a belated victory for older workers who want to continue working but have been barred by arbitrary age discrimination. Rather, such a change in policy became possible only when those in positions of power in corporate America decided that current retirement policies were too expensive and inefficient in their utilization of the labor supply. In short, in order to understand the role of the older worker, it is important to identify which values are presently being represented and whose values they are.

CONVENTIONAL POLICY DEVELOPMENT AND IMPLICIT VALUES

To illustrate where we are, as a society, with respect to a defined role for the older worker, it may be useful to examine certain contemporary policies and practices in the workplace, raise questions about the values reflected, and ask whether or not these are the values that should be implemented. The purpose of this exercise is not to engage in a systematic analysis of current policy, but to begin such an endeavor by focusing on several current practices and the implications of these practices. Then it may be possible to begin a dialogue about which values we as a society would like to support and the policies and practices that could be implemented to achieve these goals.

For the past few decades, there has been a movement in labor and industry toward the practice referred to as "30-and-out." Implementation of this policy was a victory for the worker who had spent long years at physically exhausting labor and was given an opportunity to retire before literally working himself to death. The "30-and-out" policy has been most conspicuous in the older manufacturing industries, where modernization has led to a decrease in the labor force and where there are few new opportunities for younger workers.

The benefits of the "30-and-out" policy are numerous and clearly transcend the original goal of assuring at least some time for retirement for laborers. For example, "30-and-out" tends to make room for younger workers and for promotion of those in the middle years. It has the potential to create an orderly influx of new members into the labor organizations and assure the continued need and support for such organizations. The practice also reinforces the societal belief that retirement is an earned right which workers may exercise even before reaching the age qualifying them for Social Security. For its part, industry has benefited to the extent that those in the system for a shorter time command lower salaries and fewer benefits.

On the surface, then, "30-and-out" would appear to be a practice that is desirable. However, careful scrutiny raises questions about the long-term costs of such a practice and the values that are being reinforced. For example, if an individual is capable of continued work and is not prepared for a reduction in income, this practice may be limiting his or her opportunities. Such a person is not only restricted from working but is less well able to prevent economic dependency in the future. In principle, "30-and-out" may appear to be a humane provision; in practice, it threatens the older person's access to continued employment. If there are not enough jobs to go around, the notion of full employment can be maintained if some groups are defined as outside the work force. Those groups could be the young, women, or minorities. And at various times in various ways, many groups have been prohibited access to employment. It may be convenient to treat the group of old people in this way.

It may be argued that legislation was passed in 1986 to prevent forced retirement in most employment settings. However, the law does not prevent enticements to retire such as bonuses and what are often referred to as "golden parachute" packages. Furthermore, the statistics reported above show that the average retirement age has been and continues to be below that required for Social Security eligibility. In reality, then, while there may be virtues associated with retirement, "30-and-out" and related policies may create expectations within society about who should retire and when, thereby placing a limitation on all future income for these persons.

It is the latter aspect of retirement (i.e., a limitation on future income) that may be problematic for individuals and society. As long as individuals live only a few years beyond retirement, initially adequate pensions will probably remain adequate as time passes. However, as larger numbers of persons live longer and the retirement period is extended, it becomes questionable whether existing pension programs will be able to meet the needs of individuals over their retirement life, particularly if inflationary pressure is substantial and there is no provision for cost of living allowances. When people outlive pension resources, government or other resources will be called upon to meet unmet needs, including substantial health care costs. In either case, the public purse will be drawn upon to pay for perhaps unanticipated consequences of early retirement, since these individuals will not be in a position to contribute to their own care.

In addition to the practice of "30-and-out," there are other private and public policies that encourage elders to leave the work force to make room for others. For example, persons who work part-time are limited in how much they can earn before their Social Security benefits are reduced for the period in which they are most likely to continue working, i.e., the years right after formal retirement. Further, recent changes in the tax law require recipients of Social Security to pay taxes on their benefit payments if they secure employment that raises their income over a designated maximum. The stated purpose of this practice is to ensure that elders with sufficiently high incomes are not equal beneficiaries of a tax transfer system. Another consequence of this law is that older workers are "penalized" for going into the work force. This set of circumstances is also mirrored by recent changes in federal employees' benefit packages. Essentially, a federal employee who elects to earn and then draw Social Security benefits after leaving government service is penalized for such an action. The message given by current practices is clear, whether intended or not: older persons should leave the work force.

Is this the message that we want current policy to send? Once this initial question is asked, a series of other questions emerges, all of which deserve serious consideration if we are to create policies concerned with older workers in a proactive way. Do we want workers to leave the work force at ever earlier ages? Are older persons the most appropriate group economically to force out of the work force? Do we need to force a selected subgroup out of the labor force? If not, will we need to do so in the future? Are there alternative ways of achieving full employment?

A second employment practice that is intricately tied to retirement and older worker policies is the pervasive and growing tendency to hire part-time employees. The benefits of this practice to employers are clear. They gain scheduling flexibility and major savings because part-time employees are frequently paid low hourly wages and usually are not provided key benefits. From the perspective of older workers, such jobs can be viewed favorably because they allow retired persons to supplement their retirement income on a flexible schedule. One might be tempted to assert that this practice reflects an increasing value placed on older persons. However, in reality, it reflects underlying values similar to those described earlier. Specifically, older persons are employed as marginal participants in the labor market, and often the jobs are available only because other persons are unable or unwilling to take them.

Apart from the question of whether this is the value we want to foster, there are questions related to the long-term consequences of these practices for retirement policy. Older persons are not the only group employed as part-time help without benefits. Women, youths, minorities, and those with lower levels of education are also employed in such a manner. When these persons progress through their work lives to retirement age, they arrive there with no planned retirement benefits except for minimal Social Security coverage—and even that assurance continues to be questioned. Hence the savings incurred by these service industries are likely to be at a substantial cost to the public purse. If large numbers of these marginal workers live extended lives, it is likely that minimal Social Security benefits will need to be supplemented by government programs.

The Future Role of the Older Worker

VALUE-DRIVEN POLICY DEVELOPMENT

All too often, when policy analysts and policymakers address difficult issues, they approach their task as one of fine tuning rather than one of asking more basic and difficult questions about which values are being supported by a policy and whether or not they should be supported. This reluctance to raise questions about values stems directly from the fact that many social issues are complex, involve a diverse set of values, and may be conflicting. The employment and retirement of older workers is one such issue. Debate concerning the rights and privileges of older persons as workers and retired citizens will not only reflect differences in values among different interest groups but will also reveal conflicting values among individuals.

In a brief presentation it is not possible to develop new directions for policy with regard to the older worker. However, we will suggest a few ways in which values can be stated in a forthright and direct way.

First, let us emphasize the simple notion that older persons are people like everyone else, and should not be treated any differently merely on the basis of age—that is to say, there should be no discrimination. Such a statement is more easily accepted as a generality than in application. It implies that older persons who wish to work should be judged on the basis of their qualifications, and the process of determining qualifications may create some costs. This value is now reasonably well incorporated in our federal legal system, and is reflected at other levels of government as well.

However, the other side of the coin is that older persons also should not be treated preferentially. For some, this is a position that is harder to accept. To hire without prejudice, it may be necessary to test persons' ability to do tasks. This adds administrative costs, but is fairer than making the prejudicial assumption that older persons will learn more slowly, perform more slowly, and lack the energy and alertness of young people. On the other hand, in many cases there are rewards for seniority that are routinized and may be applied without having any bearing on the efficiency of a given individual. If rewards were to be distributed on the basis of merit rather than seniority, assessment procedures would be necessary, and such procedures would add cost. It is a two-way street, and both practices, although less arbitrary and prejudicial, would add to operating costs.

In the area of retirement policies, one of the major politically sensitive issues is whether Social Security should be treated as a universal benefit or as a form of insurance. Presumably, the latter view was a prominent notion at the initiation of the program, and is evident in its title, Old Age and Survivors Insurance (now called Retirement Survivors Disability Health Insurance, or RSDHI). Many changes have occurred in the program over the years, including coverage by SSI for those not eligible by earnings, which bring the program closer to a notion of a universal entitlement. Consideration will need to be given to the question of whether the system should be moved fully to a universal entitlement. If this conclusion is reached, then attention will need to be given to how to make it work. If it is designed to provide baseline support only, then the assumption that people should get benefits on the basis of payments into the system would need to be negated. Similarly, the fiction that the payments are not a tax would need to be dispelled. Consequences of moving in such a direction would lead to other questions or consistency. For example, with the RSDHI program there are two parallel tax collection systems, and they could be combined. Presumably, the less regressive tax system would be the one to survive.

If clarification of the Social Security system were to occur, it could well have consequences for savings for retirement. On this score, again, policy has not been generated by broad reflection and planning, but has arisen out of historical circumstances. There is no reason why a parallel retirement savings plan as a form of insurance cannot exist, run either by the government or by the private sector. The principle has been established with Individual Retirement Accounts (IRAs), and could be generalized further by being made a required benefit of employment.

What is unique about the IRAs is that they constitute a notion equivalent to immediate vesting. One of the great problems that has been created for older workers is that retirement benefits have not been treated as other forms of compensation, i.e., as belonging to the worker just as wages do. Pension benefits have often been associated with funds controlled by industry or unions, and thus have been subject to many forms of abuse, ranging from actual criminal exploitation of the funds to control of workers by control of access to benefits. If pension benefits are truly a part of wages, the worker should have access to them in the form of immediate vesting and transportability.

The previous sentence may be a strong statement, but it is one that should be considered. The point is that policy development rarely, if ever, begins with such a direct statement. Most often a problem becomes apparent, and then solutions are considered within the context of the political and power structures that exist. This does not necessarily lead to good policy reflecting thoughtful consideration of values.

In sum, changes may well be on the horizon with regard to the role of older workers in America. However, it would be a mistake to view these changes as the inevitable result of demographic and economic forces in the marketplace. Such a model is not only overly simplistic and short-sighted: it has a more insidious effect. It suggests that society in general, and policymakers in particular, are somehow not responsible for the present role of the older worker in the workplace. The view presented here suggests otherwise: that social policy directly shapes roles and expectations. Unfortunately, the values shaping policy are often implicit and ill-considered. Thus the challenge confronting us is not how to respond to forces largely beyond our control. Rather, the challenge is how to develop policy on the basis of explicit statements about how we, as a society, intend to meet the economic and social challenges awaiting us now and in the years to come.

References

Adamchak, D., and E. Friedmann. 1983. "Societal Aging and Generational Dependency Relationships: Problems of Measurement and Conceptualization," *Research on Aging* 5: 319–38.

Back, K. 1969. "The Ambiguity of Retirement." In *Behavior and Adaptation in Late Life*, edited by E. W. Busse and E. P. Pfeiffer, pp. 93–114. Boston: Little, Brown.

Brody, E. 1985. "Parent Care as a Normative Family Stress," *The Gerontologist* 25: 19–29.

Clark, R. 1988. "The Future of Work and Retirement," *Research on Aging* 10: 169–93.

Fullerton, H. 1987. "Labor Force Projections: 1986–2000," *Monthly Labor Review*, September, pp. 19–29.

Gibbs, N. 1988. "Grays on the Go," *Time*, February 22, pp. 66–75.

Graebner, W. 1980. *A History of Retirement*. New Haven: Yale University Press.

Kingson, E., B. Hirshorn, and J. Cornman. 1986. *Ties That Bind: The Interdependence of Generations*. Washington, D.C.: Seven Locks Press.

Longman, P. 1987. *Born to Pay: The New Politics of Aging in America*. Boston: Houghton Mifflin Co.

Sandell, S. 1987. "Prospects for Older Workers: The Demographic and Economic Context." In *The Problem Isn't Age*, edited by S. Sandell, pp. 3–14. New York: Praeger.

Shanas, E. 1979. "Social Myth as Hypothesis: The Case of the Family Relations of Old People," *The Gerontologist* 19: 3–9.

Smedley, L. 1979. "The Patterns of Retirement," *AFL-CIO American Federationist* 86: 22–25.

U.S. Bureau of the Census. 1982. *Population Profile of the United States: 1981*. Current Population Reports, Series P-20, No. 374. Washington, D.C.: U.S. Government Printing Office.

———. 1982. *America in Transition: An Aging Society*. Current Population Reports, Series P-23, No. 128. Washington, D.C.: U.S. Government Printing Office.

U.S. News & World Report. 1978. "Work beyond Age 65? Most Would Rather Not." April 3, pp. 50–55.

Older Workers:
New Problems, New Opportunities

JOHN R. STEPP

What Stepp calls the "longevity revolution" in the United States and the decline in the proportion of children in the population raise perplexing issues relating to the composition of the work force. Moreover, people are spending less of their lifetime in active employment as incentives for early retirement have blossomed. Perhaps, this Labor Department official suggests, it is time to begin reversing the trend. Continuous education and training, redesign of jobs to make them physically easier to manage, an increase in the availability of part-time jobs, and pension portability are recommended here to keep people active in the work force for a greater number of years.

I. B.

The progressive aging of our population and our work force is bound to have major repercussions throughout our country. Directly or indirectly, it will affect all of us.

Contrary to popular impression, the aging of America is by no means a new development, although some of its more far-reaching implications only recently have come to be discussed and debated in industry, labor, and government. It's a process that has been going on, almost without interruption, throughout our two-hundred-year history. At the beginning of the nineteenth century we truly were a young country, demographically as well as politically. Fully half of the population at that time was less than 16 years old, and very few had the good fortune to survive into their sixties. Since that time, the population has aged steadily, except for the two decades after World War II when peacetime demobilization found men and women making up for lost time as "producers" of children as well as producers of goods and services for the postwar economy.

What is new and quite dramatic is the speed with which this aging trend has progressed as a result of two separate but parallel developments. First, in a relatively short span of time, we have experienced a substantial increase in the number of older people, particularly the very old. The longevity revolution of the twentieth century is a genuine American success story, standing as impressive testimony to the achievements of medical science and the growth of a public health system that markedly reduced premature mortality. Since 1900, life expectancy has been extended from 49 to 75 years, a 26-year gain that nearly equals what had been achieved over the preceding five thousand years—quite an awesome accomplishment when judged in relation to the broad sweep of history. And since 1950, in less than four decades, the number of Americans 65 and older more than doubled, while those 85 and over more than quadrupled.

The second development is the progressive decline in the proportion of children in the population. At the beginning of the 1800s, one of every two people in the country was a child under 16. As a proportion of the total population, the under-16 group declined to 35 percent as we entered the twentieth century, and to 25 percent by 1940, when the birth rate was forced downward by the economic collapse of the Great Depression. While the proportion of young Americans did increase substantially in the years between 1945 and 1964, when 76 million children were added to the population, the "baby boom" was soon after followed by a "baby bust" as the birth rate fell to its current low level.

The agenda of this volume brings into sharp focus a number of perplexing issues growing out of the changing demographics of our population. But none of these is more pressing or more challenging than those surrounding the recent and ongoing changes in the composition of our labor force. With the baby boom generation maturing and the baby bust generation entering the labor force, the average age of American workers will increase from today's 36 years to 39 years by the year 2000. However, older workers, those 55 and over, are coming to constitute an ever smaller part of the work force. While they were 17 percent of the labor force in 1972, today they are but 13 percent and by the year 2000 will be only 11 percent of the working population. Consequently, it's important to acknowledge that the increase in average age is not due to people working longer but is a joint result of the decline in the number of young labor force entrants and the maturing of that huge population bulge represented by the baby boom generation.

What conclusion can we draw from these population and labor force trends? Clearly, the longer life expectancy of the population is having little impact on the time people spend in employment. Work is coming to occupy a progressively smaller part of an individual's total lifespan as people, though principally men, have increasingly elected to, been encouraged to, or been required to relinquish employment at a relatively early age.

These demographic facts of life pose two obvious questions: first, what accounts for such a substantial decline in work activity? And second, what, if anything, should be done about it? There are a number of answers to the "why" question, but let me briefly mention just six.

1. Older workers have left the labor force because of the enhanced appeal of Social Security, through the indexation of benefits, and the option to retire with reduced benefits at age 62.
2. They have left because of the considerable expansion and liberalization of employer-sponsored pension plans, many of which have gradually reduced the minimum age required to receive full benefits.
3. More recently, they have been encouraged to leave by the added incentives many employers offer to their older workers to elect early retirement, a strategy adopted to pare down labor costs by separating their more senior and, hence, higher-paid employees and to provide career ladder opportunities for younger workers.
4. The long-standing "30-and-out" campaign of organized labor, geared to providing an earned relief from the toll taken by physically arduous jobs, also has contributed to the exodus.
5. Then there is the tendency of many employers to perceive older workers as "over the hill" because of their presumably declining physical and intellectual powers. Such misperceptions have resulted in subtle and not so subtle shoves in the direction of the retirement door.
6. And finally, for some indeterminate number of older workers, it is less the pull of a retirement "life of Riley" than the push of a work life that offers too much stress, too little satisfaction, and virtually no prospect for changing jobs or careers.

What should be our response to this trend toward earlier and earlier withdrawal from the labor force? Is it something to be applauded as a hallmark of economic and social progress? Or, conversely, are there compelling reasons to encourage the prolongation of working life into the sixties and beyond?

As a matter of public policy, the United States elected many years ago to encourage early retirement, providing, through Social Security and other pension systems, sufficient income to lessen the economic pressure to continue working beyond the point where people had the health and stamina to do so. There can be no question that these public policy decisions, made a half-century ago, were successful in achieving their aims, progressively reducing the labor force participation of older Americans and, through establishing a "safety net," lifting a great many of them from the depths of poverty.

But the conditions we face today are far different from those that prevailed at the time these policy decisions were made. Let me cite just four important changes:

1. the number of older persons in the country is growing rapidly, while young workers represent a comparatively small part of the population;
2. competition for our global market share has become so intense that we cannot afford to underutilize any of our human resources;
3. the country's occupational structure has been substantially reordered, most notably through the shift away from physically taxing jobs toward jobs that place a premium on reasoning and analytical and language skills; and
4. today's technology enables us to greatly alter the design and structure of jobs to take fuller account of the needs, capabilities, and limitations of workers.

Such profound transformations necessarily call into question the wisdom of perpetuating many of our traditional views about the allocation of work in our society and the time in each person's life to be devoted to it, particularly our notions about the role of older Americans as active participants in the labor market. It requires no heroic assumptions to foresee that as the pool of young entry-level workers diminishes, the participation of older workers in the labor force will be increasingly important to meet society's needs. Thus far we have been lucky, as serious imbalances between supply and demand have been postponed by the surge in women's labor force participation. But women do not constitute an inexhaustible supply of labor, and the potential contribution of older workers, including retirees, should not be undervalued. Older workers possess qualities that are vital to the success of American industry—maturity, stability, commitment, and well-honed skills. Their premature departure from the labor force would seriously deplete our most valuable human resource.

Our retirement system worked well so long as the labor force was growing rapidly and had only to support a relatively small number of older people, thereby maintaining a satisfactory ratio of active workers to retirees. But strains are beginning to appear as a result of our changing labor force and population demographics. Today the so-called dependency ratio is 3.3 workers for each beneficiary. Not long after the year 2000, when the first members of the huge baby boom generation reach age 65, there will be only 2.9 contributors for each beneficiary. And but a short time after that, well before mid-century, the ratio is likely to be even lower. In the light of these sobering realities, the prolongation of working life is a serious matter.

Too many employers still cling to stereotypes of aging as an inevitably disabling process, believing that beyond some arbitrarily specified age, physical and intellectual capabilities become severely impaired. Such a view flies in the face of an impressive body of data which demonstrates that age-related changes vary widely among individuals. Most recent studies of the relationship between age and productivity show that, except in the case of jobs that make unusual physical or sensory demands, the two are unrelated. It's absurd to think that a person past 65, let alone 55, must be put out to pasture.

Although skill obsolescence has come to be recognized as a major impediment to human resource development, employers have been notably reluctant to invest in the retraining of older workers to prepare them for new technologies, new jobs, and new careers. Some wrongly believe that "you can't teach old dogs new tricks." Others contend that older workers are simply not interested in being retrained, an assertion supported by neither research nor experience. But equally wrong-headed is the belief that investments in the training of older workers are not prudent because too few years remain to realize a return. Ignored in this calculus, among other things, is the fact that older employees are much less prone to turnover than young workers.

In light of the changing demographic picture and increased longevity, much more serious consideration should be given to any number of policy initiatives that can serve both to preserve employment opportunities for older workers who wish to prolong their stay in the labor force and to facilitate a more satisfactory transition to retirement for those who do not. First, there should be provision for the continuous education and training of workers throughout their working life to impart new knowledge, develop new skills, and create new job opportunities. Second, jobs and work environments can be redesigned according to ergonomic criteria which take into account the physical capabilities and limitations of individual workers. Third, older workers should be given opportunities to scale down their level of work involvement through job sharing, part-time jobs, and other kinds of reduced work schedules that allow them to experience a gradual rather than an abrupt transition from full-time work to retirement by progressively substituting leisure time for work time. And fourth, there should be provisions for pension portability to substitute for the prevailing arrangements whose "golden handcuffs" necessarily constrain workers from relocating to other employers, other industries, and other communities offering better employment opportunities.

Notwithstanding the slow pace of change, employers are beginning to appreciate the significance of the shrinking pool of young workers, with some taking serious second looks at long-established employment policies and practices. Let me cite a few illustrative cases. Many employers are abandoning their traditional preoccupation with youthful beauty and vitality. Some of the nation's airlines, for example, have begun to select flight attendants on the basis of their maturity and skills, taking on new employees in their forties and fifties—a long-overdue recognition of the more legitimate and important requirements of the job. Varian Associates, a Silicon Valley electronics company, established a retirement transition program, enabling its employees to prepare for retirement by gradually reducing their work weeks three years in advance of their retirement date. The Travelers Corporation abandoned its mandatory retirement policy before being legally required to do so and amended its pension plan so that those who wished to "retreat" but not retire could continue to work a substantial part of the year without loss of pension and health benefits. The Grumman Corporation rehires its retirees on a full- as well as part-time basis, working through a contract with an outside employment agency to enable rehirees to preserve their pension and health benefits.

Despite some of the contradictions we see today in both public and private policies, ways surely can be found to enable older people to sustain a productive role in the economy and contribute the skills and experience that will be in increasingly short supply in the years ahead. The trend today for employers to encourage early retirement has begun to create problems in some organizations, as countless numbers of tried, tested, and committed workers departing from the labor force have taken with them a substantial private as well as public investment in their "human capital." Enlightened and progressive employers now acknowledge that labor is not a cost to be minimized but an asset whose value is to be maximized. This is no less true for older than for younger workers. Adjustments can be made in human resource policies and practices which can prove equally beneficial to older workers and organizational effectiveness.

The Aging Labor Force

RONALD E. KUTSCHER
AND HOWARD N. FULLERTON, JR.

Important medium-term movements in the age structure of the labor force have been taking place. Kutscher and Fullerton point to a decline in the average age of the work force of over six years in the past quarter century but predict that it will go back up by over three years by the end of the century. The fluctuation is partly the result of the baby boom of the 1940s and 1950s, which initially reduced average age but which will increase it as the newcomers themselves age while older workers continue to retire early.

In their studies of the relationship between growth rates of industry and employment patterns of older workers, they find older workers' patterns are very similar to those of prime-age workers.

J. D. O.

Introduction

This paper explores the changing composition of the U.S. labor force by age, sex, and race with an emphasis on what the aging of the work force means. The size and structure of the labor force depends on the structure of the underlying population and on labor force participation rates. These two factors are, of course, interdependent.

Two themes will be emphasized: the changing size of succeeding generations in the labor force, particularly the group of workers aged 55 years and older, and the movement of employment within our economy from goods-producing industries to service-producing industries and what that shift might mean for older workers.

An important dimension to be emphasized is that while the share of the population over 55 years of age is increasing, in the labor force the trend is in the opposite direction. Population structure is determined by past trends in births, deaths, and migration. Labor force activity rates have changed even more than fertility rates, resulting in a labor force that has changed significantly since 1950: women's participation has increased; men's participation, particularly that of men aged 55 and older, has dropped. These changes in labor force composition by sex were not reflected in the overall population. In addition, there were important changes in the composition of the population by marital status and educational attainment.

The movement of our economy from goods-producing to service- and information-providing industries, a theme for more than half a century, is projected by the Bureau of Labor Statistics to continue. Neither the shift in industrial composition nor the shift in occupational composition should significantly affect employment among older workers, especially those aged 55 to 64, whose employment patterns closely resemble those of workers aged 25 to 54.

Population

The structure of the population is one of the important factors affecting the composition of the labor force. There are three elements affecting the structure of the population: births, deaths, and migration. Of these, by far the most important—at least over the long run—is births; changes in fertility will be translated into a changing population composition.

FERTILITY

Births have fluctuated in long cycles over the past century. During the 1920s, fertility dropped. The birth rate began rising in 1933 and continued to rise until 1958. There was a sharp increase in births with the end of World War II, but the highest level of births occurred in the 1950s. For a period of 11 years, from 1954 through 1964, births exceeded 4 million. Between the late 1950s and the middle 1970s, births dropped. Since then, births have been rising and are expected to have peaked in 1988 at 3.9 million. After that, as the baby boom generation moves beyond the peak childbearing years, the number of births is projected to drop, even as the birth rate is projected to rise slightly through the end of the century. Fluctuations in births generate different sizes of generations (cohorts), so that the age composition of the population will vary in size.

The numbers of births were also affected by trends in marital status, labor force participation, and the increasing ability to control the number and spacing of births. In the immediate post-World War II pe-

Table 1: GROWTH IN LIFE EXPECTANCY AT BIRTH AND AT AGE 65, 1920–85, WHITE WOMEN

	Annual Growth Rate	
Period	birth	age 65
	(%)	(%)
1920–30	0.7	0.0
1930–40	0.7	0.6
1940–50	0.7	0.6
1950–60	0.3	0.6
1960–70	0.2	0.9
1970–80	0.4	0.9
1980–85	0.1	0.2

Source: National Center for Health Statistics, *Vital Statistics of the United States, 1985*, vol. 2, sec. 6, Life Tables (Washington, D.C., 1988).

riod, the age of first marriage dropped, a higher proportion of the population married, and there were lots of babies. More recently, the baby boom generation has been postponing marriage (or forgoing it entirely), and the birth rate has been lower. At the same time, labor force participation by young women has risen sharply.

MORTALITY

Death rates dropped steadily over the 1920–58 period, then remained steady over the next decade before resuming their fall (Crimmins 1981). Thus, life expectancy increased by 6 years over the 1920s, 3 years over the 1930s, then 5 years over the 1940s, but only 6 years over the 1950–80 period. Life expectancy has increased by a year between 1980 and 1985, as illustrated in Table 1 for white women.

Life expectancy at age 65 increased by 2 years from the turn of the century until 1950, or 0.4 years a decade. Over the 1950s, expected life remaining at this age also increased by 0.4 years. Between 1960 and 1970, though overall mortality improved only slightly, life expectancy at 65 increased by 0.9 years. During the 1970s life expectancy increased by 1.2 years, to 16.4 years by 1980.

Changes in life expectancy do not affect the working-age population as much as they do the younger or older population. The recent changes in mortality have mainly affected the number and sex composition of the older population.

MIGRATION

Aside from births, the only way for a population to grow is by immigration. Generally, migrants are more likely to be of working age. Migration (either external or internal) is difficult to monitor. The

Table 2: POPULATION AND MIGRATION, BY DECADE, 1920–80

Year	Population at End of Decade	Immigration as Percentage of Population
	(millions)	*(millions)*
1920	100	4.3
1930	123	0.7
1940	132	0.9
1950	151	2.5
1960	181	3.2
1970	205	4.3
1980	227	—

Source: U.S. Bureau of the Census, *Historical Statistics of the United States, Statistical Abstracts.*

United States has accepted large numbers of international immigrants for years. Migration also affects the sex-age composition of the population, and thus the labor force.

Immigration was fairly high during the 1920s, then fell during the 1930s. After World War II, it returned to a level of more than two million a decade; since 1960, immigration has accounted for more than a tenth of interdecade population change (Table 2). Despite the limitations imposed by successive laws, immigration has grown during the 1970s; as a consequence, it represented 20 percent of the overall population change. The Census Bureau projects a *net* migration of more than five million for the 1990s. Further, inasmuch as population growth is projected to slow, the share of population growth which is net migration is expected to rise.

Even if all the net migrants projected to enter the country over the 1986–2000 period were to be in the labor force, they would be less than 4 percent of the labor force. Of course, they would be a more substantial component of the increment to the labor force, about a quarter.

POPULATION STRUCTURE

The consequence of rising and falling births is that the age structure of the population and the labor force fluctuates. As Table 3 indicates, there has been fluctuation in the age composition of the population. (A specific birth cohort in the table may be observed by moving diagonally down to the right.) Thus, the birth dearth of the 1930s, represented in 1950 at ages 10–19, is always smaller than its surrounding cohorts. The baby boom of the 1950s is always larger than its surrounding cohorts. However, the proportion of older people in the population, specifically those 60 and older, is growing over the entire half-century.

Table 3: AGE DISTRIBUTION OF THE POPULATION, 1950–2000

	Actual			*Projected*		
Age	1950	1960	1970	1980	1990	2000
0–9	19.5	21.8	18.1	14.7	14.7	13.1
10–19	14.4	16.8	19.6	17.3	13.9	14.3
20–29	15.8	12.1	15.0	18.1	16.0	13.2
30–39	15.1	13.7	11.1	14.0	17.0	15.4
40–49	12.8	12.6	11.8	10.0	12.6	15.5
50–59	10.2	10.0	10.4	10.3	8.9	11.5
60–69	7.3	7.4	7.7	8.3	8.4	7.5
70–79	3.6	4.2	4.6	5.1	5.7	6.0
80 and up	1.3	1.6	1.9	2.3	2.8	3.5

Sources: U.S. Bureau of the Census; for 1950 and 1960, *Statistical Abstract 1962*, Table 18; for 1970 and 1980, *Current Population Reports*, 1982, P-25, No. 917; for 1990 and 2000, *Current Population Reports*, 1988, P-25, No. 1018.

Labor Force

The labor force is influenced by the population composition and by the proportion in the labor force (participation or activity rates). The overall labor force will change as the composition of the population changes; these changes can be offset or reinforced by changes in participation. In addition to the changes in the age composition of the population, the composition of the labor force is affected by changes in marital status, parental status, and educational attainment. Further, the labor force sex structure is different because participation rates vary by sex.

PARTICIPATION BY SEX AND AGE

Men and women have different patterns of labor force participation, which have tended over time to narrow. Men's rates are higher than women's rates—at all ages. Both sexes increase participation rapidly during the teens and early twenties, but women's participation peaks in the late twenties, while men's participation peaks in the early thirties.

Participation varies by age; as a large population group moves into an age with higher participation, the labor force will grow more rapidly. When the baby boom generation entered the prime working ages, the overall labor force grew rapidly. As this group moves into the ages where participation is stable, the labor force is expected to grow more slowly, growth being dependent on increased participation as well as the entries of those born during the birth-dearth period 1965–78. These changes lag the fluctuations in births by fifteen to twenty years; youth's entry into the labor force is spread over the ages from 16 to 24 (see Table 4).

Table 4: CIVILIAN LABOR FORCE PARTICIPATION RATE, BY SEX AND AGE, 1950–80 AND PROJECTED TO 2000 (IN PERCENTAGES)

	Actual			*Projected*		
Sex, Age, and Race	1950	1960	1970	1980	1990	2000
Total, aged 16 and over	59.2	59.4	60.4	63.8	66.2	67.8
Men	86.4	83.3	79.7	77.4	75.8	74.7
16–24	77.3	71.7	69.4	74.4	73.7	74.3
25–54	96.5	97.0	95.8	94.2	93.4	92.6
55 and over	68.6	60.9	55.7	45.6	36.8	34.1
55–64	86.9	86.8	83.0	72.1	65.1	63.2
65 and over	45.8	33.1	26.8	19.0	14.1	9.9
Women	33.9	37.7	43.3	51.5	57.4	61.5
16–24	43.9	42.8	51.3	61.9	66.2	69.5
25–54	36.8	42.9	50.1	64.0	74.3	80.8
55 and over	18.9	18.1	25.3	22.8	21.0	21.4
55–64	27.0	37.2	43.0	41.3	42.8	45.8
65 and over	9.7	10.8	9.7	8.1	7.0	5.4

Source: for historical data, Fullerton 1984; for projected data, *Monthly Labor Review*, September 1987.

For the past thirty years, the participation of most groups of women has been increasing among each of the subgroups of the population just identified. Further, within each group, changes in composition moved to those groups with higher participation, for example, from married women to single women. During the 1950s, older women increased their participation, while during the late 1960s and 1970s, younger women, particularly mothers, increased their participation. The labor force rates for women aged 20 to 44 are projected to rise, but more slowly than in previous years. The participation rates for males aged 24 to 54 are expected to continue declining, although more slowly than their rates declined in the 1970s.

PARTICIPATION BY OLDER WORKERS

Older workers leave the labor force rapidly. In 1986, as an example, men aged 55 to 59 had a participation rate of 79.0 percent, but by ages 65 to 69, this had dropped by 25.0 percentage points to 54.0. Further, those aged 75 and older had a labor force participation rate of only 7.1 percent (see Table 5). Women's participation rates in 1986 at ages 55 to 59 were in fact less than the drop in male participation between ages 55 and 65. Looking at the percentage drop, the activity rate for men 65 to 69 was 68 percent lower than for men aged 55 to 59; for women, the comparable drop in participation was 72 percent. The percentage change in participation was even greater between ages 65 to 69 and 75 and older. This pattern is typical of other years.

Table 5: CIVILIAN LABOR FORCE PARTICIPATION RATE FOR OLDER PERSONS, BY SEX, 1972–86 AND PROJECTED TO 2000 (IN PERCENTAGES)

	Actual		*Projected*
Sex and Age	1972	1986	2000
Men, 55 and older	53.3	40.4	34.1
55–64	80.4	67.3	63.2
55–59	87.3	79.0	75.2
60–64	72.4	54.9	47.8
65 and older	24.3	16.0	9.9
65–74	31.1	20.4	13.9
65–69	36.9	25.0	17.9
70–74	23.2	14.3	9.3
75 and older	11.4	7.1	4.3
Women, 55 and older	24.5	22.1	21.4
55–64	42.1	42.3	45.8
55–59	48.2	51.3	55.3
60–64	35.3	33.2	33.9
65 and older	9.3	7.2	5.4
65–74	13.1	11.0	9.0
65–69	17.0	13.5	11.4
70–74	8.3	7.6	6.5
75 and older	3.4	2.2	1.5

Source: Monthly Labor Review, September 1987.

If we look across time rather than across age, we also find that labor force participation is dropping for men. Since 1972, for instance, participation by men 55 and older has dropped by 13 percentage points, while participation by women has increased by 2 points. For men 65 and older, this drop is over 7 percentage points, with a rate of only 16.0 percent by 1986. Labor force activity of older women has grown slightly, though it is still significantly lower than that of men.

Projected Changes in the Labor Force

Overall, the rate of labor force growth is projected to continue to slow down, a pattern begun in the early 1980s (Fullerton 1987). This reflects the entry of the smaller birth cohort born between 1965 and 1978. Women are projected to account for about two-thirds of the labor force growth during the 1990s, about the same proportion as the 1950s. Over the 1970s, as more and more of the men of the baby boom generation came into the labor force, the proportion of growth attributed to women steadily dropped despite the rapid increases in their labor force

Table 6: GROWTH OF THE MAJOR AGE GROUPS IN THE LABOR FORCE, 1972–2000

	Millions			*Annual Growth Rate (%)*	
Age	1972	1986	2000*	1972–86	1986–2000*
Total	[illegible]	[illegible]	[illegible]	[illegible]	[illegible]
Youth (16–24)	20.2	23.4	22.6	1.1	−.2
Prime (25–54)	52.3	79.6	100.8	3.0	1.7
Older (55 and up)	14.5	14.9	15.4	0.2	0.2

* Projected.

Source: Monthly Labor Review, September 1987.

participation rates. With the young men of the baby boom now in the labor force, the share of labor force growth attributed to women is projected to be greater over the next decade (see Table 6).

As Tables 5 and 6 indicate, growth of various age groups of the labor force is not uniform; the younger labor force did not grow until the late 1960s and 1970s. However, during the 1990s, their numbers are expected to drop. On the other hand, the prime-working-age labor force (ages 25 to 54) grew at the same rate as the labor force during the 1950s, as most were from the period of low births associated with the Great Depression. Also, this labor force grew slowly during the 1960s. As the younger members of the baby boom entered the prime working ages, and as more women entered the labor force, the rate of growth of the prime-age work force has increased (Table 7).

In developing the projections for older workers, BLS analyzed the trends for each of 48 age-sex-race groups in the age group 55 and over in detail and found no convincing evidence of any turnaround in the tendency for a smaller and smaller share of the older labor force to continue working.

The trends projected for older workers are reasonably consistent among the racial groups, though not between men and women. For example, the labor force participation rate of white men aged 55 and older is projected to drop by 6.1 percentage points, of black men the same age by 7.6 points, and of Hispanic men by 6.6 points. For older women, on the other hand, the rates for white women are projected to drop by only 0.7 percentage point, reflecting the projected rise in participation of the group aged 55 to 59; black women's participation drops by 1.2 points in these projections but still remains 2.0 percentage points above white women's participation. Hispanic women's participation is projected to be unchanged.

Participation rates of men 65 and older are projected to drop 6.1 percentage points between 1986 and 2000—to just under 10.0 per-

Table 7: DISTRIBUTION OF THE ACTUAL AND PROJECTED LABOR FORCE, BY SEX AND AGE, 1950–80 AND PROJECTED TO 2000 (IN PERCENTAGES)

Sex and Age	1950	1960	1970	1980	1990	2000
Total	*100.0*	*100.0*	*100.0*	*100.0*	*100.0*	*100.0*
Men	70.4	66.6	61.9	57.5	54.6	52.7
16–24	11.4	9.9	11.7	12.7	9.1	8.3
25–54	45.7	44.2	38.9	36.2	38.8	38.2
55 and over	13.3	12.5	11.2	8.5	6.6	6.2
55–64	9.3	9.2	8.6	6.8	5.2	5.2
65 and over	3.9	3.3	2.6	1.8	1.4	1.0
Women	29.6	33.4	38.1	42.5	45.4	47.3
16–24	7.1	6.7	9.8	10.9	8.5	8.0
25–54	18.6	21.1	22.0	26.1	32.1	34.4
55 and over	3.9	5.6	6.3	5.5	4.8	4.9
55–64	3.0	4.3	5.0	4.4	3.8	4.1
65 and over	0.9	1.3	1.3	1.1	1.0	0.7

Sources: for historical data, Fullerton 1984; for projected data, *Monthly Labor Review*, September 1987.

cent. In 1972, almost a quarter of men this age were in the labor force. By 1986, the rate had fallen to 16.0 percent. Women 65 and older in 1972 had a participation rate of 9.3 percent. This figure dropped to 7.4 percent by 1986 and is projected to drop further to 5.4 percent by 2000. Workers 65 and over would comprise just over 2 percent of the labor force in 2000 if the labor force growth projected by BLS takes place.

Since early retirement decisions under Social Security take place as early as age 62, it is important to look separately at the 62–64 age group. We are projecting the participation rates of men and of black women aged 62 to 64 to drop between 1986 and 2000 and participation of white women to increase. For white men, the drop in labor force participation in 1986–2000 is projected to be 7.3 percentage points; for black men the drop would be over 10.0 percentage points; for black women the drop would be 2.1 percentage points. The increase for white women is slight—only 0.6 percentage point. Black and white women aged 62 to 64 would have the same participation in 2000.

After 2005, Social Security eligibility will change. It is our judgment that these changes are not likely to affect significantly the participation rates of those who reach the retirement years before 2000. For older men, participation rates for those over 65 have been dropping over the entire century. The drop in participation for men 55 to 64 is of post-World War II origin (participation of women in this broad age group is still rising).

The size of the labor force aged 55 and older is projected to drop between 1986 and 1995 but then to increase between 1995 and 2000. During the period 1995–2000, the labor force 55 and older would be the fastest-growing component of the labor force. The youth labor force, which has been decreasing since 1980, is also projected to drop until 1995, before increasing more rapidly than the overall labor force. The prime-age work force (25 to 54) is the only age group which is projected to grow throughout the period, even though some age groups within this broader grouping are expected to decline for at least part of the 1986–2000 period. The prime-age work force grew by 3.0 percent between 1980 and 1986; this growth is projected to have dropped to 2.6 percent for the rest of the 1980s, 1.8 percent for the early 1990s, and less than 1.0 percent yearly for the last half of the decade of the 1990s.

Other Aspects of Older Workers' Labor Force Participation

MEDIAN AGE

The median age of the labor force in the post-World War II era peaked in 1962, at 40.6 years. With the entry of the baby boom generation into the labor force, the median age dropped, reaching a low in 1980 of 34.6 years. By 1986, the median age had increased to 35.3 years, an increase of less than one year. The median age of the labor force is projected to reach 38.9 years in 2000, an increase of 3.6 years over the 1986 level. Even though the age of the population is increasing rapidly, unless older workers remain in the labor force in greater numbers, the 1962 median age of the labor force is not likely to be attained again. As the population ages, more of it would be in the age groups which show—and are projected to continue to show—declining labor force participation rates (Table 8).

To reinforce the point about older workers, in 1972 workers aged 55 and older constituted 16.7 percent of the labor force. With the entry of the baby boom generation (and the continuing drop in participation of men aged 55 and over) in 1979, workers 55 and over comprised only 14.3 percent. In 1986, after the baby boom generation had completed its entry, the older group (aged 55 and above) was only 12.6 percent of the labor force.

EDUCATION

Americans steadily increased their years of formal schooling between 1965 and 1986. Thus, the older population has lower educational

Table 8: MEDIAN AGE OF THE LABOR FORCE, 1962–86 AND PROJECTED TO 1995–2000

					Projected	
Sex and Race	1962	1972	1979	1986	1995	2000
Total	*40.5*	*37.7*	*34.7*	*35.3*	*37.6*	*38.9*
Men	40.5	38.1	35.3	35.6	37.9	39.3
Women	40.4	37.0	33.9	34.9	37.1	38.6
White	40.9	38.0	34.9	35.5	37.9	39.2
Black	38.3	35.4	33.5	33.8	36.1	37.2
Asian and other	n.a.	n.a.	n.a.	35.5	37.2	38.0
Hispanic	n.a.	n.a.	32.2	32.6	34.1	35.1

Source: Monthly Labor Review, September 1987.

Table 9: PROPORTION OF THE LABOR FORCE COMPLETING HIGH SCHOOL OR COLLEGE, 1965–86

	Women		*Men*	
Year	high school	college	high school	college
1965	62.3	10.0	54.9	12.4
1972	70.7	11.4	63.8	15.0
1979	77.4	15.0	73.7	19.6
1986	83.9	19.0	79.7	23.1

Source: Bureau of Labor Statistics. The percentages apply to those 18 and older for 1965 and to those 16 and older for 1972, 1979, and 1976. All percentages are for March of the specified year.

attainment than the younger population. This becomes an increasingly important element in the labor force participation of older workers, since educational requirements for jobs are gradually increasing in the economy (see Table 9).

One noticeable difference in patterns of educational attainment by sex is that though a greater proportion of women complete high school, a greater proportion of men complete college. By 1986, less than a fifth of all women in the labor force had not completed a high school education, whereas over a fifth of men had not completed high school. More than a fifth of the men had at least a college education, compared to just under a fifth of the women. As education increases, the labor force participation of Americans also increases. Participation by both groups of women has been rising. The difference in participation between men and women has been dropping. By 1986, women with a college education had a participation rate only 8 percentage points less than similarly educated men. This difference was a fourth the size it was in 1965 (see Table 10).

Table 10: PARTICIPATION RATE BY LEVEL OF SCHOOL COMPLETED, 1965–86

	Women		*Men*	
Year	high school	college	high school	college
1965	46.0	60.1	89.3	92.4
1972	51.6	60.4	87.2	90.1
1979	57.1	67.1	86.0	90.2
1986	58.7	73.4	81.9	88.4

Source: see Table 9.

Table 11: ECONOMIC DEPENDENCY RATIO, 1972–2000

Age	1972	1979	1986	1995	2000
Total	*134.6*	*110.2*	*101.2*	*94.2*	*89.8*
Under 16	62.3	52.0	46.5	44.0	40.8
16–64	54.1	37.6	32.9	27.0	26.0
65 and over	18.2	20.6	21.8	23.2	23.0

Source: Monthly Labor Review, September 1987.

ECONOMIC DEPENDENCY RATIO

The economic dependency ratio is the number of those *in* the total population (including the armed forces overseas) who are *not in* the total labor force as a ratio (or per 100) of those in the total labor force.

This ratio has declined steadily over the 1972–86 period as the baby boom generation reached the working ages and entered the labor force. The largest component of the dependency ratio is made up of those under 16. However, this ratio (and the young's share in dependency) has been dropping and is projected to continue to drop throughout the 1986–2000 period (Table 11).

With the rising participation of women, the component of the dependency ratio attributed to those 16 to 64 years of age also declined steadily in 1972–86. This trend is projected to continue, particularly in the period 1986–95. The changes projected between 1995 and 2000 are modest, reflecting the slightly lower participation rates of the largest age group of men, those aged 45 to 54.

Most important, however, the dependency ratio for those over 65 has been rising over the entire 1972–86 period and is projected to continue to rise in the period 1986–95. The slight drop between 1995 and 2000 in the dependency ratio for this over-65 group reflects the movement of the smaller birth cohort of the 1930s into their mid-sixties. Thus, with the baby boom generation in their prime working years and with the smaller number of births projected between 1986 and 2000, the number working is expected to exceed the number not working.

Employment of Older Workers

We will examine two aspects of the employment of older workers, their employment by industry and by occupation. The Bureau of Labor Statistics does not make projections of employment by age or sex, but we can examine the prospects for those industries and occupations in which older workers are more likely to be employed. This will be done by examining projected employment trends both by industry and by occupation. These projected trends will be compared with current employment patterns of workers 55 and over to see whether there is any disparity among industries and occupations in which these workers are employed.

INDUSTRY EMPLOYMENT

Over 21 million new jobs are projected to be added to the U.S. economy between 1986 and the year 2000, bringing total employment to just over 133 million (Personick 1987). Many industries are projected to share in this expansion and enjoy strong job growth, but several, especially some in manufacturing, are not. The job growth of 21 million translates into a percentage increase of 19.2 percent, or a growth rate of 1.3 percent annually, 1986–2000. This compares to annual rates of job growth of 2.6 percent for 1972–79 and 1.4 percent for 1979–86. Thus, projected employment increases are expected to occur at a slower pace than in the past.

The 133 million jobs in the year 2000 will be even more concentrated in service-producing sectors than they are today (Table 12), since virtually all of the net increase of 21 million new jobs are in the service-producing sector; although some goods-producing industries are projected to grow, others are projected to decline, with a net employment change of zero. Of the 133 million total jobs projected, 119 million are expected to be nonfarm wage and salary jobs, or payroll employment. Of the nonfarm wage and salary jobs, three out of four were in service-producing industries in 1986; by the year 2000, almost four out of five are projected to be in that sector. The goods-producing sector, in contrast, is expected to show virtually no net change, as declines in manufacturing and mining just offset projected increases in construction. Manufacturing employment is projected to fall from 19 million in 1986 to 18.2 million by 2000.

As Table 12 indicates, there were only modest differences between employment patterns of older and of all workers in 1986. The

Table 12: COMPARISON OF OLDER AND ALL WORKERS, BY INDUSTRY EMPLOYMENT, 1986

Industry Sector	16–24 years	25–54 years	55 and Older: total	55 and Older: 55–64	55 and Older: 65 and older
Total	*100.0*	*100.0*	*100.0*	*100.0*	*100.0*
Agriculture	3.2	2.4	5.2	4.0	10.3
Mining	0.4	0.9	0.7	0.8	0.4
Construction	6.9	6.9	5.5	5.8	4.2
Manufacturing	14.2	20.7	19.3	21.4	10.9
Transportation, public utilities	3.9	8.0	6.3	7.1	3.1
Wholesale trade	3.2	4.3	4.2	4.2	4.1
Retail trade	33.8	13.0	14.3	13.4	18.2
Finance, insurance, real estate	6.1	7.0	6.7	6.5	7.6
Services	26.0	31.3	32.7	31.6	37.2
Public administration	2.2	5.3	5.0	5.2	4.0

Source: Monthly Labor Review, September 1987. Because of rounding, sums of columns may not total 100.0.

largest difference in percentage distribution was in retail trade. However, it is clear from the data that workers 55 to 64 and those over 65 have different employment patterns. The only industry in which workers 55 to 64 differ significantly from prime-age workers is their proportionately greater employment in agriculture. However, workers 65 and older are differently employed from prime-age workers. They are much *more* likely to be employed in agriculture and the services industry and *less* likely to be employed in mining and construction, and proportionately much less likely to be employed in manufacturing. Although these workers are more likely to be employed in retail trade than prime-age workers, the proportion is much lower than that of youth.

While examining the expected growth of these industry sectors, let us also examine the proportion of older workers in these sectors (see Table 13). Services, which employed the most older workers in 1986, had the same proportion of older workers as the overall economy and is growing at a higher rate than the overall economy. Almost a quarter of the workers in agriculture are over the age of 55, and this industry is projected to decline in employment. Of the sectors which have more older workers than the overall economy, public administration and agriculture are the only ones projected to have employment growth slower than the economy.

Manufacturing, which was the second largest employer of older workers, has about the same proportion of older workers as the overall economy but is projected to grow more slowly than the overall economy. Trade, which has fewer older workers than all employed, should

Table 13: PROPORTION OF OLDER WORKERS, BY INDUSTRY SECTOR, 1986, WITH PROJECTED GROWTH RATE, 1986–2000

Industry Sector	16–24	25–54	55 and Older: total	55 and Older: 55–64	55 and Older: 65 and older	Growth Rate
Total	*18.3*	*68.7*	*13.0*	*10.4*	*2.6*	*1.3*
Agriculture	20.2	56.5	23.3	14.1	9.1	−0.8
Mining	8.9	80.0	11.1	9.9	1.3	−0.6
Construction	18.8	70.6	10.6	9.0	1.6	1.2
Manufacturing	13.5	73.6	13.0	11.5	1.5	−0.3
Transportation, public utilities	10.2	78.2	11.6	10.5	1.1	0.6
Wholesale trade	14.6	72.1	13.4	10.8	2.6	1.7
Retail trade	36.5	52.5	11.0	8.2	2.8	1.7
Finance, insurance, real estate	16.4	70.9	12.8	9.9	2.9	1.7
Services	15.6	70.5	13.9	10.8	3.2	2.7
Public administration	8.4	77.9	13.7	11.4	2.2	0.7

Source: Monthly Labor Review, September 1987.

grow more rapidly than overall employment. This overview does not provide evidence that older workers, particularly those 55 to 64, would be affected differently from all workers by the changing structure of employment.

However, it is clear that the employment patterns of workers 65 and over are sufficiently different from those of prime-age workers (and those aged 55 to 64) to raise a question about whether employment trends favor their employment. This is particularly true given the point made earlier about the average education of older workers and the increasing educational requirements of jobs.

There are at least two reasons why there might be a higher proportion of older workers employed in an industry or occupation. First, the job may have characteristics suitable to older workers, such as flexible hours or less physically demanding labor. Second, the industry or occupation may be experiencing low growth or actual decline. In this case, there would be fewer younger workers entering the industry or occupation—resulting in an increasing median age. This would especially be the case if the rule for determining layoffs is seniority. Use of early retirement would offset the aging to some extent, but as long as there are no new hires, older workers would have to be retired at a rate high enough to offset the aging of the younger employees who are retained.

Like all workers, most older workers are employed as wage and salaried earners in private nonagricultural establishments. However, when we look at the different classes of work, we see that classes of work where the worker is self-employed have a greater proportion of older workers. Occupations and industries that have establishments with self-employed workers are more likely to have older workers (Rones 1978; Rones 1983). A further indication of the supply of time is that almost half of those 65 and older who worked did so part-time in 1982.

OCCUPATIONAL TRENDS

With this in mind, we will look at the *occupational* distribution by age in 1986 and then at future prospects. The structure of occupational employment over the 1986–2000 period is expected to shift because the change in total employment will not be evenly distributed among the broad occupational groups (Silvestri and Lukasiewicz 1986). For example, each of the three broad occupational groups with the most highly trained workers in terms of educational attainment (executive, administrative, and managerial workers; professional workers; and technicians and related support workers) is projected to continue to grow more rapidly than the average for total employment. Collectively, these three groups, which accounted for 25 percent of total employment in 1986, are expected to account for almost 40 percent of the total job growth between 1986 and 2000. In contrast, many factors, such as office and factory automation, changes in consumer demand, and import substitution, are expected to lead to relatively slow growth or decline for occupational groups requiring less education (administration support workers, including clerical; farming, forestry, and fishing workers; and operators, fabricators, and laborers). The service workers group (except private household workers), which is expected to grow at a faster rate than total employment and to account for more of the total growth in employment than any other broad occupational group, is an important exception to the general trend because its educational attainment is not in the high group.

Older workers (55 and older) were distributed much like prime-age workers (aged 25 to 54) in 1986, just as industry employment was (Table 14).

We see that older workers are represented in occupations with more flexible work hours, such as farming, sales, and service occupations. Managers, who have some control of their hours, also have a relatively higher percentage of older workers. On the other hand, in jobs that are physically demanding or in which there is less opportunity for flexible hours, such as laborers or operatives, older workers are underrepresented.

Table 14: COMPARISON OF DISTRIBUTION OF OLDER AND ALL WORKERS, 1986

			55 and Older		
Occupational Group	16–24	25–54	total	55–64	65 and older
Total	*100.0*	*100.0*	*100.0*	*100.0*	*100.0*
Executives	4.6	13.1	13.4	13.8	11.9
Professional	5.1	14.9	12.1	12.2	11.6
Technicians	2.7	3.4	1.7	1.9	1.1
Sales	15.6	11.0	13.0	12.3	15.9
Administrative support	17.8	16.0	15.1	15.6	13.3
Services	21.4	11.1	14.2	13.1	18.2
Precision production	9.8	13.0	11.4	12.3	7.6
Operators	19.1	15.1	13.5	14.6	9.4
Farming	3.8	2.5	5.6	4.2	10.9

Source: Monthly Labor Review, September 1987. Because of rounding, sums of columns may not total 100.0.

Table 15: PROPORTION OF OLDER WORKERS AND GROWTH RATE OF EMPLOYMENT, BY OCCUPATION, 1986–2000

			55 and Older			
Occupational Group	16–24	25–54	total	55–64	65 and older	Percentage Change
Total	*18.5*	*68.4*	*13.1*	*10.4*	*2.7*	*19.2*
Executives	7.4	77.4	15.2	12.4	2.8	28.7
Professional	7.5	80.1	12.4	10.0	2.4	27.0
Technicians	16.2	76.4	7.4	6.4	1.0	38.2
Sales	23.8	62.1	14.1	10.6	3.5	29.6
Administrative support	20.3	67.4	12.2	10.0	2.2	11.4
Services	29.6	56.6	13.8	10.2	3.6	32.7
Precision production	14.9	73.0	12.1	10.5	1.7	12.0
Operators	22.6	66.1	11.3	9.7	1.6	2.6
Farming	22.3	54.5	23.2	13.9	9.3	−4.6

Source: Monthly Labor Review, September 1987.

Finally, we look at the proportion of older workers in broad occupational groups and their likely growth in employment (Table 15). Three occupations had proportionately more older workers: executives, sales, and farming. Farming is projected to decline in employment; sales and executive occupations are projected to grow faster than overall employment. Occupations that may have some flexibility in hours worked, such as service and sales, are projected to grow more rapidly than the economy as a whole. However, the fastest-growing broad occupational group, technicians, has a relatively low share of older workers. This reflects the past rapid growth and the relatively lower educational attainment of older workers. The occupational group next in growth, services, has the same proportion of older workers as total employment, with the representation being high for workers 65 and older.

Summary

It appears, then, that workers aged 55 to 64 are not likely to be affected differently from all workers by shifts in the industry or in the occupational composition of employment because their employment pattern is close to that of prime-age workers, measured either by industry or by occupation. However, workers 65 and over are not distributed like prime-age workers. Their lower share of operative employment—a slow-growing occupation—could work to their advantage, but their larger share of farming jobs—a declining occupation—may work to their disadvantage. However, in 1986, almost 90 percent of those 65 and older and about two-thirds of those 55 and older were not in the labor force. The BLS projects that by the year 2000, around 73 percent of those 55 and older will be out of the labor force.

References

Crimmins, E. M. 1981. "The Changing Pattern of American Mortality Decline, 1940–77, and Its Implications for the Future," *Population and Development Review* 7: 229–54.

Fullerton, Howard N., Jr. 1984. "The Aging Labor Force, 1950 to 1995." Paper presented at Human Resource Implication of an Aging Work Force, symposium sponsored by the Aging Society Project of the Carnegie Corporation of New York and the Manpower Demonstration Research Corporation.

———. 1987. "Labor Force Projections: 1986 to 2000," *Monthly Labor Review*, September, pp. 19–29.

Personick, Valerie A. 1987. "Industry Output and Employment through the End of the Century," *Monthly Labor Review*, September, pp. 30–45.

Rones, Philip L. 1978. "Older Men—the Choice between Work and Retirement," *Monthly Labor Review*, November, pp. 3–10.

———. 1983. "The Labor Market Problem of Older Workers," *Monthly Labor Review*, May, pp. 3–12.

Silvestri, George T., and John M. Lukasiewicz. 1987. "A Look at Occupational Employment Trends to the Year 2000," *Monthly Labor Review*, September, pp. 46–63.

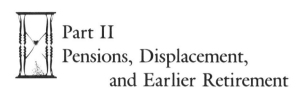

Part II
Pensions, Displacement, and Earlier Retirement

An Aging Work Force? The Dog That Didn't Bark

JOHN D. OWEN

The aging of the work force that is occurring might better be described as a "middle-aging." While it is true that there are relatively fewer younger people entering it, there is also a decline, not an increase, in the proportion of the labor force aged 55 or older.

Both the "pull" of more attractive pensions and the "push" of private and public efforts to ease older workers into retirement reduce the age at which the average person leaves the labor force, and this has been enough to offset the very large increase that has occurred in the proportion of the aged in the population as a whole: on balance, fewer older people remain employed.

J. D. O.

"Is there any other point to which you would wish to draw my attention?"
"To the curious incident of the dog in the night-time."
"The dog did nothing in the night-time."
"That was the curious incident," remarked Sherlock Holmes.

(A. Conan Doyle, "Silver Blaze")

An Aging Work Force?

Predictions by industrial gerontologists of a rapidly aging work force have not come to pass. A decade ago, Sheppard and Rix's now classic *The Graying of Working America*[1] alerted the public to this possibility. The problems that this hypothetical development would raise for

1. Harold L. Sheppard and Sara E. Rix, *The Graying of Working America: The Coming Crisis of Retirement-Age Policy* (New York: The Free Press, 1977).

industry and government have been discussed and private and public policy remedies considered.

However, the aging work force—at least in the sense of a work force dominated by those over, say, 50 or 55 years of age—has been a dog that didn't bark. This "curious incident," in Holmes's phrase, has had important social and economic consequences. Like some other well-known nonevents, it deserves serious study.

The age structure of a labor force is determined arithmetically by the age structure of the population and by the proportion of each age group that participates in the labor force. Hence one analyzes changes in the age structure of the labor force by looking at two different phenomena: changes in the age structure of the population and changes in the rates of participation of different age groups.

The U.S. population has aged, is aging, and will continue to age: the proportion of the population over 14 years of age that is 65 years old or older has more than doubled since 1920, from less than 7 percent to over 15 percent. Further substantial increases are expected early in the next century, when the baby boom generation reaches age 65. Significant increases have also occurred in the proportion of the population that is middle-aged. These upward trends have two causes, a lower birth rate and increased longevity. Immigration of younger people does tend to decrease this trend, but it is not sufficiently large to be a significant offsetting factor.

There have also been important fluctuations within this trend, largely resulting from the effects of the baby boom generation and the subsequent baby bust; for example, the arrival of baby boomers at child-bearing age now raises, temporarily, the number of newborn Americans, so that in the years immediately ahead there will be an increase in the numbers of very young (the children of the baby boomers) as well as in the numbers of the middle-aged (the baby boomers themselves). But these fluctuations do not alter the long-term upward trend in the population age structure.

The extent to which different age groups in the population participate in the economy has also changed, however, and this has offset the trend in the population structure. Both the data on participation as such and a more sophisticated measure, labor input per capita, which reflects changes in the number of hours worked per participant as well as whether an individual participates,[2] show this offsetting effect.

2. For a further discussion of this measure, and for the derivation of the historical data cited throughout this paper, see John D. Owen, *Working Lives: The American Work Force since 1920* (Lexington, Mass.: D. C. Heath–Lexington Books, 1986). See also the very interesting recent paper by Robert L. Clark,

These long-term data reveal a complex pattern. There has been virtually no change in the per capita labor supply of those in the prime-age group (25–44 years of age) in the past seventy years. For this group, declines in the average work week have been offset by increases in the proportion of women who participate in the labor force. However, sharp reductions are found in the per capita labor input of younger people (14–19 and 20–24 years of age) and of older people (over 65 years). And a smaller decline is observed in the per capita input of those 45–64 years old, especially among those 55 or older.

If we think of the cross-sectional age distribution of per capita labor input as an inverted U, with its peak at the prime-age years 25–44 and the lower levels at younger and older ages, we find that while the level of the peak has shown little change in the past seventy years, the slope of the inverted U has become progressively steeper as one moves away from the prime-age years.

These labor supply changes reflect two basic trends. Important progress has been made in raising the age of entrance into the labor force and in keeping young people in school. In recent decades, the major change has been the declining participation of the aged. Those 65 years and over and, increasingly, those in the 55- to 64-year-old group have left the labor force, reducing the average age of retirement to less than 62 years.

These contrasting trends in population structure and in participation rates have offset each other, so that the average age of the labor force has not changed very much. The mean age of the civilian labor force aged 16 or more, 39.0 in 1948, was 37.1 years in 1986, a drop of only 1.9 years.[3] There have been interesting fluctuations. The influx of young baby boomers lowered the average in the late 1970s, while the maturing of the baby boomers has now increased it somewhat. The median age of the labor force is forecast by the U.S. Department of Labor to rise further, by 3.6 years, in the 1986–2000 period.[4] But that effect will be associated with a decline in the number of youths relative to prime-age or early-middle-aged workers (i.e., those 25–54 years old), rather than with an increase

---

"The Future of Work and Retirement," *Research on Aging* 10, no. 2 (June 1988): 169–93.

3. See the paper by Mary Jablonski, Kent Kunze, and Larry Rosenblum in this volume.

4. Howard N. Fullerton, "Labor Force Projections, 1986–2000," *Monthly Labor Review* 110 (September 1987): 28. For labor market forecasts by the U.S. Department of Labor, see also the paper by Ronald E. Kutscher and Howard N. Fullerton in this volume.

in the relative numbers of older workers. Moreover, this moderate aging effect will also only be temporary and will recede as the baby boomers themselves begin to retire. In any event, a comparison of the 1948 data with the projection for the year 2000 indicates only a very small *net* increase over half a century.

Another measure of the aging of the work force—and one that directly reflects the extent to which older workers contribute to the economy—is the share of the total labor supplied to the economy contributed by those over 65. While this rose somewhat after 1920—from 4 percent then to 5 percent in 1950—it has since declined sharply, to about 1.5 percent. It is expected to fall still further in the years ahead, as retirements become even more common.[5]

The Middle-Aging of America?

When one turns from the oldest group of the middle-aged (those 45 to 64 years old), the picture is more ambiguous. This group has increased its share of labor input in the past sixty-odd years from less than a quarter in 1920 to about three-tenths today. But this figure reached its peak twenty years ago (it was at 36 percent in 1970) and has been declining since. The earlier increase in the relative size of the middle-aged group was due to declines in the proportion of labor supplied by young people (aged 14–24 years) and older people (aged 65 and older) as their participation rates fell. There was no increase in this period in the importance of middle-aged workers relative to prime-age individuals (25–44 years). The more recent decline in relative importance of this middle-aged group in the labor force was, however, associated both with changes in the population structure, especially the large number of baby boomers reaching school-leaving age, and with declines in the participation rates of middle-aged workers, especially those in the 55–64 age group.

The Department of Labor predicts that the remaining years of this century will see both increases in the proportion of the population that is middle-aged and further declines in the rate at which they participate in the labor force. The net result is likely to be an increase in the proportion of the work force that is 45–54 years old and a decline in the fraction aged 55–64 (because increased retirement rates will affect this group more).

5. See Owen, *Working Lives*, p. 157 and discussion pp. 139–55.

Why the Work Force Didn't Age: A Statistical Explanation

As we see, the work force didn't age because of the declining participation rates of older people. If age patterns of labor force participation *had* remained stable, changes in age patterns in the population would have dominated, and a very different result would have obtained: we would have indeed observed a "graying of working America." For example, as recently as 1920, the per capita labor input of the group aged 65 and over was more than three-fifths that of all those 14 years of age and over, at a time when they constituted about 7 percent of the population and contributed 4 percent of the labor supply. But the per capita contribution of the older worker has fallen to less than one-sixth of the average level: the older group constitutes about 15 percent of the over-14 population but contributes less than 2 percent of the labor supply. If older workers had just maintained their original relationship to other age groups (i.e., if their per capita labor input were still three-fifths of the average), they would now supply about one-eleventh of the total labor input—four to five times their actual contribution and more than twice their relative contribution in 1920.

This level of labor supply by the aged might be physically possible, despite what has been called the "aging of the aged" occurring as a higher percentage of people lives beyond age 70. The health of the aged has probably improved,[6] while the number of hours they must work if employed fulltime has dropped sharply: in 1920 average hours were 50 to 60 hours per week for most people, while today the aged don't have to work more than 35 to 40 hours, in most cases, in full-time jobs. Moreover, many older workers now succeed in finding part-time work.

Increased participation among late-middle-aged workers could also help to produce an aging work force. In 1920, the per capita labor supply of middle-aged workers was about nine-tenths of that of those aged 25–44, but this ratio has since fallen to about four-fifths. Much of the drop was concentrated among the late-middle-aged (55–64). A restoration of the 1920 level is certainly physically possible for this large group and would significantly contribute to an aging of the work force.

6. Though some analysts argue that medical advances have enabled more older persons in ill health to live longer.

Why the Work Force Didn't Age: Economic Explanations

Economic explanations of the reduced employment of older Americans can be found both in long-term shifts in the demand for their labor by employers and in shifts in the supply of labor by individuals. There is scattered evidence that the demand for older workers has been declining for some time. Changes in the industry and occupation mix have not been favorable to their employment: declines in sectors employing large numbers of older people, especially agriculture, and increases in the service sector and other areas where they are poorly represented have had adverse effects on demand.

Some objective evidence is available on this point. An index of changes in the proportion of employment in each of the ten major occupational categories since 1920[7] can be constructed. One can then determine how the employment of older people would have changed if they had continued to hold the same proportion of jobs in each occupation. This measure indicates that shifts in such major occupational categories as the decline of farming alone predict the decline of about 20 percent in the relative demand for workers over 65 years of age that took place in the past sixty years. Since further shifts occur within major categories, it is likely that an index based on a more detailed breakdown of occupation would show an even greater drop in the occupational demand for older workers.

A second adverse factor affecting the employment of older people has been the long-term trend toward bureaucratization of workplace relations—especially the decline of self-employment, the growth of private and corporate bureaucracies, and increased government regulation. Self-employed individuals often can gradually reduce their work effort (along with their remuneration) as they age. But older workers in a modern bureaucracy not only do not have their wages and hours reduced but often see their compensation package increase, partly because of increased health, pension, vacation, and other costs to their employers. This provides an incentive to the firm to terminate its relationship with the employee.

A partial offset is found in some protections offered the older worker in the typical bureaucracy, especially seniority rules and discrimination legislation that prevent employers from dismissing workers simply on account of age. These protections have forced employers to find other means of terminating the employment relationship.

7. See Owen, *Working Lives*, pp. 146–55.

Technical innovations may also affect the demand for older workers. But while dramatic changes in the nature of work have occurred, their overall impact here is not easy to evaluate. The acceleration in the rate of technical change has led employers to put greater emphasis on hiring young people, whom employers often regard as better educated and more adaptable, and hence easier to train. At the same time, though, technical change has greatly reduced the need for physical strength, which once put older people at a disadvantage in the labor market.

Finally, a number of writers have argued that the decline in demand for the older worker has accelerated in the 1980s as a result of intense competition and corporate restructuring. Some employers have ignored what their employees had thought was an "implicit contract" of secure employment until normal retirement age, and have either dismissed older workers or found ways to induce them to resign. Rapidly rising health care costs are also said to be a contributing factor here.[8]

These pressures have been felt sharply in industries such as autos and steel, where long-term relationships with employees have been common but which are now especially hard hit by competitive forces. These declining industries often have a disproportionately large number of older workers.

In summary, the trends affecting employer demand for the older worker are fairly complex and difficult to assess. But a persuasive case can be made that their overall effect has been negative.

Those who emphasize supply-side explanations of the long-term trend toward earlier retirement sometimes point out that most people leave the labor force voluntarily, and then go on to argue that these retirees are often responding to generous incentives, including pensions from Social Security and their employers.[9] It is important to note, though, that one can concede the importance of positive incentives for retirements without admitting that supply-side, rather than demand-side, factors are paramount. The incentives themselves may also reflect demand factors.[10]

Declining employment demand for a group can be expressed in different ways. It can take the form of a flat exclusion from employment, as when a worker is dismissed and cannot find a job at any price, or it can be felt in the form of a reduction in the price of one's services. For example, older people may find that they can only obtain employment at

8. Although the existence of retiree health plans often reduces this incentive.

9. For some individuals, though, the expectation that the size of the pension will increase with further service is likely to lead to a deferral of retirement. Cf. the discussion of "pension wealth" in the papers by Richard Burkhauser and Joseph F. Quinn and by Robert L. Clark in this volume.

10. Cf. the discussion by Harold L. Sheppard in this volume.

lower wages and in jobs that don't provide health care, employment security, and other benefits.[11]

But it can also take the form of an attractive offer to leave the labor force voluntarily. A company can use a retirement program to ease out workers over some standard age level. An early retirement program may be used to eliminate workers younger than the standard retirement age. The government can fashion a pension system that encourages retirement and a system of medical benefits that assists retirees.

A good example of this ambiguity is our Social Security system. The Social Security Act was passed in 1935, in the depths of the Depression. One major purpose of the legislation was to induce old men to leave their jobs so as to create opportunities for younger people. A second major purpose was to provide sustenance for the many older workers who had lost their jobs and couldn't find new ones.

Many private pension plans were crafted with much the same goals in mind: to create opportunities for young people (often perceived as more productive) and to provide some form of sustenance for the displaced older worker.

Such corporate and social decisions can reflect the view that the employment demand for older workers is limited and that a relatively painless method must be used to deal with that problem. Hence one can at least question the exogeneity of some of these measures. In more conventional economic terms, one can say that demand factors help determine the price to the older person for supplying labor. If the net labor supply price is the difference between the income of the worker who stays in the labor market and the retirement income of that worker, then a rise in retirement income (or in other similar incentives to retire) clearly lowers the supply price. But the underlying cause may still be found on the demand side of the labor market.

On the other hand, one can also tell a plausible, truly "supply-side story" to explain the development of these retirement programs. One can see our Social Security system as primarily a device for forcing individuals to save for their old age or (a somewhat more persuasive view) for providing for intergenerational transfers of resources from younger to older people that enable older people to enjoy leisure in their later years.

In constructing this supply-side scenario, one can begin by noting that for over one hundred years there was a long-term downward trend in male labor supply. Until the middle of this century, this reduction took the form of cuts in working hours as well as reductions in the

11. Cf. the discussion of displaced workers in Steven Sandell and Stephen Baldwin's essay in this volume.

retirement age. But once the eight-hour-day, five-day week (with an annual vacation) was achieved, attention was focused on obtaining retirement pensions.

A simple explanation of this development is to say that as income increased, workers first sought to reduce their work effort on those margins where the last hour was both painful and comparatively unproductive, and where reductions were easiest to organize. The first logical target was the long workday, the second, the work week and year. Clearly, the fatigue of long daily or weekly hours was productive of much pain and ill health and also had a negative effect on hourly productivity. Moreover, it was much easier to organize a reduction in the workday or week than it was to set up a pension scheme (easier, at least, outside government employment or other sectors where employee tenure is secure and the future ability of the employer to redeem his promise of a pension is not in question).

Once the forty-hour week was achieved, however, the next goal was inevitably a reorganization of corporate and social structures so that a comfortable retirement could be obtained. Work in the later years was often painful (especially for those in ill health or in stressful occupations), and the productivity of the older worker in these circumstances was perceived to be less. While the case for retirement on these grounds might not have been as strong as, say, that for reduction of daily hours from twelve to eight, it did have considerable force.

In practice, then, the relative importance of supply and demand forces in reducing the participation of older workers is difficult to determine. A reasonable conclusion is that both played a significant role.[12]

And, finally, one should also consider influences on the development of our retirement system that are noneconomic—or at least are outside this supply and demand framework. For example, the favorable tax treatment of employer contributions to pension plans is widely cited as encouraging firms to offer this benefit. Similarly, one can cite a number of technical and organizational advances that made possible the development of an effective and relatively inexpensive Social Security system (leading some to call it a new "social technology"). And we can look to more narrowly political considerations in explaining some Congressional amendments to the original Social Security legislation, increasing pensions and other benefits.

12. See Owen, *Working Lives*, for econometric evidence of the effect of supply and demand factors on wages and employment of different age groups. The fact that wages for older workers do not show a relative decline over time does not indicate that demand factors were not important. The supply of older workers was being reduced rapidly. A hypothetical discussion of the likely result if supply had not been cut is given in the text below.

What If the Work Force Had Truly Aged?

It is interesting to consider what would have happened if there had not been a reduction in the participation rate of the aged—if those 65 years of age and older had continued to supply about three-fifths as much labor time per capita as younger people, so that about one-eleventh of the labor supply now came from this group (which would become, say, one in ten in the years ahead, as the population aged further). Similarly, one can speculate about the effects of a restoration to earlier levels of the participation rates of the late-middle-aged (55–64).

One can plausibly argue that such a large increase in the number of older job seekers would yield a significant deterioration of their employment opportunities and wages. Some statistical calculations carried out to ascertain the sensitivity of hourly wages to the relative size of an age group indicate that substantial negative effects can be predicted.[13] Such results support the common-sense view that there is a limited supply of jobs suitable for and available to older people.

However, while it is prudent to use predictions from supply-and-demand analysis as our baseline forecast, we should not ignore the possibility that society might, if it were compelled to do so, restructure the work force so as to find new uses for older people. It is relevant to recall here that neither the recent massive entrance of women into the labor force nor the migrations of blacks into industrial employment led to a deterioration of their relative wages. A very large increase in the number of older people in the work force could well generate the necessary political pressure for federal regulations mandating special, favorable treatment for the aged in hiring, training, promotion, and other employment practices[14] and so protect their economic status.

Were large numbers of older workers integrated into the labor force by an increase in the retirement age, it could be difficult to maintain the productivity level of the remainder—at least, present retirement policies are sometimes defended on the basis that they permit increases in the level of effort that can be demanded from the work force. Some

13. See, for example, Michael L. Wachter, "Intermediate Swing in Labor Force Participation," *Brookings Papers on Economic Activity* 22 (1977): 545–74; Owen, *Working Lives*.

14. If employers regarded a worker's likely retirement age as, say, 70 rather than 60, they might be more willing to make training and other investments in employees in their fifties, even without federal coercion. These investments would increase the productivity of older workers, and so make them more competitive. A similar logic would forecast that employees in their fifties would make more extensive investments in their own workplace productivity if the retirement age were increased.

would also expect a negative effect on the flexibility and trainability of the work force[15] were older workers represented in it in numbers.

There now appears to be some self-selection in retirement, with the less fit tending to leave the labor force,[16] thus reducing the extent to which productivity declines with age. But this relationship could well change if participation of the aged greatly expanded, bringing in many less healthy people. Employers could then be expected to become more aggressive in endeavoring to terminate workers who are less fit, with concomitant increases in performance testing, litigation over age discrimination, and so on.

An increase in the retirement age is also likely to limit promotional opportunities for young people, according to some recent sociological analysis.[17] It would also reduce the rate at which the labor force is becoming female and nonwhite, since so many retirees are now white males.

Last—but certainly not least in importance—there would be significant noneconomic disadvantages for older individuals themselves if the retirement age were increased. They would lose the leisure they would have enjoyed if they were out of the work force. In some cases, retirement means escape from a stressful or unhealthy job environment, so that a delay in retirement can have ill effects on health and longevity.

But these objections to increasing the retirement age should not obscure the fact that we are now paying a very large price for *not* having an aging work force. A potential increase in national labor input per capita of from 6 to 8 percent or more is being forgone, an enormous opportunity cost. Part of this cost is now reflected in lower living standards for the aged and (perhaps) more limited bequests for their children. The remainder is experienced as costs to the rest of society in the form of forgone tax receipts, Social Security outlays, private pension outlays, and other intergenerational transfers.

Will the Dog Now Bark?

It is not surprising, then, that many have urged a reversal of the trend toward early retirement. While few would want to return to the 1920 level of participation, many would regard some increase as salutary.

15. An increase in retirement age would also provide an opportunity for a major shift of the responsibility for providing health care for older Americans from the federal government to private employers. But see the discussion below.
16. On this point, cf. the paper by Olivia Mitchell in this volume.
17. See Shelby Stewman's essay in this volume.

The prospects for such a reversal do not appear to be good, however. Recent changes were made in the Social Security system designed to increase the retirement age, but these have not yet succeeded in reversing the trend toward early retirement (though they may have slowed it down).

It has been argued that reform of the Social Security system must be accompanied by changes in the pension policies of private employers if the retirement age is to be increased.[18] There are a number of ways in which government could induce firms to increase their employment of older workers. For example, such employment could be subsidized by excusing employers from paying the Social Security taxes of older workers or by paying their medical insurance premiums. Such measures would impose costs.[19] Alternatively, the income support for the retired could be reduced, inducing many older people to remain in the labor force. Here too there are obvious social costs. But without some large-scale change in government policy, the prospects for a true graying of the American work force in the remaining years of this century do not appear to be good.

Clearly, the proportion of the population that is older will rise in the next eleven years. And this aging process will accelerate in the first decades of the next century as the baby boom ages further. But unless the trend toward early retirement is reversed, only modest increases in the proportion of work that is done by older workers is likely. Perhaps the most likely forecast is a moderate "middle-aging" of the work force, with some increase in the proportion of work done by those aged 40–55 relative to younger people.

18. The complementarities between Social Security policy and the design of private employer pension policies is discussed in the paper by Richard Burkhauser and Joseph F. Quinn in this volume.

19. These costs would doubtless include higher expenditures by the U.S. Treasury and a further intervention of the federal government in the fields of medical insurance and pensions. Reducing or eliminating the tax exemptions of pensions could be considered, but this would also have a number of negative effects, perhaps including a negative impact on savings.

Too Old to Work, Too Young to Die: A Union Program for Retired Workers

DOUGLAS FRASER

Fraser recalls the first major industrial private retirement plans negotiated in the automobile industry almost forty years ago. In response to the rapidly growing number of union retirees, over the years the UAW developed a far-reaching structure and program to accommodate the needs and desires of its retired members. At the local union level, within the international union structure, and through regional councils and in communities throughout the country, the UAW has established an active and meaningful program for its retirees that continues to involve them in the ongoing work of the union.

I. B.

Before the contract negotiations at Ford Motor Company in 1949, there was no retirement pension program for union-represented workers in the U.S. automobile industry. Workers left the shop when they became too old to work, when they were disabled, or when they died. In the 1940s, however, United Auto Workers initiated a campaign to establish a pension plan throughout the auto industry. The campaign slogan was: "Too Old to Work, Too Young to Die."

Mobilization for the Pension

In 1947 contract negotiations, in response to the union's demand, Ford Motor Company submitted a pension proposal, but it was far short of the union's objective, and in a referendum vote, the workers rejected it. In 1949, the union mounted a nationwide mobilization drive among its members and their families in support of the demand for negotiated pension plans. At union meetings and conferences, in the union newspaper and other written material, and in community rallies, members of the UAW learned about the program, and they enthusiastically rallied their forces in support of the demand. The Ford contract was the first of the auto contracts to be negotiated that year, and the pension demand stood front and center on that bargaining table. Ford rejected the UAW proposal.

Walter Reuther, as president of the UAW, led the negotiations for the union. He thereupon scheduled a mass meeting at Cass Technical High School in Detroit for all Ford workers aged 60 or older. The Cass Tech auditorium was jammed with about six thousand workers—a packed house—and the campaign was off and running. At the Ford negotiations that followed, a pension plan did emerge whose basic provisions were responsive to the union's proposal. There was to be a monthly benefit of $100, including federal Social Security benefits, for a worker retiring with thirty years of service. Of equal importance, however, were certain fundamental principles agreed to by both parties. An actuarially sound pension fund would be established. This provision obligated the company to make payments to cover both past and future pension credit accumulation, thereby guaranteeing that pension benefits would be paid, and it was a noncontributory plan—the workers did not have to contribute toward the pension fund. The plan also established a joint board of administration, with equal representation from the union and the company.

This time, the workers overwhelmingly ratified the contract. The next target was Chrysler. There the union met strong opposition—not against the basic benefit of $100 per month for thirty years of service, but against the principle of actuarially established funding. Chrysler did not want to set aside any funds labeled a "pension fund"—the company preferred to call it a "kitty." This terminology was designed to avoid the requirement of making regular payments into the pension fund to cover all past and future obligations. Chrysler argued that it had never missed a payroll and that therefore there was no need to create a pension fund. The company wanted "pay-as-you-go" benefits rather than funded guaranteed benefits. Finally, Chrysler told the union to hire its own actuaries and rejected the principles that had been agreed upon at Ford.

The union did hire its own actuaries. When they reviewed Chrysler's proposal, their professional advice was that the corporation's insistence on managing pension payments on a pay-as-you-go basis wasn't "actuarially sound." Not many in the union truly understood what that meant, but "actuarially sound" became the battle cry. Chrysler would not agree to establish a pension fund. The workers went on strike mainly over that issue, and the strike lasted 104 days. After 90 days of shutdown, on a day in February when the union was holding an outdoor rally of support for the striking workers, Chrysler made its first move. While Walter Reuther was addressing the crowd, word came that Chrysler was willing to make a one-time deposit of $90 million in a pension account as a sign of good faith. Walter interrupted his address to announce Chrysler's new proposal. From the back of the crowd a worker shouted, "Yeah, Walter, but is it actuarially sound?"

The strike lasted 14 more days before a settlement was reached, tracking the pension plan settlement at Ford. But for Chrysler's intransigent position on the issue of "actuarial funding," the strike would not have been necessary. In the annals of collective bargaining, actuarial soundness as the major cause of a strike is, to say the least, unique. The funding principle, however, was vital to ensure that pension benefits would be paid when employees retired. It was the strike at Chrysler that nailed down the principle and made funded pension plans a reality.

Private Pensions and Social Security Benefits

The UAW had quite deliberately linked the pension plan to the size of the Social Security benefit. For twelve years after the Social Security system was enacted by Congress, the Social Security benefit had not been increased. The business community had successfully opposed every effort to have Congress increase it. The union reasoned that if the amount of a company's pension payment was linked to Social Security and the pension plan was noncontributory, the companies would have an incentive to help convince Congress to increase the benefit. Since the maximum combined negotiated benefit of $100 a month was a fixed amount, any increase in Social Security would reduce the amount which would have to be paid out of the company pension fund and thereby reduce the company financial obligation.

Sure enough, about three months after the Chrysler agreement was ratified, Ernie Breech, then president of Ford Motor Company, traveled to Washington to testify before Congress in favor of increasing Social Security payments. Congress responded by increasing the basic benefit by 80 percent. Thus, the first collectively bargained pension plans in the auto industry paved the way for retirees throughout the nation to receive an increase in their monthly Social Security checks. (It is, by the way, an excellent example of the possible interrelationship between collective bargaining and social progress.)

Later in 1950, in contract negotiations with General Motors Corporation, the company pension was separated from Social Security, and from then on the company pension has been independent of the amount of Social Security payments retirees receive.

Negotiated pension plans quickly spread to the agricultural implement and aerospace industries as well as to supplier plants and other industries across the nation.

The Issue of Compulsory Retirement

Chrysler had insisted on a compulsory retirement age of 68. The UAW objected to the provision, but in the final hours of negotiations reluctantly agreed. I was a member of the bargaining committee that year and was given the task of meeting with the first group of workers who were to be forcibly retired. The pension plan actually went into effect a year after the contract settlement to allow time to work out the details of administration and prepare the workers who would be retiring. At this first meeting, I had to explain why the people in the group had to retire. One "old" fellow (he was 71) said to me, "Why are you forcing me to retire? I'll race you down the street, and if I can't beat you, I'll retire voluntarily, but if I can beat you, I'm not retiring." I was about 30 years old at the time, but this guy looked pretty vigorous, so I didn't take him on. But I started to worry about what we were doing to these workers. After all the struggle to win the pension plan, these people didn't want to be forced into retirement. They felt that retirement should be essentially a voluntary decision.

Walter Reuther often consulted with highly respected people outside the union when he needed expert advice. The UAW had a committee of gerontologists advising us on how to respond to the problem of keeping the retirees active and leading fulfilling and rewarding lives. (It was pretty presumptuous of us, when I think of it now, our trying to tell them what they should do for the rest of their lives.) While we were pondering the problem, Leonard Woodcock, who was then a UAW vice president, talked to his father about the retirement question and asked him, "What do *you* want?" His father replied, "I want to be left alone." That was probably better advice than we received from the experts.

The UAW quickly began to develop pre-retirement counseling programs for prospective retirees and their spouses. Some were designed and administered jointly by the local union and the local management. Others were undertaken directly by the local union with the assistance of the union's national headquarters.

The problem of compulsory retirement was subsequently resolved, and, in any event, with the introduction of the early retirement feature, before long over 90 percent of all auto workers were retiring well before the age of 65. In fact, with the introduction of the 30-and-out and other early retirement programs, most workers leave, at the latest, when they reach 62 and become eligible for Social Security.

The UAW Establishes Retiree Councils

Beginning in 1951, the UAW altered its constitution in response to the anticipated surge in member retirements. It established a National Retired Workers Department and a National UAW Retired Workers Council and provided for the election of a retired member to each local union executive board. Retirees also voted in local union elections and were represented by elected delegates at UAW national conventions. UAW retirees flocked to the union activities. Indeed, any incumbent who ignores the problems of the retirees does so at his or her own political peril, I can tell you!

In 1964, the companies agreed to a voluntary dues checkoff for retirees. Originally the checkoff was $1 per month. At the UAW national convention in 1986, the retirees proposed raising the voluntary dues to $2 a month; the convention delegates agreed, and the constitution was changed accordingly. There are about 413,000 UAW retirees today (1988), and over 300,000 of them pay the voluntary monthly dues. It is clear that the retirees feel that the union's program and activities in their behalf are worth paying for: recreation programs, political and legislative activity, direct involvement in local union affairs, improvements in their negotiated pension, health care, and life insurance provisions, etc.

Over time, many union retirees moved to other areas of the country. The union established "area retiree councils," and there are now 24 such councils scattered around the United States. For instance, there are 6 in Florida, 2 in Michigan, 3 in Arkansas, and 2 in the Las Vegas area—believe it or not (auto workers must be great gamblers). The most recently established retiree council is in Puerto Rico, with 910 members. These people are deeply involved in the political life of their community and the nation. In fact, many people who were never active in their local unions when they were working in the plant are now all wrapped up in local, state, and national politics and community affairs.

There is a National Advisory Committee, which is elected by the retirees through the local unions. The Retired Workers Department now has a fulltime staff of 17 and works closely with the chapters and councils around the country in the development and implementation of the various retiree programs. All these activities are financed from the voluntary dues that the retirees pay. Retirees work with many coalitions—senior citizens' groups, the National Council of Senior Citizens, the National Council on the Aging, the Black Caucus on Aging, the Consumer Federation, the Housing Federation, and the Committee for National Health Insurance.

Life after Retirement

But the bottom line is whether the UAW retirees are leading that rewarding, fulfilling, and happy life we all were worried about in 1950. People like me, who go to retirees' meetings, are convinced that the answer is "Yes." No doubt about it. These meetings have tremendous turnouts, whether at the local, regional, or national level. When you ask a retiree, "How are you doing? Are you enjoying retirement?" you get an instantaneous and exuberant reply. They say that they are having a great time, that it's a great life, that they should have retired earlier.

At a retiree meeting in Florida with 800 people in attendance (800, and this was just one of the six area retiree council meetings in the state), I asked a fellow I knew who had been a shop steward in a Chrysler plant how he liked retirement. He said, "It's the happiest period of my life. When I was a kid, I had a lot of fun, but no freedom because my parents told me what to do and what not to do. And then when I grew up, I was raising my own kids, and it was sometimes very, very tough, particularly at Chrysler, with occasional layoffs. Now that I'm retired, I have much more fun than when I was young. I make my own decisions, and I don't have the burden of responsibility."

In the 1940s, the UAW raised the slogan "Too Old to Work, Too Young to Die." It embarked on a program that is approaching its fortieth year of progress toward assuring the well-being of workers who retire. The goal was to make it possible for workers to retire with dignity, economic security, and the opportunity to continue to participate in union, community, and national life. In large measure, we have accomplished that goal and will continue to progress in the tomorrows to come.

Pensions in an Aging Society

ROBERT L. CLARK

The development of private pension plans in the United States has played an important role in limiting the labor supply of older Americans. Clark describes the various types of private pension plans and discusses how they influence the labor supply of older people. However, he advocates a cautious attitude toward government regulations designed to redirect private pension policies toward encouraging later retirements—unintended negative results could follow.

J. D. O.

Employer pensions represent an important form of compensation for many workers in the United States. The promise of benefits in retirement has a cash value that workers are willing to buy through wage reductions. Pensions also can be used by employers to achieve various personnel objectives such as reduced turnover or increased retirements. Pension costs vary with the age and tenure of workers, and pension policies can be adopted to alter the age structure of the work force. The following analysis will show that the aging of the work force increases the importance of pensions to the employer, while individual aging increases the value of pension benefits to the worker.

Other papers in this volume describe the relationship between the age structure of the population and various demographic rates such as age-specific mortality rates, fertility rates, and immigration rates. Current projections indicate that the population will continue to age over the next fifty years. With stable labor force participation rates, the aging of the population will produce an aging of the total work force; however, participation rates have not been stable. In particular, the proportion of older men has been declining rapidly, and this decline moderates the aging of the work force (Cantrell and Clark 1982). Pensions are an important determinant of job mobility and retirement and, therefore, influence the aging of the labor force.

While the age structure of the work force of individual firms is affected by the age structure of the labor force, other determinants of a firm's age structure include the rate of growth of the firm and the personnel policies that govern quit, hiring, and retirement rates. Since pension policies affect each of these rates, employer pensions also play an important role in determining the age structure of individual firm work forces.

The primary objective of this paper is to examine the relationship between pensions and the age structure of the labor force. First, information is presented on the incidence of pensions and various pension characteristics. This discussion is followed by a review of competing theories concerning the effects of pensions along with an analysis of the relationships among age, pension compensation, and earnings. These findings can then be used to illustrate the effects of pensions on job mobility, retirement, and the age structure of the work force. Finally, the regulatory environment and choice of pension type will be examined.

Pension Coverage and Plan Characteristics

Prior to World War II, the proportion of the private work force covered by employer pensions was relatively low, and coverage was expanding only slowly. Early pensions generally covered workers in the railroad, banking, and public utility sectors of the economy. In the immediate postwar period, the number of employers offering pensions and the number of workers covered by pensions increased rapidly. As a result, the proportion of wage and salary workers in the private sectorcovered by employer pensions increased from 25 percent in 1950 to over 50 percent in 1984. Most of this growth, however, occurred prior to 1975. In fact, Andrews (1985) reports that the coverage rate actually fell from 56 to 52 percent between 1979 and 1983. Ippolito (1986) estimates that in 1984 there were 788,000 private pension plans that contained 57.5 million active participants and 8 million annuitants.

The probability that any particular person will be covered by a pension plan on his job varies greatly with both personal and job characteristics. Using the May 1983 Current Population Survey, Allen and Clark (1987) determine coverage rates by various attributes and then estimate a probit equation for pension coverage. The Current Population Survey is conducted periodically by the Bureau of the Census. The survey in May 1983 included a pension supplement, and these data were used by Allen and Clark to examine pension coverage. The probit equation shows the net effect of one characteristic on the probability of pension coverage, holding all other factors constant. Both the coverage rate and the probit estimates are shown in Table 1. The sample in this analysis is restricted to fulltime private wage and salary workers. Their study showed that persons whose jobs are covered by collective bargaining agreements are much more likely to participate in a pension plan than nonunion workers. The coverage rate for union workers is 82 percent, compared to only 44 percent for nonunion workers. The probit results show that the net effect of being a union member increases the probability of being covered by a pension by 26.3 percentage points.

Allen and Clark found that the size of the workplace (establishment) and the size of the company are also important determinants of pension coverage. In establishments with fewer than 25 workers, only 28 percent of workers are covered by a pension plan. Coverage rates rise to 51 percent in establishments with 25 to 99 workers and to 86 percent in establishments with 1,000 or more workers. Using the company measure of size, the coverage rate for workers in companies with fewer than 25 workers is 17 percent, compared to 80 percent for workers in companies with 1,000 or more employees.

Coverage rates increase with higher earnings and advancing age. The coverage rate for workers earning less than $4 an hour is 13 percent, compared to a rate of 70 percent for those earning $10 or more per hour. Only about a quarter of workers aged 16 to 24 are covered by pensions. Pension coverage rises to 50 percent for those between 25 and 34 and is over 60 percent for older workers. The positive relationships between coverage and earnings and age also are shown in the probit results. Demographic variables indicate that males and married workers are more likely to have pension coverage. Finally, Table 1 reveals substantial differences in coverage across industry and occupational groups.

TYPES OF PLANS

Pension plans are of two basic types: defined benefit and defined contribution. In defined benefit plans, the company promises to pay a specified benefit to workers when they reach certain age and service requirements. The company is required by law to deposit, in an approved pension fund, sufficient funds to finance the liabilities accruing to their workers. Plans of this type comprise about 30 percent of all plans, but because they are more common among large employers, defined benefit plans cover approximately 80 percent of pension participants.

Table 1: DETERMINANTS OF PENSION COVERAGE, 1983 CPS

Determinant	Percentage Covered by Pension	Marginal Impact on Pension Coverage Probability from Probit Equation (×100)
Union contract coverage		
Nonunion	44.1	—
Union	82.2	26.3
Establishment size		
Less than 25	27.8	—
25–99	51.1	2.4*
100–499	68.9	4.7
500–999	77.6	9.6
1,000 or more	85.9	10.2
Company size		
Less than 25	17.1	—
25–99	36.7	15.1
100–499	54.6	26.5
500–999	62.7	1.1
1,000 or more	79.7	45.2
Industry		
Agriculture, forestry, fisheries	11.3	4.0*
Mining	74.0	14.4
Construction	35.9	−11.0
Durables manufacturing	72.2	9.2
Nondurables manufacturing	64.7	6.2
Transportation and utilities	70.8	2.2*
Wholesale trade	52.1	11.6
Retail trade	31.7	−3.5*
Finance, insurance, real estate	58.8	10.7
Services	39.6	—
Occupation		
Executive, administrative, managerial	60.2	—
Professional specialty	61.6	0.1*
Technicians & related support	60.0	−3.0*
Sales	42.6	−6.0
Administrative support, including clerical	55.8	3.4*
Private household service	0.0	—
Protective service	37.7	−17.7
Other service	27.6	−8.9
Precision production, craft, & repair	57.4	−1.3*
Machine operators, assemblers, & inspectors	59.5	−4.7*

Table 1: CONTINUED

Determinant	Percentage Covered by Pension	Marginal Impact on Pension Coverage Probability from Probit Equation (×100)
Transportation & materials moving	53.7	−3.6*
Handlers, equipment cleaners, etc.	47.2	−3.4*
Farming, forestry, & fishing	11.1	−17.2
Region		
Northeast	57.5	7.8
North Central	58.0	10.9
South	47.5	5.0
West	47.4	—
Sex		
Female	45.6	—
Male	56.8	3.4
Marital status		
Married, spouse present	57.6	2.9
Other	42.2	—
Age		
16–24	26.0	—
25–34	50.5	13.4
35–44	61.2	20.4
45–54	62.2	24.3
55–64	62.8	24.0
Years of schooling		
Less than 9	43.6	—
9–11	44.4	1.8*
12	52.0	7.8
13–15	52.0	7.0
16	57.2	4.8*
More than 16	66.6	10.1
Average hourly earnings		
Less than $4	13.2	—
$4–$5.99	31.8	17.6
$6–$7.99	51.8	28.6
$8–$9.99	63.2	32.9
$10–$14.99	73.3	37.4
$15 or more	79.4	41.2

Note: sample is limited to private wage and salary workers between the ages of 16 and 64, usually working more than 35 hours per week. Estimates in the second column are probit estimates of the derivative of the probability function evaluated at the means of the independent variables. All of the above variables were included in the probit equation.

*Estimates with a significance level *below* the 95 percent level.

Source: Allen and Clark 1987.

Table 2: PERCENT DEFINED CONTRIBUTION COVERAGE AMONG PENSION-COVERED WORKERS, 1982

Pension Plan Size (participants)	Union	Nonunion
1–99	12.9	63.1
100–999	4.3	31.2
1,000–10,000	3.6	11.2
Greater than 10,000	.7	4.9
Total	2.0	22.4

Source: Ippolito 1988, Table 4.

Workers covered by these plans do not bear any of the financial risks associated with the invested monies, since the firm has promised a defined benefit if they meet certain age and service requirements. However, the structure of these plans tends to weight the final years of service more heavily in benefit determination. Thus the worker must bear risks associated with job changes, and the penalty imposed on workers leaving prior to retirement will tend to reduce quit rates in firms using such plans. This backloading of benefit accruals implies that the age structure of the firm's labor force will affect the rate of pension liability accrual.

In defined contribution plans, the firm promises to contribute a fixed amount of money to an individual's pension account each period. The funds are invested by the plan and accumulate throughout the worker's life. The benefit at retirement is determined by the size of the individual's pension fund at that time. The worker bears all of the risk in connection with the rate of return on the invested portfolio. Defined contribution plans are much more common among smaller, nonunion firms. Ippolito (1988) determined the proportion of pension participants covered by a defined contribution plan on the basis of firm size and union status. The results are shown in Table 2; 63 percent of pension participants in nonunion plans covering less than 100 participants are in defined contribution plans, compared with a defined contribution coverage rate of only 12.9 percent of pension participants in small union plans and 0.7 percent of participants in large union plans.

Defined contribution plans tend to be fully funded, and the worker typically has legal rights to the entire fund. As a result, these plans do not impose penalties on workers who leave their jobs, and firms offering defined contribution plans should have the same quit rates as firms not providing pension coverage. These plans usually require that the firm contribute a specified percentage of a worker's salary to the pension fund each period. Thus these plans do not increase the cost of maintaining older workers in the labor force relative to that of maintaining younger workers.

CHARACTERISTICS

In a defined contribution plan, the primary factor governing costs is the contribution rate. This rate typically is specified as a percentage of salary that the company will contribute each pay period into the worker's account. This rate varies widely across defined contribution plans. In defined benefit plans, several plan provisions play an important role in determining the value to workers and the cost to firms. Benefit formulas usually are one of two basic types: earnings-based or dollar-amount. The most frequently used method is the earnings-based formula, in which the benefit is determined by multiplying a generosity parameter times salary average times years of service. Terminal earnings plans, in which benefits are based on the salary average over the last three or five years of employment, covered 57 percent of all participants in medium and large firms in 1986. Career earnings formula plans covered an additional 5 percent of participants. These formula-type plans are used more frequently in pensions covering professional and nonunion workers.

Dollar-amount formulas provide a fixed dollar amount to all retirees or arrive at a benefit amount by multiplying years of service times a fixed dollar amount. These types of formulas cover 26 percent of participants and are used most frequently in plans covering production workers and unionized workers. Dollar-amount plans reduce the variation in benefits among workers. Thus, the use of these formulas in collectively bargained plans is consistent with the union objective of compensation equity (Allen and Clark 1986).

Key provisions influencing the value and costs of defined benefit pensions are the age of normal retirement and the age of early retirement. The Employee Benefits Survey of Medium and Large Firms (EBS) in 1986 conducted for the Bureau of Labor Statistics found that only 36 percent of the participants were covered by plans using 65 as the normal retirement age (U.S. Bureau of Labor Statistics 1987). Another 36 percent were in plans that specified retirement ages between 60 and 64, and 4 percent were in plans with retirement ages between 55 and 59. Approximately 13 percent of plans had no age requirement at all; eligibility in these plans was determined solely by length of service. Virtually all defined benefit plans allow retirement prior to the normal retirement age at reduced benefits. In most plans, the reduction in benefits is less than the actuarial equivalent of the normal retirement benefit.

As a result, the gain in pension wealth from continued work typically falls after one has met the criteria for early retirement (Kotlikoff and Wise 1985).

The benefits that workers can accrue in some plans are limited by the integration of benefits with Social Security or the use of maximum benefit restrictions. Integration with Social Security allows firms to reduce benefits paid by taking into account the Social Security benefits of the worker in determining the pension benefit. In the 1986 EBS, 62 percent of all participants covered were in plans that integrated pension benefits with Social Security benefits. Smaller plans are more likely to be integrated. This may be done either through an excess method, where greater pension benefits are paid on earnings above the Social Security earnings limit, or through an offset method, where pension benefits are reduced by a certain fraction of the Social Security benefit. Federal regulations set maximum reductions allowed by integration, and most plans set their integration standards well below the allowed limits.

Just over 40 percent of all participants are in plans that include a maximum benefit provision. The most prevalent form of benefit limitation is limitation of credited service to a specified number of years. This type of limitation covered 36 percent of participants; the most frequently used limit is thirty years. Terminal earnings plans are much more likely to include such limits than are plans with other types of benefit formulas.

Theories of Pension Effects

A worker covered by a pension plan is exchanging his labor for current earnings, the promise of future income in the form of pension benefits, and any other fringe benefits associated with his job. The value of future pension benefits depends on the implied nature of the labor contract, survival probabilities, and government regulations. Two methods of evaluating the pension wealth of workers and liabilities to firms have been advanced in the economics literature. These competing methods of determining pension wealth are referred to as the legal method and the projected earnings method. The legal method determines pension wealth using the benefit to which a worker is legally entitled based on current earnings and pension characteristics (Bulow 1982). The projected earnings method assumes a form of implicit contract in which the worker expects to be employed with the same firm until retirement (Ippolito 1986).

These methods can be used to determine the pension wealth of a worker at each year during his work life. By comparing the pension wealth across years, the pension compensation or the gain in pension wealth associated with working one additional year can be determined. These methods yield different age-pension compensation profiles and different predictions about the impact of pensions on the labor market activities of workers.

Under the legal method, the value of pension wealth and pension compensation is determined by assuming that the labor contract is valid for a single period. Of course, the contract may be renewed, but the worker acts as if he will be terminated at the end of each period. Therefore, he is willing to pay only for those pension benefits which the firm is legally required to pay if he leaves the firm at the end of the contract period. To illustrate the implications for earnings profiles, assume that the worker is covered by an earnings-based, defined benefit formula and that total compensation is equal to earnings plus pension compensation. This implies that the worker is fully paying for his pension in the form of lower wages.

Retirement benefits are determined using the benefit formula currently in place, the worker's current earnings, and years of service. If fully vested, this is the benefit to which he is legally entitled if he leaves the current job. Pension wealth is the present value of this benefit beginning at the specified retirement age and discounted back to the worker's current age.

Using this technique, pension wealth is calculated to be very low during the early working years because workers have lower earnings, little credited service, and a waiting period of many years to receive benefits. However, pension wealth rises rapidly as long as the worker remains with the firm. The growth in pension wealth is due to increased years of service, higher earnings, and a reduction in the number of years until retirement. Each of these factors accelerates the growth rate of pension wealth over time, and, as a result, the rate of growth of pension wealth will exceed the rate of growth of earnings as job tenure increases. This continues until the worker reaches the age of eligibility for retirement benefits.

If the worker remains on the job past the normal retirement age, his pension wealth in most plans will decline with continued work, and the rate of decline will accelerate with advancing age (Clark and McDermed 1986). This results from the fact that most firms do not provide an actuarial increase in benefits with postponed retirement. In addition, approximately half of all pension participants are in plans that cease to credit wage and service accruals after the normal retirement age. Thus the annual benefit may be frozen at the normal retirement age, and, with continued employment, the worker will have fewer years to receive benefits, which produces a decline in pension wealth.

Table 3: EMPLOYEE COMPENSATION AND PENSION WEALTH: LEGAL METHOD

Age	Tenure	Earnings	Pension Comp.	Pension Comp. as Percentage of Total Comp.	Annual Pension Benefit	Pension Wealth
25	0	$ 19,959	$ 41	0.21	$ 0	$ 0
30	5	25,737	402	1.54	1,654	1,530
35	10	33,318	845	2.47	4,293	5,340
40	15	42,946	1,704	3.82	8,323	13,945
45	20	55,016	3,339	5.72	14,269	32,325
50	25	69,873	6,395	8.39	22,772	70,361
55	30	87,684	11,995	12.03	34,543	147,571
60	35	108,267	22,010	16.89	50,251	302,288
64	39	126,191	35,199	21.81	65,945	532,487
65	40	164,680	5,586	3.28	70,304	613,518
70	45	246,141	−23,610	−10.61	127,045	934,312

Source: data are based on a simulation of compensation for a male worker remaining with a firm throughout his work life. He is assumed to have been hired at age 25 with total annual compensation (earnings plus pension compensation) equal to $20,000. Total compensation grows at 5.5 percent per year. The worker is covered by a pension with a normal retirement age of 65 and a benefit formula of .015 times average earnings in the last five years of work life times years of service. The market interest rate is 6 percent.

The implied life cycle pattern of earnings and pension compensation is illustrated in Table 3 for a worker who is hired initially at age 25 with total compensation equaling $20,000. Total compensation grows at an annual rate of 5.5 percent. Pension compensation is the change in pension wealth associated with the employment contract and is based on changes in service and earnings. It does not include the change in pension wealth associated with aging, which is independent of the employment contract.

The normal retirement age is 65, and the plan offers no early retirement benefits. There are no post-retirement adjustments in benefits, and the plan has immediate and full vesting. The plan continues to credit increases in earnings and service fully as long as the worker remains with the firm. The benefit formula is .015 times years of service times average earnings in the last five years. The market interest rate is 6 percent, and workers are assumed to face mortality probabilities as shown in the 1981 U.S. life table for white men (U.S. Department of Commerce 1984). These plan provisions are used for illustrative purposes and are not intended to represent any particular pension plan. For a detailed review of average plan characteristics by industrial sectors, see Allen, Clark, and McDermed 1986.

Starting with zero pension wealth at age 25, the worker's wealth rises slowly at first and reaches $13,945 at age 40. At this age, pension wealth represents about one-third of annual earnings. Between the ages of 40 and 65, pension wealth grows by over 100 percent per five years of work. The rate of growth of pension wealth declines slightly with age during this time. At age 65, pension wealth totals $613,518, or 3.7 times annual earnings.

The projected earnings theory of pension wealth assumes that the worker and the firm enter into a long-term implicit contract. The worker promises to remain with the firm until retirement and to perform at the agreed level of effort. The firm promises to continue to employ the worker as long as he fulfills the contract. To enforce the contract, the firm requires that the worker pay for a pension that is conditional on his remaining with the firm. The "stay pension" exceeds the pension to which workers are legally entitled, which is the "leave pension." Firm reputation in the labor market is assumed to be sufficient to keep the firm from reneging on its obligation.

The difference between this model and the legal method is that, under this model, pension wealth is conditional on the worker's remaining with the firm until retirement. In each period, pension wealth is based on the plan benefit formula, current years of service, and projected earnings in the final working years just prior to retirement. Since projected future earnings typically are greater than current earnings, the "stay pension" wealth, which is based on projected earnings, will exceed the "leave pension" wealth, which is derived using current earnings. Under an implicit contract, workers pay for the stay pension, but if they quit or are laid off, they receive only the leave pension. This difference represents a capital loss in pension wealth associated with termination of employment.

Pension wealth based on the projected earnings method of calculation also follows a predictable life cycle pattern. As long as the worker remains on the job, wealth rises until the age of eligibility. Compared to pension wealth calculated through the legal method, wealth is higher early in the work life because it is based on projected final earnings rather than on actual earnings but rises more slowly with job tenure because projected final earnings do not change over time. Pension compensation drops sharply at the normal retirement age and may become negative if the worker remains with the firm. This decline after the normal retirement age is attributable to the ending of the implicit long-term contract. The worker may remain with the firm after this date, but he is assumed to be covered by an explicit, year-by-year contract. This results in benefits and pension compensation based on the legal method and actual earnings received after the termination of the implicit contract.

If the worker leaves a job, his pension wealth drops sharply from the stay pension level to the leave pension level. The magnitude of this capital loss rises during the initial working years, peaks in the late forties or early fifties, and then declines. Of course, at the normal retirement age there is no loss from leaving because the worker has completed the terms of the contract.

Capital losses in pension wealth significantly reduce the tendency of older workers to change jobs. Because of the importance of this concept, I present a simple example of the capital loss for a worker before describing the results of the numerical analysis determining the capital loss associated with the compensation pattern we have been describing. First, consider a worker who works for a single firm for forty years. For the first twenty years, the worker is paid $20,000 and for the last twenty years he is paid $40,000. He is covered by an earnings-based, defined benefit plan that has the benefit formula: $B = (.015)\ (T)\ (E)$, where B is the annual pension benefit at retirement, T is the years of service, and E is the average final earnings used to calculate the benefit. The formula indicates that the worker receives 1.5 percent of average final earnings for each year of work. In this example, let final earnings be based on the last five years of earnings. The worker's benefit at retirement is then $24,000 per year [(.015) (40) (40,000)].

This benefit can be compared to that of a worker with the same lifetime earnings who changes employers after twenty years. Assume that both employers have the pension shown above, so that the worker will receive two pensions at retirement. The sum of the two benefits will be less than the one benefit received by the one-job worker. This can be shown by calculating the two benefits: $B_1 = (.015)\ (20)\ (20{,}000) = 6{,}000$; $B_2 = (.015)\ (20)\ (40{,}000) = 12{,}000$.

The two-job worker will receive two pensions that total only $18,000, or $6,000 less than the amount received by the single-job worker. One method of explaining this difference is to note that the first twenty years of employment for the single-job worker produced the equivalent of $12,000 in pension, whereas the same twenty years for the worker who switched jobs generated only $6,000. The difference is due to the final earnings used in calculating the retirement benefits ($20,000 for the job changer as compared to $40,000 for the single-job worker). The present value of the $6,000 reduction in annual retirement benefits is the pension loss associated with job changes.

Using the pension and worker characteristics from the numerical example described above, pension wealth at various ages is shown in the last column of Table 4. After completing one year of work, pension wealth is $2,822. This value rises with additional years of work, and the rate of increase rises slightly with job tenure. Pension wealth is more than one year of earnings by age 40, when wealth is $51,752. Pension wealth grows by about 70 percent per five years of employment, grow-

Table 4: EMPLOYEE COMPENSATION AND PENSION WEALTH: PROJECTED EARNINGS METHOD

Age	Tenure	Earnings	Pension Comp.	Pension Comp. as Percentage of Total Comp.	Pension Benefit	Pension Wealth	Capital Loss
25	0	$ 18,670	$ 1,330	6.65	$ 0	$ 1,330	$ 1,330
30	5	24,353	1,786	6.83	1,562	10,717	9,272
35	10	31,762	2,401	7.03	4,074	26,414	21,346
40	15	41,415	3,234	7.24	7,969	51,752	38,399
45	20	53,982	4,373	7.49	13,853	91,835	60,452
50	25	70,303	5,964	7.82	22,564	155,076	85,357
55	30	91,432	8,247	8.27	35,245	255,654	105,082
60	35	118,664	11,612	8.91	53,434	418,048	96,610
64	39	145,802	15,587	9.66	73,290	623,494	31,700
65	40	173,397	−3,130	−1.84	79,146	690,677	0
70	45	253,590	−31,059	−13.96	134,412	988,489	0

Source: see Table 3.

ing to $690,677 at age 65. The capital loss associated with job changes rises from $21,346 at age 35 to $105,082 at age 55. The loss in pension wealth then declines to zero at age 65.

Pensions and Terminations

The preceding discussion indicates how pensions alter the incentives workers face to remain with their current employer. During the prime working years, pensions create a capital loss associated with job changes, whereas during the later working years, pensions may actually reduce total compensation as pension compensation declines with continued employment. In a recent study for the Department of Labor, Allen, Clark, and McDermed (1986) examined the effect of pensions on job changes. They concluded that pensions are one of the most important factors, if not the most important factor, influencing length of service and mobility in the labor market. Principal mechanisms through which pension coverage reduces labor mobility are the capital loss in pension plan wealth associated with job changes and the ability of firms with pension plans to attract more stable workers.

The studies by Allen, Clark, and McDermed evaluated the impact of pensions on job mobility using two national surveys. The Panel Study of Income Dynamics (PSID) is a longitudinal survey begun in 1968 by the Survey Research Center of the University of Michigan. The PSID includes economic and demographic data on a nationally representative sample of approximately 5,000 households which have been re-interviewed regularly since 1968. The National Longitudinal Survey of Mature Men (NLS) was initiated by the U.S. Census Bureau in 1966. The original NLS sample in 1966 consisted of 5,000 civilian, noninstitutionalized males between the ages of 45 and 59. Blacks were oversampled, and resurveys were conducted annually or biennially through 1983.

Estimating the impact of the capital loss on turnover probabilities for workers in the PSID, Allen, Clark, and McDermed (1987) found that a $1,000 increase in the capital loss resulted in a 3.7 percentage point decrease in the probability of a job change between 1975 and 1982. The average worker covered by a pension faced a capital loss of $5,024 in 1975 if he left his job. Thus, a worker with a potential average capital loss will have an 18.6 percentage point lower turnover probability than a worker not covered by a pension. The seven-year turnover rate among respondents in the PSID was 39.2 percent for persons covered by pensions and 62.8 percent for those not covered.

Allen, Clark, and McDermed also examined job mobility among respondents in the NLS. The average capital loss for these workers was $13,479, or over twice the value observed for the respondents in the PSID. A $1,000 increase in the capital loss is associated with a 0.6 percentage point decrease in the likelihood of turnover between 1971 and 1976, considerably smaller than the estimate for the PSID. This implies that the average pension participant in the NLS has an 8.1 percentage point decrease in turnover due to the capital loss associated with a job change. In the NLS, the turnover rate for those covered by pensions is 22.6 percentage points lower than that for workers not covered (11.7 versus 34.3 percent).

In their analysis, Allen, Clark, and McDermed tested three competing hypotheses concerning pension effects on mobility. These are: reduced turnover due to the capital loss, reduced turnover due to a tendency of workers with lower quit rates to choose pension-covered jobs, and reduced turnover due to higher total compensation associated with pension-covered jobs. They concluded that the results were more consistent with those obtained using models of implicit contracts for lifetime jobs that impose capital losses on pension participants who leave their jobs. Their findings suggest that workers covered by pensions are less likely to quit their jobs prior to retirement and that firms are less likely to lay off pension-covered workers. Although employers seemingly would gain from terminating workers who have paid for stay pensions but are legally entitled only to leave pensions, this result indicates that such opportunistic behavior is being held in check by concern about labor market reputation.

The capital loss imposed on workers who leave pension-covered jobs lowers quit rates, especially among older workers, and firms are necessarily more reluctant to lay off these workers. These responses tend to exacerbate the aging of the work force in slow-growing or declining firms. If older workers are reluctant to quit and firms are reluctant to lay them off, firms can only reduce their work force through other forms of attrition and by ceasing to hire younger workers. As a result, the firm's labor force will age rapidly.

Capital Losses across Industries

The preceding analysis has shown the importance of capital loss in pension wealth in deterring job changes among older workers. The significance of this aspect of pension coverage mandates that policymakers and analysts become aware of the magnitude of the loss in pension wealth workers face when changing jobs. Allen, Clark, and McDermed (1988) derived average pension characteristics for workers in various industry and occupational groups using data from the 1983 EBS. These data, along with information on average personal characteristics for pension participants in the May 1983 supplement to the Current Population Survey, were used to calculate capital loss in pension wealth for average workers by industry. The importance of this pension effect can be shown by determining the proportion of workers in each industry covered by a pension and hence subject to a capital loss at job termination, along with the expected magnitude of the loss.

Table 5: PENSION COVERAGE RATES OF WORKERS, BY AGE AND INDUSTRY

	Age			
Industry	25–34	35–44	45–54	55–64
Mining	62	83	68	78
Construction	30	46	42	48
Durables mfg.	65	80	80	81
Nondurables mfg.	60	64	72	40
Transportation; communication; utilities	63	72	82	72
Trade	36	40	39	46
Finance; insurance; real estate	57	64	63	58
Services	35	41	44	42

Source: Allen, Clark, and McDermed, 1988.

Table 6: PENSION LOSS FOR WORKERS COVERED BY A PENSION IN 1983, BY AGE AND INDUSTRY

	Age			
Industry	25–34	35–44	45–54	55–64
Mining	$11,054	$19,572	$12,400	$9,808
	(.42)[a]	(.65)	(.49)	(.25)
Construction	3,403	6,625	7,869	4,384
	(.13)	(.23)	(.28)	(.17)
Durables mfg.	6,048	13,947	13,112	6,944
	(.29)	(.54)	(.53)	(.33)
Nondurables mfg.	5,891	11,751	11,852	6,069
	(.30)	(.51)	(.59)	(.33)
Transportation; communication; utilities	11,501	18,529	10,630	5,452
	(.49)	(.72)	(.40)	(.21)
Trade	5,249	10,682	12,215	8,855
	(.26)	(.47)	(.54)	(.44)
Finance; insurance; real estate	6,358	14,886	19,828	10,638
	(.33)	(.60)	(.79)	(.50)
Services	4,029	9,341	10,744	9,721
	(.21)	(.35)	(.44)	(.39)

Source: see Table 5.

[a]Values in parentheses are the mean of the pension loss divided by annual earnings.

Pension coverage rates for persons working more than 35 hours per week in 1983 are shown in Table 5. These data show that coverage varies considerably across industrial categories, with the highest rates found in manufacturing and mining. Between 1980 and 1985 employment in these sectors declined by 4 to 5 percent. In contrast, low coverage rates are found in the trade, financial, and service sectors, which have been growing relatively rapidly. Employment in these sectors increased from 10 to 17 percent from 1980 to 1985. Thus the potential that pensions will reduce turnover and increase the aging of the work force is greatest in the sectors of the economy that have been declining in employment.

Table 6 presents the mean pension loss for all workers covered by a pension in the various age-industry categories. The dollar values show the loss in pension wealth incurred if workers change jobs. For example, workers aged 35 to 54 in manufacturing face a pension loss of $12,000 to $14,000 if they change jobs. This represents about half a year's earnings for these workers. Absolute and relative losses are much lower for workers in the service sector. Within an industry, benefit formulas vary considerably across occupational groups. Allen, Clark, and

McDermed divided the sample to allow for differences based on three occupational groups within each industry. Among professional workers the dollar value of the loss is much higher in the manufacturing and financial sectors than in the service sector. The loss is also higher as a proportion of a year's earnings for these professional workers. Throughout these analyses, the expected age pattern of pension loss is shown. The loss is low early in the work life and rises until around age 50, when the loss peaks. After this point, the magnitude of the loss declines until it is zero at the normal retirement age.

In summary, these number show that the average worker between the ages of 35 and 54 must forfeit approximately half a year's earnings to change jobs. This cost is in addition to any other search and moving costs the individual incurs when switching employers. A larger fraction of workers in manufacturing and mining face these costs. Thus the pension barriers to mobility are greatest in these industries, which have been declining in employment.

Public Policy, Pension Wealth, and Job Changes

If defined benefit plans had no vesting or portability provisions, a worker who left an employer would not be entitled to any pension benefits at retirement from that job. Vesting ensures that the worker will receive a benefit based on his work history with a firm. Even with vesting, we have seen that the more mobile worker will have lower lifetime pension wealth unless there is portability of pension credits, so that the worker is treated as if he had been in one pension plan throughout his work life.

Vesting of pension credits accrued to date means that workers who quit their jobs retain the legal right to a future pension benefit. This benefit is based on the current benefit formula and the worker's years of service and/or earnings. Prior to the passage of the Employee Retirement Income Security Act (ERISA) in 1974, there were no governmental regulations concerning vesting, and some firms set vesting to occur at retirement. ERISA established three alternative minimum vesting standards for pension plans; however, most plans selected the ten-year, 100-percent vesting standard.

In 1986 Congress lowered vesting standards, effective in 1989, to five-year, 100-percent vesting or graded vesting beginning with 50 percent vesting after three years. Most firms will probably adopt the five-year vesting standard. With the reduction in vesting requirement, most workers covered by a pension will remain with the company long enough to qualify for a retirement benefit. Although the service requirements for vesting may be lowered in the future, any further reduction will have only a minor impact on pension wealth at retirement because of the relatively low benefits based on only a few years of employment. Vested benefits typically remain frozen in nominal terms and do not rise with inflation or average wages. As a result, even with complete and immediate vesting, workers who change jobs will suffer a capital loss in pension wealth.

Generally, workers who have changed jobs do not have the option of transferring their accrued pension credits to their new employers. Multi-employer defined benefit plans allow workers to move across firms that are participating in the plan while retaining all service credits. Workers in multi-employer plans have full portability of pension credits as long as they move only among the firms in the pension plan. If workers move to an employer outside the plan, they will receive their vested benefits at retirement, but rarely will their service credits be portable outside the multi-employer group.

To date there has been no legislation mandating portability of accrued service credits across employers. True portability that would eliminate all pension loss associated with job changes would be extremely difficult to achieve, for two reasons. First, pensions in the United States are quite diverse, and the matching of credits across different plans would be very complex. To do so would probably require a new government agency, and regulatory costs would be quite high. Second, someone must pay for the added cost to provide the increased benefits to the job changer. Benefits for the mobile worker equal to those of the single-job worker would require either that the new employer incur higher costs for a new employee who has been covered by a pension or that the former employer make additional contributions into the pension account of the departing worker. If the old employer pays, this raises the cost of employee turnover to firms and eliminates their abilities to use pensions to reduce turnover. Of course, these costs may well be shifted back to the worker in the form of lower wages. If the hiring firm is required to fund the added costs, this will reduce the demand for workers previously covered by a pension, with older workers being the most adversely affected.

Another possible source of pension loss is the inability to gain access to pension funds at the time of job termination. The present value of future pension benefits can be calculated at the time of the job change. This value could be made available to the departing employee. For example, ERISA allowed firms to cash out workers who had a present value of pension wealth of less than $1,750, and the 1984 Retirement Equity Act raised this value to $3,500. Workers will gain in lifetime wealth from a policy of lump-sum distributions if they are able to invest these funds at a rate that exceeds the interest rate used to determine the wealth value of the cash dispersement.

Currently there is a series of proposals claiming to promote portability of pension credits. For the most part, these proposals do not require any portability among participants in defined benefit plans. Instead, they provide incentives for employers to institute defined contribution plans and allow for lump-sum distributions. These proposals will not reduce the capital loss associated with job changes among participants in defined benefit plans. Clark and McDermed (1988), in a numerical analysis of policy changes in vesting standards and changes requiring lump-sum distributions, show that large capital losses will remain even with immediate vesting and access to the cash value of one's pension account.

Pensions and Retirement

During the past four decades, the proportion of older men in the labor force has declined steadily. The labor force participation rate of men aged 65 and older fell from 45.8 percent in 1950 to 16.0 percent in 1986. This represents an average decline of 8.3 percent per ten years (see Table 7). The rate of decline has been greater in the 1970s and 1980s than in the 1960s (see Table 8). In the past twenty years, the decline in the participation rate has extended to men in age group 55 to 64. The participation rate of these men was virtually the same in 1950 and 1960; however, it declined by 3.8 percentage points—from 86.8 to 83.0 per-

Table 7: CIVILIAN LABOR FORCE PARTICIPATION RATES: ACTUAL AND PROJECTED

	Men			*Women*		
Year	45–54	55–64	65 and over	45–54	55–64	65 and over
1950	95.8	86.9	45.8	37.9	27.0	9.7
1960	95.7	86.8	33.1	49.8	32.2	10.8
1970	94.2	83.0	26.8	54.4	43.0	9.7
1980	91.2	72.3	19.1	59.9	41.5	8.1
1986	91.0	67.3	16.0	65.9	42.3	7.4
1990	90.7	65.1	14.1	69.0	42.8	7.0
2000	90.1	63.2	9.9	75.4	45.8	5.4

Source: for rates from 1950 to 1970, U.S. Department of Labor, *Employment and Training Report of the President* (Washington, D.C.: U.S. Government Printing Office, 1980), p. 224; for rates from 1980 to 2000, unpublished data from the Bureau of Labor Statistics. Values for 1990 and 2000 are projections from the Bureau of Labor Statistics middle growth path.

Table 8: DECLINES IN LABOR FORCE PARTICIPATION, 1950–86

	Interval			
Group	1950–1960	1960–1970	1970–1980	1980–1986
Men				
Aged 55–64				
Percentage point change:				
during interval	−0.1	−3.8	−10.6	−5.1
per year	0.0	−0.4	−1.1	−0.9
Percentage change				
during interval	0.0	−4.4	−12.8	−7.0
Aged 65 and over				
Percentage point change:				
during interval	−12.7	−6.3	−7.7	−3.1
per year	−1.3	−0.6	−0.8	−0.5
Percentage change				
during interval	−27.7	−19.0	−28.7	−16.2
Women				
Aged 55–64				
Percentage point change:				
during interval	10.2	5.8	−1.5	0.8
per year	1.0	0.6	−0.2	0.1
Percentage change				
during interval	37.8	15.6	−3.5	0.2
Aged 65 and over				
Percentage point change:				
during interval	1.1	−1.1	−1.6	−0.7
per year	0.1	−0.1	−0.2	−0.1
Percentage change				
during interval	11.3	−10.2	−16.5	−8.6

Source: Table 1.

cent—between 1960 and 1970. During the next decade, the decline was 10.6 percentage points, so the 1980 rate was 72.4 percent. Through the first six years of the 1980s, the decline continued at about the same rate, and the 1986 rate of these men is 67.3 percent. In addition to these declines, there have been small declines in the participation rate of younger men in the past two decades. For example, the rate for men aged 45 to 54 dropped from 94.2 percent in 1970 to 91.0 percent in 1986.

In contrast, the labor force participation rate of older women has increased throughout most of the twentieth century. The work rates of women of all ages rose steadily prior to 1970. Some of the largest increases occurred for older women aged 55 to 64. Table 7 shows that the rate for these women rose from 27.0 to 43.0 percent between 1950 and 1970, or 0.8 percentage points per year. Since 1970, the participation rates for women aged 20 to 54 have continued to rise, but the proportion of women aged 55 to 64 in the labor force has remained relatively constant. The participation rate of women aged 65 and older, which had always been low, rose slightly from 1950 to 1960 but subsequently has declined slightly.

Pensions provide income to persons conditional on their retiring from their current job. Access to benefits at the age of eligibility gives individuals a flow of income. Passing the age of eligibility also alters the gain in pension benefits from continued work. For continued employment after the worker is eligible to start receiving benefits, the worker typically must postpone the initial acceptance of benefits. This delay in acceptance of pension benefits lowers the lifetime value of the pension and therefore reduces the gain from continued work. Total compensation from work drops further if firms discontinue wage and service accruals for older workers. The decline over time in the age of eligibility for normal retirement benefits and the institution of early retirement provisions has encouraged earlier retirement of workers covered by pensions. Increases in the generosity of pensions also have encouraged workers to leave their jobs.

Pensions are an important personnel policy that can be used to encourage older workers to retire. By incorporating certain provisions into a pension plan, employers can create attractive incentives for workers to leave. Many employers periodically have instituted special early retirement plans expressly to encourage older workers to leave the firm. Such policies can be used to moderate the aging of the labor force for individual firms.

Alternatively, firms could institute pension provisions that would provide incentives for older workers to stay on with the firm. Clark and Cantrell (1986) show the importance of the retirement age in determining the age structure of the labor force. It is important to understand more about the reasons why some firms provide strong incentives for workers to stay while other firms provide strong incentives for older workers to retire.

Pension Regulations and Retirement Incentives

Many employers have instituted pension provisions that provide strong incentives for older workers to retire. Basically, these incentives reduce the value to a worker of remaining on the job by lowering pension compensation and perhaps even pension wealth for those who do not retire. Over the past two decades, regulations have been imposed that limit the employer's options in imposing these costs. Although the objective of government policy appears to have been to force firms to end the use of many retirement incentives, there remain numerous methods that employers can adopt to provide a pension penalty for continued work.

Specific government intervention can be traced to the Age Discrimination in Employment Act (ADEA) of 1967, which required that employers not discriminate against older workers aged 40 to 65. Under this legislation, it was unlawful for employers to fire, demote, or reduce the salary of workers in the protected ages without showing good cause. Pensions and pension compensation were largely excluded from the coverage of this act. Thus, many firms continued to terminate wage and service accruals at the normal retirement age, to set maximum pension benefits, to offer early retirement options, and to make no actuarial adjustments for persons working beyond the normal retirement age. In addition, firms were permitted to maintain mandatory retirement provisions at age 65.

Amendments to ADEA in 1978 raised the upper limit of the protected age range to 70 and forced firms to raise the age of mandatory retirement to this age, and in 1986 Congress eliminated the upper limit to the protected ages. These actions have effectively eliminated the use of mandatory retirement as a personnel policy. Exceptions to these laws are allowed for some public safety employees, airline pilots, policymaking executives with pensions over $44,000 per year, and university professors. While creating the option of continued work, evidence suggests that outlawing mandatory retirement has had little effect in enticing older persons to remain in the labor force (Barker and Clark 1980; Burkhauser and Quinn 1983), in part because of the continued existence of strong pension incentives to leave the job.

Also in 1986, legislation was enacted to require firms to provide wage and service accruals to persons who continue to work past the normal retirement age. This regulation affected approximately half of all participants in medium and large firms and should increase the pension compensation for workers in these plans who remain on the job. Despite these accruals, workers will continue to suffer reductions in pension compensation (and perhaps pension wealth) when they become eligible to start receiving benefits (see Tables 3 and 4). Only the provision of actuarial adjustments will eliminate this loss in pension wealth and the related retirement incentive. In addition, firms can limit the accrual of benefits through maximum benefit provisions and offers of early retirement with little or no penalty. Special early retirement options can be offered that provide large financial incentives for early departure from the firm.

In an aging society, should the government take further strong steps to encourage firms to retain older workers? If so, what actions should be taken? Certainly additional regulation of pensions could reduce the ability of firms to impose retirement incentives on their workers. Potential actions include requiring actuarial increases for work after the normal retirement age, requiring that early retirement incentive programs be offered to workers of all ages, and elimination of maximum benefit provisions. While these actions could be taken, they would have some adverse effects for both workers and firms and likely would give renewed stimulus to the trend toward greater use of defined contribution plans instead of defined benefit plans.

Regulation and the Choice of Plan Type

Since 1974, Congress has enacted a series of new regulations governing the adoption and administration of employer pension plans. These new regulations have increased the cost of maintaining defined benefit pension plans. Increased reporting standards have raised the administrative costs of ongoing defined benefit plans. Pension insurance and funding standards have increased costs and reduced the flexibility of employers in the administration of these plans. Regulations reducing vesting standards and requiring wage and service accruals past the normal retirement age limit the ability of employers to institute pension incentives to modify worker behavior in order to reduce quits or increase retirements.

These and other recently enacted regulations have reduced the benefits to firms of offering defined benefit plans while simultaneously increasing the cost of these plans. In contrast to the considerable effects on the cost and benefits of maintaining a defined benefit plan, the regulations have had only minor effects on defined contribution plans. The differential impacts follow from the full funding and relatively short vesting time characteristic of most defined contribution plans. Changes in the tax code accompanying the regulatory changes have increased options for providing defined contribution plans.

In response to these changes, there apparently is a shift among employers away from defined benefit plans toward defined contribution plans. Clark (1987) recently completed a report for the Department of Labor examining the 5,500 reporting forms which all plans with 100 or more participants are required to file each year. The total number of primary pension plans increased from 24,135 in 1977 to 37,424 in 1983 (Table 9 shows the number of plans by plan type). Although defined benefit plans increased from 18,168 to 25,772, they fell as a proportion

Table 9: NUMBER OF PRIMARY PLANS AND ACTIVE PARTICIPANTS BY PLAN TYPE

	Plans			*Participants (millions)*		
	1977	1980	1983	1977	1980	1983
Defined benefit	18,168 (75.3)[a]	23,697 (73.2)	25,772 (68.9)	22.4 (88.5)	27.2 (86.9)	27.6 (81.9)
Defined contributions	5,360 (22.2)	7,940 (24.5)	10,769 (28.8)	2.6 (10.3)	3.8 (12.1)	5.7 (16.9)
Other[b]	604 (2.5)	717 (2.2)	883 (2.4)	.3 (1.2)	.3 (1.0)	.4 (1.2)
Total	24,135 (100.0)	32,354 (100.0)	37,424 (100.0)	25.3 (100.0)	31.3 (100.0)	33.7 (100.0)

[a]Numbers in parentheses represent percentages of column totals.

[b]These plans include defined benefit plans with benefits based partly on balance separate account of participant (code section 414(k)), annuity arrangements of certain exempt organizations (code section 403(b)(1)), custodial accounts for regulated investment company stock (code section 403(b)(7)), and pension plans utilizing individual retirement accounts or annuities (described in code section 408) as the sole funding vehicle for providing benefits.

Source: Clark 1987.

of all primary plans from 75.3 percent to 68.9 percent in 1983. Similar changes are noted in the number of participants in primary plans during this period.

The trend toward greater use of defined contribution plans occurred across all major industrial groups (see Table 10), and there was a consistent pattern of expanding use of the defined contribution plan in data for all plans and for firms offering pension plans. Thus the data strongly suggest that in the current regulatory and economic climate, firms are choosing to institute and maintain defined contribution plans over defined benefit plans. This trend will tend to reduce the effect of an aging work force on employer costs and will tend to eliminate some of the barriers to mobility among older workers.

Conclusions

This review of pension economics has shown that pension costs represent a larger component of total compensation for older workers than for others. The aging of the labor force will tend to raise the cost of pensions for employers. To the extent that workers actually pay for these costs in the form of lower wages, the total labor costs of firms will not

Table 10: DISTRIBUTION OF PRIMARY PLANS BY INDUSTRY

	Defined Benefit			*Defined Contribution*		
Industry	1977	1980	1983	1977	1980	1983
Agricultural	109 (71.2)[a]	150 (67.3)	185 (60.5)	43 (28.1)	72 (32.3)	119 (38.9)
Mining	302 (81.6)	446 (77.7)	487 (69.0)	66 (17.8)	126 (22.0)	217 (30.7)
Construction	889 (74.6)	1,361 (67.7)	1,100 (60.5)	300 (25.2)	618 (30.7)	695 (38.2)
Manufacturing	9,192 (82.9)	12,597 (81.3)	13,158 (78.7)	1,851 (16.7)	2,840 (18.3)	3,503 (20.9)
Transportation, communication	1,014 (81.3)	1,276 (80.4)	1,333 (74.9)	217 (17.4)	293 (18.5)	426 (23.9)
Wholesale trade	624 (56.7)	886 (54.4)	990 (51.6)	469 (42.6)	734 (45.0)	914 (47.6)
Retail trade	609 (51.9)	951 (50.2)	981 (44.8)	560 (47.7)	930 (49.1)	1,201 (54.8)
Finance, insurance, real estate	1,593 (75.9)	1,959 (76.4)	2,228 (72.0)	494 (23.5)	585 (22.8)	847 (27.4)
Services	1,928 (73.8)	2,848 (66.8)	3,228 (60.3)	654 (25.0)	1,308 (30.7)	1,996 (37.3)

Note: Other primary plans are not shown in this table.
[a]Numbers in parentheses indicate percentage of plans in each industry.
Source: Clark 1987.

be affected. It is important to remember that firms use pensions as part of their overall personnel policy and that pensions can be used to reduce quits and increase retirements. Lowering quit rates accelerates the aging of a work force, while increasing retirement slows this process. Thus aging affects the cost of maintaining a pension, but firms can use their pension plans to affect the age structure of their labor force.

References

Allen, Steven, and Robert Clark. 1986. "Unions, Pension Wealth and Age-Compensation Profiles," *Industrial and Labor Relations Review* 39: 502–17.

———. 1987. "Pensions and Firm Performance. In *Human Resources and Firm Performance,* edited by Morris Kleiner, pp. 195–242. Madison, Wisc.: Industrial Relations Research Association.

Allen, Steven, Robert Clark, and Ann McDermed. 1986. "Job Mobility, Older Workers and the Role of Pensions." Final Report, U.S. Department of Labor Contract No. J-9-M-5–0049. October.

———. 1987. "Pensions and Lifetime Jobs. The New Industrial Feudalism Revisited." Unpublished paper.

———.1988. "The Pension Cost of Changing Jobs," *Research on Aging* 10(December): 459–71.

Andrews, Emily. 1985. *The Changing Profile of Pensions in America*. Washington, D.C.: Employee Benefit Research Institute.

Barker, David, and Robert Clark. 1980. "Mandatory Retirement and Labor Force Participation of Respondents in the Retirement History Study," *Social Security Bulletin,* November, pp. 20–29.

Bulow, Jeremy. 1982. "What Are Corporate Pension Liabilities?" *Quarterly Journal of Economics* 97: 435–52.

Burkhauser, Richard, and Joseph Quinn. 1983. "Is Mandatory Retirement Overrated?" *Journal of Human Resources* 18: 337–58.

Cantrell, Stephen, and Robert Clark. 1982. "Individual Mobility, Population Growth and Labor Force Participation," *Demography,* pp. 147–60.

Clark, Robert. 1987. "Increasing Use of Defined Contribution Pension Plans." Final Report, U.S. Department of Labor Purchase Order No. B9P63402. November.

Clark, Robert, and Stephen Cantrell. 1986. "Personnel Policies and the Age Structure of an Occupation: The Case of the Academic Labor Market," *Population Research and Policy Review* 5: 63–82.

Clark, Robert, and Ann McDermed. 1986. "Earnings and Pension Compensation: The Effect of Eligibility," *Quarterly Journal of Economics* 101: 341–61.

———. 1988. "Pension Wealth and Job Changes: The Effects of Vesting, Portability and Lump-Sum Distributions," *The Gerontologist:* 524–32.

Ippolito, Richard. 1986. *Pensions, Economics and Public Policy.* Homewood, Ill.: Dow Jones-Irwin.

———. 1988. "A Study of the Regulatory Impact of ERISA," *Journal of Law and Economics* 16 (April): 85–126.

Kotlikoff, Laurence, and David Wise. 1985. "Labor Compensation and the Structure of Private Pension Plans: Evidence for Contractual vs. Spot Labor Markets." In *Pension, Labor, and Individual Choice,* edited by David Wise, pp. 55–85. Chicago: University of Chicago Press.

U.S. Bureau of Labor Statistics. 1987. *Employee Benefits in Medium and Large Firms, 1986*. Washington, D.C.: U.S. Government Printing Office.

U.S. Department of Commerce. 1984. *Statistical Abstract of the United States 1985, 105th Edition*. Washington, D.C.: U.S. Government Printing Office.

Retirement Wealth Accrual and the Patterns of Post-Career Employment

RICHARD V. BURKHAUSER
AND JOSEPH F. QUINN

Burkhauser and Quinn argue that one unintended result of our pension system is that an increasing number of workers now find it financially advantageous to take early retirement from their principal employer, begin to draw a pension, then shift to another employer. While this enables the worker to receive two incomes and so provides a pecuniary benefit to him, it generally involves a move to less skilled employment and so represents a loss for the economy as a whole.

J. D. O.

Because most workers spend a considerable portion of their life working for a single firm, the departure from this position is an important event. Most studies of work at older ages abstract from job separation and concentrate on overall labor force participation as the variable of interest in studying retirement behavior. However, a focus on job transition rather than on labor force withdrawal offers additional insight into the way the United States retirement system influences work. Exit from a career job is not just a convenient indicator of retirement. Rather, it is crucial for considering the influences of pension plans on job exit. It reflects the fact that pensions are linked to the work decision and that the pension plan influences job exit at both younger and older ages.

What makes job transitions at older ages different from those at younger ages is that most workers leave the career job and the labor force simultaneously. This is the traditional form of retirement, and its prevalence is probably responsible for the emphasis on labor force participation in the literature. But recent research suggests that many workers pass through a transitional period of employment, often in a different industry and occupation, after leaving the career job and before ceasing work altogether. We suspect that these decisions are influenced by public policy—by the incentives built into our public and private retirement systems.

Post-career jobs are not just brief way stations on the road to retirement. Whether people who leave fulltime career status but continue to work should be labeled as retired or not is unclear. In some ways they do not seem retired: they still work, often for a considerable number of hours per year, and sometimes fulltime, but on a new job. But in other ways they do resemble the retired. Many have claimed pension benefits, some are receiving Social Security benefits, and most are earning significantly less than they did prior to the transition. Some of them describe themselves as partially retired, but many do not.

Our current pension and Social Security systems strongly encourage two distinct work states. The first is fulltime work on a career job—a job with a single firm, held for many years. The second state has usually been considered full retirement, but for a large minority of workers in the 1970s, as noted above, substantial post-career work occurs. Using data from the Retirement History Survey, a ten-year longitudinal study of men aged 58 to 63 in 1969, we will trace the work effort of these men as they left fulltime work on their career jobs. We will then discuss the possible effects of federal legislation designed to encourage greater labor force participation late in life.

Labor Force Trends of Older Americans

The recent decline in the labor force participation rates of older Americans is well known and well documented. The most readily available data are published statistics on five-year age intervals. Since some of the retirement incentives discussed below go into effect at particular ages, we are interested in trends for one-year age categories and have obtained such data by age from the U.S. Department of Labor.

Table 1 shows that male participation trends in the postwar period varied over time and across ages. The first great reduction in the work effort of men aged 65 and over occurred during the 1950s, when participation rates fell by about a quarter. Between 1960 and 1970 there were only modest declines for these older men. Labor force participation of those aged 55 and 60 actually grew during this decade of strong economic growth. Men aged 62 to 64 were first eligible for Social Security benefits in 1961, and their labor force participation fell modestly after that year. Between 1970 and 1980 substantial reductions in labor force participation occurred at each age between 55 and 70. The rate of decline has been more modest since then.

Table 1: MALE LABOR FORCE PARTICIPATION RATES BY AGE, 1950–86

Year / Age	55	60	63	65	68	70
1950	87.8	82.1	77.6	67.7	54.2	44.5
1960	89.9	83.2	75.7	53.6	39.4	33.2
1970	91.8	83.9	69.4	49.9	39.4	30.1
1972	90.7	82.1	66.5	45.2	33.8	27.1
1974	88.0	79.0	59.2	39.8	27.7	23.5
1976	87.1	75.5	55.7	36.6	26.7	22.4
1978	85.8	74.4	52.2	36.3	28.7	21.7
1980	84.9	74.0	52.3	35.2	24.1	21.3
1982	86.4	72.1	45.2	30.6	24.8	21.1
1984	84.3	70.2	48.2	30.4	21.3	18.8
1986	84.1	69.2	44.3	30.7	20.7	17.1

Source: for rates for 1950 and 1960, decennial U.S. census data; for rates for 1960–86, unpublished Department of Labor statistics, based on annual Current Population Survey labor force participation questions.

Participation data for older women show relatively little movement over time. While Americans are retiring earlier, women, especially married women, are more likely to be working than in the past, and the two trends tend to offset each other.

Figure 1 shows the total decline in male participation rates over the past two decades, by age, in both absolute and percentage terms. The largest absolute declines occur between 62 and 65, the ages of eligibility for reduced and full Social Security retirement benefits, suggesting a role for Social Security in this story. But in percentage terms, the size of the declines continues to climb. The participation rate for men aged 62 in 1986 was 30 percent lower than it was only eighteen years earlier. At age 65, it was 42 percent lower, and at age 68, 45 percent below the 1968 figure.

But Figure 1 also shows that the decrease in labor force participation starts long before eligibility for Social Security retirement benefits. The declines are substantial at age 60, a popular age for pension eligibility, where an 18 percent decline in participation rates over these two decades is observed, and even at age 55, where the decline is 9 percent.

Other employment changes are hidden by the labor force participation statistics. Fewer older Americans are working, and of the ones who are, fewer are working fulltime. In 1987, nearly half of the men aged 65 and over employed in nonagricultural industries were working part-time (fewer than 35 hours per week), compared to only 6 percent of men aged 25 to 64. (Almost all of these elderly workers claim that their part-time status is voluntary; see U.S. Department of Labor 1988,

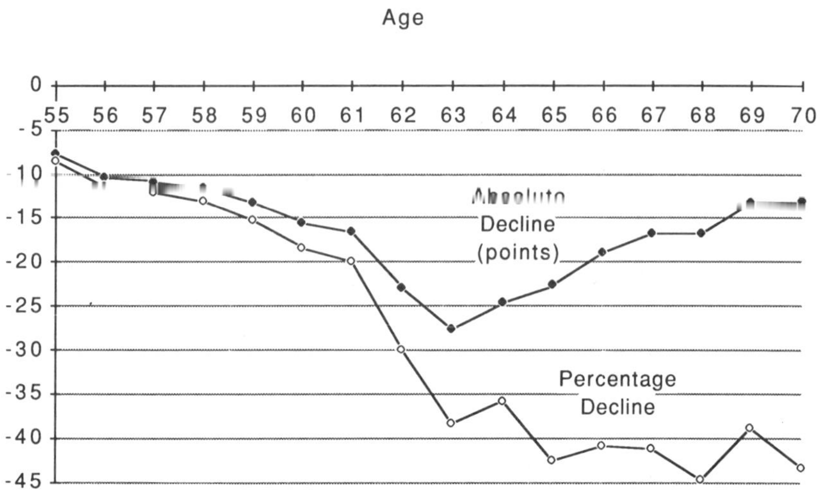

Figure 1. Change in male labor force participation rates, by age, 1968–86. Source: Unpublished U.S. Department of Labor statistics.

Table 33.) This proportion has increased steadily from only one-third in 1968. The proportion of older women working part-time has grown from 50 to 60 percent over the same time interval.

In addition, older workers are more likely to be self-employed than are members of any other age group. In 1987, almost one-quarter of all working men over 64 were self-employed, compared to less than 10 percent of those aged 16 to 64 (U.S. Department of Labor 1988, Table 23). For women, the figures were 15 and 5 percent, respectively. Both Becker (1984) and Blau (1987) suggest that the percentage of the overall nonagricultural population that is self-employed is on the rise.

What is responsible for these substantial demographic changes in the work behavior of older Americans? On what do individual retirement decisions, and, therefore, aggregate trends, depend?

Because of increases in Social Security coverage and the size of real benefits over the last two decades, much of the public attention has been focused on the impact of Social Security. But as Figure 1 shows, the recent drop in labor force participation rates begins well before age 62. Hence it is important to look also at the other major component of our retirement system—employer pension plans. Since 1950, employer pension coverage has increased from one-quarter to one-half of the wage and salary population, and the number of pension recipients has increased dramatically (Kotlikoff and Smith 1983, Tables 3.2.1, 3.5.1; Ippolito 1986, Tables 5.1, 5.2). In addition, many of these plans offer early retirement benefits well before age 62.

The tremendous growth in Social Security and employer pensions, both aimed specifically at the work decisions of the older population, must have had some impact on individual retirement behavior. But it has only been in the last decade that economists have developed a consistent method to gauge their influence, not only on retirement but on work across the life cycle.

A View of the Retirement System across Life

Eligibility for Social Security and pension benefits has long been acknowledged as an important part of a worker's compensation package. Since retirement rights are promises of income streams in the future, they are conveniently viewed as assets or wealth whose value equals the sum of all future payments discounted back to the present period. As one continues to work, the asset value of these promised future payments may rise or fall, depending on the details of the benefit calculation rules.

These changes in asset values, called "pension accrual," are part of compensation—the return to working another year. If retirement income wealth is growing, then pension accrual is positive, and true compensation exceeds the amount of earnings as traditionally defined. On the other hand, if retirement wealth is decreasing with additional work, then pension accrual is negative, and the true return is less than the paycheck by the amount of the annual loss in wealth. The benefit calculation rules encourage and discourage work at different times during the life cycle. The net result seems to be that they encourage workers to remain in a single job for most of their work lives, but not forever. Penalties exist for those who leave employment too early as well as for those who leave too late.

PENSIONS

Pension plans in the United States are generally of two types. *Defined contribution* plans establish a contribution rule, e.g., the employer and employee may each pay 5 percent of current salary into the pension fund. Contributions are invested, and the benefit paid is based on the value of the funds at retirement. Such plans play a relatively minor role in the retirement decision. The accrued value increases in accord with the contributions made in that year. But this is also true at younger ages. If workers who leave the firm have a right to the current wealth value of the pension, then (in this example) the accrual value of the pension would simply be a constant percentage of salary at all ages. Defined contribution plans are really just forced savings plans, but with significant tax advantages. Their effect on work behavior should not be substantially different from that of other forms of wealth.

Defined benefit plans are a more complex form of savings and play a direct role in work decisions. This is the dominant type of pension in America. Ippolito (1986) estimates that nearly 80 percent of covered workers have a defined benefit plan. These plans promise workers a benefit at retirement based on some agreed-upon formula. Employees usually make no explicit contribution to the plan. A typical defined pension plan offers benefits beginning at some stated age to workers who have been with the firm for a given number of years. That benefit is usually based on years of service, some average of highest nominal earnings, or both.

One method of calculating the accrual value of a pension is to estimate how the asset value of the pension plan changes with every year of tenure with the firm. After each year we calculate what the worker would get (in present discounted value terms) if he were to leave the firm at that time. This is called the current "quit value" of the pension. The change in this quit value in a given year is pension accrual. Positive accrual means that true compensation exceeds the paycheck; negative accrual means the opposite. Several economists, e.g., Barnow and Ehrenberg (1979), Gordon and Blinder (1980), Kotlikoff and Wise (1985), Allen, Clark, and McDermed (1987), and Gustman and Steinmeier (1987), have used this method to estimate pension accrual.

Tracing the actual "quit value" of a worker in a given pension plan is burdensome. Information is needed on the worker's yearly earnings, the appropriate interest rate, the life expectancy of the worker, and the often quite complex pension plan rules. Most studies that attempt to do this either by simulation (e.g., Kotlikoff and Wise) or by using actual case records (e.g. Allen, Clark, and McDermed or Gustman and Steinmeier) assume that pension accrual is zero until vesting. At vesting, which under the 1986 Tax Reform Act can occur not later than after five years of service with the firm, there is a peak. Pension accrual then rises until the age at which early benefits are first offered. The growth in accrual over time is due to the nature of defined benefit plans. Accrual grows as earnings grow, as years of service with the firm grow, and simply because the value of the pension grows as the worker nears the age when benefits can first be taken.

At early retirement age, the worker can either quit the job and accept the pension benefit or continue working and postpone pension receipt. By law, the yearly benefits a worker receives if he chooses early retirement cannot be reduced by more than an actuarially fair amount, that is, by more than the amount that would equate the present discounted values of the early and normal retirement streams. In fact, however, most early pension benefits exceed what an actuarially fair reduction would require. This means that those who continue to work are offered less than actuarially fair rewards for postponing pension acceptance. Since pension plans usually offer reduced service credit after normal retirement age, accrual is often negative past that age, and pension wealth actually falls with continued work for the great majority of workers. Those who continue to work lose retirement benefits which are not made up to them in the future. In essence, they suffer pay cuts and earn less than the amount of their paychecks.

The point at which pension accrual turns negative depends on the actuarial reduction factor and other details of the benefit calculation. Though pension accrual will peak at early retirement age if the penalty for early retirement (which is the same as the reward for delayed retirement) is less than actuarially fair, accruals may still stay positive because of wage growth and the effect of additional years of tenure with the firm. However, if these two factors are insufficient to compensate for the inadequate actuarial reward, accruals can actually turn negative after the initial early retirement age. In addition, many firms offer special early retirement bonuses that further discourage delaying job exit. Hatch (1981) finds that the majority of retirement programs with early retirement options do in fact have less than actuarially fair reduction factors at all early retirement ages.

This pattern of lifetime pension accrual has profound implications for the compensation that workers receive for continued service with the firm. Over and above the simple fact of pension eligibility, the possibility of pension wealth loss is a strong incentive for workers to leave a firm at early retirement age. For all workers the accrual value of a pension falls at this point, and for some it becomes negative. Hence, relative to previous periods, net compensation on the career job declines at early retirement age.

Defined benefit pensions also encourage workers to stay with the firm until the age of early retirement. Because the accrual value of a pension rises over time before eligibility, the return for increased tenure with the firm also increases. Workers who leave prior to early retirement give up the very large accruals at older pre-retirement ages. Hence, workers who leave a job prior to early retirement can lose a sizable portion of the pension wealth that they could have had.

SOCIAL SECURITY

Much of this discussion about pension wealth is applicable to the retirement component of Social Security. Social Security wealth and changes in that wealth are important components in the behavioral models of Burkhauser and Quinn (1983), Fields and Mitchell (1984a), and Burtless and Moffitt (1986).

Social Security is similar to a defined benefit pension plan. The government promises workers a benefit at retirement based on some agreed-upon formula, but because it is a mandatory system, backed by the taxing power of the government, it is not necessary that the benefits paid to any single individual (or cohort) equal that person's (or cohort's) payments into the plan. Hence contributions made by workers and their employers into the Social Security account need not be—and historically have not been—equal to the expected value of future benefits.

If one assumes that workers receive a constantly increasing wage rate and that they work the same number of hours each year, then the accrual pattern of Social Security benefits looks much the same as that of a private pension. Accrual during the first nine years is zero, since Social Security requires ten years of covered service before one is eligible to receive any benefits. The first peak in accrual would occur at the onset of a vested right to Social Security. Accrued benefits would then increase, as they did for private pensions, since each year of work raises average monthly earnings and reduces the time between the current year and the year of early retirement. Because 35 years of earnings are used in the average earnings calculations, the increase in average earnings associated with one more year of work may peak then, since subsequent earnings are no longer replacing zeros in the calculation. Depending on the discount rate chosen, however, accrual rates may continue to rise until age 62.

Social Security accrual after age 62 is a matter of some debate. Blinder, Gordon, and Wise (1980) argue that, at least during the 1960s and early 1970s, the accrual rate for Social Security was positive past age 62, and that this is true even after Social Security taxes are subtracted. Burkhauser and Turner (1982), on the other hand, argue that if workers can vary their labor supply over the life cycle, it is irrelevant whether accrual rates are positive or negative after age 62. What is critical is whether these rates are higher or lower than those in earlier years. If Social Security *accrual* rates do peak at early retirement, as private pensions do, this will induce workers to work more at younger pre-Social Security retirement ages and less at older ages. Most economists now agree that Social Security accrual peaks no later than age 62.

There is less consensus on when Social Security *wealth* peaks, that is, at what age Social Security accrual net of taxes becomes *negative*. The small actuarial adjustments of those who postpone acceptance past age 65 suggest that it occurs at or before this age. A first approximation

Table 2: JOB TENURE ON LONGEST JOB, MEN AGED 58–63 IN 1969 (SAMPLE SIZE, 7,818)

Years of Tenure	Percentage
0–4	12
5–9	10
10–19	23
20–29	24
30–39	18
40 or more	13

Source: Retirement History Study. See Irelan 1983 for details on this remarkable data set.

is that for a worker today with average life expectancy and increasing real earnings, taxes offset accrual, and Social Security wealth is approximately constant between age 62 and age 65.

Hence both Social Security and defined benefit plans provide incentive for workers to shift work to younger ages and away from later years, and both plans encourage long tenure with a single firm.

Patterns of Work across Life

CAREER JOBS

The falling labor force participation at older ages is the best-known change in the work effort of American men, but much more is happening. A look at the data confirms that most Americans spend a considerable proportion of their time in the labor market on a long-term career job. This is true despite the fact that the median job tenure in the United States is quite short—3.6 years in 1978, according to Hall (1982)—and despite the fact that the completed tenure of jobs ending at any given time is also very modest (3.9 and 2.8 years for whites and nonwhites in the early 1970s, according to Akerlof and Main 1981). The fact that there are many young high-turnover workers in the labor market is largely responsible for these findings. When Hall (1982) looked at the tenure of workers aged 55 and older, he found that one-third were in jobs of at least twenty years' duration.

But even this figure is misleading. Some of these workers may have recently left a job of longer duration. When we look at the figures for the longest (as opposed to the current) job of the Retirement History Study sample, we find that over half of the men had a job that lasted at least twenty years. (Nearly two-thirds of these men were still employed on their longest jobs. Of the others, half were working on another job; the rest were no longer employed.) As seen in Table 2, nearly a third of the men had held, or were currently holding, jobs of

Table 3: EXIT FROM FULLTIME CAREER JOB, WORKERS AGED 58–63 IN 1969 (SAMPLE SIZE, 2,055)

Job Status	Wage and Salary Men	Self-Employed Men	Wage and Salary Women
Part-time on same job	5%	25%	10%
Part-time on new job	10	13	10
Fulltime on new job	12	13	7
Out of labor force	73	49	74
Sample size	*1,446*	*241*	*368*

Source: see Table 2.

thirty or more years' duration, and nearly 80 percent had at least ten years' experience on their longest job.

But even these estimates are lower bounds, since some of these older workers were still employed on their longest job, and therefore adding to tenure, when they disappeared from the sample or when the surveys ended in 1979. Hall used statistical techniques to forecast the eventual tenure of his sample of men employed in 1978, and estimated that about half of those aged 40 or more were on jobs that would last at least twenty years.

POST-CAREER JOBS

Social Security and private pension plans are now an integral part of the U.S. labor market and have contributed to the current pattern of early "retirement" from fulltime work on career jobs. They have also contributed to a much less well understood phenomenon—work after retirement, or at least work after departure from a career job. Quinn (1981), Gustman and Steinmeier (1984), and Honig and Hanoch (1985) have recognized that the transition from fulltime work to fulltime retirement is not always instantaneous. They describe the decision as one of fulltime work, part-time work, or no work, but they do not link these characterizations of work to specific job changes. Exit from a fulltime career job can occur not only in terms of hours of work but also in terms of alternative jobs. Because private pensions are tied to a specific job, they most directly affect work at that job, but they generally do not restrict other employment. Hence our present retirement system provides a strong incentive for those who want to continue working to do so in another job.

Table 3 shows how workers in the Retirement History Study actually exited from their career jobs. Workers were considered to be on a career job in 1969 if they were working fulltime and had been at that job for at least ten years. About three-quarters of those employed fulltime in 1969 had been employed for ten years or more. Of the 1,446 wage and salary men in our career sample, a little over 70 percent exited their career job sometime between 1969 and 1975 and remained completely out of the work force over the next four years.

This move from fulltime work to fulltime retirement is still the most common way for workers to depart, but it is by no means the only way. About 5 percent of these men first dropped to part-time status (defined here as less than 20 hours per week) on their career job. But more surprisingly, over 20 percent left a career job and then took on new fulltime or part-time employment.

Self-employed men behaved quite differently. Less than 50 percent of them moved directly from fulltime work to full retirement. The self-employed are much more likely to be able to control working conditions, especially hours of work. Almost 25 percent moved from fulltime to part-time work on the career job. The remaining 25 percent moved to new employment. The wage and salary women behaved like their male counterparts: about 75 percent took full retirement, and the remainder were more evenly distributed among the three nontraditional options.

Work after departure from a career job is not a rare event, and the jobs in most cases are substantial. In Table 4 we follow the transitional workers for two years after the change. After one year, over 80 percent of these men and women were still at work, nearly all on the first post-career job, but a few on a second or even later job. Even after two years, three-quarters of the sample was still employed. This transitional employment, it appears, lasts long enough to be an important part of the labor force withdrawal process for a substantial proportion of older American workers.

We then looked in more detail at the subset of our sample who actually switched employers. With the exception of the self-employed, most had to do this in order to keep working after leaving fulltime status on their career jobs. A comparison of the career and new jobs reveals that most of these job switchers moved to different lines of work. About 60 percent of the wage and salary men moved to a new (1-digit) industry and occupation, and the percentage was even higher for the self-employed.

Table 4: LABOR ACTIVITY ONE AND TWO YEARS AFTER START OF POST-CAREER JOB, MEN AND WOMEN AGED 58–63 IN 1969 (SAMPLE SIZE, 743)

Year	On First Post-Career Job	On Another Job	Out of Labor Force
1 year	72%	11%	18%
2 years	57	17	25

Source: see Table 2.

Table 5: OCCUPATIONAL CHANGE OF WAGE AND SALARY MEN WHO CHANGED JOBS (VERTICAL PERCENTAGE)

	Career Job				
New Job	White-collar skilled	White-collar other	Blue-collar skilled	Blue-collar other	Total
White-collar skilled	47%	8%	7%	0%	55(17%)
White-collar other	28%	44%	9%	9%	60(18%)
Blue-collar skilled	13%	13%	50%	20%	103(32%)
Blue-collar other	11%	36%	33%	70%	107(33%)
Total	*89*	*39*	*152*	*45*	*325*
	(27%)	*(12%)*	*(47%)*	*(14%)*	

Source: see Table 2.

In ranking jobs by skill level and white-collar/blue-collar status, we noticed a drift down the occupational scale. Although about half of the job changers stayed in the same cell (see Table 5), many more slid down than climbed up. Wage rates told the same story. Wages were generally lower in the new job, especially for those moving to part-time work with a new employer. Gustman and Steinmeier (1983) report this same finding, and hypothesize that there may be a minimum-hours constraint on most of these career jobs; i.e., in order to work fewer hours, the individual must switch employers and suffer the accompanying wage loss. Although only 7 percent of our sample earned less than $5 per hour on their career jobs, about 25 percent of those with a new fulltime job and about 50 percent of those with new part-time employment earned less than $5 per hour. The new earnings levels correlate with the threshold for the Social Security earnings test, so that some of the earnings loss may be intentional. The earnings of many wage and salary men were just under that threshold, and this behavior was correlated with age. Over 25 percent of those aged 62 through 64 and over 33 percent of those over age 65 earned less than $5 per hour, compared with 9 percent of those under age 62 (and therefore ineligible for Social Security benefits).

These data suggest that work after "retirement" is not a rare event and that substantial changes are required in current Social Security and pension legislation before we can expect substantial numbers of workers to stay at work past their early sixties.

Actual and Proposed Changes in the Retirement System

MANDATORY RETIREMENT RULES

The 1977 amendments to the Age Discrimination in Employment Act raised the age of earliest mandatory retirement for most workers from 65 to 70. In 1986, mandatory retirement at any age was outlawed in all but a few jobs, but there is little evidence that this change has had or will have a significant effect on aggregate work effort.

Mandatory retirement rules were widespread before 1986. We estimated that 43 percent of employed men aged 58 to 61 in 1969 faced mandatory retirement on the job they then held (Quinn and Burkhauser 1983). But, in addition, we found that the great majority of such workers—91 percent—were also eligible for an employer pension on that job. Hence the removal of mandatory retirement for most of these workers still left in place substantial disincentives to work.

Social Security and pension accrual can have an important effect on net wage compensation. We found that for men aged 63 to 65 in 1974 employed fulltime, Social Security and private pensions did just that. For the median worker aged 63 or 64 eligible only for Social Security benefits, Social Security accrual was positive and increased true compensation by around 10 percent of traditionally defined earnings (Quinn and Burkhauser 1983). But at age 65 the median worker suffered a negative accrual, which reduced compensation by about a third. The compensation of the median worker eligible for both Social Security and a private pension was augmented by about 10 percent at age 63 but was reduced by 3 percent at age 64 and by almost half at age 65. This suggests that attempts to increase work effort after age 65 that do not address these dramatic reductions in pension and Social Security wealth may be doomed to failure.

SOCIAL SECURITY RULES

There is little doubt that the work incentives embedded in Social Security have altered the behavior of older Americans, although the size of the aggregate effect is hotly debated. In the early years of the twenty-first century, the costs of this policy in lost manpower will grow. The changing demographic structure makes policies that drive older men and women away from work more and more questionable. These considerations, together with the budget crises of the early 1980s, were at the heart of the 1983 amendments to the Social Security Act that grew out of the Greenspan Commission report.

The amendments will increase work effort in two ways. Paradoxically, it will be stimulated both by reducing benefits and by increasing benefits. The gradual increase in the normal retirement age from 65 to 67 lowers the benefits of those who retire before age 67, but the increase in the annual reward for delayed receipt of benefits past age 65 from 3 to 8 percent per year increases the marginal return to work past age 65. These are important changes in the incentive structure, but it is unclear how much of an effect this will have on future work effort.

Social Security benefits will continue to be offered at age 62, and Social Security accrual will continue to peak at this age for most workers. But for those who choose to take such benefits, the actuarial reduction will reduce yearly benefits to 70 percent of normal rather than the current 80 percent. Two studies done before the actual rule changes were announced simulated the effect of similar proposals. In one study, Burtless and Moffitt (1985) found that delaying the normal retirement age to 68 would delay retirement, but by a modest amount—less than half a year, on the average. In another study, Fields and Mitchell (1984b), using a slightly different behavioral model, also found that the increase in work effort from such a change would be small. They found that an increase of retirement age to 68 would increase average retirement by under two months.

Gustman and Steinmeier (1985) simulated three actual changes initiated by the 1983 Social Security amendments—the increase in normal retirement age to 67, the increase in the delayed retirement credit after age 65 from 3 to 8 percent, and the decrease in the benefit reduction rate (the earnings test) from 50 to 33 percent. The predicted effects are long-run, in that the study assumes that workers know that these are the rules over their lifetime. But they do not allow other aspects of the retirement system to change; in particular, the details of private pension plan accrual are assumed to be unaltered.

These researchers predicted a larger effect of the amendments than did the other studies cited. The percentage of men over age 65 working fulltime would increase, and the percentage working part-time would decrease. For example, they found that the fulltime participation rate of men aged 66 would increase from 18 to 23 percent, with similar or larger increases for other age categories above age 65. While these are dramatic percentage increases, they are based on such a small group of the total that the overall effects on the labor market would still be small. Gustman and Steinmeier predicted more modest effects on retirement prior to age 65. The majority of the impact on work effort is found to result from the increase in the delayed retirement credit rather than the postponement of normal retirement age.

EMPLOYER PENSION PLANS

Information on individual pension plans is more difficult to obtain, and hence it is more difficult to estimate the full effect of these plans on work behavior. Burkhauser and Quinn (1983) and Fields and Mitchell (1984c) have shown that negative pension accrual does influence the age that a worker leaves a firm. Allen, Clark, and McDermed (1987) and Kotlikoff and Wise (1987) have used more recent data to show that pension accrual is, on average, negative well before age 65 for most defined benefit pension plans. But because pension plans vary widely across the economy, no one has been able to estimate the impact of these plans on overall work effort.

Because private pensions play an important role in the job exit decision of workers, simulations of the type discussed above can be dramatically affected by assumptions about how the accrual patterns of employer pensions will change over the next several decades. Although there is very little empirical evidence on this important issue, it is unlikely that they will remain the same, as is implicitly assumed by these simulations. Mitchell and Luzadis (1988), using a small sample of actual pension plans and sixty illustrative workers, suggest that the incentives have changed significantly over the past thirty years, from encouraging late retirement during the 1960s to encouraging early retirement today. Firms have therefore been willing to change pension structures to adjust to changes in their environment. The federal government is now proposing major changes in the retirement environment. The response by employers is a critical but generally unknown factor.

Changes in Social Security legislation alone will have some effect on aggregate behavior. For instance, there is evidence that workers do bunch earnings just below the level of the earnings test. But the currently slated changes in that level, in the normal retirement age, and in the actuarial adjustment past age 65 will not in themselves have dramatic effects on length of stay in a career job. And it is this labor market decision which most strongly drives total work effort at older ages.

Many defined pension plans encourage exit from a career job at the earliest possible retirement age. It is likely that changes in pension rules, rather than in the Social Security system, will have the greatest effect on fulltime work in such jobs. For instance, the 1986 amendments to the Age Discrimination Act require firms with pension plans to continue to provide service credit to those who continue with the firm past normal retirement age. But firms can make early retirement benefits more generous in order to offset this rule.

But the ability to offset government policy does not necessarily translate into such action. Rather, one might argue that the opposite will occur. One reason that the majority of pension plans in the United States chose age 65 as their normal retirement age was that Social Security was pegged at that age. One of the original purposes of Social Security was to encourage older workers to leave the labor force. Until 1972, earnings above some small amount were taxed at a rate of 100 percent, and benefits postponed beyond age 65 earned *no* actuarial credit.

Given the strong disincentives to fulltime work in any job by such a national retirement system, it is not surprising that firms developed institutional relationships that conformed to this government institution. To do otherwise would have required employers to pay workers higher wages past age 65 to offset the losses in Social Security wealth associated with working fulltime past that age. The establishment of Social Security benefits at age 62 in 1961 further encouraged employers to follow a policy of early retirement. The changes in Social Security benefit rules scheduled to begin in the next decade will reduce the fall in accrual after age 62 and, to some extent, will change the institutional structure on which employer pensions were built. Thus it is possible that employer pensions will move with, rather than against, the flow of these changes.

A final speculation concerns the influence of these rule changes on the type of work done at older ages. If pension rules do not adjust, we can expect increased part-time and fulltime work after a fulltime career job because an easing of Social Security work rules will make part-time and even fulltime work on new jobs a relatively attractive alternative to complete retirement. But the current changes are unlikely to have much of an effect on the timing of that exit from fulltime career work unless pension rules also change.

If private firms disagree with those who believe labor will be in short supply in the next century and counter Social Security rule changes with even stronger early retirement incentives, then we will see even more part- and fulltime work in post-career jobs. If, however, firms foresee labor shortages and make similar attempts to flatten pension accrual across the life cycle, then the age at which workers quit fulltime career work will rise.

A final and important variation on this theme is the possibility of part-time work in a career job. Self-employed workers are much more likely to take this step than are others, as we have seen; at present, defined benefit pension rules make this a very poor choice for those who desire part-time work. Even if actuarial adjustment and service credit rules are changed for fulltime career work past normal retirement age, this will not have a major effect on those who want to work only part-time in a career job, since many defined benefit pensions are still importantly affected by highest-earnings rules. Hence, even if firms allowed workers to work part-time, it is not clear how many would take advantage of such an opportunity.

Conclusion

Our modern retirement system is responsible, in large degree, for breaking the link between old age and poverty, but in so doing, it has had an important influence on labor supply over life. Social Security and defined benefit employer pensions encourage fulltime work on a single job prior to "retirement" age. To the degree that work is performed after that age, employer pensions encourage it to be with another firm. While the majority of older workers go directly from a career job to fulltime retirement, a substantial percentage of workers take post-career jobs. Policy changes meant to encourage work at older ages should recognize the difference between proposals that will increase time in a career job and those likely to increase post-career employment.

References

Akerlof, George A., and Brian G. M. Main. 1981. "An Experience-Weighted Measure of Employment and Unemployment Durations," *American Economic Review* 71 (December): 1003–11.

Allen, Steven G., Robert L. Clark, and Ann A. McDermed. 1987. "Pensions and Lifetime Jobs: The New Industrial Feudalism Revisited." Unpublished paper.

Barnow, Burt S., and Ronald G. Ehrenberg. 1979. "The Costs of Defined Benefit Pension Plans and Firm Adjustments," *Quarterly Journal of Economics* 79 (November): 523–40.

Becker, Eugene H. 1984. "Self-Employed Workers: An Update to 1983," *Monthly Labor Review,* July, pp. 14–18.

Blau, David M. 1987. "A Time Series Analysis of Self-Employment in the United States," *Journal of Political Economy* 95 (June): 445–66.

Blinder, Alan S., Roger H. Gordon, and Donald E. Wise. 1980. "Reconsidering the Work Disincentives of Social Security," *National Tax Journal* 33 (December): 431–42.

Burkhauser, Richard V., and Joseph F. Quinn. 1983. "Is Mandatory Retirement Overrated? Evidence from the 1970s," *Journal of Human Resources* 18 (Summer): 339–58.

Burkhauser, Richard V., and John A. Turner. 1982. "Labor Market Experience of the Almost Old and the Implications for Income Support," *American Economic Review* 72 (May): 304–8.

Burtless, Gary, and Robert A. Moffitt. 1985. "The Joint Choice of Retirement Age and Postretirement Hours of Work," *Journal of Labor Economics* 3 (April): 209–36.

———. 1986. "Social Security, Earnings Tests, and Age at Retirement," *Public Finance Quarterly* 14 (January): 3–27.

Fields, Gary S., and Olivia S. Mitchell. 1984a. "Economic Determinants of the Optimal Retirement Age: An Empirical Investigation," *Journal of Human Resources* 19 (Spring): 245–62.

———. 1984b. "The Effects of Social Security Reforms on Retirement Ages and Retirement Incomes," *Journal of Public Economics* 25 (November): 143–59.

———. 1984c. *Retirement, Pensions, and Social Security.* Cambridge, Mass.: MIT Press.

Gordon, Roger H., and Alan S. Blinder. 1980. "Market Wages, Reservation Wages and Retirement Decision," *Journal of Public Economics* 14 (October): 277–308.

Gustman, Alan A., and Thomas L. Steinmeier. 1983. "Minimum-Hours Constraints and Retirement Behavior," *Contemporary Policy Issues* 3 (April): 77–91.

———. 1984. "Partial Retirement and the Analysis of Retirement Behavior," *Industrial and Labor Relations Review* 37 (April): 403–15.

———. 1985. "The 1983 Social Security Reforms and Labor Supply Adjustments of Older Individuals in the Long Run," *Journal of Labor Economics* 3 (April): 237–53.

———. 1987. "An Analysis of Pension Benefit Formulas, Pension Wealth, and Incentives from Pensions." Final Report to the U.S. Department of Labor, July.

Hall, Robert E. 1982. "The Importance of Lifetime Jobs in the U.S. Economy," *American Economic Review* 72 (September): 716–24.

Hatch, Sara. 1981. "Financial Retirement Incentives in Private Pension Plans." Urban Institute draft project report to the U.S. Department of Labor, J-9-P-0-0163, September.

Honig, Marjorie, and Giora Hanoch. 1985. "Partial Retirement as a Separate Mode of Retirement Behavior," *Journal of Human Resources* 20 (Winter): 21–46.

Ippolito, Richard A. 1986. *Pensions, Economics and Public Policy.* Homewood, Ill.: Dow Jones-Irwin.

Irelan, Lola M. 1983. "Retirement History Study: Introduction," *Social Security Bulletin* 35 (November): 3–8.

Kotlikoff, Laurence J., and Daniel E. Smith. 1983. *Pensions in the American Economy.* Chicago: University of Chicago Press.

Kotlikoff, Laurence J., and David A. Wise. 1985. "Labor Compensation and the Structure of Private Pension Plans: Evidence for Contractual vs. Spot Labor Markets." In *Pensions, Labor, and Individual Choice,* edited by David Wise, pp. 55–85. Chicago: University of Chicago Press.

———. 1987. "Pension Backloading, Wage Taxes, and Work Disincentives." National Bureau of Economic Research Working Paper 2463, December.

Mitchell, Olivia S., and Rebecca Luzadis. 1988. "Changes in Pension Incentives over Time," *Industrial and Labor Relations Review* 42 (October): 100–108.

Quinn, Joseph F. 1981. "The Extent and Correlates of Partial Retirement," *The Gerontologist* 21 (December): 634–43.

Quinn, Joseph F., and Richard V. Burkhauser. 1983. "Influencing Retirement Behavior: A Key Issue for Social Security," *Journal of Policy Analysis and Management* 3 (Fall): 1–13

U.S. Department of Labor, Bureau of Labor Statistics. 1988. *Employment and Earnings*, January.

Adequate Pensions: A National Obligation

OWEN BIEBER

The president of the UAW points to the success in negotiating basic private pension plans in the auto industry in the late 1940s and early 1950s and to their improvement in the years that followed, including provision for voluntary early retirement. Pension costs, however, are rising at a rapid rate as the number of active workers shrinks in relation to the number of retired workers. Health care costs are also increasing markedly. Joint private sector responses are needed, but cannot alone solve the problems of the aging work force. Bieber emphasizes that the national government has responsibilities that must be met in order to ensure adequate income and health care for the elderly.

I. B.

A number of other contributors to this volume touch on the national policy dimensions of the maturing work force, and, while I will emphasize the United Auto Workers' experiences in that industry, I too will outline some of the broader social and philosophical considerations that guide our approach.

First, let me describe briefly the history of UAW's involvement with older workers and retirement-related issues.

Many will recall the slogan, made famous by Walter Reuther, that was heard around the auto plants, especially in the 1940s, "Too Old to Work, Too Young to Die," which Doug Fraser uses as the title of his paper. Auto companies in those days were notorious for using up workers and spitting them out in what we now would consider their prime years. Often, workers in their fifties and even their forties were released so that the company could hire someone younger who could work just a little bit faster.

It goes without saying that one of the union's first objectives was to put a stop to that kind of abuse. The contract and the grievance procedure soon succeeded in blocking capricious firings and layoffs for such phony reasons as a worker's age. At the same time, however, the union recognized the desire of older workers to leave the plant after years of toil—making room for the unemployed who needed jobs and enjoying leisure time after a life's work was completed. Provisions had to be made for a decent retirement. So we put a premium on winning company-paid pensions, and by 1949 we had made the breakthrough at the Ford Motor Company, with the nation's first fully funded employer-paid pension plan, administered jointly by the company and the union.

From that point forward, our union continued to champion the cause of retirees and to negotiate pension increases not only for future retirees but for the current group of retired members as well. Our approach has always been guided first and foremost by the needs of the older worker and the retiree.

30-and-Out

While the growing strength of the union certainly made working conditions much better than they had been, we never kidded ourselves that work on the line in an auto plant was easy or that, after a couple of decades or more, it wouldn't begin to take its toll on the individual worker. We also anticipated that it would be necessary to create job openings for those seeking work and promotional opportunities for employees with low seniority. We therefore sought to make it possible for our members to leave the plant with a good pension before age 65, depending on years of service. Our rallying cry became "30-and-Out," and in the 1973 Chrysler agreement, following a brief strike, we won the opportunity for our members to collect a full pension at any age after thirty years of service.

In the years since then, we have chipped away still further at obstacles to early retirement options for workers covered by our major contracts. We have also raised the pension amounts dramatically to make it more attractive for individuals to make the decision to retire.

Pensions and the Shrinking Work Force

Let me be very clear. We know how expensive it is to achieve pension increases in the current environment. Not only are UAW employers facing unprecedented competitive challenges but the cost of increases in relation to units sold is constantly shooting upward because of the high ratio of retired to active members at these companies. At the

Chrysler Corporation, for instance, the ratio of retired to active workers is already at 1.3 to 1, and that's obviously the direction in which other auto companies are heading. As many of the older manufacturing industries shrink in size, they encounter the same problem; in fact, the Steelworkers Union faces an even bigger headache in its industry, as Lynch points out in his remarks.

It is important to understand why this crisis has come about. It is not the natural result of *demographic* changes: there is currently no scarcity of younger people who would like to work in an auto plant or a steel plant. On the contrary, there are hundreds of thousands eager to get in. They can't get jobs, however, because employers in the auto, steel, and other industries are drastically downsizing their work force. Chrysler, for example, permanently eliminated some 40,000 UAW jobs in the reorganization that accompanied its brush with bankruptcy. Ford today has 50,000 fewer UAW workers than it had in 1979. At General Motors, the number is down by nearly 150,000 and still declining.

It could be argued, I suppose, that these are structural adjustments to a new competitive situation. That's partly correct, but it is by no means the whole story. Even when sales and profits at the Big Three rebounded after the terrible sales slump of 1982–83, the companies never called our people back in numbers reflecting the expanded production. The reasons included introduction of new technology, increased reliance on overtime schedules, and, beyond question, outsourcing and foreign sourcing of work previously performed by our members. It is important to bear this in mind because it relates directly to the challenge of winning pension increases in this new environment.

As I have had occasion to tell the auto companies across the bargaining table, we agree that it's very expensive to raise pensions with such a high ratio of retired to active people, but you made it expensive when you made the decision to trim the work force so drastically. We are not at all shy about demanding substantial increases in pension benefits despite the cost. Our position is that the employers owe that to us as the price for making such drastic cuts in our numbers. What is more, by making it clear to the companies that we will continue to seek significant pension increases, we feel we can help create job opportunities for younger workers that might not otherwise exist. And perhaps employers won't be so quick to drop people from the active payroll if they know it's going to cost them on the pension end.

Even if that doesn't convince the companies, it is clear that raising pension benefits is one means among several to help manage overall work force reduction in a reasonably humane way. If we can raise pensions high enough to induce senior workers to leave voluntarily, not only is more security created for workers further down in the seniority list but also some slots may be opened for our laid-off brothers and sisters or possibly even for new people off the street.

Living on Retirement Income

One of the most troubling issues during my tenure as president of the UAW has been that of balancing the legitimate concerns of high-seniority workers with the insecurity and layoff fears of younger people. A look at the back issues of our national magazine, *Solidarity*, would show an extended debate being played out in the Letters-to-the-Editor section between younger workers and their spouses, who write in to accuse members with high seniority of depriving them of job opportunities, and older members, who reply—with equal feeling—that they are fully entitled to keep on working. After all, the older people say, their generation built the union, and what is more, they can't afford to live the life they want to live on a combination of their UAW pension and Social Security—that point is made in different ways again and again.

The members who make this point are right. While we are very proud of the good pensions we have negotiated in the UAW, even the best of them is disappointing in comparison with what that member makes in the plant. We should bear in mind, however, that the private pensions benefit was *never intended* to carry the whole load of retirement. The expectation was that a retired person would be sustained by a combination of that private pension, a Social Security check, and accumulated personal savings. The foundation, of course, is Social Security. Our Social Security system is without doubt one of the more effective and stable and well-understood public programs in America. Two-thirds of our nation's elderly today rely on Social Security for over half of their income. Social Security also has the advantage of being universal and completely portable.

Compared to Social Security, the second tier of the American retirement system—private pensions—is a very mixed bag. The biggest problem derives from people's perfectly reasonable expectation that their living standard in retirement will be considerably higher than the basic Social Security level. But only 25 percent of our elderly today have any kind of private pension at all, which means that the majority of employers are skipping out on what should be a basic responsibility to their employees. Moreover, because of vesting standards and frequent job changes, fewer than half of the active workers now employed by companies with pension plans will ever receive a pension from these employers.

Pensions as Public Policy

It should concern our elected leaders that those charged with negotiating pensions in the private sector *cannot* use pension increases to encourage early retirement as effectively as we might wish because of too much reliance on this single source of retirement income. It should likewise concern our elected leaders that our nation's practice of relying extensively on private pensions to sustain workers in their retirement places significant added financial burden on our industries at home, while national social welfare policies among many of the nations which compete with us ease the financial impact on their industries. And it should also concern our elected leaders that the close link between advancing age and increasing health care needs makes our privately funded approach look even more vulnerable and inadequate when we compare it with the approach taken by our competitors. Anyone with a retired parent who becomes ill or incapacitated in some way while living on a fixed income is familiar with the inadequacy of our national policies in this regard. It is obvious that the health care needs of that individual consume more and more of his or her income. And it should be equally obvious that if we as a people provided more adequately for the long-term health care needs of retirees, a good measure of the pressure on our private pension system would be relieved.

In this connection, I am pleased to say that the UAW hopes to help point the way to a cost-effective and humane model of how government can and should handle the long-term care issue. In our recent contract settlements with Ford and General Motors, we were able to negotiate pilot programs in this area—programs that we will encourage government planners to examine and learn from as this issue grows in national significance and enters the public policy arena.

Ultimately, the pension issue really boils down to a question of means, not ends. As long as we intend to remain a reasonably civilized people, and continue to recognize the contributions made by workers throughout the course of their lifetimes, we will be paying to provide for a dignified retirement for those workers.

I would not argue for one minute that it is the responsibility of government to assume all responsibility for retirees or that employers should be let off the hook—especially when they so clearly derive very tangible benefits from their workers' years of active service. But I do think that now is the time to consider whether it is in our national interest to continue to manage the needs of retirees exactly as we do now, or whether some other approaches might be tried.

Our recent presidential national political debates have not come close to addressing these issues in any depth. We witness a barrage of charges and counter-charges on how this or that candidate voted on Social Security, but there is little dialogue about how ensuring adequate income and adequate health care for America's seniors relates to the challenge of rebuilding America's economic strength and competitiveness. Candidates for public office and commentators must devote more of their attention to these issues because the elected officials will have to face them soon enough.

During the 1980s, we have had a form of governance at the federal level that amounts to what psychologists would call an "avoidance response." Americans seem to have preferred to listen to Mr. Reagan tell us comforting stories rather than face squarely what are sometimes depressing realities. It is dangerous to live in a world of make-believe, however. The Reagan administration, in typical fashion, told us not to worry over the loss of industrial jobs—that the tremendous growth of the service economy will assure us a secure economic future. And as for my comments above about the impact of pensions on private sector competitiveness, I suppose a Reagan-type response would be that yet another advantage of the new service economy is that pension costs aren't a competitive problem—because most of the new service jobs don't include a pension benefit. Such a response would indicate exactly how shortsighted it is to pin our hopes on a service-based economy. Our service sector may be able to compete with any in the world, but there ***aren't any takers*** in that kind of competition. Service jobs without a solid, viable manufacturing base are not considered strategically significant by people who are truly serious about building a nation's economic future. That fact alone should lead the American people to demand national leaders who *do* take seriously the pension issue and how it relates to the survival and strengthening of the goods-producing side of the U.S. economy. We can find and elect such leaders, but only if we ourselves raise the key issues with clarity and conviction.

Older Workers and Employment Shifts: Policy Responses to Displacement

STEVEN H. SANDELL
AND STEPHEN E. BALDWIN

Some economists have emphasized the role of labor market changes and corporate reorganizations in pushing older workers out of the labor force. Sandell and Baldwin identify three groups of dislocated workers: those who lose their previous jobs but stay with their employers; those who leave, but stay in the labor force; and those who quit the labor force altogether. They find that older workers are less often retained by their employers when skill upgrading is involved and that displaced older workers often do not take advantage of programs to upgrade their marketable skills or to acquire new ones. In practice, many displaced older workers opt for earlier retirement. More federal and other programs are needed, the authors say, to retain these individuals in the work force.

J. D. O.

Plant closings, mass layoffs, or organizational changes can be caused by the introduction of new technologies, the reduction of product demand, or other factors. The treatment accorded workers in such situations, as well as their own expectations and plans, can vary by age. Displacement outcomes and related policy issues fall into three general categories. The first includes workers who lose their previous jobs but stay with the employer. The second includes workers who leave the employer but stay in the labor force. The third contains workers who leave the employer and, either immediately or within a relatively short time, the labor force as well. The first group makes demands primarily on the firm; the second makes demands primarily on the employment security and training system; the third makes demands primarily on the income security system.

Employment year-round and fulltime (more than 35 hours per week) is especially important to the economic security of older displaced workers. Displacement sometimes implies the end of fulltime work. Pre-

Table 1: INCOME BY AGE, SEX, AND EMPLOYMENT STATUS, 1985

	Age				
Category	15+	55–59	60–64	65–69	70+
All men					
No.	88,474	5,313	5,036	4,241	7,031
Median income	$16,311	$22,693	$17,835	$12,581	$10,023
Year-round, full-time, men					
Civilian income recipients	54.5%	66.0%	45.4%	13.7%	3.8%
Median income	$24,999	$28,967	$27,483	$27,714	$23,694
All women					
No.	96,354	5,899	5,813	5,173	10,876
Median income	$7,217	$7,680	$6,833	$6,524	$6,225
Year-round, fulltime, women					
Civilian income recipients	31.7%	36.8%	21.2%	4,8%	0.9%
Median income	$16,252	$16,716	$16,835	$17,882	$19,178

Source: U.S. Bureau of the Census 1987, Table 34, pp. 126–27.

vious, current, and anticipated earnings from employment are central to the economic well-being of older persons. They are not only the major component of income for persons of working age but are the basis for Social Security benefits and pension income in retirement.

Table 1 shows the sizable income advantage enjoyed by older persons with fulltime employment. For example, among men between the ages of 55 and 59 the median income for fulltime year-round workers is almost $29,000, while the median for all men in that age bracket is $22,700. For men aged 60 to 64 the comparable figures are even more dramatic: $27,500 for fulltime year-round workers and $17,800 for all men. The pattern for women is similar, although income is substantially lower and a lesser proportion of women work fulltime year-round.

Thus, the loss of a fulltime job will have substantial economic consequences. While retirement from this type of job is voluntary for many older persons, for older workers who are displaced, problems often ensue.

Displaced older workers tend to follow one of three patterns of labor force experience. There are mainstream workers whose earnings normally increase over their working years, with real income peaking in the fifties and leveling off at the end of their careers, prior to retirement.

There are workers following this track who experience unanticipated midlife events, such as major health or disability problems or the loss of a long-held job. There are disadvantaged workers, people with histories of intermittent employment and low earnings who often have severe labor market problems as they reach old age.

This paper focuses most of its attention on a subset of the second category—the displaced worker—and also examines government training programs targeted at the third group, the disadvantaged, because many older displaced workers are eligible to participate.

Initial federal concern about worker displacement caused by technological change was expressed in the Manpower Development and Training Act (MDTA) of 1962 (Johnston 1980). Policy concern soon shifted, however, to focus on disadvantaged workers, and displacement did not resurface as a priority until the start of the 1980s. By January 1984, when the Bureau of Labor Statistics conducted its first Displaced Worker Survey as a supplement to the monthly Current Population Survey, the country had been through the worst recession in fifty years, and a separate federal program, Title III of the Job Training Partnership Act, had been established. This, along with other expressions of concern, is evidence that once again dislocation is perceived to be a problem needing a national approach.

Being an unemployed worker from an industry or occupation experiencing declining employment nationally was not a particularly good predictor of long-term unemployment, according to one of the first of the studies of displacement in the 1980s (Bendick and Devine 1981). However, living in a declining region was associated with increased re-employment difficulty. Lack of mobility made matters worse. Moving could be a problem for relatively affluent workers who owned their own homes, which they were unable to sell because of depressed markets or which would not yield enough money to finance a home purchase in areas of expanding employment (Zornitsky 1987).

Being displaced is only half the story: why people lose their jobs may have little to do with why they have difficulty getting new ones. Recent analyses of worker dislocation have used Bureau of Labor Statistics survey data and data from unemployment insurance records to investigate these issues (Podgursky and Swaim 1986; Crosslin, Hanna, and Stevens 1984, 1986). These studies confirm the importance of local labor market conditions in affecting re-employment experience. They also emphasize certain background characteristics as "risk factors" increasing the likelihood that a displaced worker will have difficulty finding re-employment.

The two risk factors most associated with significant reemployment difficulty are being older and being a high school dropout. A concomitant negative factor, especially for men, is having been a factory-based blue-collar worker. The economic events of the early 1980s hit manufacturing with a double whammy. Not only did the economic downturn affect sales but the appreciating dollar cut away U.S. export business and caused a surge of imported goods into U.S. markets. As orders dropped, many firms reduced employment: they cut their work forces further, altered the mix of skills when forced to introduce new technologies, or took other actions to stay competitive.

Displaced Workers Who Stay with the Present Employer

SELECTION OF THOSE RETAINED

Most workers strongly prefer staying with their present employer. In addition to a firm's preferences on whom to retain, there may be other factors that affect who stays and who goes. Influences on who is retained/retrained include: anticipated productivity in the new job(s); seniority or other selection rules; and age, sex, and/or race preconceptions.

Older workers and women are less often retained than younger workers and men when skill upgrading is involved, according to case studies (Flynn 1988). This is probably the result of perceived educational deficiencies combined with notions about the lower productivity of older persons. The case studies reviewed by Flynn indicated that problems were greatest for blue-collar workers in factory situations. Older workers were said to be less able or willing to be retrained than younger workers in the same firm. If the change also involved a new location or different work shifts, reluctance to adjust was greater for older than younger workers. Office clerical jobs were less likely to involve age-related displacement, in part because there are relatively more younger workers in predominantly female office occupations.

The retention chances of senior, mostly older, employees in a situation of less than complete shutdown depend on the number of other jobs into which they may transfer (the seniority district). "Bumping rights" allow workers to transfer across organizational lines within the firm, replacing other workers, who in turn can bump other workers, in domino fashion. Such arrangements may conflict, either prospectively or actually, with management's desire to retain particular employees. The wider the district, the less the likelihood of a worker of high seniority being displaced by a reduction in his own division but the greater the likelihood of a low-seniority worker being displaced by reductions in other divisions.

Technological change also affects selection/retention decisions. If there is some discretion over whom to keep, firms may rank employees on the basis of how well they are expected to do in the new work environment. "Anticipated productivity" can be affected by attitudes to change as well as by the presence or absence of the requisite job skills. Effective implementation of advanced technology often requires changes in the operating structure of the organization (National Academy of Sciences 1986). Such changes in the "corporate culture" include devolving decisionmaking to the actual operating units, increasing the two-way flow of information between managers and workers, and eliminating intervening levels of supervision. Managers, as well as workers, can find this an unsettling and unwelcome change, and resistance to the new structures and procedures can lower performance of specific work groups or of the entire organization. Selection criteria for retention and upgrading may thus need to take explicit account of individuals' willingness and ability to function in a new operating environment.

PROGRAMS FOR WORKERS AT OR NEAR RETIREMENT AGE

Where some employees are at or near normal retirement age, an intermediate arrangement may be established in which such workers fill contingent or part-time slots, with or without retraining. Older workers in office jobs are more likely than those in factory jobs to be participants in such programs (Root 1987). Such programs are successful when they benefit both the firm and the worker. They tend to be abandoned under poor business conditions.

Sometimes these programs can be characterized as a way station between retention and displacement. These almost-retired workers are on what National Football League teams call the "taxi squad" of readily available players not on the active roster, but just a taxi ride away. Temporary or contingent worker programs are constrained by regulations, such as the "1000 Hour Rule" for pension contributions (Paul 1987). Advocates of expanded programs have urged the modification of this and other regulations that thwart their development.

Displaced Workers Who Leave the Original Employer

Displaced workers include more people than those who stay until the last possible moment. Most displaced workers do work up to the point of layoff (Barenbeim 1986). Workers who quit because they anticipate or have been told of an impending layoff but who would not have quit otherwise are also classified as displaced. Once the employment relationship is terminated, there are a number of possible outcomes.

Unemployment, in the everyday sense of the term as well in the sense used by economists, means being without a job and searching for a new one. Implicit in this search is a "reservation wage," or the minimal acceptable rate of pay. Experienced workers are typically not interested in low-wage, entry-level jobs, and workers with above-average earnings histories are typically not interested in low-wage jobs at all.

Unemployment for some displaced workers consists of waiting for recall without actively searching for a new job. This behavior depends in part on the degree of enforcement of the "work test" for unemployment insurance (UI) recipients. To receive UI, a person is ostensibly required to be actively seeking, and ready to accept, new employment. In practice, especially in mass layoff situations, the job search requirement is often not enforced. Temporarily laid-off workers with a definite recall date, or workers in an industry with seasonal employment fluctuations, are also not regarded as displaced.

Most displaced workers without definite recall dates still hope to be recalled to their original employers when business picks up or when attrition brings one's name to the top of the recall list. Accepting recall, even if one has had intervening jobs, depends on seniority and pension considerations as well as salary and promotion prospects and is generally the preferred option for displaced workers (Crosslin, Hanna, and Stevens 1986).

Displaced workers generally prefer working in the same or a similar job for a new employer or self-employment in the same area. Such an outcome takes advantage of most of the human capital acquired on the old job, so that earnings losses are limited to firm-specific knowledge and job seniority. Working in a different job, after or without formal training, and for which only the most general work skills are transferable, is another step down on the desirability scale. The new job could be self-employment or could be located in a different area, both of which add to adjustment costs.

Displaced workers, especially older ones, are typically not keen to obtain training to upgrade skills or to acquire new ones, either on their own or with the aid of employer-based or government-funded programs. There is a general reluctance to return to a classroom environment after many years away, and workers are especially reluctant to take training without any assurance of a job at the end of the course.

OLDER WORKERS AND JOB LOSS

Other things being equal, older workers are less likely to be displaced and more likely to be recalled than are younger workers because they typically have more seniority than younger workers (Horvath 1987). In addition, older workers' great reluctance to leave the immediate labor market area to secure new jobs tends to make them easier to recall than younger, more mobile workers, who may have left the employer's area.

Older workers with less than a high school education and men with long tenure with the pre-layoff employer are at particular risk of longer durations of joblessness. Interestingly, workers with these characteristics show the *highest* rates of return to the previous employer (Crosslin, Hanna, and Stevens 1986). In particular, older workers who are displaced from industries that dominate local labor markets return to employers in these industries even though the number of jobs is shrinking and prospects for future displacement might seem serious. In part, pension eligibility considerations are likely to be involved, as is the fact that such employers typically are relatively high-paying and represent the best job that the worker ever had. There may be some foundation for the reluctance of employers in lower-wage industries to hire displaced workers because they believe that such employees will leave to accept recall by the old employer.

Despite the protection of seniority, technological changes that call for additional training are more likely to lead to the displacement of older workers (Flynn 1988), perhaps because of educational shortfalls, perhaps because of preconceptions on the employer's or the employee's part. Lack of education worsens the chances of qualifying for external training programs.

Geographical mobility is lowest for displaced workers over the age of 55, although those older workers who did move had markedly higher re-employment rates than nonmovers. Selection bias may be involved if it was the more employable workers who moved or were offered jobs requiring a move. Thus, although older displaced workers surveyed who had moved voluntarily had much lower rates of being out of the labor force than did nonmovers (Horvath 1987), a strat-egy encouraging greater mobility is unlikely to generate favorable re-employment experiences. Family responsibilities, need for medical insurance coverage, etc., may inhibit mobility or limit retraining options.

Although older workers as a group are less likely to lose their jobs than younger workers, for some older workers the loss of long-held jobs can have devastating consequences. The unexpected loss of a job is not only a matter of the loss of current income; it may make the difference between severe economic hardship and financial stability in retirement, based on the accumulation of pension and Social Security credits as well as savings. This is especially true for the dislocated worker whose place of employment or occupation is permanently eliminated. Two-thirds of the displaced workers in the Bureau of Labor Statistics 1986 Displaced Worker Survey aged 55 and older lost jobs because of plant closings, while only about half of the displaced workers aged 25 to 34 were unemployed for that reason (Horvath 1987). Analysis of data from the 1984 BLS Displaced Worker Survey indicated that for workers who lost fulltime jobs and subsequently became re-employed, the new job yielded earnings that were 96 percent of that at the old job for workers aged 20 to 40 but were just 86 percent of former earnings for workers in their fifties (Podgursky and Swaim 1986, Table 12).

Older job losers have less schooling on average than both older workers in general and young job losers (Shapiro and Sandell 1987; Podgursky and Swaim 1986). College graduates are particularly under-represented among job losers, and blue-collar workers are harder hit by job loss than workers in other occupations. For example, Shapiro and Sandell found that 50 percent of all male workers were craft-workers, operatives, and laborers from 1966 through 1978, but that these occupations accounted for more than 70 percent of the male job losers.

Differences between the personal characteristics of job losers aged 22 through 44 and those 45 and older are similar to differences between younger and older workers in general. Older male job losers have less education, are more likely to be white, have health problems, and have greater tenure on their jobs, higher previous wages, and slightly higher annual earnings than younger job losers. Similarly, older female job losers have less education than younger female job losers, but young and old are equally likely to be white or have health problems. Older female job losers had longer tenure on their jobs but had lower wages, were more likely to have clerical and sales jobs, and were less likely to have professional or technical occupations than younger female job losers (Johnson, Dickinson, and West 1987).

Length of Unemployment When older workers lose their jobs, they are likely to remain unemployed longer than younger job losers. The median duration of joblessness was 20 weeks for older male job losers, compared with 13 weeks for younger males in a study of State Employment Service registrants (Johnson, Dickinson, and West 1987). Among women, the median duration of joblessness was 21 weeks for older workers and 16 weeks for younger workers.

Because older job losers are more likely to drop out of the labor force than their younger counterparts, the effect of age on the potential length of unemployment is even greater than these figures indicate. Taking the relationship of age and the probability of dropping out of the labor force into account, older job losers face potentially much longer periods of unemployment than younger job losers (Sandell and Shapiro 1987).

Before reaching conclusions about the specific effects of age and job loss on the employment problems of older workers, it is important to take into account the effects of such characteristics as education and previous work experience. Such analyses yield different results for men and women (Johnson, Dickinson, and West 1987). Among older male job losers, black men, men with health problems, and those with less formal education are likely to remain unemployed longer than otherwise similar male job losers. The fact that older men have, on average, lower education and poorer health than younger men makes the average duration of their job search longer. However, being older seems to affect the length of women's unemployment even after other factors are taken into account. This could be an indication that older women are discriminated against in hiring.

Previous earnings can affect the length of time people spend looking for new jobs because, quite naturally, they try to find jobs that pay as well as or better than their previous jobs. To the extent that employers are unwilling to meet these salary demands, these persons will remain unemployed until they lower their earnings expectations, and previous earnings can thus become a barrier to finding employment.

This is the crux of the personal dilemma facing older displaced workers. Realism about job prospects may diminish the worker's hopes for a comfortable future, and it is painful for operators of employment and training programs to describe the predicament and undermine these hopes. Assistance for older job losers that focuses on developing more realistic expectations of the labor market might nevertheless encourage more displaced workers to take advantage of training opportunities. Realistic expectations might also reduce the amount of time spent in looking for jobs that will pay them what they earned on their previous jobs and that are rarely available in changed local labor markets (Cook 1987). However, even with lowered earnings expectations, displaced workers will not be hired by some employers, who expect them to leave these new jobs if recalled.

Earnings Older job losers who previously had relatively low pay or who possess skills that are readily transferable to new jobs do not, on average, experience large reductions in pay in their new jobs. Earnings reductions are greatest among older workers who are looking for work in poor labor market conditions, who have substantial nontransferable skills and knowledge associated with seniority, or who are aged 65 and older (Shapiro and Sandell 1985).

Earnings reductions are largest under unfavorable labor market conditions. Among men aged 45 and older who lost their jobs between 1965 and 1978, the average loss in hourly earnings on subsequent jobs was 3.5 percent. Older workers who lost their jobs between 1966 and 1969, a period of relatively low unemployment, generally did not experience a wage loss. However, older workers who lost their jobs between 1969 and 1978, a period of higher unemployment, experienced an average reduction in hourly earnings of 6 percent and had, on average, two more years of seniority than did job losers during the low unemployment period. Thus, in times of low unemployment, a high demand for workers appears to compensate for the loss of seniority. Conversely, job loss in periods of high unemployment results in greater earnings loss because affected workers have greater seniority and correspondingly larger wage reductions.

The drop in pay experienced by most re-employed workers was greater for older than for younger job losers—but this does not necessarily reflect age discrimination: 90 percent of the wage loss can be explained by the nontransferability of the workers' firm-specific skills and knowledge (the knowledge and skills presumed to be useful only to a specific employer) or by seniority (Shapiro and Sandell 1985). New employers are often not willing to pay for seniority earned and firm-specific experience gained in a previous job.

Because older workers on average have more seniority and, presumably, more firm-specific skills than younger workers, their reduction in average hourly earnings from one job to the next is correspondingly greater. For example, workers studied by Shapiro and Sandell (1985) who were age 60 when they lost their jobs averaged more than 11 years of job tenure; their average wage loss was 6 percent. Workers aged 45 through 49 averaged 6 years of job tenure when they lost their jobs; their average wage loss was 3 percent. Because most older workers forced to change jobs have more seniority to lose in the job change, the drop in average hourly earnings on a new job is greater than the drop for younger workers in otherwise similar situations. A negative impact of tenure on the re-employment earnings of older blue-collar men of approximately 6 percent was found by Podgursky and Swaim (1986) for workers displaced between 1979 and 1983.

Shapiro and Sandell (1985) found greater earnings losses for persons over 65 than could be explained by loss of firm-specific training alone. Some of the loss in earnings for this group can be attributed to changes in the occupations and hours of work of the job losers: for instance, workers in the sample over 65 who returned to work were more likely to change occupations and to work part-time than were workers between the ages of 45 and 49.

DISPLACED WORKERS WHO LEAVE THE LABOR FORCE

Older job losers are much more likely to retire than are older workers of the same age who have not lost their jobs. For example, if the national unemployment rate were 6 percent, almost 30 percent of male job losers aged 60 would retire. In contrast, less than 10 percent of all males aged 60 still employed would retire at that time (Sandell and Shapiro 1987).

High unemployment rates disproportionately increase the number of older job losers who retire early. For example, although an estimated 18 percent of all 60-year-old job losers would retire if the economy were at 4 percent unemployment, almost one-half (44 percent) would retire if the economy were at 8 percent unemployment. Moreover, once retired, these workers tend to stay retired.

Although this retirement may be considered voluntary, in the sense that workers prefer retirement to searching for or accepting new jobs, it is clearly induced by economic conditions. They would not have retired if they had not lost their jobs or if conditions had proved more propitious for finding new ones. As a result, job loss and high unemployment have significant long-term costs for the economy both in terms of the loss of potentially productive workers and in terms of increased Social Security benefits, private pensions, and other payments.

Federal Employment and Training Programs

Federal employment and training programs aim to improve the employment prospects of displaced workers, as well as other older workers. These programs include those in which older persons as well as other eligible persons can participate, primarily financed under the Job Training Partnership Act (JTPA), and programs specifically designed for older persons, such as the Senior Community Service Employment Program (SCSEP), Title V of the Older Americans Act. Income-eligible displaced older workers can participate in JTPA and SCSEP programs. (This discussion is largely based on a chapter in an Industrial Relations Research Association volume; see Sandell 1988.)

Several questions must be answered in order to evaluate the usefulness of these programs for older workers. The key ones are: Do older persons receive their fair share of training opportunities? Is the size of the program adequate? What is the net increase in earnings due to the program? And, for programs that provide subsidized jobs, what is the value to society of program activities engaged in by participants?

JOB TRAINING PARTNERSHIP ACT

JTPA has been the federal government's primary vehicle for providing employment services since it replaced the Comprehensive Employment and Training Act (CETA) in 1982. JTPA establishes the framework and funding formula for employment and training programs for economically disadvantaged persons (Title II) and dislocated workers (Title III); 3 percent of the Title II training funds are set aside for persons aged 55 and older.

Title II programs are administered by the states and run through local service delivery areas, while the states are fully responsible for Title III programs. JTPA emphasizes training to increase earnings in unsubsidized jobs. The act also establishes nationally administered programs, such as the Job Corps, and amends the Wagner-Peyser Act, the authorizing legislation for the federal/state Employment Service (ES), in order to provide for greater ES/JTPA coordination.

In addition to the regular Title II programs, 3 percent of each state's Title II-A allocation is set aside for employment and training services to economically disadvantaged persons aged 55 and older. One-fourth of the states delegate the responsibility for administering these programs to state units on aging, while three-fourths administer them through the units responsible for other JTPA programs.

Participation in JTPA Title II-A programs is affected by many factors. The broad statutory definition of eligibility is met by a large segment of the population. Approximately 39 million persons, or about 20 percent of the population aged 14 and over, were eligible for JTPA Title II-A programs in 1985 based on their incomes. Nevertheless, only 2.3 percent, about 738,000 persons, of the 31.7 million eligible persons between the ages of 16 and 64 participated in JTPA II-A in program year 1985 (July 1985 to June 1986).

The fraction of eligible persons participating in JTPA II-A declines even further with age. Only 0.4 percent of the 4.4 million eligible persons between the ages of 55 and 64 participated in these programs in 1985. The rate for eligible persons aged 55 to 64 is less than one-fifth of the rate for persons 22 to 44 (Sandell and Rupp 1988).

The difference in labor market interest of older people as compared with other eligible adults substantially accounts for the dramatically lower participation rates among older eligible persons. All persons with incomes below the poverty level (or 70 percent of the Office of Management and Budget's lower living standard income, if that is higher) are eligible for JTPA programs. However, interest in obtaining a job is necessary for seeking the available training or job-search assistance. Thus persons who are both unemployed and income-eligible make up most of the de facto eligibility pool, and only 5 percent of eligibles

Table 2: ELIGIBILITY AND PARTICIPATION IN JOB TRAINING PARTNERSHIP ACT PROGRAM, UNEMPLOYED ADULTS, BY AGE, 1985

	Men		*Women*	
Age	No. eligible (000s)	Participation rate (%)	No. eligible (000s)	Participation rate (%)
22–44	1,428	10.2	1,047	14.3
45–54	226	5.3	151	8.7
55–64	146	4.6	64	11.1

Source: Sandell and Rupp 1988.

aged 55 to 64, compared to 13 percent of eligibles aged 22 to 54, were unemployed in March 1986.

Title II-A participation rates by age and sex among unemployed eligible adults are shown in Table 2. Unemployed older men have substantially lower program participation rates than other unemployed adult men. The JTPA participation rate for unemployed eligible men aged 55 to 64 can still be considered low, at 4.6 percent. However, it is about half the rate for unemployed men aged 22 to 44, a favorable comparison in view of the fact that the rate for all eligible men in the older group is less than one-fifth of the rate for all eligible men in the younger group.

Smaller age differences in participation rates are observed among women. The JTPA participation rate for unemployed eligible women aged 55 to 64, 11.1 percent, is close to that of unemployed eligible women aged 22 to 44 (14.3 percent) and is higher than the 8.7 percent participation rate for unemployed eligible women aged 45 to 54. Thus JTPA may be a useful training vehicle for older displaced homemakers, a group mentioned in the act as especially likely to be unemployed.

Overall, much of the age-related difference in training program participation is fundamentally shaped by age-related patterns of labor force participation. Explicit age discrimination by program operators seems to be a minor factor, although some programs may be structured to appeal to younger persons. Analysis of factors affecting participation in CETA, the predecessor of JTPA, has shown that more than one-third of the difference in CETA participation rates among adults of different ages can be explained by factors other than age (Rupp et al. 1987); that is, older persons are more likely than younger persons to have characteristics, such as poor health and low levels of formal education, that are associated with low program participation.

Credible studies of the impact of JTPA are not yet available. However, impact analyses of CETA programs suggest that JTPA, like the earlier program, may be useful for improving some older workers' employment prospects. Participation in CETA led to a net increase of 4.5 weeks of employment and a 20 percent increase in the employment rate among participants 45 and older, after other factors affecting employment and earnings were taken into account (Rupp et al. 1987). These results compared favorably with those of other demographic groups, indicating that the program worked for older persons who participated.

SENIOR COMMUNITY SERVICE EMPLOYMENT PROGRAM

SCSEP, authorized by Title V of the Older Americans Act, provides part-time minimum-wage jobs for low-income older persons in community service agencies. The provision of training for subsequent unsubsidized jobs is often secondary to providing income support via the participants' performing useful community services.

In 1983 an estimated 12.7 million persons, 26.4 percent of the eligible population (aged 55 and over), met the SCSEP income criterion of family income less than 125 percent of the federal poverty level (Rupp et al. 1986). However, less than 1 percent of the eligible population, about 100,000 persons, participated during program year 1983–84.

Those eligibles who reported experiencing at least one week of unemployment (750,000 people, or about 6 percent of the eligible population) could be considered to be the population most in need of SCSEP services. Employed eligibles are usually not interested in the program because they have jobs; eligibles who are out of the labor force by choice are generally not interested in employment. (Discouraged workers, persons who are interested in working but are not looking for jobs because they believe none are available, are an exception.) Thus, although being unemployed is not part of the formal eligibility requirements, it approaches a condition for participation. SCSEP served 13 percent of this population in 1983–84.

Subsidized employment is an important component of employment policy for older persons with few years of work expected before they leave the labor force. The Senior Community Service Employment Program is popular among the participants, sponsors, and agencies that benefit from older workers' subsidized employment. Expanding this approach by providing fulltime, year-round employment at the minimum wage to persons between the ages of 50 and 62 has been recommended by a private nonpartisan panel of employment policy experts (National Council on Employment Policy 1987). The council felt that this group, not yet old enough to be eligible for reduced Social Security benefits but old enough to be affected by age discrimination in the labor market, should be eligible for a new program of public sector employment.

CHARACTERISTICS OF SUCCESSFUL OLDER WORKER EMPLOYMENT PROGRAMS

Older worker programs can recruit, train, and place older persons (Lester 1987). Successful programs usually have these elements in common:

1. the major program components of assessment, occupational skills training, job search training, job development, and job match form a system of services;
2. assessment of participants' skills, abilities, and interests is considered the key to effective job matching;
3. the program staff has extensive knowledge of the participants' employment potential and of the local labor market;
4. occupational skills training is provided;
5. additional resources for participants are obtained through coordination with other programs and agencies; and
6. good staff management, including staff assessment and program experimentation, is present.

DISPLACED WORKER PROGRAMS

As already discussed, older workers are less likely than younger workers to receive or benefit from services available under federal/state employment and training programs. In particular, older displaced workers participate in programs funded under Title III of the Job Training Partnership Act in lower numbers than their share of the displaced unemployed population (U.S. General Accounting Office 1987a). In 563 programs operating in 1984–1985 studied by the GAO, 8 percent of enrollees were 55 and above, compared to 20 percent of unemployed dislocated workers in the Bureau of Labor Statistics Displaced Worker Survey of January 1984.

Some of the reasons for low participation of older workers advanced by project officials interviewed by GAO were that older workers may lack the background for training; that they sometimes have qualms about entering an educational setting; that projects may screen out older workers as less likely to be re-employed; and that older workers may be receiving assistance through other programs, such as the 3 percent set-aside under JTPA. Tellingly, the GAO reported: "Project officials told us that, based on their experience, employers were reluctant to hire workers over age 55" (U.S. General Accounting Office 1987a, p. 43). Evaluating projects, in part, on their placement rates thus provides an incentive to program operators to screen out interested older persons solely on the basis of age.

Some programs, however, attract above-average proportions of enrollees aged 55 and above. Older workers tend to be a higher percentage in projects that are employer- and/or union-operated but a lower percentage in projects operated by educational institutions. Projects which focus on specific worker groups or dislocation events and in which all applicants are accepted (as opposed to projects that screen applicants) have greater-than-average representation of older participants. Projects linked to specific job openings (customized training) and those in which remedial or classroom training is provided to a large proportion of participants tend to have below-average representation of older participants.

GAO identified 80 of the 563 Title III projects as "exemplary," based on their above-average placement and wage rates (U.S. General Accounting Office 1987b). Two characteristics of "exemplary" projects are operation by an employer and/or union and focus on a specific dislocation event. Better knowledge of and connections in the local labor market than programs operated by schools and service delivery areas and the ability to intervene before the actual event were factors accounting for the better outcomes. This program configuration was also favorable to participation by older workers. Because of their lack of recent job search experience, individual counseling and support seem to be especially important to older workers.

A recent volume of case studies provides further information on implementation of Title III projects (Cook 1987). Although each of the successful projects studied provided a different mix of services, all were flexible and responsive to individual worker choices. An important part of the process was "reality counseling," designed to acquaint workers with the wage levels and jobs they could expect in the open labor market. The studies found that training was not the preferred choice for many experienced workers. Workers often need continued earnings and have skills that are not specific to their former jobs. Thus they prefer job search or on-the-job training to longer-term training, especially if the training is not directly linked to a job.

Provision of an array of program interventions and a significant increase in federal funding were among the recommendations of a recent study of displaced worker issues. In 1986 the Task Force on Economic Adjustment and Worker Dislocation submitted its report to the Secretary of Labor. The group, composed of labor, management, and public representatives, was unable to agree on whether to recommend mandatory advance notice of employment reductions but did agree that more resources and attention should be directed toward the re-employment needs of displaced workers. Legislation implementing many of these recommendations, including increased funding, is part of the trade bill enacted in August 1988.

THE EMPLOYMENT SERVICE AND OLDER WORKERS

ES has a long history of providing services to clients of all ages, including displaced and older workers. Most ES clients received only job referrals, even though other services (i.e., counseling, testing, job development, and referral to training or supportive services) are sometimes provided. Older workers were substantially less likely to receive referrals than younger job seekers (Johnson, Dickinson, and West 1987). While about one-third of men and women between ages 25 and 44 received referrals, only 15 percent of the older men and 22 percent of the older women did. These differences did not seem to reflect differences in education and other characteristics across age groups.

The researchers concluded that the Employment Service staff were not referring older applicants to all the jobs for which they were qualified, perhaps because of a belief that older workers were less likely to be hired. Many of the low-paying, entry-level jobs listed at the Employment Service in fact may not be appropriate to the skills and interests of some older workers. Furthermore, a requirement that job losers register with the Employment Service in order to collect unemployment insurance can mean that some older registrants are not really interested in employment but are collecting UI before formally retiring (although this is a violation of UI statutes).

Older women benefited from ES referrals, but older men did not (according to Johnson, Dickinson, and West 1987). Older women with job referrals had 7 fewer weeks of unemployment and almost $600 more in annual earnings than women who did not receive referrals, after statistically controlling for the effects of other characteristics. The earnings increase stems from more weeks of work, not higher hourly or weekly pay. Older men with ES referrals did not receive statistically different earnings from nonreferred older men.

Implications for Policy

Any attempt to resolve policy issues involves tradeoffs among diverse objectives. In the case of displaced worker programs and other programs for older workers, there are at least five major dimensions along which policy choices can be structured. These are: targeting, identification, creaming, cost-effectiveness, and institutional responsiveness (Baldwin 1986).

TARGETING

Is there a continued need for making older workers a target group for employment and training purposes? Are there targeting strategies that are most effective and appropriate? In part, answers to these questions depend on one's view of the sources of the employment problems of older workers. If "the problem isn't age" (Sandell 1987) but a set of other factors such as lower educational levels, then the appropriate targeting is on individuals with those characteristics. In part, answers depend on the degree to which employers respond to differing targeting strategies. If wage subsidies attached to new employees are viewed by employers as signals of "distressed merchandise" (Burtless 1984), and workers realize this, then job applicants will not disclose their eligibility until after being hired, if at all. Then the subsidy, if claimed, will be a pure windfall to the employer. Subsidies for retraining employees to prevent dislocation should involve jointly targeting workers and firms.

IDENTIFICATION

This term refers to the ability of program administrators to select those most in need of assistance within the broader target group. If former manufacturing production workers with less than a high school education can be apprised of their prospects before their UI runs out, for instance, they may be aided in a more timely manner. Antidiscrimination programs can take a preventive identification approach by educating managers, educators, and workers themselves about older worker potentials.

Much of the feelings about older worker inadequacy for retraining (feelings shared by workers themselves as well as employers) may be based on stereotypes and attitudes that will not withstand objective analysis. The relative success of individualized, situation-specific programs for displaced workers indicates that some of the problems may be caused by the way in which educational institutions structure their programs.

CREAMING

If program operators are providing upskilling opportunities to disproportionate numbers of those perceived as costing less to train or place in jobs, "creaming" is taking place. Older workers and minority group members may be the victims of this practice. Setting of group against group in this way inhibits the ability of workers to perceive their common problems and interests and act together to support allocation of more resources to training programs.

COST-EFFECTIVENESS

When displacement occurs, the major burden is on the affected workers. The loss of a job can also mean loss of medical coverage and other valuable fringe benefits (Podgursky and Swaim 1986). The 1986 federal budget reconciliation bill mandates that workers be allowed to retain their group insurance coverage if they pay the premiums themselves. That helps, but even this right involves a substantial outlay from a drastically reduced income. Similarly, pension rights, vesting, and portability provisions affect the willingness and ability of workers to move to jobs in which they could both earn more and contribute more to national output and productivity.

Such costs need to be offset against the direct costs of worker assistance programs, as well as the costs of income transfers such as UI that might be reduced by getting workers re-employed sooner. There has been considerable interest on the part of some states in programs that would increase the amount of upgrading by employers, so that more workers would be retained. The argument is that employers respond to their own perceptions of costs, ignoring the external costs that layoffs and turnover impose on workers, communities, and other firms—the costs to workers because of the trauma of unemployment, to communities because of the reduction in the tax base and the need for expanded support and social services, and to other firms because of the cross-subsidies that exist within the tax structure of the UI system.

One argument often heard is that older workers have fewer years of working life remaining, so that the payback from training will be less for them than for other potential workers. The relevant comparison should be for years expected with the firm providing the training, in relation to the expected life of the technology being implemented (Morse 1979). To the extent that turnover rates are higher for younger workers, it is possible that firms can expect to receive more years of upgraded service from older employees than from younger employees. We also know that once unemployed, older workers have a harder time finding new jobs, so that the burden on the UI system is increased if older workers are disproportionately excluded from training opportunities.

INSTITUTIONAL RESPONSIVENESS

Can the UI/ES/JTPA system work well with educational institutions and employers in delivering the services needed by displaced older workers? Rewards and sanctions need to be appropriate; e.g., the evidence presented about the lower rate of referrals of older workers from the Employment Service indicates that the reward structure perceived by ES personnel gives less weight to their experience. Another area of concern is how a system structured with blue-collar manufacturing workers in mind will handle displaced managers and clerical workers.

Another question relating to institutional responsiveness is: should part-time work be more actively promoted for older workers, as a phase-in to complete retirement? Wages for part-time work are substantially lower than full-time pay, so that relatively few older persons find these jobs attractive (Jondrow, Brechling, and Marcus 1987). Individuals who have retired from one job (i.e., who are receiving job-related pensions) may also wish to engage in part-time work, especially if their pensions are not reduced for doing so. The earnings test under Social Security reduces benefits for persons aged 65 to 69 by 50 cents for each dollar earned above the exempt amount, currently (1988) $8,400. Thus, limited work by persons 65 to 69 is encouraged by allowing them to receive full Social Security benefits as well as their earnings, but more substantial work efforts are penalized. Should the income security system favor, inhibit, or be neutral with respect to such arrangements?

Concluding Comments

The aging of the work force will remain a critical issue for years to come. The problems of older workers may receive even more attention and resources in the future as the population ages and the number of older workers experiencing employment problems rises. The changing economy may make the incidence of older worker problems so great that increased resources will be needed just to respond minimally to growing needs for help.

Awareness of these problems led the National Commission for Employment Policy to recommend that "the Federal Government should establish a new priority for employment in the development of its overall economic policies. In the tradeoffs that inevitably must be made in developing national economic policy, Federal policymakers should recognize the often hidden but substantial long-term costs to the economy and to older individuals that result from induced retirement caused by high unemployment" (National Commission for Employment Policy 1985).

In any case, we believe that for the United States to maintain high living standards while remaining technologically competitive, we have to use our human resources fully. Older workers cannot be relegated to the scrap heap if demand for their specific skills diminishes. They must be helped to acquire the new skills needed to maintain their participation in the labor force.

References

Baldwin, Stephen E. 1986. "Comments." In *Measuring Structural Unemployment,* edited by Stephen A. Wardner, pp. 132–34. Washington, D.C.: U.S. Department of Labor.

Berenbeim, Ronald E. 1986. "Company Programs to Ease the Impact of Shutdowns." Report 878. The Conference Board, New York.

Bendick, Marc, and Judith Devine. 1981. "Workers Dislocated by Economic Change: Do They Need Federal Employment and Training Assistance?" In National Commission for Employment Policy, *Seventh Annual Report,* pp. 175–226. Washington, D.C.: U.S. Government Printing Office.

Burtless, Gary. 1984. "Manpower Policies for the Disadvantaged: What Works?" *The Brookings Review,* Fall.

Cook, Robert F., ed. 1987. *Worker Dislocation: Case Studies of Causes and Cures.* Kalamazoo, Mich.: W. E. Upjohn Institute for Employment Research.

Crosslin, Robert, James Hanna, and David Stevens. 1984. "Identification of Dislocated Workers Utilizing Unemployment Insurance Administrative Data: Results of a Five-State Analysis." Research Report 84-03. National Commission for Employment Policy, Washington D.C.

———. 1986. "The Permanence of Dislocation: 1979–83 Evidence." Research Report 86-21. National Commission for Employment Policy, Washington, D.C.

Flynn, Patricia. 1988. *Facilitating Technological Change: The Human Resource Challenge.* Cambridge, Mass.: Ballinger Publishing Co.

Horvath, Francis. 1987. "The Pulse of Economic Change: Displaced Workers of 1981–85," *Monthly Labor Review,* June.

Johnson, Terry, Katherine P. Dickinson, and Richard W. West. 1987. "Older Workers, Job Displacement, and the Employment Service." In *The Problem Isn't Age: Work and Older Americans,* edited by Steven H. Sandell. New York: Praeger Publishers.

Johnston, Janet W. 1980. "An Overview of Federal Employment and Training Programs." In National Commission for Employment Policy, *Sixth Annual Report,* pp. 49–139. Washington, D.C.: U.S. Government Printing Office.

Jondrow, Jim, Frank Brechling, and Alan Marcus. 1987. "Older Workers in the Market for Part-Time Employment." In *The Problem Isn't Age: Work and Older Americans,* edited by Steven H. Sandell. New York: Praeger Publishers.

Lester, Brenda. 1984. *A Practitioner's Guide for Training Older Workers.* Washington, D.C.: National Commission for Employment Policy.

———. 1987. *Job Placement Systems for Older Workers,* vol. 1: *Research Findings, Case Studies, Program Models.* Washington, D.C.: National Caucus and Center on Black Aged, Inc.

Morse, Dean. 1979. *The Utilization of Older Workers.* National Commission for Employment Policy Special Report 33. Washington, D.C.: U.S. Government Printing Office.

National Academy of Sciences, Committee on Effective Implementation of Advanced Manufacturing Technology. 1986. *Human Resource Practices for Implementing Advanced Manufacturing Technology.* Washington, D.C.: National Academy Press.

National Commission for Employment Policy. 1985. *Older Workers: Prospects, Problems and Policies.* Washington, D.C.: National Commission for Employment Policy.

National Council on Employment Policy. 1987. "Policy Statement on the Labor Market Problems of Older Workers." National Council on Employment Policy, Washington, D.C.

Paul, Carolyn. 1987. "Work Alternatives for Older Americans: A Management Perspective." In *The Problem Isn't Age: Work and Older Americans,* edited by Steven H. Sandell. New York: Praeger Publishers.

Podgursky, Michael, and Paul Swaim. 1986. "Job Displacement, Reemployment and Earnings Loss: Evidence from the January 1984 Displaced Worker Survey." Research Report 86-18. National Commission for Employment Policy, Washington, D.C.

Root, Lawrence S., and Laura H. Zarrugh. 1987. "Private-Sector Employment Practices of Older Workers." In *The Problem Isn't Age: Work and Older Americans,* edited by Steven H. Sandell. New York: Praeger Publishers.

Rupp, Kalman, Edward Bryant, John Brown, Caricia Fisher, Helene Hennings, Robin McEntire, and Dave Wright. 1986. "The Senior Community Service Employment Program: Participant Selection, Program Experience, and Outcomes." Westat, Inc., Rockville, Md.

Rupp, Kalman, Edward Bryant, Richard Mantovani, and Michael Rhoads. 1987. "Government Employment and Training Programs and Older Americans." In *The Problem Isn't Age: Work and Older Americans,* edited by Steven H. Sandell. New York: Praeger Publishers.

Sandell, Steven H., ed. 1987. *The Problem Isn't Age: Work and Older Americans.* New York: Praeger Publishers.

———. 1988. "Public Policies and Programs Affecting Older Workers." In *The Older Worker,* edited by Michael E. Borus, Herbert S. Parnes, Steven H. Sandell, and Bert Seidman. Madison, Wis.: Industrial Relations Research Association.

Sandell, Steven H., and Kalman Rupp. 1988. "Who Is Served in JTPA Programs? Patterns of Participation and Intergroup Equity." Research Report 88-03. National Commission for Employment Policy, Washington, D.C.

Sandell, Steven H., and David Shapiro. 1987. "Economic Conditions, Job Loss and Induced Retirement." Unpublished paper.

Shapiro, David, and Steven H. Sandell. 1985. "Age Discrimination in Wages and Displaced Older Men," *Southern Economic Journal* 52 (July): 90–102.

———. 1987. "The Reduced Pay of Older Job Losers: Age Discrimination and Other Explanations." In *The Problem Isn't Age: Work and Older Americans,* edited by Steven H. Sandell. New York: Praeger Publishers.

U.S. Bureau of the Census. 1987. *Money Income of Households, Families, and Persons in the United States: 1985*. Current Population Reports, Series P-60, No. 156. Washington, D.C.: U.S. Government Printing Office.

U.S. General Accounting Office. 1987a. *Dislocated Workers: Local Programs and Outcomes under the Job Training Partnership Act*. GAO/HRD-87-41. Washington, D.C.: U.S. Government Printing Office.

———. 1987b. *Dislocated Workers: Exemplary Local Projects under the Job Training Partnership Act*. GAO/HRD-87-700BR. Washington, D.C.: U.S. Government Printing Office.

Zornitsky, Jeffrey, Jane Kulik, and Adam Seitchik. 1986. "Worker Mobility in the U.S. Economy." Research Report 86-24. National Commission for Employment Policy, Washington, D.C.

The Older Worker in a Fast-Shrinking Industry

LEON LYNCH

The rapid downsizing of the steel industry and the aging of the work force in steel which accompanied it have led to intensified collective bargaining on issues such as employment security, pensions, health care programs, overtime control, and training. Lynch reports on the progress being made at the negotiating table by steel companies and the United Steelworkers Union but stresses the importance of government's role in helping to stabilize the industry and attend to the welfare of its work force. He believes that close coordination is needed between state and federal government, as solutions will not be found at the bargaining table alone but in the political and legislative arena as well.

I. B.

I was admonishing a friend of mine recently about some vacation plans he had abandoned and the rut he had settled into. For emphasis, I added, "You're not getting any *younger,* you know." To which he replied, "Do you know anybody who is?" We're all getting older—as a nation and as workers. As a result, the labor movement is faced with a new and markedly different set of issues today. I would like to raise some questions that may lead to answers to the problems generated by this phenomenon—problems affecting the wages, working conditions, health, and safety of active workers and the pensions and health care of retirees.

Steel: A Troubled Industry

At the United Steelworkers of America, the graying of the workplace came upon us with a rush. Fifteen years ago, when membership in our union was at its peak, the average age of a worker in the basic steel industry was 41 years and 5 months. In 1983, only five years ago, even in the midst of a precipitous membership drop, the average age had increased only slightly, to 41 years and 6 months. But just one year later it jumped to 43 years. More recent figures are not available, but—given the continued decline of the steel industry in particular and basic industry in general our union estimates that the current average age is 46 years.

This sharp change has brought with it a major shift in the ratio of retirees to active workers in our union. In 1980 there was one retiree to every four active workers. Today there are two retirees to every three workers. The ratio is much higher at some companies. For example, at LTV, retirees outnumber actives by slightly more than two to one; at USX the ratio is almost three to one.

What we have, then, is a smaller, older work force and a larger and growing group of retirees across a widening age spectrum. There are divergent needs between and within the two groups which must be addressed, but trade unionists and the academics who study the labor force cannot achieve this goal alone. We need the full involvement of employers and government.

We have reached this point in the steel industry for a number of reasons:

- a continuing world-wide oversupply
- surging imports
- flawed trade policies
- a 30 percent cut in domestic production capacity
- questionable management practices, including inadequate modernization
- elimination of almost 60 percent of the hourly work force, which now numbers about 130,000—the lowest figure since such recordkeeping began

During the past seven years, the Steelworkers—along with many others—have been agitating and lobbying for changes in national trade and fiscal policies to help stop the hemorrhaging. Trade legislation is awaiting final action in Congress (a trade law was enacted in 1988), and voluntary restraint agreements and the declining value of the dollar against other currencies have helped to stabilize the industry, even if only temporarily.

Many workers in basic steel are working at lower hourly wage rates today than they were in 1982. Thousands of them are receiving profit-sharing checks and/or productivity bonuses, but these payments are only reimbursements—in many cases, partial reimbursements—for past wage and benefit reductions.

The work force reduction and improved business climate have resulted in a glut of overtime work, which increases take-home pay to a degree but raises questions at other levels. First, excessive overtime deprives younger laid-off workers of employment opportunities. The current amount of overtime being worked in our industry is the equivalent of 20,000 jobs. (We are attempting to resolve this dichotomy in our collective bargaining agreements by restricting the use of overtime work.) Second, excessive overtime may compromise health and safety if it leads to fatigue, a speedup of work, or laxness in maintaining safety standards.

We are especially troubled by an examination, conducted by the union safety and health department, of steel mill fatalities during the eight-year period 1980–1987. Workers between the ages of 45 and 64, who now make up 41 percent of the work force, accounted for 60 percent of the accidental deaths. This was not a scientific study by any means, but its implications are nevertheless ominous.

Finally, overtime can lead to increased absenteeism, creating the need for more overtime, thereby perpetuating and exacerbating the problem.

The Steelworkers Union Response

What recourse do workers and retirees have? What protections are available? Fortunately, the union leadership, past and present, has secured some legislative and contractual action on these matters. I refer to such things as Employee Stock Option Plans (ESOPs); employment security; retiree health insurance; early retirement pension benefit provisions to ease the trauma of plant closings; the Employee Retirement Income Security Act (ERISA), which guarantees pensions; and training and retraining on and off the job for those too young to retire and to old, too settled, or with too few skills to move easily into other occupations.

The Pension Guarantee Issue

In 1986 LTV filed for protection under the bankruptcy laws and stopped paying premiums for retiree health insurance. The payments were reinstated following a strike against the company, and legislation is now before Congress to require companies in bankruptcy to continue providing insurance to retirees.

While the legislative branch has had an interest in protecting retirees, the same cannot be said of the executive branch. The Pension Benefit Guaranty Corp. (PBGC) went to court to overturn a new pension plan negotiated with LTV as a result of its bankruptcy. The move is rich with irony. Because the PBGC terminated the existing LTV pension plan, about 8,000 of the 48,000 LTV retirees had their monthly checks reduced by $400, the amount of the supplement they were paid to accept early retirement but which is not guaranteed under ERISA. Our new agreement restored an average of 92 percent of the lost income and created a new defined contribution pension plan for active workers. The PBGC stated that it wants to overturn the new agreement, on the grounds that it does not inflict sufficient pain—and "pain" is the very word the agency's director used. This dispute is now (summer 1988) in the courts.

In a number of other instances, employers have forced the union into court by flatly refusing to meet their health care obligations to retirees. Although the union position has been upheld consistently, the process is lengthy and expensive—an inexcusable waste of time and money that could be used to help the membership in other ways.

Keeping Plants Operating

In an attempt to forestall or circumvent the application of contractual provisions for severance pay or supplemental retirement benefits, steel companies will cease production and lay off the work force, but will delay for years a formal announcement of permanent plant closing. This kind of dallying creates other problems for workers as well. Thousands of eligible participants have passed up opportunities for job retraining because their income maintenance is exhausted by the time shutdowns are declared. The efforts of workers or third parties to purchase facilities that otherwise would be closed have also been stymied by reluctance to announce shutdowns. Where members have had adequate notice, they have sometimes been able to put together employee buyouts in which they own varying degrees of the operation. Such buyouts have taken place at a number of locations, including McLouth Steel and the Copper Range Company in Michigan.

Where communities have been given adequate warning of a shutdown, they too have stepped in. At the former USX plant in Provo, Utah, 1,500 jobs were saved because the workers, the union, and the community closed ranks and brought a buyer into the picture. The plant, written off by USX, is thriving, and the workers have retained well-paying jobs.

Ultimately, that's what this is all about—decent jobs at decent wages in a safe workplace so that workers can provide for themselves and their families and live as part of the total society.

Training Programs

When jobs are unavoidably lost, there must be just and humane treatment for those leaving the work force to enter retirement—and our contracts have generally provided for that. There must also be retraining for those left behind. We have been involved in the training process since the first massive wave of layoffs hit the steel industry earlier in this decade, when we expanded contractual provisions for joint union-management efforts to train and retrain the affected workers. For the most part, although there are exceptions, the companies' role here has been financial—a total contribution of $6.7 million. The union provided in-kind services and expertise. In our 1988 round of negotiations, we secured additional annual commitments of $2.6 million. The bulk of the funding—$33 million—came from the Job Training Partnership Act. Our experience in retraining can be broken down into four categories: good news, not-so-good news, bad news, and it-gets-worse news. The good news is that we have helped 21,000 of our former members to find new jobs. The not-so-good news is that the jobs pay only about half what these people were earning in steel mills. The bad news is that another 10,000 people who participated in the retraining have *not* found jobs. Another 66,000 who were eligible for retraining did not enroll, and that's the worst news of all.

Most of the placements have been in the lower-paying service sector because that's where job growth is concentrated. These workers had held obsolescent, repetitive jobs. In the main, skilled craftsmen found comparable jobs but, again, at much lower wages. The new wages for all placements averaged between $6.50 and $7 an hour.

There are varying reasons for nonparticipation in retraining programs, some quantifiable, some not. In addition to lack of notice and insufficient or nonexistent income maintenance, there also is a psychological factor—loss of self-esteem. We have had to find ways to motivate people who suddenly found themselves without jobs, without incomes to support their families, without confidence or ability to change careers in midlife . . . people who were, in a word, desperate.

A former Steelworker who has been deeply involved in helping dislocated workers describes them this way: "In the early 1980s, they believed they could take the skills they had and get something else. Now they know they can't. Reality has set in. They're lost human beings. They're pretty certain they're untrainable, and, even if they do retrain, they think nobody will hire them."

There is another disturbing aspect—illiteracy among both those who participated and those who did not. To deal with all of these problems, we are broadening our efforts as much as possible. We have two programs under way, one in Pennsylvania and one in Ohio, to confront the problem of illiteracy, and plans are in the works for more.

We have also found a need for spousal support programs in such areas as child care, counseling, money management, drug and alcohol abuse, health care—indeed, almost the full range of domestic relationships. Spousal involvement, with guarantees of absolute confidentiality, helps to expose and resolve problems that the trainee otherwise would not divulge, particularly the long-term unemployed.

Whatever we do, income maintenance and early notice are absolutely vital ingredients. It's almost impossible to persuade people to enroll for retraining when they're worried about whether their lights are going to be turned off or whether they can pay for their child's medical care. Then there is the related problem of minimum wage. Some of our people declined to accept employment for months after they were laid off, finding it uneconomical to work for $4.25 an hour when they were receiving more than that from unemployment compensation. We have dealt with these elements in collective bargaining. In some cases, we have negotiated increases in benefits for both present and future retirees. We've achieved unprecedented worker involvement in the actual operation of their enterprises.

There is new language in the Steelworkers' contracts strictly limiting the contracting out of work, which has resulted in increased job security, callbacks, and prevention of layoffs. There are bonuses and profit sharing—sometimes as high as $4 and $5 an hour—to compensate for wage and benefit sacrifices. And there is an increased commitment to job training for active and dislocated workers. Again, however, we've been forced into unnecessary and expensive litigation over violation of the new language and over the excessive overtime. Our negotiations have been based in part on surveys of our members, who ranked employment security high on their list of contract objectives, along with improved wages and benefits.

We wrapped these elements into one package in our contract with National Steel Corporation, which guarantees employment security . . . and guarantees profit sharing even if the company fails to post a profit. Instead of being laid off, employees are placed in an employment pool, with no reduction in pay. They are being assigned in several ways: to traditional jobs that would otherwise be contracted out, to temporary vacancies that would otherwise be filled by overtime, and to nontraditional jobs such as work redesign teams, training and retraining, customer service, statistical process control, and technical problem-solving groups. They are also involved in virtually the full range of corporate decisionmaking, ranging from safety issues on the job to capital expenditures. There have been concomitant improvements in productivity, product quality, and workplace safety and an increase in attempts to resolve problems before they become grievances without diminishing the integrity of the basic labor agreement.

These initiatives cannot succeed without trust and commitment from both sides. Too often, mutual goals and benefits have been sacrificed to managerial prerogatives, particularly the long-held but increasingly invalid view that success comes only when managers manage and workers work. This *noblesse oblige* posture has deprived many companies of substantive contributions from their employees and caused a deterioration in labor relations.

Joint Action Anchored in Collective Bargaining

I want to emphasize also that cooperative ventures can only be adjuncts to, and not substitutes for, collective bargaining. Differences have always existed between unions and employers on the questions of wage levels, job conditions, and the distribution of profits. To assume that easy agreement is possible is to deny human nature, so we have to be realistic about what we can accomplish through cooperative endeavors. The situation is not advanced by skirting contract compliance, or by such union-avoidance efforts as the Committee for a Union-Free Environment formed under the aegis of the National Association of Manufacturers.

Need for Government Programs

As valuable as our efforts are, and as successful as we have been in training and placing our unemployed members in jobs, we still are treating only the symptom and not the major cause of our difficulties. Unfair trade has been the single largest factor in the downsizing of American industry, throwing more than 300,000 Steelworkers out of their jobs in this decade. That is why we lobbied vigorously in support of the trade bill (finally enacted in 1988). We're also pushing for public works programs, with emphasis on refurbishing the infrastructure. Such projects would be beneficial to the total economy not only by improving transportation and water delivery and removal but by creating jobs, directly and indirectly. In Pennsylvania a study of state bridges, conducted by the University of Pittsburgh for the Steelworkers, projects 116,000 man-years of work in the rehabilitation and replacement phase alone, with a multiplier effect in related service and supply industries—quite apart from the benefits of a modern infrastructure. We're working also on the state level. We helped formulate an office of labor-management cooperation in Pennsylvania under the auspices of Governor Robert Casey. Our president, Lynn Williams, served as a member of a similar body created in New York by Governor Mario Cuomo. We're working for improvements of such things as unemployment and workers' compensation benefits and the minimum wage, even though we recognize that such programs would be better served under federal auspices.

We do not, nor should we, sanction the pitting of state against state to see who can offer the lowest wages or benefits or the weakest labor laws. Nonetheless, where there are voids, states have been stepping in to fill them. *Governing* magazine estimates that tax collections by states between 1983 and 1986 increased by one-third—or $43 billion—to a total of $228 billion, as the federal government's role in various programs diminished. State legislatures *can* and *do* exert significant pressure to change things for the better. For instance, the Hazardous Materials Communication Standard—commonly known as the "Right-to-Know Law"—was promulgated by the Occupational Safety and Health Administration only when forced to act because the standard had been passed by state after state. That's the way universal health insurance was created in Canada. There have been similar initiatives in Ohio, with Governor Richard Celeste's high-speed rail proposal, and in Massachusetts, with Governor Michael Dukakis's health plan.

But these individual state efforts are financially and administratively onerous. Ideally, what should occur is close coordination between states and the federal government that results, when appropriate, in state implementation of programs with federal guidelines. The Steelworkers favor this approach. It would give coherence to such things as workers' compensation, where we have been unable to get any guidelines to speak of, and unemployment compensation, with its uneven distribution systems and qualification standards.

As we deal with these difficulties on a daily basis, it's obvious that the key to restoring our national psyche is in the political arena. That's where the power lies, and power is the name of this game. To help us in this struggle, we are tapping a huge reservoir of political clout—our 410,000 retired members operating under the acronym SOAR, the Steelworkers Organization of Active Retirees. And, following the lead of the AFL-CIO, we have begun an associate membership program. As members of many other unions did, Steelworkers ran for election as delegates to the Democratic Party nominating convention so that we could have voice in fashioning the party platform and in choosing the presidential candidate. I myself am privileged to serve as a member of the Democratic National Committee and the Democratic Institute for International Affairs. We consult with our members concerning the advocacy of social and economic policy aimed toward building a better life for all Americans.

It is the effective combination of collective bargaining and enlightened national policy, with labor, management, and government working together, which will create the climate needed to meet the challenges today and in the years ahead.

The "New" Early Retirement: Europe and the United States

HAROLD L. SHEPPARD

The continued decline in labor force participation by older people in the United States and Europe cannot be explained simply by better pension systems, according to Sheppard, who points out that it also reflects the efforts of employers to rid themselves of older workers and of governments to reduce competition for jobs. The unemployment crisis of the past ten years has led many European governments to the mistaken conclusion that society is made better off by continued declines in the average retirement age.

J. D. O.

This chapter on the issue of early retirement in the United States is derived in part from the author's participation in a multi-country project in 1979–81 and from the valuable contributions of a U.S.-European team of policy researchers from Great Britain, France, Sweden, the Netherlands, and West Germany.[1] The project focuses on such topics as the conditions, policies, and "pathways" leading to worker exit from the labor force before a country's "normal" or conventional retirement age, the costs and consequences of such patterns, and the political dimensions of this recent—and perhaps permanent—phenomenon.

The relationship to early retirement of joblessness and of disabilities is one of the central themes of this chapter, especially in the early sections. One question raised is whether benefits under disability programs, even those not explicitly created to meet the labor market

1. These contributions consist of working papers (country reports) for the International Early Exit Project, to be synthesized in a forthcoming publication by Martin Kohli, Martin Rein, Anne-Marie Guillemard, and Herman van Gunsteren, under the tentative title *Time for Retirement: Comparative Studies of the Decreasing Age of Exit from the Labor Force.*

problems of older workers, may actually function as new routes into "premature" retirement.

Employer-based (or occupational) pension programs are also discussed, with special attention to the British scene, including critical policy issues and proposals for reduction in full-pension retirement age, cost dimensions, and medical and demographic developments.

France represents an interesting case. Retirement age was recently (1983) reduced to 60, pointing up the interplay between demographic and pension age trends. Labor force participation rate trends in France are compared with those in five other countries (including the United States). These data strongly suggest that students of early retirement policy should shift attention from the group aged 60–64 to the 55–59 group.

Trends and programs in West Germany and the Netherlands are presented and discussed next, again in the context of joblessness and early retirement. Greater attention, however, is given to Sweden because of its deviation from trends and policies in most (if not all) of western Europe and the United States and because Sweden does not correspond to the American image of an "advanced welfare state" as far as early retirement is concerned.

The chapter concludes with a general discussion (and questioning) of the importance of social legislation and progressive public policy, the part played by market mechanisms, the early retirement "opportunities" associated with a variety of forms of nonwork income programs, and organizational and technological restructuring. The consequences (including costs) of the seemingly inexorable downward trend in age at retirement for the individual and the general economy or society are discussed, as is the question of one possible result of the trend (at least in the United States), a growth in resentment of retirees among younger people.

Frank Laczko's observations about Great Britain may be applicable to modern industrial (or post-industrial) society in general:

> The spread of retirement and the transformation of old age into a social category to which one gains access by virtue of reaching a specified age is a relatively recent phenomenon, which is associated with the establishment of a set of age-based income entitlements administered by the state, i.e., the public pension. Throughout the nineteenth century and well into the twentieth century, the majority of old people did not retire.... it was not until after World War II that old age became retirement.[2]

Retirement can now occur before reaching conventionally defined old age ("retirement" here means exit from the labor force, not simply leav-

2. "Patterns of Early Exit from the Labour Force in Britain," unpublished working paper, International Early Exit Project, 1987.

ing one job, possibly with a pension, and moving on to another). Laczko believes that "the life span is being socially re-defined in a more complex fashion than is often suggested," i.e., that re-entry into the labor force, temporary and permanent part-time work, career changes, etc., typify the new era.

Unemployment and Retirement

The statistics for the United Kingdom are startling to us in the United States (where jobless rates for older workers tend to be relatively low), even if we adjust for differences in definitions of unemployment. A comparison of 1985 unemployment rates in six countries (Table 1)

Table 1: 1985 UNEMPLOYMENT RATES FOR WORKERS AGED 55–64, BY SEX AND COUNTRY

Sex	France	U.K.	Sweden	Germany	Netherlands	U.S.
Men	6.7%	13.4%	3.5%	10.2%	5.3%	4.3%
Women	7.6	n.a.	4.6	10.9	3.8	4.3

Source: Klaus Jacobs, Martin Kohli, and Martin Rein, "The Evolution of Early Exit: A Comparative Analysis of the Labor Force Participation of the Elderly," unpublished working paper, International Early Exit Research Project, 1987.

Table 2: 1975 AND 1985 EMPLOYMENT RATES FOR MEN AGED 55–64, BY COUNTRY (ROUNDED)

Year	France	U.K.	Sweden	Germany	Netherlands	U.S.
1975	67%	82%	81%	65%	71%	71%
1985	47	58	73	52	51	65

shows that the jobless rate for the United Kingdom is by far the highest of the group. In 1985, for example, the jobless rate of British men 55–64 years old was over 13 percent; Germany was the only other country studied with a double-digit figure, slightly over 10 percent, while Sweden's rate for men was lowest.

Table 2 gives employment rates (the number of employed as a proportion of persons in a given age group) as a method of measuring both employment and labor force participation. As we see, in 1975 the United Kingdom, along with Sweden, had by far the highest employment rate for men in the 55–64 age group—over 80 percent. But the U.K.'s employment rate was substantially reduced by 1985, while the Swedish rate declined but remained the highest, at 73 percent (we return to Sweden later, as a special case). The labor market and special early retirement programs are important factors in this phenomenon. Furthermore, the full-pension age for women in Britain is only 60, while it is 65 for men; in fact, several European countries provide for earlier full-pension ages for women than for men.

Since 1977, the United Kingdom has had a special early retirement program explicitly designed to meet the problem of unemployment in younger age groups—the Job Release Scheme (JRS), which allows some older workers to retire early. Presumably this program is temporary. Officially, according to Laczko, JRS is supposed to be "primarily and essentially an unemployment measure rather than a move toward early retirement." It remains to be seen how long it takes before a "temporary" measure becomes a long-term one, and perhaps an institution. Among the requirements for such an early retirement benefit are the hiring by the retiree's company of an unemployed younger person. Officially, early retirees under the scheme are not allowed to seek other employment.

Eligibility provisions under the JRS have undergone several changes. When first established, it covered both employed and unemployed men aged 64 and women aged 59, and only in high-unemployment areas of Britain. By May of 1979, the program was opened to men aged 62 or older and women aged 59 and older and to disabled men aged 60 and 61—but not to workers already unemployed, who presumably were and are covered by a special unemployment insurance program. On April 1, 1984, the ages were raised to 64 and older for men (they remained at 59 or older for women) and to 60–63 for disabled men.

Participants in the JRS have been overwhelmingly (80 percent) men. Coverage reached a peak of 95,000 in early 1984, but by June 1987 only 22,000 were receiving JRS allowances, and the scheme's impact on the jobless rate has been negligible. Laczko claims that this small number is due to the raising of the eligibility age to 64 and older for able-bodied men, instituted in 1984. It is also possible that if an employer must hire a replacement for the JRS participant, economic or labor-saving considerations would also have a negative effect on employer participation. Nor is it coincidental that the benefit under JRS is not earnings-related, but is a somewhat low flat rate. Thus "the overwhelming majority of recipients are low-paid semi- and unskilled workers," according to Laczko.

The critical point is that job loss, or unemployment, is clearly a factor in the United Kingdom's early retirement phenomenon (to use the word "decision," as in "retirement decision," has the inaccurate connotation of an activist, virtually voluntary act), as it is in other countries. British studies point out that large proportions of unemployed

Table 3: JOB LOSS AS MOST IMPORTANT REASON FOR EXIT FROM LABOR FORCE, BY GENDER, MARITAL STATUS, AND EXIT AGE

Gender/Marital Status	*Exit Age*[a]		
	Under 62	62	63 plus
Married men	10.6	8.3	7.4
Unmarried men	19.0	22.0	14.7
Married women	14.0	12.0	9.1
Unmarried women	18.7	14.5	9.9

[a]As percentage of all exits.

Source: U.S. Social Security Administration, New Beneficiary Survey; analysis of these data was done for the Retirement Research Foundation and the International Early Exit Project.

workers in age groups 50–59 years state that they have given up looking for new employment because they believe that no jobs are available.[3] Such studies carried out in most, if not all, countries in western Europe and North America would reveal the same pattern—that is, once unemployed, the older the worker, the greater the likelihood of remaining unemployed and/or dropping out of the labor force.

Job loss is clearly a factor in early retirement. Among reasons given for early exit (at age 62 or under) from the labor force in the U.S. Social Security Administration's New Beneficiary Survey, "job loss" is cited as the most important reason for retirement more frequently than among beneficiaries leaving the labor force at later ages (see Table 3).

What may be even more significant is that the age at which re-employment of job-losing older workers is possible may be going downward, and might become a very serious problem. Furthermore, the younger the age at which employers *retire* workers, or allow them to retire, the younger the age at which employers *hire* people.

We will return to the topic of unemployment and retirement below, in describing features of Germany's policies.

Disability and Retirement

It is significant that in some European countries, hiring bias (or re-employment problems) appears to be recognized and taken into consideration in formulating the eligibility conditions for early retirement income benefits; that is, disability or "invalidity" pensions can be obtained by older unemployed workers even if they are in good health or have no disability as defined in the United States. Their "disability" is defined as being too old to find re-employment, but too young to be

3. See survey data cited by Laczko, e.g., *Employment Gazette,* October 1985, p. 394.

eligible for the regular public or private pension scheme. In other words, "labor market chances" are a basis for early exit income eligibility. In the Netherlands, for example, there is a new pension program for unemployed workers as young as 50.

Great Britain does not have such a program. Nevertheless, there is "a rise in the proportion of older men defining themselves as disabled. . . . an individual in the United Kingdom does not have to have a fixed level of disability before he or she can receive an invalidity benefit. It is usually left to a person's doctor to judge whether they are incapable of working and to provide the relevant medical certificate. No doubt such judgements vary according to the labour market situation" (Laczko, "Early Exit," p. 7).

The increase in disability benefits among British men 55–59 and 60–65 years old, during the 1970s, was due in part to the overall increase in unemployment in the United Kingdom. David Piachaud, in an analysis of 1971 and 1981 English county census data, demonstrated a relationship between changes in disability and shifts in jobless rates.[4] Swedish research points to similar results.[5] In the United States, applications for disability benefits under Social Security appear to rise a few years after a peak in unemployment rates.[6]

The role of disability in the British case may also be attributable to the fact that benefits for the disabled are greater than for the unemployed. Furthermore, unemployment compensation is limited to only twelve months, whereas disability benefits in such circumstances end at age 70. In the Netherlands, too, disability benefits are more attractive than jobless benefits.

The significance of disability (or "sickness" or "invalidity") benefit programs lies in their function as a route or pathway out of the labor force for unemployed or discouraged workers (including ordinarily disabled middle-aged and older workers finding it difficult to

4. David Piachaud, "Disability, Retirement, and Unemployment of Older Men," *Journal of Social Policy* 15, no. 2 (1986), also cited by Laczko in his working paper. A similar study in Sweden showed that the percentage of "premature" (disability) pensions in 278 municipalities was closely related to local jobless rates: Hans Berglind, "Unemployment and Redundancy in a 'Post-Industrial' Labour Market," in *Work and Technology*, edited by Marie Haug and J. Dofny (Beverly Hills, Calif.: Sage Publications, 1977). See also Berglind's "Older Workers and the Labor Market in Sweden" in his *Growing Old in Sweden* (Tampa, Fla.: International Exchange Center on Gerontology, University of South Florida, 1985).

5. Berglind, *Growing Old in Sweden*.

6. Cf. H. L. Sheppard, *Employment-Related Problems of Older Workers: A Research Strategy* (Washington, D.C.: American Institutes for Research, 1978), published in edited form as R&D Monograph 73 by the U.S. Department of Labor in 1979; see p. 6 of the monograph.

gain re-employment after layoffs). This pathway may serve as a substitute for other routes into retirement not otherwise available. As stated elsewhere in these comments, several European countries officially allow early exit through this route for older workers not disabled in American terms but deemed at a disadvantage in the labor market.

It is nevertheless striking that while our own disability benefit program is not deliberately or officially constructed to alleviate problems of long-term unemployed older workers (or those in distressed industries or areas), disability benefit awards have increased at a rate far in excess of the rate of increase in retired worker awards.[7]

From 1965 to 1985, disability awards increased by 61 percent, compared to only 42 percent for retired worker awards. When we add to the disability trend the trend toward retired worker awards at age 62, we find that *both* pathways (disability and age 62 retired worker awards) have dramatically exceeded the overall retired worker benefit program. These two pathways, in other words, may be serving the same function as "invalidity" pensions in Europe as a route into early retirement.[8]

Occupational or Private Pensions

The most important base for British workers in general, as far as early retirement is concerned, is what the British call the occupational pension program—what we would call an employer-based pension, including public employers. Actually, only a little over one-third of private sector employees have such coverage, with wide discrepancies between males and females. Given the so-called normal retirement age in several public and private sectors in the United Kingdom, Laczko estimates that there are roughly 3 million men (about 25 percent of all employed men) who could retire with a full pension before the age of 65.

The more important point is that the opportunity for early retirement has been increasing. Few companies in the 1960s had much in the way of such provisions, but by the 1980s, about 95 percent of the occupational pension plans had such voluntary early retirement pension provisions. The early retirement "decision" or policy is today, much more than in the past, a mechanism for managing manpower reductions. More than one study has shown that early retirement provisions on a

7. *Social Security Bulletin Supplement,* 1986, Table 2.

8. Even among workers (with the exception of married women) who receive retired worker awards but who actually retired before age 62, 30 percent cited poor health as the most important reason for exiting, compared to 27 percent who retired at 62 and 23 percent who retired at 63 or older, according to my analysis of the U.S. Social Security Administration's New Beneficiary Survey.

widespread basis are used to bring about personnel reductions: "They are associated with manpower pruning rather than wholesale rapid shutdowns."[9] This is a growing pattern in many countries.[10]

Laczko's main conclusion from 1983 data provided to him by the U.K. Department of Health and Social Security is that occupational pensions are important in "facilitating early exit from the labour market for those taking different routes. Roughly half of the men aged 60–64 who were unemployed, disabled or receiving [Job Release Scheme] benefits were also receiving an occupational pension."[11] Could it be that in the absence of such occupational (that is, private) pensions, unemployed or so-called disabled older workers would not actually leave the labor force? And if so, under what conditions would they retire?

Additional insights and factual information about early retirement in Great Britain can be found in a valuable publication by Michael Fogarty, now retired from the Policy Studies Institute in London, *Retirement Age and Retirement Costs.*[12] Fogarty's analysis of early retirement points to the demand side—in other words, the increasing unemployment of older workers—in keeping with more recent data provided by Laczko in his 1987 working paper. The prospects for regaining employment when the unemployment rate is generally high are poor. As Fogarty puts it, "For some, it may be a case of becoming formally retired on such occupational pensions as they may have. For others it may be a matter simply of re-labeling unemployment—of men who are living on unemployment or sickness or invalidity benefit, but describe themselves as retired because their prospects of obtaining work are too dim to be worth pursuing. Either way, it is a case of involuntary retirement and not of early retirement by choice."[13]

Fogarty's study is important for at least three reasons: first, his opinion about the British so-called provisional or temporary schemes (programs) of early retirement; second, his stress on the costs of early retirement pensions—of lowering the regular age at retirement; third, his discussion of the topic in terms of biomedical and demographic developments.

9. Laczko, "Early Exit," p. 11.
10. For example, see U.S. Department of Labor, Bureau of Labor Statistics, *Employee Benefits in Medium and Large Firms. 1986,* ch. 6.
11. Laczko, "Early Exit," p. 13.
12. Published by the Institute in 1980. This publication is based on a working paper prepared by Fogarty for the multi-country report directed by H. L. Sheppard for the U.S. German Marshall Fund and the U.S. Administration on Aging. Cf. Sara E. Rix and Paul Fisher, *Retirement Age Policy: An International Perspective* (New York: Pergamon Press, 1982).
13. Michael Fogarty, *Retirement Age and Retirement Costs* (London: Policy Studies Institute, 1980), p. 11.

Fogarty instructs us that "an accelerated trend towards early retirement, even if it originates in employers' rather than employees' own decisions, or in a semi-voluntary way . . . , may set a new pattern of custom and practice which will extend in due course to other employees as well. It would be rash to assume that if employment recovered, activity rates among older men would simply return to the trend which prevailed till the middle of the 1970s."[14]

His statement reflects the view of the U.K. Department of Unemployment, published in 1978.[15]

Fogarty's second point—the costs of early retirement—is not given adequate scrutiny in all the countries involved. He discusses the demands of the Trades Union Congress that the standard pension age for men be lowered to 60 from 65, starting in hazardous industries, as already possible in mining, and extended to workers over 60 who effectively leave the labor force. All of these demands assume, of course, that the early benefit be at least the same as at age 65 retirement. The aim is obviously not "more years in poverty." In response, the Department of Health and Social Security estimated that for 1980, if men 60–64 were retired at the same rate as those currently 65–69, the net public funds costs (allowing for reductions in income tax receipts and social security contributions, etc.) would have been £3.6 billion per year.[16]

The third factor that must be reckoned with in any serious and comprehensive perspective on the early retirement issue (especially when early retirement benefits are not actuarially adjusted for longer years in retirement, and under conditions of slow or no economic growth) is the demographic factor. Fogarty used a Policy Studies Institute paper by B. Benjamin and Elizabeth Overton[17] on mortality projections in the United Kingdom over the next several decades. Policy discussions about retirement age policy (actually, pension age policy) are relatively useless unless this dimension is also taken into consideration.

Under three different sets of mortality rates by age and sex, involving different rates of reduction in deaths from diseases of early infancy, reduction in deaths from cancer of the lungs from cigarette smoking avoidance, reduction in cardiovascular-related deaths, etc., Benjamin and Overton project marked changes by the year 2016 in the number of British men 65 and older, British women 60 and older, and the percentages they would constitute depending on a set of assump-

14. Ibid.
15. "Measures to Alleviate Unemployment in the Medium Term: Early Retirement," *DOE Gazette,* March 1978.
16. Fogarty, *Retirement Age,* pp. 28–29.
17. *The Prospects for Mortality Decline in England and Wales* (London: Policy Studies Institute, 1980).

tions concerning different fertility rates. The bottom line is that the cost per capita for pensions would be 40–50 percent greater than the 1980 costs. Only one-half of such an increase would be due to any increase in the average pension benefit. The other half represents the increase in the number of pensioners living longer than under 1980 mortality realities.

Incidentally, Benjamin and Overton, in labeling the different population scenarios of the future, call the low mortality/high population estimate "optimistic." In macabre fashion, U.S. government demographers and economists, on the other hand, call the very same type of projections "pessimistic" because a larger population of older persons (with or without differences in fertility rates) would mean greater costs to our different pension programs, especially Social Security.

The overall perspective presented by Fogarty, and one which is applicable to all similar societies in the Western world, is that even if only some of the possibilities examined by Benjamin and Overton become reality,

> the balance of population will be less favourable to the elderly, and perhaps in the long run much less favourable, than current official forecasts indicate. But this is not an immediate reason for alarm. But it is a reason for moving carefully, for watching how trends actually develop, and for caution in adopting policies whose implications could look very different if some of the possibilities . . . were fulfilled. It could be risky to allow a new pattern of early retirement to establish itself before it is clear that the future "active" population will be large enough—and willing—to ensure an acceptable standard of living to the new pensioners. So it also could be risky to enter into pension commitments whose costs might come to look very different, well within the lifetime of today's younger workers, if Benjamin and Overton's "optimistic" projection—or even, what is *prima facie* more likely, their "medium" plus low fertility projections—proved to be near the mark.[18]

The demographic issue has been even more dramatically, and less technically, posed by the famous French demographer/philosopher Alfred Sauvy. Sauvy is an adamant high birth rate, or fertility rate, advocate. At a Lisbon conference on aging in 1970, he recounted the reactions to an article that he had published in *Le Monde* the year before, in which he argued that France needed more young people, if only to pay for the pensions of the old. One woman wrote a letter to the editor complaining that such pensions have nothing to do with the number of young people working: "That pension—the 'bête noire' of many selfish people . . . I paid for that pension by my work . . . . So please do not say such stupid things, and think before you write an article."

Sauvy thought a little more, and in another essay discussed the pros and cons of an increase in the French population and the problems

18. Fogarty, *Retirement Age*, p. 20.

resulting in a declining birth rate. This time, he received a letter from an engineer, "presumably an educated man." "In spite of everything you can say," wrote the engineer, "I believe that the French people would be better off from the material standpoint if instead of numbering fifty million, there were ten million of them." Now, in order to reach a population of only ten million, Sauvy calculated that it would require that the fifty million French have no children at all for a period of sixty years. After sixty years of childlessness, France could then attain the engineer's ideal goal of ten million people. And all of the ten million people would be at least 60 years old.[19] But this is not the main point of Sauvy's story. Not to be daunted by such demographic facts, the engineer wrote back: "So much the better—they could all live happily on their pensions."

The moral of the story applies not just to our forms of so-called transfer payment systems to provide retirement income to older nonworkers, but even to private pension schemes, which must be based on production of goods and services in the future, in order to provide retirement benefits.

Labor Force Participation Trends

FRANCE

The situation in France highlights the interaction between demographic trends and retirement-age (actually, pension-age) policy. France today provides a dramatic instance of early retirement policies: in 1983, that country lowered the *full* pension-benefit age from 65 to 60. Accordingly, it has, among the countries involved in the multi-country project (see Table 4), the lowest participation rate of older men aged either 55–59 or 60–64 years. It must be pointed out, however, that early retirement—as reflected in lower labor force participation rates—has begun to emerge in groups as young as 55–59 in many countries other than France, but their rates are not as low as those for France.

The latest figures available, for 1985, show less than a 68 percent participation rate for French males aged 55–59, almost 19 percent less than the 1975 figure. This decline is higher than for any of the four other European countries in the International Early Exit Project. The comparative figure for the United States was slightly less than 15 percent. The lowest rate of decline was in Sweden, only 2.3 percent. The pattern for the last decade is much more dramatic than for 1965–75. It is ironic that France, with the highest decline rate for the recent decade,

19. Quoted in H. L. Sheppard and S. E. Rix, *The Graying of Working America: The Coming Crisis of Retirement-Age Policy* (New York: Free Press-Macmillan, 1979), p. viii.

Table 4: MALE LABOR FORCE PARTICIPATION RATES, AGES 55–59 AND 60–64, 1975–85, AND RATE OF DECLINE, SELECTED COUNTRIES

Year	France	U.K.	Sweden	Germany	Netherlands	U.S.
			Age Group 55–59			
1975	83.3	93.4	89.7	84.5	30.5	83.3
1985	67.8	82.3	87.6	76.9	70.2	71.2
1975–85 decline rate	18.6	11.9	2.3	9.0	12.8	14.5
1965–75 decline rate	+0.5*	2.4	3.3	6.6	n.a.	2.8
			Age Group 60–64			
1975	56.7	82.5	74.1	56.2	65.0	64.5
1985	30.8	52.0	65.1	33.2	36.2	48.0
1975–85 decline rate	45.6	37.0	12.1	40.9	44.3	25.6
1965–75 decline rate	17.3	7.5	10.8	27.9	n.a.	18.6

*The only participation rate which increased rather than declined.

Source: OECD sources and Swedish labor force surveys, cited in working papers prepared for International Early Exit Project. Rates of decline figured by H. L. Sheppard.

experienced virtually no decline rate for the recent decade but rather a 0.5 percent increase.

Table 4 also shows the relative rates of decline for the 60–64 age group of males, the bracket which *until recently* was typically defined as the one in which "early retirement" was beginning to show itself. It is clear that we must now begin to look at 55–59 as the "successor" of that 60–64 age group as far as patterns of early retirement are concerned. (In the United States, nearly 40 percent of all new Social Security beneficiaries, as of 1980–81, had left the labor force *before* age 62, the earliest official eligibility age for receipt of reduced retired worker benefits.) As one more way of dramatizing the new period into which we may have entered, let us again look at French data. In 1975, the 60–64 participation rate, as a proportion of the same year's rate for men aged 55–59, was 68.1 percent, but by 1985 the same measure was only 45.4 percent. As Table 4 shows, the 60–64 group rate dropped far faster than the 55–59 group rate. But the participation rate for the *new* early retirement cohort is fast approaching the rate for the 60–64 group in earlier decades.

The picture for European women may be more complicated than that for men (Table 5). In general (but only in general), the labor force participation rates of middle-aged and older women have been on the rise, in contrast to those for men in the same countries. At the same

Table 5: FEMALE LABOR FORCE PARTICIPATION RATES, AGES 55–59 AND 60–64, 1975–85, AND RATE OF CHANGE, SELECTED COUNTRIES

Year	France	U.K.	Sweden	Germany	Netherlands	U.S.
			Age Group 55–59			
1975	43.5	52.6	60.8	37.9	17.8	47.5
1985	42.8	52.0	74.5	37.8	20.4	50.1
1975–85 change	−1.6	−1.1	+22.5	−0.3	+14.6	+5.5
1965–75 change	+5.6	+18.2	+30.5	+4.4	n.a.	+5.8
			Age Group 60–64			
1975	29.8	28.7	38.3	15.5	10.8	33.0
1985	18.9	19.0	46.6	10.6	8.5	33.2
1975–85 change	−36.6	−38.8	+21.7	−31.6	−21.3	+0.6
1965–75 change	−6.0	+11.2	+23.9	−33.5	n.a.	−4.3

Source: see Table 4.

time, some countries do not have a common full-pension age for both sexes: women are eligible at an earlier age, usually five years before men. So far, in contrast to men, signs of "early" exit are showing up among females in the 60–64 age group (*participation* rates are, of course, lower among women in all countries).

But the critical point, as in the case of men, is that the past decade, by and large, shows a decline in the 60–64 group's participation rates that is greater than the comparable pattern for the 1965–75 decade. For example, in France the rate from 1975–85 for the 60–64 group dropped at a rate of nearly 37 percent, compared to only a 6 percent drop from 1965 to 1975.

THE NETHERLANDS

The case of the Netherlands, too frequently bypassed in the general literature, deserves some special attention. As Martin Blomsma and Bert De Vroom point out,[20] despite the official pension age of 65, the actual pension age is moving toward 60. Even though the participation rate for women 50 to 59 has been increasing (and decreasing among men of the same age), the data on the 60- to 64-year-old population of both men and women show that labor force participation rates have dropped considerably from 1973 to 1985—more than 52 percent for

20. "Exit and Older Workers in the Netherlands," Leyden Institute for Law and Public Policy, 1987, paper prepared for International Early Exit Project.

men, 29 percent for women. In more general terms, Blomsma and De Vroom describe the exit pattern of older workers as having four basic characteristics: (1) it is male-specific; (2) it is disproportionate to other age groups; (3) exit patterns demonstrate industry-specific features; and (4) the exit rate has been accelerating.

GERMANY

Germany should be of special interest as far as a policy or program of private pensions is concerned. Such pensions are not as important as they are in Europe and North America. In fact there has even been a reduction in the importance of such programs in recent years.[21] The German story is interesting also because of the strikes in recent years by some member unions of the DGB (the central labor organization) aimed at lowering weekly working hours, while other unions have advocated a lowering of the working life, i.e., a reduction of the eligibility age for full-benefit pensions. The first step includes the metal workers, while the second consists of such unions as the chemical workers.

In the view of Klaus Jacobs and his co-authors, "Early exit has become the focus of political conflict and negotiations on several levels. It obviously concerns labor market and social policy, but it also extends into basic questions of industrial relations and of the moral economy."[22]

Unemployment in Germany is now a major pathway to retirement as early as age 57 plus 4 months; what this means is eligibility for jobless benefits at this age, continuing until one is eligible to enter the regular pension system at age 60 because of poor labor demand.[23] In cases of plant shutdowns, extended jobless benefits are available for 32 months. When the worker reaches approximately 58.5 years, means-tested unemployment help is available for an unlimited time until age 60. At that age, the regular pension is available.

In Germany, as a matter of fact, a program of unemployment-based pensions for male workers at age 60 has been in force for over thirty years (women can retire regularly at age 60 anyway), but it was rarely used until the early 1980s. Now in Germany one can find many long-term male unemployed workers exiting through this route. More general observations concerning the German scene are: (1) its relatively low percentage of part-time workers, only 5 percent; (2) its relatively low rate of decline in participation rates among both males and females

21. Klaus Jacobs, Martin Kohli, and Martin Rein, "Early Exit from the Labor Force in Germany," paper prepared for International Early Exit Project.
22. Ibid., p. 25.
23. Ibid., p. 13.

aged 55–59 over the past decade; and (3) its extremely low participation rate of women aged 60–64 (in 1985, for example, this rate was only 10.6 percent, compared to 33 percent in the United States).

THE SWEDISH CONTRADICTION

Sweden is an exception to the general developments in Europe, and its performance in this area provides a sharp antidote to the belief that it, as one of the most developed, advanced "welfare states," would have the lowest participation rates for both men and women, certainly for persons aged 60–64. The concept of a "welfare state" conjures up the notion of retirement, especially *early* retirement, as an index of social progress. The earlier the retirement, the greater the social progress. But an examination of the two accompanying tables shows that for Swedish men, the decline rate has been the *lowest* over the past decade (see Table 4). As for women in Sweden, Table 5 shows that in age group 55–59 there has been not a decline but an *increase* in their participation rate (22.5 percent) from 1975 to 1985. Even more remarkable is the fact that for the 60–64 age group of women, Sweden registers a marked *increase* in the participation rate (21.7 percent), while other countries have experienced a decrease in rates for women in this age group.

I do not deal here with Sweden's widely publicized program of partial pensions, largely because it is not truly a retirement program, nor was it originally legislated as a measure to combat high unemployment problems among younger workers. Its original purpose was largely driven by a belief that gradual or targeted retirement was better than "sudden death" departure from the work force. During recent recessions, however, its "take-up" rate did increase.

To repeat, Sweden represents a remarkable, interesting case study because it does not fit the traditional theory that countries with so-called advanced social legislation will be characterized by early labor force exit rates. In Sweden, the recession of the 1970s was followed by such special developments as the Security of Employment Act, which was aimed at the protection of all workers. It pays special attention to older workers and handicapped workers; for example, it emphasizes advance notice of dismissal for workers 45 and older. Special Adjustment Programs were created to find new job assignments for older workers in situations involving employment changes. The basic thrust is directed at *preventing* their unemployment by maintaining their current jobs. Swedish labor market policy is, it seems, driven by an emphasis on keeping and finding jobs for older workers, with early or complete retirement as a last, and not a first, resort. Paradoxically, Sweden has "all the supporting legislation needed to produce early retirement [but nevertheless

Table 6: MALE LABOR FORCE PARTICIPATION RATES, AGES 55–64, 1985, SELECTED COUNTRIES

Sweden	France	Germany	Netherlands	U.K.	U.S.
76.0	50.1	57.5	53.8	66.4	64.5

does] not show the same rates of high exit" as in other countries without such legislation.[24]

Sweden is not so unique that it was spared the economic stagnation beginning roughly with the oil crisis of the early 1970s, but it has nevertheless witnessed an increase in overall labor force participation, and even a relatively low rate of unemployment, during the past decade and a half. Most of us are already aware of some of the possible explanations for this difference between Sweden and other western European and American economies. I refer especially to its deliberate and positive labor market policy.

Thus, while the early exit trend also characterizes Sweden, its participation rate for older men remains the highest among the European countries and also when compared to the United States. In recent years, Sweden has experienced a relatively slow decline in the percentage of employed men 55 and older, as Table 6 shows.

The "Troubled Industry" Hypothesis

Popular among researchers in the arena of retirement analysis is the "troubled industry" hypothesis, namely, that declining industries are a critical factor in the declining labor force participation rate of older persons. But in a detailed analysis of comparative data pertaining to this notion, Jacobs, Kohli, and Rein conclude that, contrary to what they originally expected, "It is not the troubled industries that are the leaders in rejuvenating their age structure, but the services industry, especially of the public sector."[25] The "troubled industry" explanation of early exit was not the comprehensive factor they had anticipated. Equally important, they found, was that even *growing* industries experienced a decline in the number of older workers—*except in Sweden.*

24. Helen Ginsburg, *Full Employment and Public Policy: The United States and Sweden* (Lexington, Mass.: D. C. Heath-Lexington Books, 1983).

25. Klaus Jacobs, Martin Kohli, and Martin Rein, "Testing the Industry-Mix Hypothesis of Early Exit," paper prepared for the Nordic Council Research Conference on Social Policy and Labor Markets, Bergen, Norway, June 4–6, 1987.

What *is* happening, according to the authors?

> The expanding industries of the past decades brought in young skilled workers who developed long term work attachment to their relatively high paid jobs. . . . When these firms were forced to reduce their work force in response to technological change and/or declining market shares they shed their older workers. This was especially true when these industries could "push out" the workers they no longer needed by using the available tools of public policy. Workers, in turn, could accept and even find attractive the incentive to exit, and the boundary between voluntary exit and expulsion became blurred.[26]

But there remains the intriguing policy analysis challenge of a country which has managed, despite the process just described, to have a relatively low rate of early exits or to have an early retirement trend matching that of so many modern economies in the past few decades. If social legislation and "progressive" social policy (and "troubled industries") are not unambiguously related to early retirement, is there some other set of social, cultural, political, and economic forces at play? According to Jacobs, Kohli, and Rein, another dimension may relate to

> an extreme structural perspective because it assumes that the process of early retirement is driven by deeper, less accessible structural features of economy and society, such as modernization, changing work values, and increasing productivity. In this view, institutional arrangements do not matter. Early exit takes place regardless of what institutional routes are available. Social policy cannot stop the early retirement process from unfolding.[27]

Perhaps social policy is not unimportant, however. "It can mold the retirement process so that it is more or less acceptable to different actors. . . . The process of early retirement cannot be reversed."[28] What does change, according to Jacobs and his colleagues, is the means or the pathway through which the early retirement phenomenon is realized.

This proposition or policy theory may be closely associated with my own interpretation of the American case, and it also might have some bearing on the paradox, contradiction, or confusion of many European observers of that American case. The paradox has to do with our own age discrimination in employment legislation, as well as the intended thrust, as reflected in the early 1983 amendments to the Social Security Act, toward deferred or later retirement.

Despite these two American developments, Europeans are surprised to find that there has been no meaningful halt of the early retire-

26. Ibid., p. 36.
27. "Early Exit in Germany," p. 16.
28. Ibid.

ment process, including retirements even *before* the Social Security pension age of 62. It is my interpretation, coming back to the "substitution" theory, that what is involved is the market mechanism (involving unemployment problems), along with incentives to retire early under selected pension plans (including disability benefits and both private pension and Social Security retired worker benefits). "Incentives" might not be the right term because it implies carrots resulting in truly voluntary retirements. The stick can also be operative, even when the exit from an employer's establishment technically or legally is categorized as "voluntary." Perhaps the word "conditions" for early retirement is a more appropriate one than "incentives."

These two elements, the market mechanism and the early retirement pension conditions, are apparently more powerful than both our legislation and our rhetoric about the continuing potential of older workers, based in large part on research in a field that has come to be called "industrial gerontology." American society and, to a lesser extent, European societies may be distinguished by a form of schizophrenia when it comes to this issue. On the one hand, we push for the increases in pension coverage and improved pension benefits that form part of the conditions of early retirement, along with defining retirement as a sign of social progress; on the other hand, we have special projects and programs, along with pro-older worker, anti-compulsory retirement legislation, and studies that are motivated by the need of employers to retain, retrain, and hire older workers.

In any event, it appears that unemployment, economic cycles, and financial, organizational, and technological restructuring are forces too powerful to be sufficiently influenced by legislation and scientific knowledge. Nor can we ignore the less measurable influence of sociocultural and social-psychological nuances of ocean-wave dimensions and force. I refer here to the intangibles of values and attitudes; the qualitative nature of a panoply of work tasks that can encourage or discourage work continuity; so-called spiritual values affecting tradeoffs between paid work and unpaid leisure; and so on *ad infinitum*.

But to return to the more comfortable plane of the concrete and the empirically measurable, there has been an increase in the number of early retirement plan *provisions,* and of *people* actually retiring early—both with pension benefits that are not actuarially reduced. The statistics on discouraging job-seeking behavior (the "discouraged worker" phenomenon) demonstrate what I call the "flaking" process, whereby after each major recession or layoff, older workers are the least likely to return to the labor force (or, at best, obtain lower-paying, often temporary employment). Many of them exit from the labor force even without pensions, and often before the age of 62, at which age they are then eligible for severely reduced retired worker Social Security benefits.[29] The new phenomenon of corporate mergers and buyouts (in place of corporate job-creating investments in this country) is accompanied by remarkable "golden handshakes"—company carrots for very early retirements—again without truly actuarial reductions.

We are witnessing very dramatic developments in very early exits from the labor force. But it is still not clear, or settled, whether such developments are to be looked upon as positive, wholesome phenomena or as portents of new burdens on the working population or the general economy. We still don't have enough reliable information as to whether they represent positive experiences for the individuals involved during their ostensibly long (and increasing) years in retirement. And just how truly voluntary are such retirements, even those at later but still "early" ages of retirement from the labor force?

On the financial cost side, it may not be enough to use the conventional demographic approach, that is, the body-count method involving measures of nonworking population as a percentage of working population. Other elements enter into the equation, such as productivity. Theoretically, given some unexpected miracle in productivity, the American economy could afford to support growing numbers—both relatively and absolutely—of nonworking adults with acceptable retirement incomes and services. Other cost questions include the following:

1. Given early-exit pensions at benefit levels close to or equal to those for later-exit pensions (i.e., not actuarially reduced), are the costs passed on to consumers in the form of higher prices? To the remaining workers in the firm in the form of lower wage increases or none at all?
2. Are the costs compensated for by corresponding productivity improvements?
3. Since there are preferential corporate tax exemptions for the private pension system in the United States, how much of a loss is there to general revenues? A 1986 Government Accounting Office report estimates that about $88 billion were lost in that year.[30]

29. Among workers exiting before age 62 because of job loss, 52 percent received no retirement pension other than Social Security (obtainable at age 62). This should be compared to the 32 percent of all *other* workers exiting before age 62 for other reasons who received no pensions (data from U.S. Social Security Administration New Beneficiary Survey, 1982, analyzed by H. L. Sheppard).

30. *Retirement before Age 65: Trends, Costs, and National Issues* (Washington, D.C.: General Accounting Office, 1986), p. 4.

4. What cost impact does the secular trend of increase in life expectancy at age 60 or 65 have?

Another element has to do with social policy as internalized by the supporting working population, i.e., the willingness to support—directly and indirectly—a large nonworking population. I am talking about values and intergenerational reciprocity—keeping in mind that the old, when they were younger, made contributions to the social and economic base that obtains today, and that they supported younger adults of today when those adults were unable to support themselves. Furthermore—contrary to the image most of us have today of the elderly simply as takers and not as givers—the proportion of the old who today give to younger age groups is greater. It may even be greater than the proportion of the young adults who give to an older parent, according to a 1987 Commonwealth Fund study.[31]

Such questions or issues form part of the context or conditions, it seems to me, for the emergence—so far in the United States more than elsewhere—of an anti-older generation mentality, partly propagated by the mass media, partly by some academics, and partly even by an organization presumably devoted to "generation equity." The development or growth of persons with somewhat adequate retirement pensions; the incomplete understanding of the so-called economic dependency of the old; recent economic studies pointing to a slower rate of economic progress (or none at all) for the younger working generation compared with the rates for older adult workers and retirees; the use of statistics showing differences in public expenditures for the old; etc.—all of these and other selected data are being used to generate a tension between generations.

Even in Sweden, I have seen negative public reference to its retirees as the "richest pensioners in the world." This does not mean, of course, that anti-elderly propaganda has succeeded yet in creating actual intergenerational conflict or tension. In fact, public opinion surveys have so far not tapped such feelings, to any meaningful extent. But this does not mean that such scapegoating of the older generation (and I see this movement partly as a new type of scapegoating, as a way of "explaining," for example, child poverty and the wage and income problems of younger families and workers) will not, in time, gain large numbers of adherents.

One of the best scholarly and empirical refutations of the doctrine that the progress of the elderly in the United States has been at the expense of younger Americans can be found in an article by Richard

31. *Problems Facing Elderly Americans Living Alone* (New York: Louis Harris and Associates, 1987), p. ii.

Easterlin of the University of Southern California, in the journal *Population and Development Review* for June 1987. A major target of Easterlin's rebuttal is essentially the provocative piece by Samuel Preston in *Scientific American* for December 1984, "Children and the Elderly in the United States." Pitting the experience of children (and even of youth and younger adults in the economy) against that of the elderly as Preston does, "lends itself," writes Easterlin, "to the view that the gains of one have been at the expense of the other; more specifically, that expanded government programs underlying the improved status of the elderly have been purchased by sacrificing programs for the young."[32] Easterlin's analysis presents an alternative perspective and explanation of the differential rates of progress or lack thereof. The divergent trends "chiefly reflect two different and largely independent causes":

> Whereas the improved status of the elderly is largely attributable to government action, especially advances in social security . . . the rise in the poverty rate of children is, to an important extent, a result of market forces and would have occurred even in the absence of programs improving the lot of the elderly. . . . This is not to say that there is no need for improving government programs for children.[33]

Returning to the main topic of this paper, the overall story for the countries as a whole is perhaps one of the more telling ones. Regardless of country (with the prominent exception of Sweden) and regardless of whether we focus on the 55–59 or the 60–64 age group, the last decade—compared to earlier ones—has witnessed a radical decline in labor force participation, especially among men. One burning policy issue is: does this seemingly near-universal trend signify progress, or does it reflect serious economic growth problems? Does it portend a new problem—on the level of the economy or society or the state? Or on the level of the lives of individuals, who face longer years of nonwork existence and for whom we have apparently not yet institutionalized a life style (or a mosaic of life styles) that can be said truly to constitute a positive quality of life?

32. "The New Age Structure of Poverty in America: Permanent or Transient," *Population and Development Review,* June 1987.

33. Ibid., p. 195.

"Work for Everyone"—
A Swedish Commitment

BO ADOLFSSON

Swedish policies toward older workers are different from those in many other European countries. In contrast to the negative European attitudes described by Sheppard, Adolfsson says, the Swedish government understands the economic and social need to make use of older workers and has developed labor market and pension policies to further this goal. As a result, the trend toward earlier retirement is not so marked in Sweden as in many European countries or the United States.

J. D. O.

The most important political goal in Sweden is, without a doubt, full employment. Achieving this goal means, in practice, economic development leading to a low level of unemployment. But a low unemployment level is not itself a sufficient goal, as it can be achieved by reducing the supply of labor, for example, by encouraging women to leave the labor market to return to housework.

"Work for everyone," on the other hand, is an expression used by Swedish policymakers since the mid-1970s to mean providing an increased number of people with the opportunity to participate in the labor market, the real base for equal opportunity (see Figure 1).

Economic policy must create an economic climate in which demand for labor can keep pace with supply and in which other goals of economic policy can be realized. Full employment requires full demand. However, Sweden's experience shows that using general economic policy until full employment is achieved puts pressure on wages and salaries and generates inflation.

The Swedish labor union movement has been united in its belief that the political goals of growth, stabilization, and distribution must be incorporated into economic policy in order to achieve the country's em-

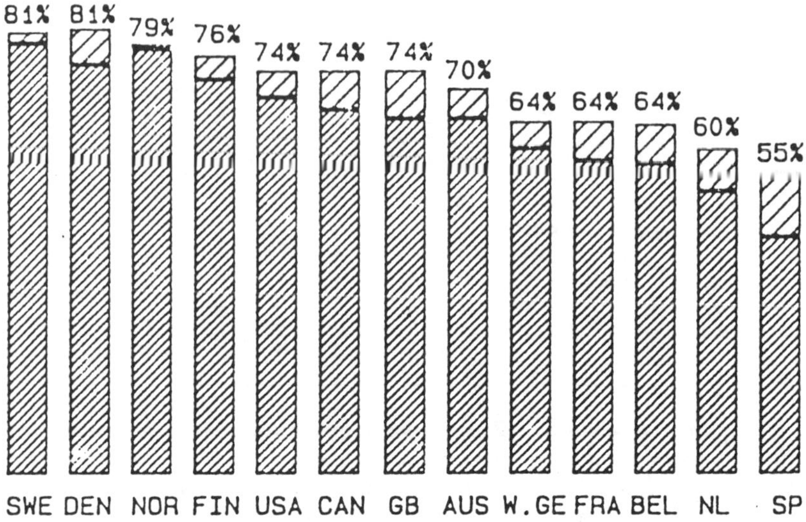

Figure 1. Employed and unemployed workers as percentage of total labor force, selected industrialized countries, 1986. *Key: heavily shaded,* employed workers; *lightly shaded,* unemployed workers. Source: Organization for Economic Co-operation and Development 1986.

ployment goals. It is necessary that general policy be aimed at full employment and economic growth, in this view, while labor market policy gives priority to work and/or training; passive cash unemployment benefits are to be given only if there is no suitable alternative.

Of the government budget, 6–7 percent, which corresponds to 2.5 percent of GNP, is utilized for labor market programs. Total expenditures on such programs are almost $5 billion, in a labor force numbering 4.4 million. Almost 70 percent of the labor policy funding goes to active programs; 30 percent goes to unemployment benefits (priorities in most western European countries are the reverse, with 70–80 percent going to unemployment benefits and only 20–30 percent to programs).

There are both economic and social reasons for making such an effort: work is an important part of the good society, and everyone who is willing and able to work should be given the chance to do so. Unemployment is a waste of resources, and the government has found that most active programs break even in the short run and are highly profitable in the longer run.

The Public Employment Service

An active labor market policy must find ways to improve the functioning of the whole labor market, and an efficient public employment service is the best and cheapest employment policy. The placement service must cover the whole market, serving both the unemployed and those who have a job and are looking for new opportunities, both job seekers with a strong position and those with a weaker position. The older workers' special problem is that their basic knowledge of mathematics and Swedish is poor. For this reason, it is common to supplement retraining with some education on the elementary school level.

Sweden's public employment service covers 90 percent of published vacancies and 60 percent of all job openings. More than 80 percent of the unemployed and more than 30 percent of other job seekers are registered at its offices. Officials in the job exchanges work closely with business as well as with job seekers. A nationwide computer-based information system allows job seekers in any employment office to get information on vacancies all over the country.

Human Resource Development Programs

For many job seekers—young people who need counseling, women entering or re-entering the labor market, displaced workers who need training or retraining to find new employment, disabled workers who need counseling, rehabilitation, and retraining—supply-side measures are required. In a rapidly changing economy, people need to improve their skills and abilities. These measures stimulate labor supply in general as well as various parts of the labor market, thereby avoiding bottlenecks in production.

During the 1970s and the first half of the 1980s, resources were concentrated on eliminating the high level of youth unemployment. These efforts were rather successful. The Labor Market Board is now focusing its resources on preventing the elimination of older workers, as there are already signs of the labor shortage that will not become fully apparent until the mid-1990s, caused by the drop in the numbers of young people.

To be competitive, Sweden must be a high-skill economy, which is more than a high-tech economy. Policymakers are convinced that Sweden must not only be advanced in technology but must also develop a high level of skill and competence in all trades and sectors of the economy—and a high degree of flexibility in work organization. The educational system, personnel training, and employment training, as well as learning by doing, are important elements in the development of this high-skill society. The importance of employment training can be illustrated by the fact that an increasing number of vacancies are reserved for persons with such training and/or experience. In 1980 employers required training and/or experience in 55 percent of vacancies; in 1987 that figure had jumped to 78 percent.

Employment training absorbs an increasing part of the labor market portion of the national budget, more than 25 percent in 1987. The average number of persons engaged in employment training and retraining at any given time is about 40,000, about 1 percent of the labor force. In any year about 130,000 persons, almost 3 percent of the labor force, are trained for new jobs and opportunities.

These programs are important in bringing people who are unemployed or at risk of being unemployed back to work. According to follow-up studies six months after the training, 70 percent of the participants are working. The human resource programs, especially the training program, continue to be an important bridge to employment for women entering or re-entering the labor market.

Job Development Programs

For some job seekers, neither the placement service nor the human resource programs are sufficient or adequate. Demand-side measures, or job development programs, are necessary. These measures are based on economic incentives to employers to stimulate the demand for labor where and when necessary by hiring the unemployed. Though these efforts are directed at teenagers and the disabled, incentives are also used to create an employment alternative for older workers in place of early retirement and other social programs. Early retirement of older people doing heavy manual work has often been the most convenient solution, but even in this area there have been changes in policy in Sweden. The Labor Market Board is now trying to relocate rather than retiring workers, and often combines this strategy with retraining.

Labor Market Policy in Practice: Shipbuilding

The programs described above, in various combinations, are used all over the country to meet individual needs for jobs and security and producers' needs for flexibility.

The shipbuilding industry provides an example of how they work. In the 1960s Sweden was second only to Japan in shipbuilding. In the 1970s the market changed, and other countries moved into the industry. The last two Swedish shipyards, Kockums and Uddevalla, were closed in the mid-1980s.

The town of Uddevalla has 45,000 inhabitants, and shipbuilding had been the dominant employer, with 2,200 workers. Great efforts were made to help these workers find new jobs. The government presented a vigorous program of investment in Uddevalla, made a deal with Volvo to establish a new auto plant in the town, and started massive labor programs. An employment office was established at the shipyard a year before it closed. More than 30 placement officers and counselors attempted to find a satisfactory employment solution for every worker.

Most of these workers now have new jobs, either directly or as a result of employment training; some are still in training for new skills and professions; some have started their own businesses; some have retired. All workers who received retirement payments were 60 years old or older. New enterprises have been developed in the region, and the economic structure is more healthy now than at the beginning of the 1980s. There are fewer people unemployed in Uddevalla today than there were before the shipyard shut down.

The Labor Movement

The Confederation of Trade Unions (Landsorganisationen i Sverge, or LO) has never accepted job sharing as a measure to reduce unemployment, nor does it believe that reducing working hours will solve the unemployment problem. Each time working hours have been cut in Sweden, the result has been increased labor costs because weekly or monthly wages are guaranteed.

Because production must finance a reduction of working hours, an increase in productivity is required. Only increased productivity can provide an improved standard of living: this means that the employee has to decide whether to demand a higher salary or shorter working hours (when economically feasible). LO believes that unemployment is a political matter and a problem for the government to resolve. Under such conditions it will never be possible to fight unemployment through a reduction in working hours.

Both employers and workers are well-organized and powerful. Business can talk with one voice, through the Swedish Employers' Confederation, and therefore is strong. Union membership is high—95 percent of blue-collar workers and 85 percent of salaried workers are organized, giving the unions a great deal of influence and responsibility.

The unions are not only organizations for struggle but social builders as well. They generally cannot confine themselves to the short-term interests of their members but must view their role in a broader context. As a contribution to Sweden's transformation to a high-tech, high-skill economy, the unions accepted wage restraints and lower wage increases in order to improve future real earnings.

SOLIDARITY IN THE LO

In the postwar period the labor movement, and above all LO, has had a policy of solidarity in wages. Groups who are better off are expected to help those with a lower income by loyalty to their wage demands. This policy has been successful, and the result has been that the wage spread among workers in Sweden is minor compared to that in other countries. An employee at McDonald's in Sweden earns about half a mine worker's wage. A person who has lost his job because of plant closings, etc., and who has to change occupation or trade rarely has to worry about being paid a dramatically lower rate at the next job. Furthermore, the system of social insurance is almost entirely fixed by law; this means that pension benefits, for example, remain the same if a person changes jobs.

Older Workers

In spite of all this, middle-aged and older workers in Sweden do not like to change jobs and hesitate to do so. Between 75 and 85 percent of all workers have been with the same employer for more than ten years, and between 35 and 40 percent have been with the same employer for more than twenty-five years. In 1984, among workers in the private sector 28 years of age or older, 82 percent worked for the same employer during the entire year, and another 15 percent changed employment only once.

It seems that once a person has found a place in the labor market, he hopes to remain there until retirement, even though, as noted above, there is little risk of losing income or earned social benefits by job changes. In view of this preference, as well as projections of the labor market ten to fifteen years from today (see Figures 2–3), it is easy to understand that employees, employers, and society have a difficult road to travel.

The Labor Force in the Year 2000

It is not easy to predict demand for different sorts of labor in the work force in future. Such predictions are often pure guesswork and are very uncertain, as postwar economic history well illustrates. From 1945 to about 1970, the growth of production and productivity in the Western Hemisphere, from a historical point of view, was quite unique. There was a combination of conditions behind this growth: increased

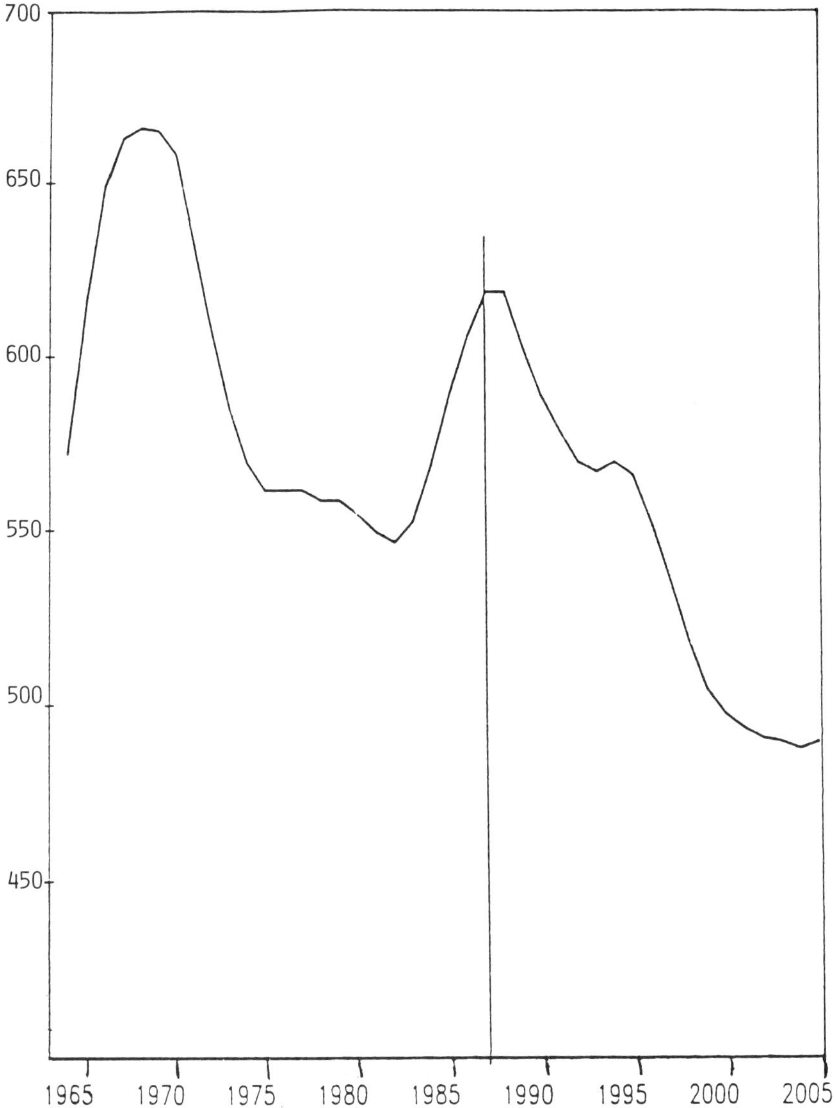

Figure 2. Number of persons aged 20–24, Sweden, 1964–86 and projected to 2005. Source: Swedish Ministry of Labour. (Unit of measurement: thousands of people.)

internationalization, increased free trade and migration across borders, large investments in infrastructure, and improved production techniques.

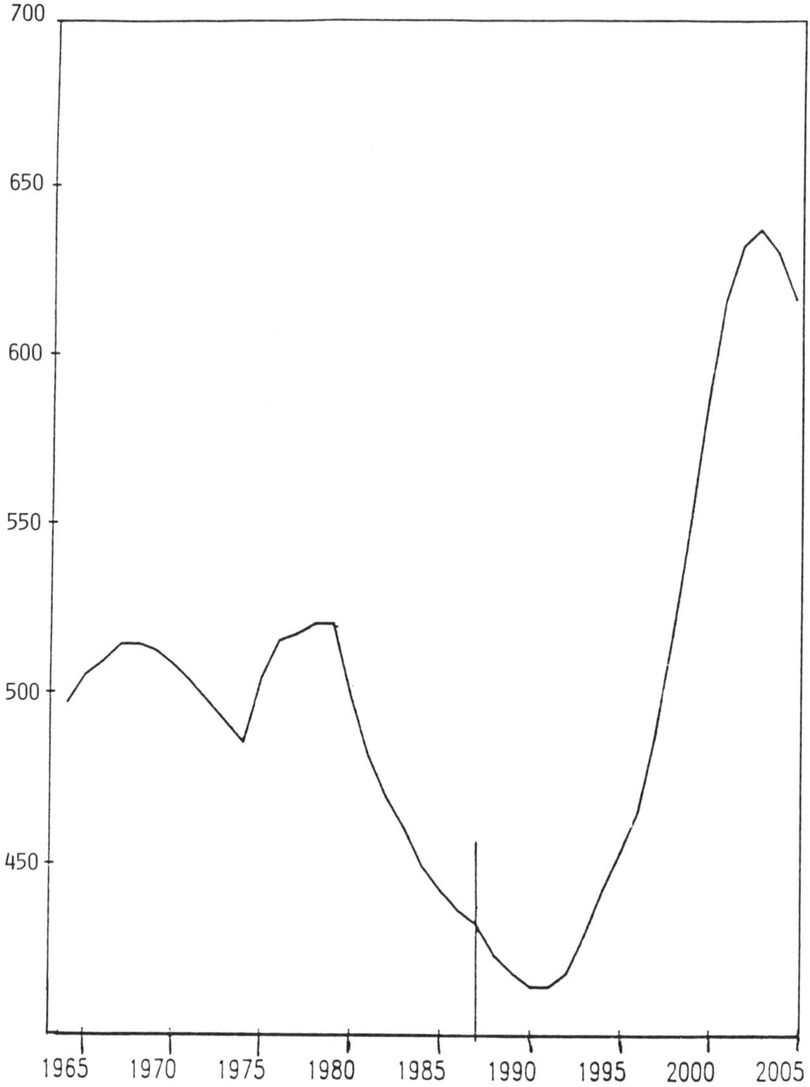

Figure 3. Number of persons aged 55–59, Sweden, 1964–86 and projected to 2005. Source: Swedish Ministry of Labour. (Unit of measurement: thousands of people.)

A few years into the 1970s, however, economic development had changed radically because of economic ups and downs and structural crises. A high rate of unemployment and a reluctance to invest became important factors. Many of the conditions that reinforced one

Table 1: PERCENTAGE OF POPULATION AGED 0–15 YEARS, 16–64 YEARS, AND 65–, SWEDEN, 1960–2005

Year	Age Group 0–15	16–64	65–	Total Population (millions)
1960	23.9	64.3	11.9	7.498
1965	22.4	64.9	12.7	7.773
1970	22.2	64.1	13.7	8.081
1975	21.1	62.9	15.2	8.208
1980	20.9	62.7	16.4	8.318
1985	19.4	63.2	17.4	8.358
		Projected		
1990	18.7	63.3	18.1	8.432
1995	18.9	63.2	17.9	8.498
2000	19.2	63.4	17.4	8.539
2005	18.9	63.8	17.3	8.542

Source: Central Bureau of Statistics, Government of Sweden, 1986.

another during 1945–1970 and favored economic growth in the 1970s now hampered it. In recent years we are again in a phase of high economic growth, and there is an increased interest in investment but a lack of well-trained and specialized workers.

When it comes to predicting the size of the labor force in future, the supply by and large is determined by present demographic developments (Table 1). The percentage of the total population of Sweden in age bracket 16–64, the working years, will remain largely unchanged at the turn of the century; at present, it is slightly more than 63 percent. But since the total population will increase slightly, the actual number of persons in the work force will increase by about 100,000, or 3 percent.

There will be some great changes within the group in the productive age category which will greatly influence the labor market in future. The number of youths entering the market on a yearly basis over the next twenty years can be determined fairly precisely, as it reflects the number of births during the period 1965–86. The total number of 20-year-olds in the labor force will drop by 350,000–400,000 annually because of the dramatic decrease in births.

IMMIGRATION

Gross immigration to Sweden would have to increase enormously to compensate for the reduction in the number of youths. A gross immigration of between 350,000 and 400,000 would be needed to keep the number of 20-year-olds at the 1986 level. However, during the period 1976–85 the gross immigration to Sweden averaged 35,000 persons a year. There is no reason—political, social, or economic—to believe that there will be an influx of the magnitude needed; in fact, should it take place, it would double the Swedish population in twenty years. We also know that births in countries of emigration will decrease to roughly the same extent as in Sweden (Table 2). The prospects for young workers in industrialized nations seem brighter than ever before, as youth will be in such short supply.

Another reason why immigration is not a solution is the fact that the salaried sector will expand most in future, and the most basic requirement for employment within this sector is ability to speak and write the language of the country. Within the manufacturing sector, there is a great demand for highly skilled workers, and this demand will only increase over time, while unskilled work opportunities vanish.

YOUNG WORKERS

Figure 2 shows the number of youths in Sweden aged 20–24 years in the 1964–86 period, as well as the number projected for 1987–2005. We can see that at the turn of the century this age bracket will drop 20 percent from the 1970 level. In ten years the yearly influx of young people into the labor force will be about 15 percent less than now, and at the turn of the century the total will be about 30 percent less. In certain sectors of the labor market—for example, manufacturing and health care, where the employment of younger persons is desirable, though for quite different reasons—this shortage is already apparent.

OLDER WORKERS

The population reaching upper middle age will greatly increase up to the year 2000: the number of persons aged 55 to 59 will increase more than 35 percent, compared to the situation today, because the large number of children born during the 1940s will reach upper middle age. To illustrate this, Figure 3 shows the number of persons in age bracket 55–59 in 1964–86, as well as the projections in this category for 1987–2005. We can assume that this age imbalance will be accentuated at the turn of the century, when the number of youths entering the labor market is at its lowest, while the number in upper middle age is at its peak. This imbalance can be simply illustrated: presently we have 14 youths aged 20–24 for every 10 persons aged 55–59. At the turn of the century this number will be cut in half, to 7.

What will be the consequences in the labor market of the 1990s? The possibility of replacing young workers with older people will be limited and cannot be done easily. We will probably see a reduction in unemployment among young people, a tendency to increase starting pay, and favorable long-term contracts offered to youths. Many

Table 2: TOTAL FERTILITY RATE, SELECTED INDUSTRIALIZED COUNTRIES, 1965–84

Country	1965	1970	1975	1978	1979	1980	1981	1982	1983	1984
Eastern Europe										
Bulgaria	2.03	2.18	2.23	2.15	2.15	2.05	2.01	2.02	2.00	NA
Czechoslovakia	2.37	2.07	2.43	2.36	2.33	2.16	2.10	2.10	2.08	2.07
East Germany	2.48	2.19	1.54	1.90	1.90	1.94	1.85	1.85	1.79	NA
Hungary	1.82	1.96	2.35	2.07	2.01	1.91	1.88	1.79	1.72	1.73
Poland	2.52	2.20	2.27	2.20	2.25	2.26	2.22	2.31	2.40	NA
Romania	1.91	2.89	2.60	2.52	2.48	2.43	2.35	2.19	2.00	NA
Northern Europe										
Denmark	2.61	1.95	1.92	1.67	1.60	1.55	1.44	1.43	1.38	1.40
Finland	2.47	1.83	1.68	1.64	1.64	1.63	1.64	1.72	1.74	1.70
Iceland	3.71	2.81	2.65	2.35	2.49	2.48	2.33	2.26	NA	NA
Ireland	4.03	3.87	3.41	3.24	3.23	3.23	3.08	2.96	2.74	NA
Norway	2.93	2.50	1.98	1.77	1.75	1.72	1.70	1.71	1.65	1.65
Sweden	2.42	1.92	1.77	1.60	1.66	1.68	1.63	1.62	1.61	1.65
Great Britain	2.83	2.44	1.82	1.77	1.88	1.92	1.84	1.78	1.77	NA
Southern Europe										
Greece	2.32	2.43	2.33	2.29	2.29	2.21	2.09	2.02	1.94	NA
Italy	2.55	2.37	2.19	1.85	1.74	1.66	1.57	1.57	1.53	NA
Portugal	3.07	2.62	2.59	2.28	2.17	2.12	2.04	2.02	1.96	NA
Spain	2.97	2.87	2.80	2.53	2.31	2.16	1.99	1.87	NA	NA
Yugoslavia	2.71	2.29	2.27	2.15	2.12	2.13	2.06	NA	NA	NA
Western Europe										
Austria	2.68	2.30	1.83	1.60	1.60	1.65	1.67	1.66	1.56	1.52
Belgium	2.60	2.24	1.73	1.69	1.69	1.68	1.66	1.60	1.56	NA
France	2.84	2.47	1.93	1.82	1.86	1.95	1.95	1.91	1.79	1.81
West Germany	2.50	2.01	1.45	1.38	1.38	1.45	1.43	1.41	1.33	1.29
Netherlands	3.04	2.58	1.66	1.58	1.56	1.60	1.56	1.49	1.47	1.49
Switzerland	2.01	2.10	1.61	1.50	1.52	1.55	1.54	1.55	1.51	1.52
Soviet Union	2.46	2.39	2.41	2.32	2.28	2.26	2.25	2.29	2.37	2.41
Australia	2.97	2.85	2.14	1.95	1.90	1.89	1.93	1.93	1.93	NA
Canada	3.15	2.33	1.90	1.75	1.75	1.73	1.70	1.69	1.67	NA
Israel	3.19	3.97	3.67	3.26	3.21	3.14	3.12	3.12	3.14	NA
Japan	2.14	2.13	1.89	1.77	1.74	1.73	1.75	1.75	1.80	1.81
New Zealand	3.53	3.17	2.36	2.10	2.10	2.03	1.95	1.95	1.92	NA
USA	2.93	2.48	1.77	1.76	1.81	1.84	1.82	1.83	1.79	1.82

enterprises will be forced to rethink the design of their internal training and working conditions to make jobs more attractive to young people. Furthermore, attempts will probably be made to recruit the young at even earlier ages in order to give them company training, especially in the health care and manufacturing sectors. Even elsewhere, employers will be using various strategies to attract the young labor force.

As the baby boomers reach middle age, a lot of people at the middle levels in companies will find further advancement blocked. In some cases older people will be laid off, as is already happening, especially in larger companies, to correct their imbalanced age structure in the work force. It is clear that some serious social and psychological problems could result among individuals who reach upper middle age during the 1990s.

The problem of youth unemployment today will be transformed into the problem of the middle-aged unemployed in the 2000s. A number of programs will be necessary—retraining, frequent in-company training, designing of alternate career routes, therapeutic measures, aid to older persons attempting to establish businesses, and so on. The labor market of 2000 presents a great challenge, and its ingredients are here today among us, as we can see.

Human Rights and the Older Worker: The ILO Perspective

STEPHEN SCHLOSSBERG

International Labor Organization deliberations and resolutions are aimed essentially at the advancement and protection of human rights. The author calls special attention to ILO Recommendation No. 162, directed toward the enlightened treatment of older workers, and describes the problems of and prospects for aging populations as essentially human rights issues. He notes that the ILO is undertaking a major comparative study of a number of countries throughout the world designed to learn how older citizens are treated within their respective nations, and thus point the way toward the further advancement of human rights and social justice for the elderly.

I. B.

The International Labor Organization, a body comprising management, labor, and government representatives from nations throughout the world, is concerned with the treatment of people at work and the field of labor-management relations. At present, the ILO is vitally interested in the aging work force.

Friend or Enemy?

Throughout the industrialized world, concern is being expressed about the problems inherent in a work force and a population which are rapidly growing older. In some quarters, the treatment given to older workers by management results in actions that are more hurtful than helpful to the older worker. Subtle—and often not so subtle—pressures to induce workers to leave the work force before they are really ready to do so, for instance, foster resentment and often impose economic and emotional hardship on those affected.

What some self-styled friends of the older workers and retirees are doing when they think they are being helpful reminds me of the story of the medieval knight who was gone from the castle for about three weeks. When he returned, battering on the drawbridge with his lance to be let in, one of the king's servants peered out and saw him, beaten half to death, covered with blood and mud, armor dented, and horse exhausted. The servant rushed to tell the king, who came to see the sight. When he saw the knight's state, the king demanded to know where he had been. The knight replied, "I have been in the west, your majesty, pillaging, raping, plundering, and robbing your enemies." The king asked in surprise, "Enemies in the west? I didn't know I had any." Came the quick reply: "You do now."

A Human Rights Issue

What we are discussing in this book is really a human rights issue. I recently talked with two distinguished visitors from France, one a training director, the other a management development expert. I mentioned to them that I was very excited about the ILO activities regarding the problems of the aging work force and that I was about to participate in a conference on these problems at Wayne State University. One of these fellows exclaimed: "Well, if you're worried about the human rights of older people, what about the human rights of younger people who need jobs? You have to get those older people out of there and make room for the younger people. Stop worrying about those older people." As a matter of fact, he added, "in France a law passed in 1971 forbids the expenditure of money for job-related training for workers 55 and older because you never get your investment back."

His comments reminded me of how, a few years ago, I used to hear similar comments about women—"Why are you worried about jobs for women," people would ask, "when there are young men and older men and middle-aged men with families to support who have to have jobs?" My answer to these people is that if we pit man against woman, young against old, one group against another, we will bring nothing but disaster to each group and to society as a whole.

Our nation is experiencing a rising wave of older people. Economists, demographers, and sociologists project that, with the aging of the work force, there will be a shortage of young workers. It seems to me that society had better learn to live with that problem, and that it is wiser to begin to address it now than when the shortage is upon us. Fortunately, our older citizens will be available as a backstop when that time comes, and businesses, governments, and economic planners must learn to use that valuable resource effectively. With this in mind, the ILO is presently undertaking a research project on the subject. Harold Sheppard, a contributor to this volume, is one of our consultants in this study, which I will describe later.

I was intrigued to learn some years ago of a study undertaken in the United States of television portrayals of the elderly. The study found that four out of ten older people shown on television were victims, either of muggers or of shrewd young people who took advantage of them. They were often shown in an unflattering light, and women, particularly elderly women, were portrayed as victims more often than men. Instead of looking at individual ability and capacity to perform, older people are treated in statistical generalizations and stereotypes, and individual potential is ignored (it seems particularly ironic that the medium of television should discriminate against older people, since they are among the most avid viewers).[1]

The ILO and Human Rights

The ILO was founded in 1919, at the close of World War I, as part of Article 13 of the Versailles Treaty. The American movers and shakers were Woodrow Wilson and Samuel Gompers. Human rights—workers' rights—were to be protected in a multilateral forum all over the world rather than being a basis for competition between and among nations. The premise was that nations should trade on the basis of creativity, ingenuity, service, quality, and all those other sound values and not on the basis of human misery, and that the vicious exploitation of fellow human beings, such as child labor, slavery, forced labor, unsafe and unhealthy conditions, and every manifestation of discrimination, could be eliminated from the world.

Typically, the ILO considers and adopts resolutions and conventions. Conventions are like treaties: they are ratified by the national governments. Even though many of the resolutions and conventions of the ILO are based either on the U.S. Constitution or on its most forward-looking national laws, it was only in 1988, after 25 years, that the United States ratified them. Title VII of the U.S. antidiscrimination law, which prohibits discriminatory practices for reasons of race, color, national origin, or sex, is copied almost word for word in ILO Convention No. 111, which the United States has not yet ratified.

The ILO is a tripartite organization, not just an organization of governments. Governments are affiliated—150 of them—but they share

1. G. Gerbner et al., "Aging with Television: Images on Television and Conceptions of Social Reality," *Journal of Communication*, Winter 1980.

voting power in the controlling bodies with employers and unions. The union contingent represents workers; the employer contingent represents business; and the governments represent the interests of the public at large. The ILO is the only forum that I know of in the United Nations system or in any other multilateral organization in which there are active nongovernmental participants. This is vitally important because tripartitism is the hope of the future. This model permits a social compact to be formed which will enable people to live more decently than they have in the past—and to achieve that social compact by negotiation and consensus and not by force.

Many of the ILO conventions and resolutions deal with basic human rights. The resolutions do not have the force of treaties, but every member is expected to work toward implementing those recommendations. Recommendation No. 162, passed in 1980, applies to all older workers—poor people, hand workers, professional workers, managers, supervisors—everybody. It promotes the idea that government, management, and labor cooperate in seeking solutions to the problems of the older worker. It is noteworthy that the United States seems to be somewhat ahead of much of the rest of the world in this matter. There are several sound reasons for this, among them the political power of seniors in our society. Organizations of the elderly, such as the National Council of Senior Citizens, the AARP, and many other groups, have translated their hopes, needs, and dreams into action programs that speak to the legislatures of the country and to the Congress. Credit must also be given to the leadership of one man, Congressman Claude Pepper, who was one of the foremost spokespersons in behalf of older people.

Age Discrimination

There is still much work to be done to fulfill the needs of our older citizens in the United States and around the world. For instance, we should enact legislation and promote access to vocational and placement services. There are now some programs that not only do not discriminate but in fact are particularly designed for older people. Older people should be able to find employment of their choice in both the public and private sectors—employment that takes account of their skills, experience, and qualifications. Certain age limits may have to be established because of special requisites and conditions for certain types of employment. Even then, however, care must be exercised to avoid any hint of discrimination.

Opportunities should be made available for paid educational leave, especially for the purpose of training, as new technology requires new qualifications. The U.S. Secretary of Labor, Ann McLaughlin, recently noted that in the years to come, workers could be expected to change careers perhaps four or five times in their lifetimes. That means more training, more and better education, and opportunities for promotion. We must not push people out of the work force but must provide the means to keep them employed if they desire to continue working and are able to do so.

Voluntary Retirement

Sometimes voluntary retirement is no more voluntary than the "voluntary restraints" that the Japanese automobile manufacturers imposed upon themselves with respect to exports to the United States. Evidence of this is the fact that a good portion of the approximately 27,000 charges filed each year under the Age Discrimination Act are against "voluntary retirements." Compounding the problem is that, from time to time, people are assigned to enforce policies to which they themselves are hostile. I am advised that the EEOC actually *lost* some 900 or so age discrimination complaints shortly before they were ripe for litigation in the courts. When the chairman of the EEOC was asked by a Congressional committee how such a thing could have happened, he replied, "You cut us back. You don't give us very much money, and computers don't work well if they don't have a lot of money." That certainly tells us something about the kind of attitude some enforcement agencies bring to the job.

It is essential also that the optimism which generally permeates our society must be shared by older people. One's outlook on life and events can often determine whether one can succeed in managing the problems that arise. What do I mean by that? Well, most of us have children. When a child says, "I failed because there is something wrong with me," you try to instill confidence in the child—a sense of optimism, of "can do." Failure may be the result of not trying hard enough or not exercising enough self-discipline, but it can also be caused by external factors beyond our control. It is almost never the result of something genetically or inherently lacking in the child. Everyone needs that spark of optimism, of hope, of self-confidence—older people along with the rest of us.

ILO Research on Older Workers

The ILO, as mentioned earlier, is studying the treatment of older workers in Switzerland, Italy, Japan, the German Democratic Republic, the Netherlands, Spain, Sweden, the Soviet Union, and other countries. Are older workers forced out of the workplace? What policies and procedures exist for continuing education? What plans, programs, laws, and regulations exist for retraining for new jobs? What about outplacement programs? How do such programs manage problems of discrimination? Should there be a national agency that handles age problems exclusively? What role do trade unions and management groups play, as compared with intervention by government?

These are issues of enormous interest and concern. As the demographers' projections concerning the growing proportion of older people become reality, we will have to find ways to utilize their talents effectively. The ILO study, which will be completed in about three years, will probably culminate in a major international conference followed by a publication for broad distribution. In the meantime, we already know, in general terms, what is the right thing to do.

Joe Glazer sang the coal miner's plaint in his "Once a Man, Twice a Boy." I have a picture of breaker boys outside a coal mine. They ranged from six years to nine years old. They worked outside the mine; when the coal came up from inside the earth, they would break the coal away from the slag with hammers, for which they were paid a pittance. When they got big enough they were sent down into the mines. After years in the mines, they contracted emphysema and black lung disease; then they became breaker boys again. That was their Social Security; that was their pension; that was the way society treated them.

We don't have breaker boys anymore. Instead, there are some very ingenious plans in place. For example, at Xerox, the Amalgamated Clothing and Textile Workers Union and management have a unique agreement. When a worker can no longer perform a high-paid and demanding job but could perform a lesser job, that person can be assigned to the lesser job on his or her own motion. The worker is then paid 50 percent of the lower salary plus 50 percent of the higher salary. There is a myriad of similar, thoughtful responses to the problems posed by the aging work force, for people of understanding and goodwill are finding answers. Today and in the years ahead, a society which prides itself on the advancement of human rights and social justice has the opportunity to assure that its older workers' interests are protected.

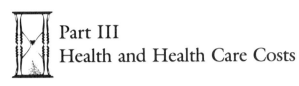

Part III
Health and Health Care Costs

Needed: More, Not Less, Government Intervention

IRVING BLUESTONE

The escalation in private pension and health care costs as the work force grows older points to the need for more, not less, government involvement in assuring an adequate benefit structure and continuity of coverage for the entire population. Historically, the business community has generally opposed such intervention. Cost pressures, however, are increasingly burdensome. There are now signs that management is rethinking its opposition to programs such as national health insurance and accepting the notion that more comprehensive national policies are necessary.

I. B.

The quality of any society may well be measured by how it treats its children and its older citizens. By that standard, the promise that is the United States, the most powerful nation in the world, remains unfulfilled.

Needed: A Child Welfare Policy

Our infant mortality rate is among the highest of the world's industrialized countries.[1] Recent studies indicate that one out of every

1. The Children's Defense Fund issued a report on February 2, 1987, on the subject of infant mortality, based on U.S. 1984 government figures, the latest then available. The report found that the infant mortality rate in the United States was one of the highest in the industrialized world, at 10.8 infant deaths per 1,000 live births. The lowest infant mortality rates are found in Japan, Iceland, and Finland, with 6 deaths for every 1,000 live births. The incidence of infant deaths has risen since 1950, when the United States reported one of the lowest such rates among the industrialized countries. The Children's Defense Fund report attributed the high rate in the United States

five children aged 6 lives below the official U.S. poverty line,[2] while at the same time the major national program aimed at assisting the young—Aid to Families with Dependent Children—has been cut back and AFDC payments have been eroded by inflation. The U.S. Department of Education finds that our educational system is faltering and that our schools suffer a frightening dropout rate among teenagers.[3] Illiteracy and functional illiteracy remain high, and the unemployment rate among our young people continues in the double-digit figures.[4] As the number of two-career families proliferates, child care programs fall far short in terms of filling the need and providing quality care, thereby depriving hundreds of thousands of children of the day care they need for stimulation and growth.

Indeed, our nation lags in its concern and care for its children and thereby for the future social and economical health of the nation.

Needed: A Policy for Older Workers

As for its older citizens, the needs and problems are obviously different, but any impartial assessment of national policy (or lack of it) reinforces the conclusion that, here too, the United States is failing, es-

---

to cuts in federal programs, including Medicaid and AFDC, which have left poor families without access to adequate prenatal and postnatal care. A UNICEF study on the same subject for the year 1985 found 11 infant deaths per 1,000 live births, and among the black population 19 deaths per 1,000 live births. Again the United States stood at the lower end of the ladder among industrialized nations.

2. The U.S. Bureau of the Census, in a report issued in March 1987, noted that, in 1986, 22.1 percent of American children below the age of 6 lived below the poverty line. Altogether, 4,796,000 children, or 1 out of every 5 in the total population below the age of 6, were in the poverty category.

3. In May 1988 the U.S. Department of Education issued a report titled "American Education: Making It Work," a follow-up to the report entitled "A Nation at Risk," published five years earlier. Secretary of Education William Bennett, in reporting on the latter study, declared: "We are doing better [but] we are still at risk." SAT scores among high school graduates had not improved over the previous three years, and the national high school dropout rate continued to average at least 25 percent. In some cities (Chicago, for instance) the dropout rate borders on or exceeds 50 percent.

4. In May 1988 the U.S. Department of Labor Bureau of Labor Statistics reported that for the previous month the unemployment rate for youth aged 16 to 19 was 19.2 percent. Its summary report for the unemployment rate of that age group indicated that it had risen to 18.3 percent for 1986 from 17.8 percent for 1980. Similar figures for the age group 20 to 24 were 10.1 percent for April 1987, down from 11.5 percent for the year 1980.

pecially as compared with the programs of other countries.[5] Our current failings will loom even larger in the years ahead, as the proportion of the elderly in the total population increases. The most recent statistics confirming that ours is rapidly becoming an aged society prompted the U.S. Census Bureau to caution that "rapidly expanding numbers of older people represent a social phenomenon without historical precedent [that] has various economic implications for individuals, families and public policy makers."[6] The aging of our society has major implications for business and for labor as well. The fact that U.S. social policy is woefully weak compared with its global economic competitors highlights the significance of the demographic changes in the population, and particularly in the "active work force," as they affect private sector responsibilities and decisions.

In July 1987, the Bureau of National Affairs, Inc., issued a special report entitled "Older Americans in the Workforce: Challenges and Solutions," which noted the country's lack of preparation for the new situation:

> The United States seems unprepared to deal with the complex challenges presented by the unprecedented influx of older Americans into the workforce in the coming decades. While some corporations and governments have initiated "activist" approaches toward older workers, in general, no coherent, coordinated public or private policies have been developed in response to this projected domination of the workforce by older workers.[7]

The headlines and titles of research reports one sees nowadays underscore the variety of challenges posed by the phenomenon of the aging work force: "Forced Retirement, Age Bias—Problems for Older Workers"; "Managing a Changing Workforce"; "Older Americans—The Challenge to Business and Labor"; "An Older Workforce Burdens Big Producers in Basic Industries"; "Work Ability of the Aged"; "The Economic Marginalization of Older Workers"; "Aging, Job Satisfaction and Productivity: A Problem for Tomorrow"; "Firms Stunned by Retiree Health Costs"; "Sick Retirees Could Kill Your Company"; "Labor Market Problems for Older Workers"; "Management Hotline: Age Discrimination in Employment"; "Private and Public Responses to the Employment Problems of Older Workers"; and "Pension Costs Rising Sharply."

The papers in this volume describe a broad and multifaceted range of social and economic policy issues that an aging work force and

5. For policies regarding the elderly in Sweden, Denmark, and Finland compared with the United States, see Tad Szulc, "How We Can Help Ourselves Age with Dignity," *Parade Magazine,* May 29, 1988, pp. 4–7.
6. Quoted in ibid., p. 6.
7. Bureau of National Affairs, Daily Labor Report, July 9, 1987, p. c-1.

an aging population present for both government and the private sector. The subject matter ranges through an array of concerns which bear, among others, upon national policy toward older workers, business decisions, employer-employee relations, collective bargaining, individual choice, pre-retirement planning, post-retirement activities, re-entry into the active work force, community activities, and the general problem of discrimination against the elderly.

The most burdensome economic issues for business and unions alike are health care costs, pension plan costs, training and retraining, and eldercare. Some contributors to this volume discuss the escalation in health care costs (older people require more medical care), the fast-dropping ratio of active to retired employees, and the special training programs required to adapt the work force to changing technology. The need to address the subject of eldercare (home care/nursing home care, hospice care) has become more and more apparent. The questions are complex, the possible answers highly controversial, and the costs steep. Yet if our nation is to continue to meet its social and moral obligations and to prosper, satisfactory solutions must be found.

Needed: A National Health and Pension Policy

None of the business costs of labor is rising more rapidly than the cost of health care protection. Health care cost containment has become one of the foremost concerns of both management and labor. Health care coverage for retirees and their families at Ford Motor Co., for instance, cost $160 million in 1984. The projection is that those costs will escalate to $300 million by 1990, an increase of 87 percent in the comparatively short period of six years.[8] Among industries across the nation, cost increases of this magnitude are no longer unusual or surprising. They constitute a particularly urgent problem.

Similarly, the pension labor cost per active, productive employee is escalating. In part, this is attributable to the effort to raise pension benefits in order to sustain a decent living standard. In large measure, however, and particularly in cases in which the work force has been curtailed, these escalating costs result from a sharp drop in the ratio of active to retired employees. Thus, at Chrysler, the ratio of active to retired employees, 2.6:1 in 1977, is projected at 0.9:1 for the year 2015.[9] In the steel industry the ratios are, in some cases, even more

8. For these figures see the comments of Ernest Savoie in this volume.
9. Report by Coalition: Health Policy Agenda, quoted in *New York Times*, June 28, 1988.

startling. Companies have even declared bankruptcy in part as a means to get out from under the pension cost obligation (the case of LTV Corporation is a recent example). Obviously, however, long-service employees will continue to demand early retirement despite these constraints.

For all those considering retirement, comprehensive pre-retirement planning programs for the prospective retiree and spouse are a valuable benefit, and many such programs are already in effect, some of which are jointly designed and implemented by management and union representatives.

As unions bargain for employment security provisions (a major issue, particularly in companies undergoing retrenchment), special training programs must be devised and paid for to ensure the continual utilization of older employees. Early retirement inducements, reflecting management's wish to avoid retention and retraining of older employees, are obviously an expensive enterprise. They may become even less attractive as the proportion of young people in the work force as a whole declines and the need to utilize fully the capabilities, knowledge, and experience of older active employees increases. Reemployment of the already retired will, in all likelihood, become a common practice.

The disparities in the treatment of older employees across the nation as a whole exacerbate the problem of the disparate distribution of financial burden and responsibility among the various companies and industries. At the same time, the failure to adopt adequate national policies means that vast inequities in income and health care protection will persist both in the work force and among citizens in general.

THE FACTOR OF FOREIGN INVESTMENT

Foreign investment in the manufacturing and service sectors of the United States is a source of newly created jobs. At the same time, it adds to the competitive challenge faced by well-established U.S. firms. The newly organized greensite firms start out with a younger work force, and, even if they provide health care protection and a pension plan, their medical costs are lower because of the lower age of the work force, and there are no past-service pension liabilities to pay for. Even when wages and salaries are equal and the rate of productivity is essentially the same, the substantially lower obligations in health care and pensions (plus, of course, other benefits such as vacation pay, life insurance, etc.) provide these new firms a competitive advantage in labor cost, to say nothing of other advantages, such as newer, more efficient facilities and world-class technology.

Needed: A National Health Care Program

Consider, then, the factors which compel us to re-evaluate current national policy on the subjects of retirement income and health care protection. In recent years, approximately 1 million people join the rolls of the medically uninsured each year. In 1988, 37 million Americans had no health care insurance protection of any kind, while health care costs rose at a rate considerably faster than the national rate of inflation. At the same time, 30 to 40 million more people paid for health care protection that was inadequate.[10] Moreover, it is estimated that of those with no coverage, about 70 percent are employed fulltime or are dependents of persons employed fulltime.

Social Security coverage, while improved and with a measure of protection against inflation, still falls considerably short of assuring a decent standard of living. The minimum monthly Social Security benefit is $377, or $4,524 a year. By current standards, that amount falls below the poverty level. Auto workers are believed to enjoy a higher than national average hourly wage, yet the average monthly Social Security benefit for a 65-year-old auto assembler retiring in 1988 is $813, or $9,756 per year—somewhat above the poverty level for a married couple. Supplemental private pensions are far from universal, and, where they are provided, benefits and cost vary widely, depending upon corporate policy and/or collective bargaining contracts.

Health care protection—and giving Medicare and Medicaid their due—is at best a hodgepodge, even for those who have health care insurance. It is essentially a non-system, especially for the 37 million without any protection at all. Costs and ranges of benefits for the privately insured, whether through employer programs or individual payment plans, vary by program, by community, and by insurance carrier. The financial burden borne by employers varies from firm to firm and industry to industry, ranging from zero, where no health insurance is offered, to full cost of comprehensive programs. The burden to the employer has little or no connection with the competence of management, which, after all, is one of the fundamental requirements for business success or failure. For the individual who is unemployed, looking for work has become as much a search for health insurance protection as for a job, for if no health insurance is offered, the out-of-pocket expense may be too great to bear even if fully employed.

THE FREE MARKET AS SOCIAL POLICYMAKER

The so-called free market cannot be relied upon to define who (apart from Medicare recipients) will receive health care protection. In

10. See the comments of Anthony P. St. John in this volume.

fact, as Professor Rashi Fein of the Department of Social Medicine and Health Policy at the Harvard University Medical School has noted:

> The market is not designed to worry about fairness. Producers of health care and insurance companies are not in the business of producing equity. Competition, based on efficiency, is one thing, but in the health care field most of the competition designed to offer lower cost health insurance would be around risk selection—around excluding those who are sick and those who are older and those who are poorer from coverage.[11]

Similarly, while the "free market" has established supplemental income plans for millions of workers when they retire (including early retirement features), it has failed to fill the need of other millions who require something more than Social Security to make ends meet in retirement.

Striking confirmation of the importance of the national health insurance system in the competitive marketplace is evidenced among multinational corporations with facilities in both the United States and Canada. Canada's national health insurance program has proven to be an asset in lowering labor costs in comparison with those in the United States. In the auto industry, it is estimated that health care costs in Canadian auto facilities are approximately one-half of the same company's cost in the United States, a fact attributable, of course, to the lower cost of Canadian health insurance.[12] And coverage and quality of care in Canada are at least equal to the best private insurance coverage in the United States.

Business Attitudes Shift

For decades, the U.S. business community has been opposed to the adoption of national health insurance, ostensibly on the basis of principle; in fact, the National Association of Manufacturers opposed the original passage of both Social Security and Medicare legislation. Recently, however, recognition of the cost savings which could result from a national approach to health care appears to be softening management's hard line, and recent comments by corporate executives indicate that earlier positions on this issue are being re-evaluated. For example, on March 15, 1988, John Butler, general director of employee benefits at General Motors Corporation, stated: "At one time, the unequivocal answer would be 'no' to supporting national health insurance. In terms

11. "Issues in Health and Approaches to Solutions," address to the Women's National Democratic Club, Washington, D.C., May 7, 1984.
12. United Auto Workers and Social Security Department study covering 1984 and 1985.

of our competition I would say that is something we are looking at. I'm not saying we are endorsing it, just thinking about it."[13] In a more direct statement, Walter B. Maher, director of employee benefits at Chrysler Corporation, testified on June 24, 1987, before the U.S. Senate Committee on Labor and Human Resources, expressing Chrysler's support for the principles underlying the Minimum Health Benefits for All Act of 1987. His testimony concluded as follows:

> Chrysler is pleased to appear here today and express our support for what you seek to accomplish through this Bill. We are convinced it represents both good social policy and is equitable for the business community. It may not be perfect legislation; adjustments may be required. However, whatever adjustments one may seek, we share your belief that there is no convincing argument against the need to assure basic access to essential health care to all American workers and their families.[14]

It is increasingly evident that the pressures of change stemming from the age composition of the work force and the population at large must move the nation toward adopting policies to ensure adequate income in retirement and health care protection. National systems of income maintenance for workers entering retirement and of health insurance as a matter of right for the entire population are increasingly a social and moral imperative. They are, moreover, an important factor in creating a level playing field in the economic race among private firms to maintain their viability and, in some cases, perhaps even their existence.

The business community must come to realize that adequate health care and retirement income are national concerns requiring national solutions. It is a certainty that supplemental pensions and coverage for health care, as well as retraining employees for different skills and responsibilities, will continue to be issues for collective bargaining and/or company policy. However, labor, management, and government, working together out of mutual self-interest, can surely develop rational social policy solutions which will advance the welfare of the entire nation and all its people.

13. *Detroit News,* March 16, 1988, p. 1c.

14. U.S. Congress, Senate, Committee on Labor and Human Resources, Public Hearing, June 24, 1987, Minutes.

Health Care Costs for Older Workers and Retirees: Social Needs in a Changing Benefit Structure

JUDITH K. BARR

Barr describes the greater use of both institutional and home care services that has resulted from the increase in chronic conditions and decrease in acute conditions in recent years. Employers have modified their traditional role, introducing flexible benefit packages, alternative delivery options, and cost-sharing measures to limit costs. Similarly, benefit packages have been redesigned to limit costs of retiree health care. Barr cautions that the structure of retiree benefits offered by employers must be viewed within the context of federally financed health care for the aged, which has been altered through a series of federal acts, with no clear policy direction.

R. J. V. M.

The "cost" issues in employer-provided health care benefits and employee health care needs are two-fold: the cost to employers of providing health care for an aging work force and the cost to society of caring for an aging population. Let us begin with a review of changing patterns of disease, disability, and health services utilization among older workers themselves, including employees who care for elderly and chronically ill dependents at home. Next, we will examine the changing nature of the health benefits employees and retirees receive: the increased out-of-pocket costs to employees and the new benefits being offered by employers in response to changing patterns of health care. Finally, we will consider the federal government's role, both in paying for and in constraining the costs of health care for older workers and retirees and the consequences of those federal actions for employer-provided health coverage.

Health Issues in an Aging Work Force

HEALTH CHARACTERISTICS OF OLDER PERSONS

Perhaps the most dramatic statistics we have seen in recent times are those describing the aging of the population. Projections indicate that people over 65 will increase to nearly 15 percent of the population in the year 2000 (Fullerton 1987), while the older working population, those aged 45 to 64, is expected to increase from just under 20 percent in 1980 to 23 percent of the population in the year 2000 (Rice and Feldman 1983). Labor force participation of men in this age segment will decrease by the year 2000; however, women in the same age group are projected to increase their labor force participation (Fullerton 1987).

At the same time that the proportion of older persons is increasing, the health needs of that population are changing also. The major causes of death and disability today are chronic diseases, which most often affect the middle-aged and elderly. Heart disease and other chronic conditions continue to increase, often burdening the families who must provide or arrange for care and the health insurance system that must pay for it.

Using data from the federal government's National Health Interview Survey (which provides annual reports of individuals' perceptions of health and health problems derived from random household interviews, i.e., a "social record" of health), Verbrugge (1984) examined trends in acute and chronic morbidity, restricted activity and bed disability, and long-term limitations as a result of chronic conditions. Evidence shows that the general decline in the incidence of acute conditions from 1958 to 1980 has been accompanied by an increase in activity reduction, suggesting that more days are being spent caring for acute conditions. Chronic conditions show a somewhat different pattern. Morbidity has risen among those aged 45 to 64 years for most chronic conditions which can be fatal, especially cancer, diabetes, heart disease, and hypertension, with accompanying activity limitations but declining mortality rates. Among chronic conditions which are not fatal, increases in respiratory problems, arthritis, and hearing impairments are notable. Most chronic conditions affect more women than men; exceptions are heart disease, digestive diseases, and visual and hearing problems.

Major activity limitations associated with these chronic conditions have increased since 1958 among middle-aged persons, with implications for work force participation. Functional limitations in routine activities—such as difficulties in stooping, crouching or kneeling, standing for long periods, lifting or carrying heavy weights, and using fingers to grasp or handle objects—have increased with age in both men and women, although women have higher work disability rates than men at every age. In an analysis of work disability rates over the decade

1970–1980, Feldman (1983) noted that the percentage unable to work increased with age. This trend was most striking in those with less than 12 years of education. With continued expansion of jobs in the service industries, the proportion of physically demanding jobs and those requiring more education may increase, bringing less opportunity for these workers to remain employed. Further, projections by the National Center for Health Statistics indicate that the proportion of persons with limitations of activities of daily living will increase in the period 1980–2000, especially in the over-75 age group (76 percent), but also to almost 40 percent among those aged 45–64 years (Rice and Feldman 1983). Currently, one out of five elderly persons is estimated to have at least a mild degree of disability.

MANAGING WORKER DISABILITIES

The implications of these findings for restructuring work are interesting to consider. Feldman (1983, p. 439) concluded:

> Some individuals could continue working despite a physical limitation if they could find a job that would permit them to work intermittently, i.e., during periods of remission of their symptoms. Others could work regularly on a part-time basis but not full-time. Still others could work at a physically less demanding job but not at their regular jobs. ... The state of health and the requirements of the job for a majority of workers reaching their mid-sixties would permit them to continue their regular line of work with only minimal, if any, job redesign. It is the sizable minority with a rather wide discrepancy between the demand of their regular jobs and their remaining functional capacity for whom there is a problem.

The rate of disabilities among workers was estimated by the Menninger Foundation at 5 per 1,000 in 1985, representing the number of workers who are so severely disabled that they are unable to work for five months or more; the rate is expected to increase in the future. This report on worker disability (Hester, Decelles, and Hood 1986) points to the need for employer-sponsored return-to-work programs. Increasingly, employers are coming to recognize the importance of disability management in the workplace. They can address the issue of chronic disabling conditions through several strategies: early recognition of physical problems, institution of worksite programs to prevent illness and injury as well as to assist in rehabilitation, encouraging return to work, and adapting jobs and work assignments to employee limitations (New York Business Group on Health 1987). Some companies are viewing disability management programs, such as on-site rehabilitation, as a cost-containment strategy (Schwartz 1986).

Whether the incidence of work disability will grow in the future seems uncertain. On the one hand, declines in mortality from diseases such as diabetes can be expected to be accompanied by an increasing prevalence of disabilities from chronic medical problems (e.g., vision loss and cardiovascular complications). On the other hand, it has been argued that improvements in personal health habits (e.g., declines in obesity, smoking, and drug use) will result in a "compression of infirmity," delaying the onset of disabling conditions. It seems reasonable to expect that health improvements resulting from the increasing adoption of "healthy" life styles and the avoidance of "risk" behaviors will take some time to emerge, and that the more immediate issue for employers and older workers will be the need to consider adapting jobs to the functional limitations of otherwise healthy older workers.

A recent report by the Commonwealth Fund Commission on Elderly People Living Alone (Louis Harris and Associates 1987) found that 17 percent of the elderly had worked at a paying job or business sometime during the past year; the proportion was 26 percent for those in the 65–69 year age group. Another 10 percent would like to be working, probably part-time, and only 18 percent said that they were not able to work. Fuchs (1984) argues that the sharp drops in labor force participation among men aged 65 and over (from 46 percent in 1950 to 19 percent in 1980) and among men aged 55 to 64 (from 83 percent in 1965 to 72 percent in 1980) are not due to declining health. Rather, several factors must be considered: the decline in self-employment, which decreased the number of workers who are able to shift hours or alter working conditions without leaving the job; the growth in the number of elderly at a time when the hierarchical structure of work organizations leaves few openings for upward mobility; and the significant growth in Social Security benefits relative to wages.

One way to accommodate more older workers in the work force might be simply to change the definition of who is old. For example, in 1935 life expectancy at 65 was 12.5 years, while in 1984 the average 72-year-old had that same life expectancy. Mechanic points out that factors which motivate early retirement "could change substantially with altered views of the lifespan, economic pressures and incentives, and new conceptions of what it means to be elderly" (1987, p. 24). Indeed, companies are beginning to recognize the value of experienced workers and to develop programs to recruit and retrain retirees for part-time, temporary, or regular employment.

Changes and Needs in Health Care Utilization

USE OF INSTITUTIONAL HEALTH SERVICES

What changes in the utilization of services can be observed as morbidity and functional health status have changed? The elderly are the heaviest users of health services, accounting for 30 percent of all hospital discharges and one-third of the nation's personal health care expenditures, although today they comprise only 12 percent of the population. However, to understand changes and needs in the health care system, we must look at trends for those under 65 as well. Data on the use of health services by age suggest the relative vulnerability of the older worker. According to results of the National Health Interview Survey, persons aged 45–64 have more than twice the number of hospital discharges per 1,000 population, on the average, as those aged 17–44 (U.S. Department of Health and Human Services 1986). Since 1980, discharges for middle-aged persons have remained stable, while there has been a sharp decrease for the younger age group. Although average length of stay has decreased for all groups over age 17, it is only slightly lower among those aged 45–64 than among those 65 and over.

Among the elderly, per capita expenditures for health services have increased overall from 1965 to 1981, relative to those under 65 (Fuchs 1984). It is interesting that physician expenditures increased more sharply than hospital expenditures. The number of physician visits is projected to increase 73 percent among those aged 75 and older and 37 percent among those aged 45–64, from 1980 to the year 2000 (Rice and Feldman 1983). However, recent analysis of cohort data from the 1972, 1976, and 1980 National Health Interview Survey casts doubt on the explanations of the trends toward increasing utilization of services with increasing age. Wolinsky et al. (1986) found a decrease in the use of physicians' services among the oldest old (age 80 and over). One possible explanation is that family and informal help is being substituted for formal services, with implications for the older worker as new norms of family care-giving emerge (we shall return to this topic shortly). The latest Robert Wood Johnson Foundation survey (1987) found a reversal in the trend toward increased use of services, particularly physician visits, since 1982. For example, one-third of the survey respondents reported no ambulatory visits during the prior twelve months, compared to only 20 percent reporting no visit in 1982; hospitalizations decreased from 9.3 percent to 6.6 percent of the respondents. The results may indicate that access to services is more difficult and that there is a greater need for family care.

With the increasing prevalence of chronic and disabling conditions, the need for long-term care can be expected to increase. Only about 5 percent of the population over 65 are in nursing homes; however, this proportion increases with age: 10 percent of those aged 75 and over and 22 percent of those aged 85 and over are in nursing homes (Wetle and Pearson 1986). Evidence indicates that the functional status of nursing home residents is deteriorating (U.S. Department of Health and Human Services 1986). For example, a recent study of nursing home residents in Georgia found that patients discharged from a hospital after the Medicare prospective payment system went into effect were significantly more likely to have conditions which required constant nursing care than a comparable group of patients discharged prior to this change (Carroll and Erwin 1987). These results suggest that more intensive treatment and greater use of resources will be needed in nursing homes. To accommodate these more seriously ill patients, others in need of home care may be discharged.

HOME CARE

Most of the elderly live in the community: 30 percent live alone, 54 percent live with a spouse, and 16 percent live with others, usually an adult child or other relative (Louis Harris and Associates 1987). In the recent Commonwealth Fund study on the elderly, 12 percent say they have physical limitations and need help routinely to do usual activities such as meal preparation; one-fourth of those living alone mention receiving help from formal programs in the community (Louis Harris and Associates 1987). The need for home care services is well documented (National Association for Home Care 1985). Overall, the number of home health agencies has more than doubled since 1977, to more than 5,000 in 1984. This growth has been most striking among proprietary agencies, which have increased to 1,569, or 30 percent of the total number of home health agencies (Balinsky 1985). In New York City, the certified capacity of long-term home health care programs increased over 700 percent from 1980 to 1985, and the unduplicated patient count increased by about the same proportion; home health visits increased from 1.3 million in 1980 to over 2 million in 1984 (Bell 1987).

Along with this growth, the home health care industry is facing issues of regulation, standardization of training, quality of care, and reimbursement, as well as increasing needs in the community. Recent national home care demonstration projects sponsored by the Health Care Financing Administration have shown that formal services do not substitute for care provided by family and friends (Kemper, Applebaum, and Harrigan 1987). Rather, community services, such as home health aides, complement the informal care-giving, improving the quality of life and satisfaction for both the elderly person and the care-giver. Indeed, there is evidence that entry into the formal system of in-home nursing and aide services is more likely to occur in situations of care-giver stress: activity restrictions, deterioration of the health of the elderly person, and overburdening of the care-giver (Bass and Noelker 1987).

The combination of forces resulting in more persons in the community in need of care include the more recent impetus of prospective hospital payment for reducing hospital length of stay, as well as the growing adoption of managed care strategies to reduce admissions, decrease length of stay, and substitute ambulatory services for in-patient care. The employer's role in managed care will be reviewed below, but first it is useful to focus on the needs of employees responsible for the care of chronically or critically ill dependents.

The Needs of Employee Care-Givers The elderly rely heavily on informal support and care-giving from spouses, children, and other relatives and friends. In 1984, relatives provided approximately 84 percent of all community care to disabled elderly men. The Commonwealth Fund study found that over 40 percent of the elderly who need help and care receive assistance from their children (Louis Harris and Associates 1987). A national study of informal care-givers for the disabled elderly (Stone, Cafferata, and Sangl 1987) describes their characteristics: their average age is 57 years; they are predominantly female (72 percent); 29 percent are daughters; and they are usually the primary care-givers (70 percent).

Of importance to this discussion is the employment status of these care-givers: 31 percent were employed, including 44 percent of the daughters, but about 9 percent had left the work force in order to care for the disabled elderly person. These data are consistent with other reports of the care-giver experience. For example, one report indicates that 28 percent of nonworking women had left their jobs to care for their elderly and ill mothers; others had cut back work schedules and were considering quitting (Brody and Schoonover 1986). Similar observations were made among care-givers of brain-damaged adults, with 22 percent of the unemployed having quit work to give care fulltime. More dramatically, nearly half of the adult daughters who had worked quit to become care-givers (Petty and Friss 1987); and 55 percent of those working part-time had reduced their work hours to accommodate care-giving demands.

A Travelers Corporation (1985) study found that 28 percent of the employees surveyed had some care-giving responsibilities for elderly parents or friends; over half of these employee care-givers were between the ages of 41 and 55, and 18 percent had had no vacation for two years. Workers who have care-giving responsibilities for elderly and ill relatives rearrange time, take time from their own families, and place stress on their other role obligations. It appears, however, that they do not skimp on care-giving. Brody and Schoonover (1986) found no significant differences in the amounts of help given by working and non-working daughters to their elderly mothers (about ten hours per week); the working women did spend somewhat fewer hours in personal care and meal preparation, the only task difference noted. The employed care-givers for brain-damaged adults averaged 34 hours at work each week and another 35 hours caring for the disabled family member (Petty and Friss 1987).

The results of such heavy duties are stress and strain. A care-giver's assistance program in Buffalo reported that two-thirds of those who come for counselling services are working women no longer able to balance competing demands of care-giving and employment (Nowak 1986). The pressures of balancing work and care-giving responsibilities may be particularly acute for those workers close to retirement age themselves, who may risk retiree benefits if they leave their jobs at this point, adding economic stress to an already difficult family situation. The average age of employed care-givers of brain-damaged adults was 52 years, and over half were employed as professionals or managers (Petty and Friss 1987). While work provided an "outlet" for some, there were also negative consequences: they missed over a day a month from work, and they sometimes worked more slowly due to care-giving concerns.

In the national study (Stone, Cafferata, and Sangl 1987), employed care-givers of the elderly experienced conflicts between work obligations and care-giving duties (20 percent), resulting in changed work schedules (29 percent), fewer work hours (20 percent), and time off without pay (19 percent). Other burdens included time constraints (34 percent), conflicting expectations about the dependent person's behavior (22 percent), limitations on their own social activity (22 percent), and negative effects on their well-being (13 percent) (Cafferata and Stone forthcoming).

Helping Employee Care-Givers These strains have been felt in the workplace. In the first study of employers' perceptions of the care-giving issue, the New York Business Group on Health found, in a small sample study, that about one-half of the employers were aware of employee care-giver problems (Warshaw et al. 1986). The major problems were the need for time, as evidenced by lateness, absenteeism, and the use of unscheduled days off, mentioned by two-thirds to three-fourths of the responding companies. Even on the job, these employees needed time to telephone home or to call medical and social service agencies; two-thirds of the companies reported excessive use of the telephone. In addition, decreased productivity or quality of work performance was reported by nearly half the companies. In another study of care-givers employed in five firms, 40 percent had been employed by the same company for over ten years, suggesting that it may be costly to replace loyal and experienced workers (American Association of Retired Persons 1986).

It appears that these pressures will mount for both care-givers and the workplace and that employers must assist in order to retain these experienced workers. Recently a number of companies have undertaken programs designed to meet at least some of these needs.[1] Such programs may be off-site, such as the recently implemented IBM Elder Care Referral Service, designed to provide information and referral to community health resources for employees who are caring for an elderly parent, spouse, or relative. Two large corporations in New York, the American Express Company and the Phillip Morris Company, have contracted with the New York City Department for the Aging to provide an information and referral service for employees, with a special telephone number to call with questions and to get help in arranging needed services.

On-site programs such as lunchtime seminars on aging and the health needs of the elderly have been implemented by the Travelers Company, among others. Pepsico commissioned a 67-page eldercare resource guide for employees to provide information on the normal aging process, physical and mental health, and sources of information about programs and services. The New York Business Group on Health sponsored a training session for counseling and human resources personnel in business and industry to help them recognize care-giver problems in the workplace, provide information on community resources, and conduct care-giver support groups. Another type of help from the employer focuses on respite care, aimed at giving the care-giver some relief from daily duties, either by providing funds or by supporting community respite programs. Various ways of using the employee benefit structure to assist care-givers will be discussed below as employer-sponsored health benefits are considered.

Health Insurance at Work: Shifting Choices and Costs

THE ROLE OF THE EMPLOYER

A recent national survey places total medical costs per employee at over $1,900 (Foster Higgins 1987).[2] In general, average cost rises as

1. The New York Business Group on Health is planning an evaluation of various care-giver programs to determine which program or program components are most appropriate for a company of a given size and work force composition.
2. Much of the information reported comes from two major national surveys. The Bureau of Labor Statistics of the U.S. Department of Labor conducts periodic surveys of employee benefits in medium-sized and large firms in eight industry categories. The 1986 survey (published in 1987), the eighth in the series, presents data for 21.3 million fulltime employees in a cross-section of

the number of employees increases. Among employers with half or more of the work force under union agreements, costs averaged over $2,300, indicating the importance of health benefits in employee compensation packages (Foster Higgins 1987). An average of 9.7 percent of payroll goes for the employer share of the health benefits program (medical, dental, vision, prescription drug, and hearing benefits).

The employer has traditionally been the "enabler" for health care, making health benefits coverage available for employees, which enables workers to purchase health services and thereby enhances their access to care. Most of this coverage has been for hospital care through basic benefits and/or major medical benefits in a service or indemnity package. The enabler role is being modified in at least two ways: more employers are promoting individualized selection of benefits by employees, and more are requiring increased cost-sharing by employees.

SHIFTING CHOICES

Flexible benefits allow employees to choose the types and levels of benefits most suitable to their own needs and family circumstances (Employee Benefit Research Institute 1987). Surveys (Foster Higgins 1987; Business Roundtable 1987) indicate that 15 to 20 percent of employers offer a choice of benefit levels, including substitution of nontaxable benefits or reimbursement accounts from which employees may select that combination of benefits which best meets their needs. However, a Bureau of Labor Statistics survey found that only 8 to 9 percent of white-collar workers and 2 percent of blue-collar workers have a choice among two or more types of benefits (U.S. Department of Labor 1987). Flexible benefits allow older workers to select greater coverage for themselves, including long-term or dependent care benefits for a dis-

1,503 firms, ranging in size from 50 employees to over 10,000. The Foster Higgins Health Care Benefits Survey for 1987 reports data from 2,016 employers from 50 states in 15 industry categories and covers over 13 million individuals; 39 percent of the responding companies have under 500 employees, and 12 percent have 10,000 or more. These two sources appear to be the most comprehensive in terms of information about health benefits, the most representative in terms of respondents, and the most enlightening in terms of differentiating employer characteristics relating to health benefit coverage. The Labor Department survey compares different types of workers: professional/administrative, technical/clerical, and production; data are reported on percentage of employees in a random sample of companies across the nation. The Foster Higgins study compares companies by geographic region, size of firm (number of employees), and industry; it may be the only national survey of companies which systematically reports data by these company characteristics. Though not random, the sample of companies is broader than other corporate surveys.

abled spouse, child, or parent. Of approximately 2,000 companies in the Foster Higgins survey, only 15 percent offered flexible benefit plans. Although two-thirds of those with flexible benefits offered dependent care expense accounts, enrollment in these accounts averaged only 6 percent. In a recent survey by the Washington Business Group on Health (Levin and Frobom 1987), in less than 20 percent of the 147 companies surveyed were flexible benefits or spending accounts being used by employees to pay expenses of elderly dependents.

The provision of benefits directed to specific health problems and medical needs of the older worker is not uniform. For example, according to the Employee Benefit Research Institute (1987), vision care coverage is available to only a small proportion of the working population; a Johnson and Higgins survey (1986) found that only 16 percent of companies offered vision care benefits. However, the U.S. Department of Labor survey for 1986 reported that 40 percent of employees were covered for vision care expenses, an increase from 19 percent in 1979 to 35 percent in 1985 (the greatest gains were in plans for blue-collar workers). Hearing care was covered for 20 percent of the employees. Prescription drug coverage is often included in major medical benefits packages, although separate prescription plans are also used; over 25 percent of the companies in the Johnson and Higgins survey offered a discount drug program. Dental coverage was provided by 70 percent of the firms, and about 70 percent of employees participated in plans which included dental expenses (U.S. Department of Labor 1987). In 1986, about two-thirds of surveyed employees were covered for drug abuse treatment and 70 percent were covered for alcoholism treatment; 87 percent of employers offered coverage for care at drug and alcohol rehabilitation centers, and 39 percent provided employee assistance programs (Johnson and Higgins 1986).

In recent years, employers have offered alternative delivery options which tend to include more comprehensive benefits. For example, health maintenance organizations (HMOs) typically include vision and hearing care, prescription drugs, out-patient mental health care, and other services. A large majority of companies (62 percent) offer HMO coverage, with a 29 percent average participation rate among employees (Foster Higgins 1987). Another option is the preferred provider organization (PPO), in which selected providers agree to accept lower reimbursement for covered services; employees selecting this option are given incentives for using the preferred providers. Often, a PPO is developed to provide specific services, such as alcoholism treatment. In the Foster Higgins survey, 21 percent of employers contract with a PPO, nearly all with hospitals (91 percent) and/or physicians (85 percent). HMOs and PPOs may be particularly attractive to older workers because of the comprehensive coverage, prepayment rather than reimbursement of expenses, centralization of medical records, ease of access, and built-in quality review mechanisms.

Alternative care coverage, also important to older workers, is becoming more widespread. About two-thirds of all employees in medium-sized and large firms participate in health plans which cover home health care, and over 30 percent are covered for hospice care (U.S. Department of Labor 1987). According to the latest company survey, 87 percent offer home care and 73 percent offer hospice care. More emphasis is also being placed on prevention, with periodic voluntary physical examinations covered by 41 percent of the companies for some or all employees. Reports indicate that 20 to 45 percent of companies surveyed offered wellness, fitness, or health promotion programs in the workplace, such as alcohol and drug abuse counseling, stress management or hypertension screening, smoking cessation, exercise classes, and weight loss and nutrition education (Kittrell 1984; Johnson and Higgins 1986). These programs can be important to older workers in helping them adopt and practice health behaviors and to maintain their health as they age.

Companies are just beginning to address the need for long-term medical and nursing home care, and a small percentage (9 percent) are considering offering such insurance through their flexible benefit program (Foster Higgins 1987). The gap in long-term care coverage is discussed below in relation to retiree health benefits.

SHIFTING COSTS

At the same time that the benefit structure is changing, employers are attempting to influence employee utilization of services through cost-sharing for health care expenditures in the form of increased employee contributions to plan premiums, deductibles, and copayments. In 1986, 54 percent of employees made no contribution to premiums; just a year earlier that figure was 61 percent (U.S. Department of Labor 1987). In the Foster Higgins survey, 61 percent of companies required no employee contributions to premiums. Free coverage is offered most frequently by government employers, those with more than half the work force unionized, and companies with fewer than 500 employees. However, for dependent care coverage, contributions to premiums are required by over two-thirds of the companies.

It is more and more common for employees with basic hospital coverage, as well as those with major medical plans, to pay a deductible and coinsurance (Jensen, Morrisey, and Marcus 1987). Self-insured plans more often require employee cost-sharing than do traditional insurers. The assumption is that employees use fewer and less costly services if faced with more out-of-pocket expenses (Herzlinger and Schwartz 1985; Manning et al. 1984). Today, most employers (81 percent) include an employee deductible in their health benefit plans (Foster Higgins 1987). For half the companies, the amount is between $100 and $150, but 40 percent have higher deductibles. Further, a majority (55 percent) have increased the amount of the deductible in the past few years. The same trend was reported in the Labor Department's most recent survey; the percentage of employees paying deductibles of $150 or more increased to 35 percent in 1986 from 19 percent in 1983. Nearly all employees in major medical plans were also required to pay coinsurance for hospital in-patient services, although most (83 percent) set an out-of-pocket maximum, usually between $500 and $1,500 for individuals.

These costs form the context in which older workers must pay for health services. As their health care needs and utilization increase, they can expect to have more out-of-pocket expenses.

CONTROLLING UTILIZATION

The trend in employee health benefits toward managed care includes the imposition of reviews and sanctions to control utilization and enhance quality. While HMOs and PPOs focus on specific providers in their panels, other strategies being used by insurers and employers focus on specific interventions at the point of utilization. Perhaps the most widely used are second surgical opinion programs, preadmission testing, and incentives for ambulatory surgery (Barr 1986). Hospital preadmission certification was required by nearly two-thirds of the companies surveyed by Foster Higgins. Older workers for whom cataract removal or total hip replacement is recommended, for example, are likely to be required to obtain a second opinion prior to surgery or face penalties in the form of reduced benefits for hospitalization and physician costs. More companies are adding mandatory second surgical opinion programs each year. Of particular assistance for older workers and retirees are programs for individual case management of complex cases. This intervention puts a professional nurse or social worker in charge of the case to assess needs for services, find the most appropriate ones, and help individuals and families make necessary adjustments to illness and disability. The intended effect is to improve access and quality and reduce costs. Half of the companies in the Foster Higgins survey have plans which provide case management for catastrophic illness.

Health Insurance for Retirees

COVERAGE AND COSTS

Perhaps one of the major issues facing employers and workers in the 1990s is the provision of health care benefits for retirees. Data from 2,000 employers indicate that 12 percent of total health plan costs represents the costs for retirees; these costs are over 15 percent in firms with more than 10,000 employees (Foster Higgins 1987). Retiree health costs amount to as much as 2 to 3 percent of payroll or even higher (Mercer-Meidinger 1985). Further, they are likely to increase even more than health costs for active employees because the number of retirees is growing: according to a recent report, approximately seven million retirees and their dependents are covered by employer-sponsored health plans, and current benefit packages allow some 25 million workers to expect post-retirement health coverage (Chandler 1987). Estimates cited in another report suggest that, by 1996, corporate health care benefits will be provided to one retiree for every two active employees (Liebtag 1987).

While 75 percent of the employees in the Department of Labor survey were in health plans which extended coverage into retirement, 64 percent of the employers in the Foster Higgins 1987 survey offered health benefits for retirees under age 65, and 57 percent covered retirees over 65. Coverage for retirees was considerably more prevalent as the size of firm increased; just over one-third of companies with under 500 employees offered retiree health benefits, compared to 75 percent or more of those with over 1,000 employees. Another report confirms the extent of retiree health coverage by size of firm but indicates that, even among small companies with 50 to 99 employees, 42 percent provide these benefits (Dopkeen 1987). Generally, retiree benefits are the same as those of active employees (U.S. Department of Labor 1987), and most companies adjust retiree benefits as the active employees' program is changed. Coverage is slightly less prevalent for retirees over age 65 than for younger retirees; production workers and those in the health services industry are less likely than others to have retiree benefits regardless of age (U.S. Department of Labor 1987; Foster Higgins 1987).

It should be noted that eligibility for retiree health benefits is limited to employees who retire from a firm and are vested in its retirement plan (with the exception of a few larger multi-employer plans); those who leave prior to retirement do not receive the health coverage in retirement even if they qualify for pension benefits (Dopkeen 1987).

Post-retirement medical plans may be structured in different ways: as reimbursement plans, Medicare supplement plans, or cash plans (Rappaport and Kalman 1987). Most retiree health benefits are provided in a reimbursement plan which pays for specified medical services (including HMOs); it may require deductibles and coinsurance to be paid by the employee and may include cost management mechanisms such as preadmission certification. These plans coordinate with Medicare, for eligible retirees, to cover expenses not paid by Medicare. The Medicare supplement plans pay for gaps in Medicare coverage and may even specify fixed dollar amounts. Although deductibles and copayments, out-patient prescription drugs, and private duty nursing are covered, benefits are generally less comprehensive than in the reimbursement plans. Cash plans specify a predetermined amount for payment of medical expenses or medical insurance premiums. In these plans, the risk to the employee can increase because there is no way to guard against future inflation of medical care prices. The retiree can purchase insurance, shifting this risk to the insurer, but continuation of coverage would not be guaranteed.

SHIFTING THE RISK TO RETIREES

The high cost of retiree benefits has spawned a number of attempts to redesign them so as to limit costs—for example, requiring or extending minimum length of service for eligibility for benefits, putting a dollar limit on employer payments, or increasing cost-sharing. Already, only half the employees in the Labor Department survey for 1986 have the cost of retiree health benefits paid in full by the employer, and, according to the Foster Higgins survey, 63 percent of the companies require premium contributions from retirees under 65, and 53 percent require contributions from those over 65. Further, in about 40 percent of employer plans which require contributions, the retiree must pay the full cost of the premium. The health services industry is least generous in paying in full for retiree benefits, with only 20 to 30 percent of employers paying in full for retiree coverage for both those under and those over 65 years of age (Foster Higgins 1987). The cost burden for retirees can be expected to increase. In one survey of large companies (Mercer-Meidinger 1985), nearly two-thirds of the 886 responding CEOs would consider requiring retirees to pay more for their coverage. In another survey of 312 major companies (Liebtag 1987), nearly all stated their intention to modify retiree benefits in ways that will affect future retirees rather than those currently retired.

Reports of legal cases against companies that change their retiree health care plans, whether due to bankruptcy or other reasons, indicate the uncertainty facing employers (Greenwald 1986; Mercer-Meidinger 1985). One employer, trying to cut costs by cutting the retiree programs which had been collectively bargained with the United Steelworkers Union, was permanently enjoined by the court from failing to provide established retiree coverage, although the company offered a new employer-sponsored plan in exchange (Employee Benefit Plan Review 1987). Congress is reportedly developing legislation to deal with the issue of retiree benefits in companies which are failing or trying to reorganize (Liebtag 1987). As it is now, when companies have attempted to modify, reduce, or eliminate retiree medical plans, subsequent court rulings on challenges to such actions have generally been in favor of the retirees: the courts' view seems to be that the "status" of retirement is, in itself, indication of the employer's intention and promise to provide health benefits and to do so unchanged from what they were at the time of retirement.

The Federal Role in Health Care Financing

MEDICARE AND MANDATED BENEFITS

The structure of retiree benefits offered by employers must be viewed within the context of federally financed health care for those aged 65 and over and federal requirements.

Expenditures for Medicare, the federal health insurance program for the elderly and disabled, totaled over $70 billion in 1985, according to the Health Care Financing Administration (Waldo, Levit, and Lazenby 1986). While 41 percent of total spending for health care in 1985 came from the government, only 17 percent came from Medicare. In comparison, private health insurance paid for 31 percent and 25 percent was paid directly. Federal programs and legislation are attempting to shift more of the costs to individuals and the private sector. Beneficiaries are being required to pay larger amounts out of pocket in the form of deductibles and noncovered expenses. Retirees under age 65 are not eligible for Medicare, yet they are more likely to be required to pay a contribution to premium than retirees over age 65 (Liebtag 1987; Foster Higgins 1987).

In addition to the pressure exerted on employers by the growing number of retirees and the costs of retiree benefits, recent legislation has increased the employer burden in relation to Medicare. The Tax Equity and Fiscal Responsibility Act of 1982 and the Deficit Reduction Tax Act of 1984 (DEFRA) made Medicare the secondary payer to employer plans for Medicare-eligible employed workers and their dependents. This means that the employer-sponsored health plan continues in force for active workers and their spouses between the ages of 65 and 70. COBRA, the Consolidated Omnibus Budget Reconciliation Act of 1985, eliminated the age 70 cutoff, extending this provision regardless of age. COBRA also contains provisions for the continuation of employer-provided health coverage for an employee and dependents for up to 18 months after an employee has been terminated, retired, or otherwise left the work force (except for gross misconduct). Although COBRA requirements for continuation of coverage are not as liberal as some existing practices, the new law does require coverage in situations not usually included, such as coverage to a terminated employee or to the dependents of a deceased employee (Rappaport and Kalman 1987). Further, in 1986, new nondiscrimination rules on retiree medical coverage were imposed (DEFRA and the Tax Reform Act of 1986) which require comparison of benefit levels between higher- and lower-paid workers.

These requirements are likely to affect the design and provision of retiree benefits. One concern is that these mandated benefits and liability for Medicare-eligible employees may disproportionately affect different employers. For example, small firms are reported to have three times as many Medicare-eligible employees as larger companies, yet they are least able to pay for health care benefits, especially mandated benefits (Rasmussen 1987). Employers in cyclical or depressed industries also would find it difficult to comply with these requirements. Further, self-insured plans are currently exempt from the mandated provisions; this means that many of the large companies that represent over half of all employee health coverage (McDonnell et al. 1986) are not required to provide the benefits mandated nor to deal with attendant costs.[3] An analysis of the effects of the 1982 legislation on the employment of older people found that Medicare payment changes may reduce employer demand for workers aged 65 through 69 by only about 1 percent, a small effect which is likely to be less important than other considerations regarding older workers (Anderson, Kennell, and Shiels 1987).

A major issue in the public/private mix of funding for health services is the lack of coverage for long-term care. Many active employees and retirees mistakenly believe that Medicare will pay for nursing home costs (Equicor 1986); 15 percent of the elderly people living at home believe that Medicare will pay for nursing home or other long-term care (Louis Harris and Associates 1986). A survey by the American Association of Retired Persons (1986) found this belief even more widespread. Nor do employer-based health insurance plans provide for long-term custodial care. Only one company in a recent Washington Business

3. A national survey in 1984 by the Health Care Financing Administration (McDonnell et al. 1986) found that 8 percent of all employment-related health plans are self-insured, and that the larger the plan the most likely it is to be self-insured. The Foster Higgins 1987 survey found that 49 percent of employers self-fund health benefits, predominantly the largest companies; this finding is consistent with other employer surveys.

Group on Health study of 147 large corporations, most of which have self-insured plans, offered such long-term care, although nearly all provided medical coverage for retirees (Levin and Frobom 1987). While many companies offer so-called Medigap coverage to coordinate with costs for care approved but not paid by Medicare, it is estimated that only 1 percent of nursing home costs are paid by private insurance and less than 2 percent are paid by medicare (Schramm 1987). Individuals pay over half of these costs out of pocket, and Medicaid pays for 42 percent (individuals must be impoverished to qualify for Medicaid coverage). More insurers are currently investigating options for financing long-term care, and one suggestion is that employers provide long-term care benefits in an indemnity insurance plan linked to retirement benefits. Regardless of the difficulties to be overcome in designing such benefits, it seems clear that the public must be educated about the limitations of current coverage.

FUNDING RETIREE BENEFITS: GOVERNMENT DISINCENTIVES AND PRESSURE

A growing concern for employers providing health benefits to retirees is how this coverage is to be funded. Generally, retiree benefits are on a pay-as-you-go basis; 80 percent of the employers in the Foster Higgins 1987 survey funded this way, and only 20 percent had determined the extent of their liabilities. According to the Health Benefits Research Institute, unfunded liability for current retirees is $85 billion, and estimates of liability for employer-obligated retiree health benefits range from $95 billion to $2 trillion (Chandler 1987). A problem is that federal laws have made it both unattractive and financially risky for companies to establish a fund for future payment of retiree medical benefits. Prefunding through a pension plan or a welfare plan trust is discouraged by the Internal Revenue Code, secs. 401(h) and 501(c)(9) (Rappaport and Kalman 1987).

One approach to prefunding is through volunteer retirement health plans (VRHPs), an alternative in the proposed Retiree Health Protection Act of 1987 (H.R. 2860) (Chandler 1987). These accounts would be funded by employer tax-deductible contributions with the interest tax exempt. Actuarial estimates would be used to plan for lifetime coverage, but limits would be set on the amount of annual contributions. Two important features relate to vesting and age: employees would be vested after five years and then could take the VRHP account to a new job with an employer who also funds these accounts, and VRHPs would not be activated before age 65 (except for the disabled) so as not to encourage early retirement. An anticipated advantage to this proposal is that it would encourage the development of group health insurance for long-term care. This bill is currently under consideration.

Another suggestion includes changing legislation to allow and encourage the use of surplus in pension funds to fund health benefits. In this plan, known as Voluntary Employee Beneficiary Associations (VEBAs), the employer would have tax incentives to prefund retiree health benefits, as with pensions. Both annual contributions and earned interest would be deductible from unrelated business income tax (Dopkeen 1987). Supported by the business and insurance community, VEBAs are not new, but their implementation has been curtailed by the imposition of restrictions in DEFRA (Chandler 1987).

A third suggestion advocates a cash benefit approach, with voluntary prefunding for near-term employees encouraged through favorable tax policy and, for younger workers, through incentives similar to pensions (e.g., no tax on accumulated interest). Essentially a medical IRA, contributions under this plan would go with the employee to different jobs. However, a recent analysis (Smallwood, Simon, and Brody 1987) concluded that IRAs for long-term care would not provide adequate coverage for most of the population and that the costs of long-term care will have to be contained to make IRAs attractive propositions.

The federal government has suggested a number of approaches, including a Medicare capitation concept whereby the Health Care Financing Administration would contract with employers, union welfare funds, or insurers for group insurance coverage for retirees, with HCFA paying the premium. The assumption is that the same managed care components and options of traditional insurance programs would be available to retirees.

At the same time that legislative disincentives for employers to prefund retiree benefits persist, employers are being required to account for these plans and their liabilities more fully. A 1985 interim ruling of the Financial Accounting Standards Board (FASB) required retiree liabilities to be identified in financial reports. FASB is currently considering requiring employers to recognize retiree health obligations, in most cases unfunded liabilities, on corporate balance sheets, accrued as an annual expense against corporate earnings over the working lives of covered employees rather than as current operating costs when benefits are paid. These proposed accounting procedures have the potential for reducing earnings ratios in many companies (Mercer-Meidinger 1985; Rappaport and Kalman 1987). Clearly, the issue of retiree benefits is volatile because of these changes: "With the aging of the American population, there is no question that this liability will grow and become a major financial factor for many corporations" (Chandler 1987, p. 21).

Other funding problems in health care are coverage for catastrophic care and for the employed uninsured. Proposals to mandate coverage for high-cost care for all employees will add expenditures at a time when the public and private sectors are attempting to cut back on health care spending. Yet these needs must be addressed, and they can be expected to affect the way that benefits are provided for older workers and retirees. For example, the recently enacted Medicare Catastrophic Coverage Act, effective January 1, 1989, is likely to require employers with health plans that appreciably duplicate Medicare benefits to expand benefit offerings or return funds to employees for duplicated benefits, as a one-time offset. This legislation is also likely to mean more costs to the beneficiary. The effects of Medicaid expansion for low-income workers and the effects of requiring or giving incentives for employers to insure all workers are unclear (Wilensky 1987).

Conclusion

What we are presented with is a series of cross-pressures in the arena of health care costs for older workers and retirees and no clear direction as to resolution. The health needs of the population are exerting pressures on employers: pressures to modify jobs to accommodate altered health status and pressures to provide workplace support and assistance to employee care-givers. The economic strains in the health care system are exerting pressures on employers to provide health insurance coverage for an aging population, including retirees, and to expand benefits to cover long-term care needs; at the same time, there is pressure to control health expenditures.

What is critical as we move ahead to redesign benefits, coordinate public and private financing of health services, and deal with cost-control issues is that we balance these concerns against the needs of older workers and their families. Changing the structure of health benefits is both a challenge and an opportunity for employers.

In addition to resolving the benefits issues which confront them, there are three important areas for employer activity to meet the health and social needs of their employees, especially older workers.

First, flexibility in job design and scheduling in the workplace will assist disabled and older workers, as well as employees with care-giving responsibilities, to adapt to and maintain employment. Second, the employer can provide a critical link between the formal services of the community and the informal support system of family and friends in order to facilitate and ensure access to care. Third, as they adopt cost-management strategies, employers can become increasingly involved in reviewing quality of care for employees and can encourage studies of the long-term effects, for example, of delaying surgery or of earlier hospital discharges under a prospective payment system.[4]

Along with employment levels, housing, education, and public safety, the health of the nation is a major indicator of how we, as a society, are faring, over time and in comparison with other countries. Today's employer must look beyond the more limited role of the enabler who provides coverage for health care costs to a broader responsibility, which may include advising employees about health benefits options and even acting as a mediator between employees and the health care system.

References

American Association of Retired Persons. 1986. "Caregivers in the Workplace Survey Results: Overall Summary." October 31. American Association of Retired Persons, Washington, D.C.

Anderson, Joseph M., David L. Kennell, and John F. Sheils. 1987. "Health Plan Costs, Medicare, and Employment of Older Workers." In *The Problem Isn't Age: Work and Older Americans,* edited by Steven H. Sandell, pp. 206–17. New York: Praeger.

Balinsky, Warren. 1985. "Home Care: Current Trends and Future Prospects." The New York Business Group on Health, Newsletter Discussion Paper 5, suppl. 3. The New York Business Group on Health, New York.

Barr, Judith K. 1986. "Employee Health Benefits: Structural Incentives for Cost Containment." Paper presented at the annual meeting of the American Sociological Association, New York, August.

Bass, David M., and Linda S. Noelker. 1987. "The Influence of Family Caregivers on Elder's Use of In-Home Services: An Expanded Conceptual Framework," *Journal of Health and Social Behavior* 28 (June): 184–96.

Bell, Dale. 1987. "Home Care in New York City: Providers, Payers and Clients." March. United Hospital Fund of New York, New York.

Brody, Elaine M., and Claire B. Schoonover. 1986. "Patterns of Parent-Care When Adult Daughters Work and When They Do Not," *The Gerontologist* 26 (August): 372–81.

Business Roundtable. 1987. *Corporate Health-Care-Cost Management and Private-Sector Initiatives: Results of the 1986 Business Roundtable Health, Welfare, and Retirement Income Task Force Survey.* July. Indianapolis, Ind.: Business Roundtable.

4. Evidence indicates that under the Medicare prospective payment system, hospitals are differentially affected, with some profiting while an estimated 25 percent of rural hospitals operate at a loss. Although adjustments are likely, it is possible that small, less profitable, and rural hospitals will be forced to cut back on services or close, and that quality of care will suffer as hospitals try to discourage admissions for unprofitable diagnoses or to discharge patients sooner than medically prudent (Sheingold 1986).

Cafferata, Gail Lee, and Robyn Stone. "The Caregiving Role: Dimensions of Burden and Benefits," *Comprehensive Gerontology,* forthcoming.

Carroll, Norman V., and W. Gary Erwin. 1987. "Patient Shifting as a Response to Medicare Prospective Payment," *Medical Care* 25 (December): 1161–67.

Chandler, Rod. 1987. "Pursuing Funding for Retiree Benefits," *Business and Health* 4 (December): 21–25.

Dopkeen, Jonathan C. 1987. "Post-Retirement Benefits: A Bottomless Liability?" *Business and Health* 4 (June): 9–14.

Employee Benefit Plan Review. 1987. "Another Employer Taken to Task for Changing Retirees' Medical Benefits," *Employee Benefit Plan Review* 41 (January): 70.

Employee Benefit Research Institute. 1987. *Fundamentals of Employee Benefit Programs.* Washington, D.C.: Employee Benefit Research Institute.

Equicor. 1986. *Looking to the Future of Retiree Health Benefits: The Equicor Health Care Survey—VI.* New York: Equitable HCA Corporation.

Feldman, Jacob J. 1983. "Work Ability of the Aged under Conditions of Improving Mortality," *Milbank Memorial Fund Quarterly/Health and Society* 61 (Summer): 430–44.

Foster Higgins, A., & Co., Inc. 1987. *Foster Higgins Health Care Benefits Survey.* Princeton, N.J.: Foster Higgins.

Fuchs, Victor R. 1984. "'Though Much Is Taken': Reflections on Aging, Health, and Medical Care," *Milbank Memorial Fund Quarterly/Health and Society* 62 (Spring): 143–66.

Fullerton, Howard N., Jr. 1987. "Labor Force Projections: 1986 to Year 2000," *Monthly Labor Review* 110 (September): 19–20.

Greenwald, Judy. 1986. "Firms Can Cut Retiree Health Benefits: Court," *Business Insurance,* May 12, pp. 7–8.

Herzlinger, Regina E., and Jeffrey Schwartz. 1985. "How Companies Tackle Health Care Costs: Part I," *Harvard Business Review* 63 (July–August): 69–81.

Hester, Edward J., Paul G. Decelles, and Layne E. Hood. 1986. *The Relationship between Age and Physical Disability among Workers: Implications for the Future.* Topeka, Kan.: Menninger Foundation.

Jensen, Gail A., Michael A. Morrisey, and John W. Marcus. 1987. "Cost-Sharing and the Changing Pattern of Employer-Sponsored Health Benefits." Paper presented at the annual meeting of the American Public Health Association, New Orleans, October.

Johnson and Higgins. 1986. "Corporate Health Care Benefits Survey 1986." Johnson and Higgins, Princeton, N.J.

Kemper, Peter, Robert Applebaum, and Margaret Harrigan. 1987. "Community Care Demonstrations: What Have We Learned?" *Health Care Financing Review* 8: 87–100.

Kittrell, Alison. 1984. "Wellness Programs Used to Cut Costs: Study," *Business Insurance* 9 (July): 10–11.

Levin, Robert, and Rebecca Frobom. 1987. *The Corporate Perspective on Long Term Care: Survey Report*. Washington, D.C.: Washington Business Group on Health.

Liebtag, Bill. 1987. "Health Benefits for Retirees," *Journal of Accountancy*, October, pp. 100–107.

Louis Harris and Associates, Inc. 1987. *Problems Facing Elderly Americans Living Alone: A National Survey*. The Commonwealth Fund Commission on Elderly People Living Alone. Baltimore, Md.: Louis Harris and Associates.

McDonnell, Patricia, Allbie Guttenberg, Leonard Greenberg, and Ross H. Arnett III. 1986. "Self-Insured Health Plans," *Health Care Financing Review* 8 (Winter): 1–15.

Manning, William G., Arleen Leidowitz, George A. Goldberg, William H. Rogers, and Joseph P. Newhouse. 1984. "A Controlled Trial of the Effect of a Prepaid Group Practice on Use of Services," *New England Journal of Medicine* 310 (June 7): 1505–10.

Mechanic, David. 1987. "Challenges in Long-Term Care Policy," *Health Affairs* 6 (Summer) 22–34.

Mercer-Meidinger, William M., Inc. 1985. "Understanding the Cost of Post-Retirement Medical Benefits."

National Association for Home Care. 1985. "Toward a National Home Care Policy."

New York Business Group on Health. 1987. "Managing Disability in the Workforce." Discussion Paper 7. New York Business Group on Health, New York.

Nowak, Carol A. 1986. "Familial Caregiving to the Elderly," *Business and Health* 3 (June): 23–25.

Petty, Diana, and Lynn Friss. 1987. "A Balancing Act of Working and Caregiving," *Business and Health* 4 (October): 22–26.

Rappaport, Anna M., and Robert W. Kalman. 1987. "The Future of Employer-Sponsored Retiree Medical Plans," *Inquiry* 24 (Spring): 26–35.

———. 1987. "Vesting Issues in Retiree Medical Plans," *Business and Health* 4 (June): 24–34.

Rasmussen, Brian. 1987. "Mandated Coverage: An Employer Debate," *Business and Health* 4 (April): 12–24.

Rice, Dorothy P., and Jacob J. Feldman. 1983. "Living Longer in the United States: Demographic Changes and Health Needs of the Elderly," *Milbank Memorial Fund Quarterly/Health and Society* 61 (Summer): 362–95.

Robert Wood Johnson Foundation. 1987. "Access to Health Care in the United States: Results of a 1986 Survey." Special Report Two. Robert Wood Johnson Foundation, Princeton, N.J.

Schramm, Carl J. 1987. "Why Restructuring Medicare Will Not Work," *Business and Health* 4 (September): 12–13.

Schwartz, Gail E. 1986. *State of the Art: Corporate Behavior in Disability Management: Survey Results*. Washington, D.C.: Institute for Rehabilitation and Disability Management.

Sheingold, Steven H. 1986. "Unintended Results of Medicare's National Prospective Payment Rates," *Health Affairs* 4 (Winter): 5–21.

Smallwood, Dennis E., Harold J. Simon, and Barbara L. Brody. 1987. "Questioning the Adequacy of Long-Term Care IRAs," *Health Affairs* 6 (Summer): 132–43.

Stone, Robyn, Gail Lee Cafferata, and Judith Sangl. 1987. "Caregivers of the Frail Elderly: A National Profile," *The Gerontologist* 27 (October): 616–26.

Travelers Companies. 1985. "The Travelers Employee Caregiver Survey." June. Travelers Companies, Hartford, Conn.

U.S. Department of Health and Human Services. 1986. *Health: United States, 1986*. Public Health Service, National Center for Health Statistics, DHHS Pub. 87-1232. December. Hyattsville, Md.: Department of Health and Human Services.

U.S. Department of Labor, Bureau of Labor Statistics. 1987. *Employee Benefits in Medium and Large Firms, 1986*. Washington, D.C.: Bureau of Labor Statistics.

Verbrugge, Lois M. 1984. "Longer Life but Worsening Health? Trends in Health and Mortality of Middle-aged and Older Persons," *Milbank Memorial Fund Quarterly/Health and Society* 62 (Summer): 475–519.

Waldo, Daniel R., Katherine R. Levit, and Helen Lazenby. 1986. "National Health Expenditures, 1985," *Health Care Financing Review* 8 (Fall): 1–21.

Warshaw, Leon J., Judith K. Barr, Irene Rayman, Mark Schacter, and Theodore G. Lucas. 1986. *Employer Support for Employee Caregivers*. New York: New York Business Group on Health.

Wetle, Terrie T., and David A. Pearson. 1986. "Long-term Care." In *Health Care Delivery in the United States,* edited by Steven Jonas, pp. 214–36. New York: Springer Publishing Company.

Wilensky, Gail R. 1987. "Public, Private Sector Options to Cover Uninsured Workers," *Business and Health* 4 (January): 42–43.

Wolinsky, Fredric D., Ray R. Mosely II, and Rodney M. Coe. 1986. "A Cohort Analysis of the Use of Health Services by Elderly Americans," *Journal of Health and Social Behavior* 27 (September): 209–19.

The Aging Issue: Challenges and Opportunities at Chrysler

ANTHONY P. ST. JOHN

As the work force grows older, Chrysler is experiencing sharp increases in the cost of pensions, health care programs, training, etc. Together with the UAW, Chrysler is involved in a research project concerning Medicare plan options, leading toward a pilot program as part of a demonstration project. A wellness program has been instituted, and a joint UAW-Chrysler EAP is being implemented, as well as a retirement planning program. The UAW and Chrysler, working together, are seeking solutions to the challenges of the aging work force and are already making progress.

I. B.

America is growing older—it's no secret. All you have to do is look at the headlines in our newspapers: "America's Gray Wave of the Future," "Today's Baby Boomers—Tomorrow's Elderly," "The War between the Generations," "Baby Boom—Then Bust," "And Now the Fun Years." The large percentage of older individuals in the work force will influence promotional decisions, training opportunities, benefit plans, and retirement policies. The question is: how will we in human resources management confront this issue?

The Chrysler Statistics

Let me describe the current demographics of the Chrysler work force, review our future projections, and discuss some of the changes we are implementing to accommodate an aging Chrysler active and retiree population.

At Chrysler today, the average age for hourly employees is 44, for nonmanagement salaried employees 41, and for management employees 40. For hourly employees, the average age has risen from a recent low of 36 in 1977 to 44 in 1987; however, for salaried employees, the averages have remained essentially constant over the last ten years. The average corporate service for hourly employees is 17 years, for non-management salaried employees 13 years, and for management employees 16 years.

The current number of Chrysler retirees is 83,000, compared with an active work force of 115,000. In 1977, the ratio of active employees to retirees was 2.6:1. It reached a low of 0.99:1 in 1982, when the recession hit bottom. Currently, the ratio is about 1.3:1. Our projections indicate that the ratio will further decrease to 1.1:1 in 1990 through 1995, 1.04:1 in the year 2000, and 0.94:1 by 2015. This ratio will continue to remain low because retirees and their surviving spouses (the great majority of whom continue receiving pension and health insurance benefits after the spouse's death) are living longer and because a significant number of employees elect to retire early. It may be of interest to note that during the last three years about 90 percent of employees who retired did so before the normal retirement age of 65. The average age at retirement is now less than 60.

In 1987, pension benefit payments totaled $400 million, and retiree health and life insurance benefits totaled $202 million. The two benefits alone are equal to about 17.5 percent of the Chrysler payroll, and these costs have been constantly escalating. Over the last five years, health and life insurance benefit costs for employees and retirees increased by over 50 percent, from $414 million to $625 million. Insurance costs for retirees increased by 39 percent and for active employees by 57 percent. In the same period, pension costs increased by 24 percent.

Health Care Challenges

Health care costs are and have been a particularly troublesome subject. As the number of retirees continues to grow, Chrysler will be confronted with a two-fold challenge: maintaining the quality of care and coverage while reducing and containing benefit costs. Even though Chrysler is only number three in the auto industry, the cost of these benefits is rather staggering.

WHAT'S BEING DONE?

The company has implemented and will be implementing measures to meet the challenges of an aging work force successfully. In the area of cost control, we have refused to subscribe to the myth that aggressive cost containment reduces the quality of care. We have worked to provide a greater variety of efficient alternative health care delivery options, with the result that last year we increased employee and retiree enrollment in managed health care plans (PPOs and HMOs) by 43 percent and 48 percent respectively, *without* compromising the quality of care and coverage.

We have also implemented an "individual case management" program, designed for individuals in an in-patient care environment. An example may help to explain how it works. John Doe is hospitalized and has become dependent on a ventilator. If nothing changes, he will spend the rest of the year in a hospital bed. His health care cost per day is $1,000, and he has 100 days of coverage remaining. Chrysler is at risk of spending $100,000. If Chrysler determined that the cost of re-wiring John Doe's house to accommodate a ventilator plus provision of skilled home nursing care will cost only $500 per day, then John Doe's coverage is extended by 100 days without increasing Chrysler's total cost. There are many other instances as well in which the program can serve to reduce Chrysler's cost. The overall goal of the program is to control costs and improve a patient's quality of life.

COST-EFFECTIVE MEDICARE

Although private health care insurance costs have risen significantly in the last several years, the cost of government-sponsored programs, such as Medicare, has accelerated at a much faster rate. Chrysler and the United Auto Workers have jointly proposed a research and demonstration project under a cooperative agreement with the Health Care Financing Administration (HCFA) to determine whether the Medicare program can be administered in a more cost-effective manner through the private sector of the economy. This project will be conducted in three independent phases. Phase 1 is a data analysis phase, during which the feasibility of the effort will be explored. Phase 2 involves the design of benefit plan options with the UAW and financing arrangements with HCFA. This stage should take no more than nine months and, we hope, much less.

Assuming the successful completion of Phases 1 and 2, we plan a three- to five-year pilot program. During the operational phase of this project, Chrysler Medicare-enrolled retirees will select from several health plan options through which to receive their Medicare and Medicare supplemental health benefits. These options will include one or more plans which will be developed by Chrysler and the UAW as part of the research and demonstration project. This project will address important problems of employers, Medicare beneficiaries, and the HCFA. The Medicare Insurance Group Approach (or MIG, the label used by Medicare for such private sector demonstration projects) will allow Chrysler to implement cost-containment efforts and strategies proven effective for our active population, which Medicare regulations prohibit for Medicare enrollees.

The current dual Medicare and Medicare supplemental claim system is often confusing and frustrating for retirees. Under the proposed demonstration, MIG enrollees would have a single, integrated system for handling claims and inquiries. The MIG health plan options also offer a means to reverse the growth in out-of-pocket expenditures by Medicare beneficiaries. For the HCFA, the MIG model provides a means of expanding Medicare enrollment in alternative delivery systems, thereby reducing federal Medicare expenditures.

We hope to demonstrate through this project that we in the private sector are better able than government to contain the cost of the Medicare program and that this nation, unlike England, need not resort to the rationing of health care services to reduce costs.

WELLNESS PROGRAMS

Another approach to controlling health care costs is to offer employees a program designed to create and maintain a healthier work force. Chrysler has instituted an education program for its employees and retirees on three fronts that we believe will pay dividends in the long run. First, a major health promotion and disease prevention effort, entitled "Staywell," has been mounted to keep people out of the hospital and in good health. Employees are informed about the dangers of smoking and urged to quit. The benefits of proper diet, exercise, and rest are discussed. "Staywell" programs are in operation at four locations, and there are plans to expand to nine this year (1988). Eventually, we hope to have "Staywell" at all Chrysler facilities. Second, a joint UAW-Chrysler employee assistance program is being implemented. Joint local programs will sponsor educational and informative training sessions about the dangers of alcohol and drug abuse.

Third, a corporate communications program explains to our employees some of the inefficiencies in the health care system and, most important, the fact that they can make choices and get better or equally fine health care at far less cost. These communications efforts include special employee presentations and company publications; a regular newspaper feature is planned, entitled "Staywell."

Retirement Planning Program

A planned, comfortable, and secure retirement is the ultimate goal of every employee. A life-planning seminar has been designed to help salaried employees plan for retirement. The seminar consists of six modules covering financial planning, the issues and myths of aging and health, interpersonal relationships, housing decisions, and leisure vs. work options following retirement. Each module runs for approximately 2½ hours, and they are held after work or on weekends. Attendees are encouraged to bring a spouse or guest. To be eligible for enrollment, employees must be 45 years old and have ten years of corporate service. The eligibility time frame for this pre-retirement program allows employees to participate in the seminar without specifically committing to retirement and to plan for retirement emotionally, physically, and financially. It does not focus simply on retirement benefits, but encourages employees to view retirement as part of the career development process. A similar program is being developed for hourly employees by the UAW-Chrysler National Training Center.

We recognize that the challenges posed by an aging population will require a great deal of imagination and ingenuity on the part of private industry, labor, the government, and academia to develop programs and implement measures designed to accommodate an older population. However, this planning process has to begin now—we can't wait another five to ten years when problems begin to surface.

Chrysler has taken some initial steps in this direction, but the company is aware that there is a long way to go. Nevertheless, with Chrysler and the UAW working together and drawing upon the resources of the academic community, we can properly position ourselves to meet the challenges that lie ahead.

Rolling Along toward Retirement: GM and Its Older Workers

ALFRED S. WARREN, JR.

Intensified competition in the automobile industry, work force reductions, and a virtual cessation of hiring have turned the spotlight at General Motors on its aging work force. Like Stempel, this GM executive points to new retraining programs, pre-retirement counseling, and concern with health care management in the face of rising costs as key elements in the company's response. The UAW-GM effort has as its goal healthy and productive lives at work and in retirement for GM's older workers.

I. B.

"Old Man River, he don't say nothing. He *must* know something. That Old Man River, he just keeps rolling along." I was thinking of that song when I realized recently that I will be 62 years old. The last time I looked, I was 40. I don't know how I got here all of a sudden. Age is a factor, not just for me, but for the nation as a whole. The median age of the U.S. population continues to rise. For my company, General Motors, the age of the work force presents a particularly serious problem, however.

It is common knowledge that the American auto industry is struggling to become competitive on its own turf—the United States—which is the major automobile market in the world. In 1965 there were only four auto companies selling in significant numbers in this country; by 1975 that number had jumped to twelve; today there are almost thirty. In other words, thirty companies are now cutting up the pie that four once divided. It's obvious that adjustment to this situation is difficult. Ten years ago a number of pundits took a look at their crystal balls and said that a shakeout by the year 2000 in the auto industry would leave only five major auto companies in the world. It's obvious that Yugoslavia, Taiwan, Korea, and a few other places weren't even considered in that particular scenario.

This uncertainty creates an environment where change is inevitable and planning essential if organizations like GM are to participate as leaders in the world marketplace. All functional areas of our company, including industrial relations, are currently evaluating how best to participate in this new environment, and the aging of the work force is a major item on the agenda.

Training Programs

Because of its agreements with the United Auto Workers Union and the protections provided workers in its union contracts, GM does not anticipate hiring many new employees for a long time to come. In fact, in the past twelve months not a single new worker has been hired except in about half a dozen areas where the skills required have changed and current workers could not be trained to fill the need.

In addition, we are involved in the most extensive training program in our history, our JOBS bank. This arrangement, negotiated with the UAW, allows an employee who would otherwise be laid off to elect to enter the JOBS bank program. There that worker will be taught the new skills needed to perform other jobs in the plant or will be prepared for employment in other GM plants or perhaps other industries. Millions and millions of training hours are involved. The contract stipulates that employees who enter the JOBS bank continue to receive their full wage and benefits while there—a true "safety net" for our employees.

Assisting employees to better prepare themselves for the future is another challenge facing the GM organization. One of the most popular subjects the company offers its workers is a course in literacy. In the aging GM work force, there are many people who, unfortunately, cannot read or write. This situation requires great sensitivity and compassion, since without the program these employees would be unequipped to perform any new job requiring basic skills. At high-school graduation ceremonies recently for some workers who were receiving their equivalency degrees, one man approached me and said, "I want you to watch me do something." He then took out a new checkbook, with check No. 1 on the top, and filled it out in front of me. He told me that it was the first check he had ever written in his life because in all his 52 years he had not learned to read or write. This was a glorious moment for him.

Pre-Retirement Training

The very thought of retirement makes employees apprehensive and anxious. At GM we are trying to assist them during this period of transition by establishing pre-retirement training programs. These programs provide prospective retirees with information concerning pension benefits, health care coverage, and continuing life insurance. In addition, employees can get information concerning legal matters, nutrition, moves to another location, health care, wills, finances, etc. In the last two years about ten thousand people have taken pre-retiree training. In the past, many GM workers retired without proper preparation for their new life, but the company feels it is essential that some kind of training for retirement be given. In fact, the first such pre-retirement programs were offered in some locations about fifteen years ago, sponsored jointly by the UAW and management.

Ratios of Retirees to Active Employees

GM has learned that taking the ceiling off the mandatory retirement age hasn't made a lot of difference. Very few people stay around to age 70, though more people are working closer to age 65 than was expected, despite the 30-and-out retirement option, and that pattern is continuing.

To give some idea of the GM retiree group in terms of age, here are some simple statistics. In age group 65–74 at the present time there are 128,000 retirees. The company projects that retiree totals in this group will climax in 1997, at close to 150,000 people. In age group 75–84 at the present time there are 60,900 retirees. By the year 2002 there will be 87,900. In the group 85 and over at the present time there are 11,800 retirees. By the year 2002 there will be 25,500. The present ratio of retirees to workers at GM is 1.6:1 (that is, 1.6 active employees for every retiree).

Health Care Costs

The current numbers and accelerated projections are having a significant impact on GM's current operations. Last year the company had to sell 230,000 vehicles just to meet its health care costs. To meet the cost of the benefit program as a whole, 550,000 vehicles had to be sold. These costs will increase, since it is clear that people are living longer now and that young people are going to live longer in the future.

Technology is also playing a major role. In recent years, technology has advanced most vigorously in the health care area, with heart and other organ transplants, laser surgery, hi-tech medication, and so on. I talked to a man the other day who was 91 years old; his main fear was that a whole host of cures would be discovered right after his death, so he wanted to stay on earth a bit longer. That's a real possibility.

Though I admire the technological sophistication of the medical profession, I have become extremely irritated with some aspects of it, particularly as it affects GM workers. For example, I found recently that there has not been a natural birth among GM employees in the city of Flint, Michigan, in ten years. I'm not a mother myself, but this seems more than a little odd to me! In another of our plant cities, I found that if you visit the doctor complaining of a backache, you will spend three days in the local hospital, no matter what the medical diagnosis is. These are the kinds of costs that we simply have to get under control.

There are over 800,000 people in the GM family, and over 300,000 of them are retirees. Retirees use more health care benefits than active employees. In 1987, retiree health care cost GM $900 million. In the age group 65–75, about four days of hospital stay per year are used by each person. In age group 75 and over, each person averages about six hospital days per year. A lot of people are in hospitals for a great deal longer than that, of course. Hospital costs account for about 56 percent of GM's health care costs. Because of the significant dollars involved and our concern for proper treatment for our employees, special attention was paid to this matter during the last round of negotiations with the union.

Our goal was to put together a health care program focused on long-term care. The UAW and the company agreed to have a joint committee on health care benefits develop a pilot program, based on guidelines worked out by both parties during the negotiations, which responds to the concern for the chronically disabled population in a cost-effective manner. By their very nature, chronically disabling illnesses require services which go beyond medical and therapeutic coverage under the health care program. So the parties agreed that any approach to this problem should be interdisciplinary in nature, considering such issues as the appropriate utilization of health care, including non-medical assistance.

To explain what that means, we all have an idea of the problems people face when a mother or father becomes ill in their retirement years. Those kinds of problems are not really medical in many cases. For example, some kind of day care is often needed for retired people who cannot be left alone. What about the daughter who works and has a mother who can't stay by herself? What about the elderly people who are unable to take care of their homes and need a housekeeper or home helper to come in several days a week? The Meals-on-Wheels program has been filling a need in many places; someone is often needed just to run errands for an elderly house-bound person. The family of caretakers has to be able to place the aging ill person somewhere from time to time to get a respite from the intensity of the task.

As a retiree grows older and savings shrink, he or she is often not able to pay for the kind of health care needed. I am on the board of a local hospital. One of the problems we hear about is that of the retired person the hospital is caring for who has money to pay the bills for a time. But that money is eaten up fast. Pretty soon only Medicaid and Medicare are left. Caring for that patient costs, let us say, $500 a day; suddenly the government program is providing only $300 a day. The hospital has to find some way to make up the difference. That's a problem that not only GM but the United States as a nation absolutely must face.

Let's hope we don't face it like one of my favorite characters, the clergyman caught in a flood. He was standing with the water washing around his knees when a rowboat came by. The people called to him, "Father, may we take you to safety?" "Oh no," he said. "I'm going to stay here because God will take care of me." A little later, when the water had reached his shoulders, another boat came by and the people cried to him, "Father, please let us get you out of here!" "Don't worry about me," said the clergyman, "God will take care of me." Finally, as the water had reached his nose, a helicopter flew over, came down to him, and the people called, "Put up your arms—we will save you." "God will take care of me," said he again. And so he drowned. In heaven, at the Pearly Gates, he said angrily to St. Peter, "What happened up here? I prayed to God to save me, and he didn't help me." St. Peter replied, "Didn't help you?! He sent you two rowboats and a helicopter!"

If, like this unfortunate clergyman, we rely on a miracle to solve the problems of our aging work force and our retired folk, we'll drown in a sea of red ink. We must work together, exploring the opportunities to provide the necessary good quality health care at costs we can afford. That means working at solving the problem together. And that's what the UAW and GM are doing on this issue of common interest and concern.

One last item I want to mention is the need to teach the aging worker and retirees to recognize the need for good health care. Often retirees are stuck in a small town somewhere, perhaps with no access to advice as to the medical treatment they need and how to avoid becoming victimized by professionals. They need proper training in how to use the health care system. The UAW has established retiree centers and local union retiree chapters across the country. One of the benefits of these centers and chapters is the advice the aging worker and the retiree can get from them as to the best use of the health care dollar. Though a great deal of assistance for retirees and aging workers is available, it is up to each individual to determine what support is required.

When prospective retirees ask me for some pointers, I often encourage them to do three things:

- Think ahead—do not wait until the last minute to plan for retirement and, once retired, periodically check to see whether the pre-retirement "game plan" is still appropriate.
- Understand the available benefit programs and use them wisely. Abuses can often lead to increased costs and possibly a reduction in the level of benefits.
- Evaluate any recommended medical treatment carefully to avoid being victimized, especially by professionals recommending excessive treatment.

The theme underlying the GM approach is that we care about our workers, active and retired. We hope that, as a result of careful planning and administration, they won't have to worry about being rescued at the last minute and can concentrate on living productive, healthy, and fulfilled lives.

Aging, Job Satisfaction, and Job Performance

OLIVIA S. MITCHELL
WITH THE ASSISTANCE OF PHILLIP B. LEVINE
AND SILVANA POZZEBON

Is conventional wisdom wrong in doubting whether older workers are healthy, satisfied, and productive employees—sometimes even more so than their younger counterparts? Mitchell reviews the evidence, notes its shortcomings, and uses data from a nationally representative survey of workers to shed some light on the relationship. She finds little evidence for a link between aging and either job performance or job satisfaction and no evidence of a negative effect of aging on health. She also considers the possibility that her results may reflect a pattern of selective retirements, in which older persons who remain in the labor force have fewer physical impairments or other health problems than those who retire.

J. D. O.

In 1950, almost 90 percent of men aged 55–64 were in the labor force in the United States. Today, fewer than three-quarters of men in that age bracket are working or seeking work. An even more stunning decline in labor force attachment occurred among men aged 65 and older—down to only 20 percent from about 50 percent after World War II.

The drop in market attachment among older workers is surprising in the light of the conventional wisdom holding that older workers are equally, if not more, healthy, satisfied, and productive employees than their younger counterparts. This paper examines whether conventional wisdom is wrong by correcting several shortcomings of previous studies, including the fact that they often analyze unrepresentative data, lack controls for variables correlated with age, and use inappropriate sta-

Special thanks are due to Vivian Fields for excellent computer programming assistance. Tove Hammer, John Owen, and Robert Smith provided useful suggestions on an earlier version of this chapter. Opinions expressed herein remain solely the responsibility of the author.

tistical methodology. The overall question posed is: are older workers less satisfied and/or less productive on the job than are their younger counterparts? If so, the evidence may help explain the trend toward early retirement in the U.S. economy over the last three to four decades.

The plan of the paper is as follows: a first section reviews previous studies which examined the links between aging, job satisfaction, and job performance, and presents new hypotheses regarding these relationships. These hypotheses are then tested empirically in a second section using a nationally representative data set known as the Quality of Employment Survey. A final section offers discussion and conclusions.

I. Job Satisfaction and Aging

Over a decade ago, Locke (1976) enumerated over three thousand studies of job satisfaction. Because the present review focuses only on age-job satisfaction profiles, attention here is limited to a subset of literature. A brief discussion of how job satisfaction has been quantified is followed by a review of findings on how job satisfaction profiles change with age. A set of hypotheses is then given, to be tested empirically.

A. DEFINITIONS AND MEASUREMENTS OF JOB SATISFACTION

Many very elaborate definitions of job satisfaction have appeared in the literature, but Organ and Hamner's (1982) is easily grasped and is perhaps the most complete: "Essentially, job satisfaction is a person's attitude toward his job." The simplicity of this definition belies the difficulty researchers have had pinning down the concept empirically. In industrial relations studies, individuals are often asked to assess their own job satisfaction, usually using one or a combination of three methods. The first is a simple, direct evaluation based on a single question, such as the one in the National Longitudinal Survey: "How do you feel about the job you have now? Do you like it very much, like it fairly well, dislike it somewhat, or dislike it very much?" The second method is also a global measure of overall job satisfaction but uses several detailed questions pertaining to job aspects rather than a single overview query. Individuals' scaled responses to these questions indicating the degree of worker satisfaction or dissatisfaction (termed "attitude scales") are then summed or averaged to arrive at an overall assessment. A third method asks employees to rate specific facets or components of the job (e.g., pay, supervision, pace, etc.) using one of the approaches described above. Though some authors advocate an attitude scale termed the Job Descriptive Index (Hulin and Smith 1965; Locke 1976;

Muchinsky 1978), there is no single generally accepted and widely used scale for any of these three measures of job satisfaction (Borjas 1979), perhaps because self-assessment measures are subjective, and as such are somewhat difficult to interpret across individuals.

Despite these many differences in method, evidence suggests that most workers are satisfied with their jobs. Quinn, Staines, and McCullough (1974) note that roughly 80 percent of all workers consistently report themselves as satisfied. Wright and Hamilton (1978) concur, identifying the least satisfied workers as those under age 30, but even here discontent levels are still fairly low—from 14 to 25 percent.

B. AGE AND JOB SATISFACTION

Tables 1 and 2 summarize findings from the recent literature on the empirical linkages between age and job satisfaction. Table 1 focuses on overall satisfaction measures; individual job facets are examined in Table 2. The general consensus appears to be that age is positively related to overall job satisfaction. Early analysts suggested a U-shaped age-satisfaction profile (Hulin and Smith 1965). However, subsequent research indicates that this U-shaped profile might be positive and linear when other factors are controlled (Hulin and Smith 1965; Gibson and Klein 1970; Hunt and Saul 1975).[1]

Six specific job facets have been examined most frequently in the industrial psychology literature (Cohn 1979). These are: satisfaction with work, pay, promotions, supervision, working conditions, and co-workers. Having a positive feeling toward the work itself is generally labeled "intrinsic" satisfaction, while "extrinsic" satisfaction is associated with tangible job rewards, including pay, promotion, supervisory relationships, and working conditions. In addition, aggregate measures are sometimes used instead of those based on single components (Schwab and Heneman 1977).

As Table 2 indicates, there is no consistent link between age and individual job facet variables. Only one generalization can be drawn from the evidence reviewed: satisfaction with the content of the work itself appears positively and linearly related to age among male employees. For women, no significant relationship is discerned for any measure.

1. Previous studies are not unanimous in their conclusions, since some report no significant differences in satisfaction by age (Holley, Field, and Holley 1978; Phillips, Barret, and Rush 1978; Cohn 1979). However, such studies utilize broad age groups, as compared to other studies in which the age variable is more narrowly defined. For example, Phillips, Barret, and Rush (1978) define the old as those over age 47 and the young as those under age 47. In general, however, researchers do seem to concur that age is positively related to overall job satisfaction.

Part of the inconsistency in the research on aging and job component satisfaction may be due to the fact that job facet measures differ from one analysis to the next. Data samples are also nonrepresentative, since they are usually specific to one or a few firms and/or cover only a subset of workers (e.g., blue-collar workers only, white-collar workers only, males only). This may also explain the insignificant results for females. The fact that many studies do not hold constant other important variables, such as pay and experience, may also explain the observed lack of agreement. Finally, the evidence is also compatible with the conclusion that job facet questions measure something rather different from what overall job satisfaction queries measure.

C. LIMITATIONS AND IMPLICATIONS OF PREVIOUS RESEARCH

Existing research does not fully specify the links between age and job satisfaction patterns. Measurement problems in the dependent variable, job satisfaction, tend to render results noncomparable across studies. Lack of sophisticated methodology is also a serious limitation. In several instances, no appeal is made to statistical tests at all, and though some researchers do employ statistical techniques, they limit themselves to simple ones (e.g., zero-order correlations) without controlling for other variables which are correlated with age (e.g., pay, experience, and education). A related methodological limitation characterizing all existing studies is the fact that none corrects for the possibility that older job incumbents are a nonrandom sample, but if workers move out of more demanding jobs as they accumulate seniority, those older workers remaining in their jobs are more likely to be satisfied because they are a self-selected group. Another shortcoming of existing studies has to do with the data samples employed. Most use case studies, which are far from being nationally representative. Because of the reliance on cross-sectional surveys, the link between age and job satisfaction for the same workers over time has not been thoroughly assessed. Finally, each paper defines "old" and "young" differently, making comparisons difficult.

Though the evidence is far from complete, older workers seem generally more satisfied with their jobs than younger employees. A possible explanation for this phenomenon is that job satisfaction rises with age because older workers have more attractive jobs than younger employees. This view is termed the "life cycle" hypothesis. One implication of this theory is directly testable: after controlling for job characteristics like occupation and industry, there should be no remaining systematic age effects in a job satisfaction model. Early empirical analyses of this hypothesis did demonstrate a positive correlation between age and job satisfaction, but focused only on broad occupational groupings; for in-

Table 1: RELATIONSHIP BETWEEN AGE AND

	Study				
	Gibson and Klein (1970)	Quinn et al. (1974)	Hunt and Saul (1975)	Stagner (1975)	Glenn et al. (1977)
Sample	(1) 385 blue-collar workers, mainly women, rural South (2) 1,682 blue-collar males, 18 plants, disperse locations	7 national surveys, 1958–73	3,253 male/ 550 female white-collar workers, large Australian govt. organization	cites unpublished study of large sample, auto-related blue-collar workers	1,080 white males/461 white females; probability sample U.S. population for 1972/ 73/74
Methodology	analysis of variance for (1) and (2); partial correlation for (2) (diff. age and tenure groups in each sample)	simple tabulations (% satisfied in each age category)	multiple regression	simple tabulation	zero-order correlation
Other control variables	tenure	none	tenure	none	none
JS measure	one question	one question	attitude scale	attitude scale	one question
Estimated effect of age on JS	+ linear	6 or 7 surveys; + increasing	males, + linear; females, n.s.	+	males, + corr.; females, +corr.

Note: all effects reported are statistically significant unless coded n.s.

[a]Quality of Employment Survey, conducted annually by the Institute for Social Research, University of Michigan.

OVERALL JOB SATISFACTION

Study				
Holley et al. (1978)	Phillips et al. (1978)	Wright and Hamilton (1978)	Cohn (1979)	Janson and Martin (1982)
362 female para-professionals, Alabama Extension Service	71 blue-collar workers, large auto plant	QES[a] 1972–73; males 16–64	subsample of males 21–64 from national sample	QUES[a] 1972–73; 1,455 workers
T-tests	individual data, corr.; group data, analysis of variance	simple tabulations	analysis of variance	simple tabulations (derivations from grand mean of JS score)
none	education tenure	none	none	none
attitude scale	Job Descriptive Index	one question	attitude scale	attitude scale
n.s.	individual data, n.s.; group data, no diff. in satisfaction between young (≤47) and old (≥47)	+	no diff. in satisfaction between age groups 21–34, 35–44, 45–54, and 55–64	+

Table 2: RELATIONSHIP BETWEEN AGE AND JOB FACET SATISFACTION

	Study						
	Hulin and Smith (1965)	Gibson and Klein (1970)	Hunt and Saul (1975)	Schwab and Heneman (1977)	Holley et al. (1978)	Muchinsky (1978)	Cohn (1979)
	(1)	(2)	(3)	(4)	(5)	(6)	(7)
Sample	185 males/75 females, random sample of New England electronics manufacturing workers (verified results on sample of 700 from 4 companies in East and Midwest)	(1) 385 blue-collar workers, mainly women, rural South (2) 1,682 blue-collar males, 18 plants, disperse locations	3,338 males/579 females, white-collar workers, large Australian government organization	96 males/177 females, Midwest, blue-collar operatives, one firm	362 female para-professionals, Alabama Extension Service	494 workers, statewide public utility	subsample of males 21–64 from national sample
					T-tests	Scheffe test checks for diff. in mean scores between age groups	analysis of variance
					none	none	none

Methodology	multiple regression analysis	analysis of variance for (1) and (2); partial correlation for (2) (diff. age and tenure groups in each sample)	multiple regression analysis	partial correlation (corrects for multicollinearity between age and tenure)	one question	Job Descriptive Index	one question
Other control variables	age; job tenure; company tenure; job level; salary; salary desired minus salary received	tenure	tenure	tenure	none	none	none
JS measure	Job Descriptive Index	one question	one question	Job Descriptive Index[a]	one question	Job Descriptive Index	one question

RESULTS: Nature of Relationship of Age and Job Satisfaction with

	Males	Females		Males	Females	Males	Females		
Work	+linear	n.s.	+linear	+linear	+ linear	+	n.s.	18–29 less satisfied than ≥30	21–34 less satisfied than ≥35

Table 2: CONTINUED

	Study									
	Hulin and Smith (1965)		Gibson and Klein (1970)	Hunt and Saul (1975)		Schwab and Heneman (1977)	Holley et al. (1978)	Muchinsky (1978)		Cohn (1979)
	(1)		(2)	(3)		(4)	(5)	(6)		(7)
Pay	+linear	n.s.	+; not completely linear; flat to 40, linear after 40	n.s.	− linear	n.s.	n.s.	≥57 more satisfied than ≤47	− monotonic	n.s.
Promotions	n.s.	n.s.		− linear	− linear	n.s.	n.s.		− monotonic	
Supervision	n.s.	n.s.	+; linear to 50, then levels off	curvilinear	n.s.	n.s.	n.s.	n.s.	n.s.	
Working conditions	n.s.	n.s.		curvilinear	n.s.	n.s.	n.s.	n.s.	≥50 less satisfied than <50	
Coworkers				curvilinear	n.s.					

Note: all effects reported are statistically significant unless coded n.s.

[a]This study also used the Minnesota Satisfaction Questionnaire and concluded that age is not significantly related to an extrinsic satisfaction measure for both sexes. Age is positively related to intrinsic work satisfaction for both males and females, and the coefficients are statistically significant.

stance, Wright and Hamilton (1978) examined white-collar workers as a whole, with no finer occupational breakdowns given. More recent research (for instance, Janson and Martin 1982) has found that controlling for occupation and industry has little discernible impact on the correlation between age and job satisfaction. The ongoing empirical controversy underscores the value of a further examination of the evidence.[2]

A competing explanation for the positive empirical link between aging and job satisfaction we call the "self-selection" hypothesis, the view that satisfied workers are more likely to remain with their employer and that older workers are most likely to have long tenure. Hence job satisfaction may appear higher for older workers when tenure is not held constant, simply because tenure is correlated with age. This theory can be tested on the basis of its prediction that the positive age-job satisfaction link should decrease (if not disappear) when time on the job is controlled for.

Using a data set to be described in more detail below, we propose to differentiate between these two explanations for the positive age and job satisfaction link.[3] The data set we use contains measures of

2. A variant on this life cycle hypothesis is consistent with recent research in labor economics on long-term contract theory (cf. Hutchens 1986; Lazear 1979). In this view, some firms find it advantageous to underpay workers when they are young in exchange for overpayments when they grow older. Such a "backloaded" compensation scheme has the effect of raising productivity by tying workers to their jobs, with a consequent reduction in turnover, search, and hiring costs. An older worker in this setting may thus report himself as satisfied with his job because at that firm his pay exceeds marginal product (and his pay at that firm is also greater than he could expect to draw at some alternative firm where wage would equal his marginal product).

To eliminate this possibility it would be necessary to control for productivity differences across firms due to backloaded pay schemes. Unfortunately, productivity is only imperfectly represented by the other control variables usually available in most data sets. Nevertheless, such a spurious age-job satisfaction relationship should be lessened once tenure is controlled, since a Lazear-style long-term contract should apply to long-term employees rather than to older workers *per se*.

3. Two other social and psychological explanations for the age-job satisfaction link have been mentioned in the literature but are not directly testable with available data. One is the "cohort theory," which holds that today's young workers are less satisfied because they are the product of a different, less materialistic generation which seeks more fulfillment from its employment than did the earlier cohort. (Aronowitz [1973] advanced this notion, among others.) One reason why this hypothesis is impossible to test directly is that no available data sets contain the necessary longitudinal information on several different cohorts. An indirect test by Janson and Martin (1982) employed proxy variables to control for factors like education which vary by cohort, and rejected the hypothesis.

workers' job satisfaction, tenure, and job characteristics, providing many of the variables needed to distinguish between the theories.[4]

II. Aging and Job Performance

Existing studies on aging and productivity profiles are of two types. One set of analyses, which we examine first, seeks direct empirical confirmation of productivity changes with age using longitudinal data on worker output. However, direct measures of workplace performance are typically unavailable to social scientists. Therefore, a second set of studies which contains indirect evidence on factors like workers' health and job limitations due to health problems is also examined in order to reveal further age-job performance linkages.

A. MEASURING PRODUCTIVITY CHANGES WITH AGE

There is a large literature on the impact of age on physiological and psychological functioning (cf. Bourne 1982; Brousseau 1981; Coates and Kirby 1982). Many analysts argue that age has a "decremental" effect on physical and mental capabilities on average, though some have suggested that the variability in individual capabilities also increases with age. Age-related physiological changes include a deterioration in sensory functions (hearing and vision), lung capacity, muscular strength, and bone structure (Coates and Kirby 1982; Fleisher and Kaplan 1980; and Riley and Foner 1968 review several studies of these issues). There is also some evidence of decline in mental capabilities with age. Psychomotor skill (measured by response speed) peaks in the mid-twenties and declines slowly thereafter. Bourne's overview (1982) reports that older people tend to be more anxious, exhibit greater caution, and take longer to make decisions than younger people. Time pressure and increased

---

A different view, termed by some the "grinding down" hypothesis, holds that older workers are more satisfied with their jobs because the process of aging lowers youthful expectations. A direct test of this hypothesis is also impossible at present, since longitudinal data are not available on how job satisfaction changes with age for a given worker, holding other factors constant. Lacking longitudinal data, previous studies compared older and younger workers' expectations, and concluded that aspirations are generally similar (Wright and Hamilton 1978). Hence this hypothesis is not supported with available data.

4. Self-selection may affect empirical job satisfaction measures for older workers in another way as well: older workers who are unhappy with their jobs may be more likely to retire. The data set analyzed below also excludes retirees, so this possibility cannot be directly addressed here either. Future research should consider this issue in more depth.

task complexity also tend to reduce older people's efficiency. For example, the ability to learn new tasks is comparable among the young and the old as long as time constraints are not imposed (cf. Baugher 1978; Fleisher and Kaplan 1980). On the other hand, longitudinal analysis which controls for cohort effects (via education) indicates that intelligence does not decline until around age 70 (Brousseau 1981). Verbal skills and information-processing capacity have been found to remain constant or to increase with age.

Unfortunately, most of these general findings on age and performance pertain to overall functioning in laboratory settings and thus may not be relevant to performance on the job. A few productivity studies which were conducted at the workplace indicate that older workers perform, on the whole, as well as their younger counterparts; indeed, in some cases, their greater experience, training, and judgment resulted in superior performance (Brousseau 1981; Fleisher and Kaplan 1980; Sonnenfeld 1978).

Nonetheless, several problems make it difficult to draw reliable conclusions about the shape of age-job productivity profiles based on these studies. First, job productivity (output produced per labor hour) is inherently difficult to quantify. One direct approach to measuring output uses piece rates, a practice common, for instance, in the garment industry. But pay scales depend solely on an individual worker's output in only a tiny minority of jobs. In addition, measuring productivity using piece rates does not hold quality of output constant. A different method relies on worker self-reports, but here too data accuracy has been proven to be problematic. The method preferred by personnel practitioners is performance evaluation. It involves observers' interpretations of jobs using rating and ranking schemes, descriptive essays, job content checklists, and the like. These approaches are also prone to error, however, and further refinement is currently being attempted (Gibson et al. 1982).

Because of the difficulties inherent in measuring worker productivity, a second group of analysts has chosen to use proxy variables to reveal productivity changes with age. These include indicators of absenteeism, turnover, illness, and accident rates. Here the data show that older workers tend to be absent for reasons of illness less often than the young but to experience longer recovery periods and lose more workdays per year when illness does occur (Coates and Kirby 1982). Health problems therefore appear to affect the labor market attachment of older workers (Coates and Kirby 1982; Giniger, Dispenzieri, and Eisenberg 1983; Riley and Foner 1968; Sonnenfeld 1978).

On-the-job accidents and injuries are alternative indicators of age-linked productivity problems. Data on frequency of accidents indicate the probability of injury, usually expressed in terms of the number of injuries per worker per time period exposed. Severity of injury data, on the other hand, measure the degree of impairment associated with an injury received; severity is usually classified as temporary disability, permanent disability, or fatality. Most studies on the link between aging and worker accidents report that young employees are more likely to be injured on the job than are older or prime-age workers by virtue of their lack of work experience. For instance, Kossoris (1940), using evidence on American, Swiss, and Austrian workers, found that the frequency of occupational injury fell with age. Later studies by Dillingham (1979, 1981a) and Root (1981) support his conclusion. However, the exact shape of the relationship remains a matter of controversy; it is still an open question as to whether injuries decline smoothly with age or whether some other pattern is present. Root, who tabulated 1977 U.S. information collected from Workers' Compensation files in thirty states, found a declining incidence of injuries with age. Using New York State data, Dillingham found that males under age 25 had the highest injury rates, with the rate for those over 25 only half that of the younger group. My own study (Mitchell 1988) is one of the very few to test for statistically significant differences in injury frequency by age after controlling for other variables. In general, I found that injury rates rise with age only for workers aged 65 and older.

Though the evidence shows that older workers do suffer fewer injuries, it has been conjectured that their injuries are more serious than younger workers'. Kossoris (1940) concluded that older workers, when injured, were more likely to sustain a longer recovery period if temporarily disabled and had higher rates of permanent disability and death than the young. Root (1981) agreed that job-related death and disability rates are higher among older employees. In addition, he noted that temporary disabilities are more prevalent among the young. Dillingham's (1979) work supported these inferences in general, though he argued that permanent disability rates were highest among those under 25.

As with the frequency rates, the exact shape of the age-severity of injury relationship is the subject of controversy. Kossoris detected a positive trend in the severity of injury with age in his Swiss and U.S. data, where severity was defined as the proportion of deaths and permanent disabilities per thousand injuries. Death rates caused by injury were somewhat higher for workers in their fifties, with greatly increased rates for those over age 60. The pattern for permanent disabilities, while similar, was less clear but still suggestive. In contrast, evidence from New York State shows U-shaped profiles (Dillingham 1979): workers under age 25 suffered the highest permanent disability rates, while those 45 and over had the highest fatality rates. Both death and permanent impairment rates were lowest for the group aged 25–44. Root (1981) found no distinct relationship between age and severity. None of these studies tested for statistically significant differences in severity by age.

Only one study, that by Root (1981), dealt with injury characteristics by age. Though he examined the nature, source, and type of injury as well as the part of the body affected, he noted that the percentage of workers in all age brackets suffering each kind of injury appeared about the same. Generally, older workers seemed to have more hernias, heart attacks, and fractures but fewer cuts, lacerations, and burns than the young. Injuries due to falls rose with age. However, no tests were provided to indicate whether those general patterns were statistically significant.

There is also evidence on poor health and age patterns as they vary across occupations and industries (Mitchell, Levine, and Pozzebon 1988). For instance, surveys administered to retirees aged 55 and over indicate that their reasons for leaving their previous occupation often include poor health (U.S. Department of Labor 1980, 1982, 1985). My calculations using these data imply that poor health is offered more often as a reason for retirement by men leaving blue-collar occupations (about one-quarter reply that poor health induced them to leave) than by white-collar males (only 15 percent of this group cited poor health).

A positive relationship between poor health and age is corroborated by studies which use longitudinal rather than cross-sectional data; Schwab (1974) computed the percentage of men aged 58–63 with self-reported health-imposed work limitations by tenure in longest job, and found that blue-collar employees (e.g., craftsmen, operatives, nonfarm laborers) were more likely to report health-related work limitations than those in white-collar occupations (professionals, managers, clerical and sales).[5] This is compatible with Andrisani's (1977) report as well as more recent work by Gustman and Steinmeier (1985). While the evidence clearly shows that blue-collar workers with health limitations leave the labor force far more often than do white-collar employees, it is not yet clear whether health limitations hinder productivity more powerfully in blue-collar jobs or whether distaste for work is stronger among blue-collar employees, so that a given health limitation has more of a deterrent effect than it does among white-collar workers.[6]

5. Since Schwab's data sample included workers and nonworkers, this analysis is less likely to be subject to sample selection problems described elsewhere.

6. In addition to these indirect studies of age-productivity profiles, there is some direct evidence gathered from case studies of white-collar workers (e.g., scholars, scientists, and artists; managers; sales and clerical workers; and paraprofessionals) and blue-collar workers (e.g., manual laborers and printing press workers); see Mitchell, Levine, and Pozzebon 1988.

Very little information exists on intersectoral differences in job risk by age. The U.S. Department of Labor (1980, 1982, 1985), Root (1981), and Dillingham (1979) showed that blue-collar jobs are more dangerous in absolute terms than other jobs, particularly in the construction and manufacturing industries. Dillingham (1983) also found that (1) the frequency of injury was lower for older workers than for those younger than age 25 in blue-collar, white-collar, and service jobs; (2) injury severity generally worsened with age for all three occupational groupings; and (3) aging was associated with the highest absolute fatality risk in blue-collar jobs. The frequency of temporary and permanent disabilities, as well as fatalities, was also highest in absolute terms for blue-collar workers in corresponding age groups relative to other workers. My own regression analysis (Mitchell 1988) confirmed that age and occupational status were the primary determinants of injury risk among males. Dillingham (1981b) further claimed that age and injury rates were positively linked for women workers.[7]

B. LIMITATIONS AND IMPLICATIONS OF PREVIOUS RESEARCH

A serious problem confronting researchers interested in investigating how productivity patterns change with age is the absence of nationally representative data containing productivity information. Because no survey contains all the information necessary to assess productivity patterns by age, many authors have resorted to using other types of information which attempt to measure productivity indirectly. Few existing studies test for age effects using modern statistical tools or control for other relevant variables. Even when age is held constant, aggregation of age groups makes it virtually impossible to evaluate differential risk patterns for particular subsets of older workers. Seniority on the job is rarely controlled, so that it is impossible to determine whether age or inexperience is the factor more closely associated with risk. It is evident that a more detailed statistical analysis of age patterns by sector would be informative.

While studies on health, age, and job performance indicate that older workers are often as productive as younger workers and are injured less frequently, it is not clear whether age is the explanation for the negative age-job risk profile or whether age might be reflecting a "life cycle" phenomenon. It is known that older workers are employed in somewhat different occupations and industries than younger ones and are thus exposed to fewer and different health risks (e.g., they are more likely to be supervisors than production-line workers). One testable implication of this life cycle hypothesis is that the correlation between age

7. Also important is the relationship between age and job-related illness, but data on occupational illness are extremely poor due to the difficulty of collection.

and performance problems should drop and perhaps disappear altogether when job characteristics like occupation and industry are controlled. In addition, it would be useful to explore further Dillingham's (1979) finding that older workers suffer more severe health repercussions when injured, though the incidence of injuries seems to fall with age. More severe problems among older workers may simply be the result of cumulative exposure to job risks, since many health problems take years to develop (e.g., those associated with exposure to environmental hazards in particular industries and occupations). This "exposure hypothesis" has a testable implication, in that, if we control for tenure, we would anticipate that the effect of age on productivity problems due to poor health would be moderated or eliminated.[8]

III. Aging and Health Status: An Empirical Analysis

Let us turn to an empirical analysis of how workers' health status and health limitations on the job change with age, as we seek to determine whether age exacerbates or moderates general and specific work-related health problems. The greater severity of older workers' job-related health problems may be due to greater exposure, a hypothesis which is also tested.

A. DATA EMPLOYED

To investigate how aging affects workers' performance and job satisfaction, a sample of 787 wage and salary workers (61 percent males and 39 percent females) was taken from the 1977 Quality of Employment Survey (QES) file. Collected by the University of Michigan Institute for Social Research, the data set contains extensive information on a nationally representative sample of workers and their jobs. The QES contains many different questions useful for delving into employee dissatisfaction and performance. For the present purposes, these are organized into two main types: job dissatisfaction variables and problems with worker productivity and health variables (see Table 3).

Indices for job dissatisfaction range from general indicators ("unsatisfied," "meaningless") to several detailed questions regarding a worker's compensation ("pay bad") and intrinsic job content ("fast pace," "danger," "contaminants"). Variables indicating perceptions of productivity and health problems are of two types. One set of factors indicates workers' perceptions of their own health status. The second set

8. This assumes that tenure on the job is a reasonable proxy for tenure in the sector. Since this correlation is low for some workers, tenure in the occupation and industry would be more useful, but very few data sets report it.

Table 3: INDICES OF JOB CONTENT/SATISFACTION AND WORKER PRODUCTIVITY/HEALTH

Variable	Rating System	Mean
Job satisfaction		
Unsatisfied	1 if somewhat or very unsatisfied with job; 0 otherwise	11%
Meaningless	1 if work is not main satisfaction, or job meaningless or uninteresting, or job requires little learning, or work repetitive; 0 otherwise	3%
Pay bad	1 if pay or fringe benefits are bad; 0 otherwise	22%
Job content		
Fast pace	1 if required to work fast or not enough time to do job; 0 otherwise	29%
Danger	1 if exposed to dangerous equipment; 0 otherwise	28%
Contaminants	1 if exposed to pollution, fire, chemicals, extreme temperatures indoors; 0 otherwise	59%
Health status		
Weeks sick	no. of wks. away from work due to illness or injury	1.31
Tired	1 if worker tires in short time; 0 otherwise	26%
Breath	1 if worker has difficulty breathing; 0 otherwise	19%
Back	1 if worker has back trouble; 0 otherwise	36%
Health and job limitations		
Circulation	1 if worker has circulatory ailment limiting work; 0 otherwise	1%
Musc/Skel	1 if worker has muscular/skeletal ailment limiting work; 0 otherwise	3%
Nerves	1 if worker has nervous disorder limiting work; 0 otherwise	2%
Respiratory	1 if worker has respiratory problems limiting work; 0 otherwise	4%

reveals employees' perceptions of strain and limitations on the job due to health factors.

Because self-assessment health indices of this sort are imperfect measures of true health status (Bazzoli 1985; Parsons 1982), we focus on the more objective measure available in the data—work time lost due to illness or injury ("weeks sick"). If a worker mentions specific ailments (e.g., tiredness, back problems, or shortness of breath), those too are noted. Finally, the individual is asked to indicate the existence of circulatory, respiratory, nervous, muscular, or skeletal afflictions exacerbated

Table 4: AVERAGE VALUES OF JOB CONTENT/SATISFACTION AND PERFORMANCE VARIABLES, BY AGE GROUP

	Age	
	Under 55	55 and Older
Job content/satisfaction		
Unsatisfied	12	6**
Meaningless	4	0**
Pay bad	22	18
Fast pace	73	60
Danger	29	26
Contaminants	59	57
Worker productivity/health		
Weeks sick	1.39	0.78**
Tired	25	32
Breath	19	22
Back	36	40
Circulation	0.3	6**
Musc/Skel	2	7**
Nerves	2	1**
Respiratory	0.1	2**
Total N	686	101

**Statistically different at $p=0.05$.
Note: for definitions of variables, see Table 3.

by working conditions; these too are examined in some depth. Except for the "weeks sick" variable, which is continuous, all outcome measures take on a value of 1 if the worker indicates dissatisfaction with the job or its content and 0 otherwise.

Before evaluating the specific theories linking aging with job satisfaction and performance indicators in a multivariate context, it is useful to obtain a general impression of the patterns by age in this data set. Table 4 presents, for this nationally representative sample of workers, a breakdown of the values of job satisfaction and performance outcomes for workers in two age groups, those under 55 and those 55 and over.[9] In this survey, older and younger workers' answers to the questions differ at conventional statistical levels for only half of the fourteen variables. Specifically, workers' opinions about whether their jobs are dangerous or expose them to contaminants do not differ by age; there is

9. The QES sample analyzed here contains 153 workers under age 25, 241 aged 25–43, 156 aged 35–44, 136 aged 45–54, 88 aged 55–64, and 13 aged 65 and over. Analysis of finer age categories is precluded by the relatively small sample sizes at the older end of the age spectrum.

also no difference by age in workers' assessment of their pay. Older and younger workers also prove to be equally likely to report breathing problems, difficulties with their backs, and fatigue.

Where responses do differ statistically across age groups, older workers prove to have fewer (rather than more) complaints than their younger counterparts in four out of seven variables. With regard to the general job satisfaction index, the data agree with findings elsewhere in the literature: older workers are statistically more likely to be satisfied with their work, and far fewer criticize their jobs as meaningless than do younger workers. In general, then, the QES survey offers no evidence that older workers are less satisfied with their jobs than younger employees, either in general or when asked about specifics.

A more mixed picture prevails for the indicators of worker productivity and health limitations on the job. Older workers report a significantly lower rate of time off due to sickness and lower rates of limitations due to nervous conditions. On the other hand, older workers attest to being more hampered on the job by circulatory, respiratory, and muscular/skeletal conditions than their younger peers.

In general, the simple tabulations imply that there is no unidirectional empirical link between aging, job satisfaction, and job performance, suggesting the importance of further analysis before firm conclusions can be drawn.

B. MULTIVARIATE ANALYSIS

A multivariate format is needed to probe age differences while holding constant measurable job and worker characteristics that differ by age. This is accomplished by controlling measurable differences across jobs and workers with models of the form $y=f(\mathbf{A}, \mathbf{X}, e)$, where y is the dependent variable of interest; **A** is a vector of age terms; **X** is a vector of other explanatory terms; and e is a random disturbance term. Two empirical approaches are employed: multinomial Logit, which takes into account the fact that most of the dependent variables of interest are dichotomous rather than continuous,[10] and linear regression in the one case where the dependent variable is continuous rather than qualitative ("weeks off").

Two sets of models are presented here for the job satisfaction and content variables, differing in the way in which the age variables are formulated. Table 5 uses age and age-squared as controls, indicating whether the outcome in question becomes more or less prevalent with age and also whether the outcome becomes more or less prevalent with

10. Other authors who use qualitative variables in the QES data set do not employ nonlinear models (cf. Janson and Martin 1982; Wright and Hamilton 1978).

increasing age. To assess the robustness of the aging variables in a different way, we also estimate models in which binary age controls indicate whether the respondent is under age 25 or aged 55 and over (the reference category is workers aged 25–54). These results appear in Table 6. In general, if an explanatory variable has a positive (negative) coefficient, this should be interpreted as a direct (inverse) association between that variable and the outcome in question. For instance, when age is negatively associated with the outcome "Unsatisfied," this indicates that older workers are less likely to report that they are dissatisfied with their jobs. In all cases coefficient estimates must be statistically significant at least at the 10 percent level (indicated by one asterisk) or the 5 percent level (two asterisks) in order to warrant attention in the discussion below.

For each outcome variable we estimate both a simple model, which includes only age terms, and an extended model. The extended formulation, in addition to controlling for age, also includes tenure, industry and occupation controls, and three additional variables: the worker's union status, gender, and firm size. The union variable indicates the degree to which workers have input into and can alter their working conditions (Freeman and Medoff 1984). A separate intercept for female respondents is included to determine whether sex differences mentioned in some of the studies above persist in multivariate analysis. Firm size is a proxy for the degree of supervision and monitoring at the workplace; workers at larger firms are probably less closely monitored (Parsons 1980). The industry and occupation controls, while not of primary interest in their own right, are included to test the life cycle hypothesis discussed earlier. (Table 7 lists definitions for explanatory variables employed.)

C. FINDINGS FOR JOB SATISFACTION AND JOB CONTENT VARIABLES

It will be recalled that the general finding of previous studies, in which other variables were not controlled, was that of a positive relationship between aging and overall satisfaction on the job. Less unanimity prevailed regarding specific job facet or content variables. We hypothesized that the life cycle hypothesis might explain this finding if the relationship between age and performance problems disappears when job characteristics like occupation and industry are controlled. Another view, the "self-selection" view, held that the positive age/satisfaction pattern should decline if tenure is controlled.

A first conclusion from the QES models is that aging has a surprisingly small effect on the available indicators of job satisfaction and job content when tested using conventional statistical tools (see columns

Table 5: AGE AND OTHER DETERMINANTS OF JOB SATISFACTION, PRODUCTIVITY, AND HEALTH

	Unsatisfied (1)		*Meaningless* (2)		*Pay Bad* (3)		*Fast Pace* (4)		*Danger* (5)		*Contaminants* (6)	
Age	−.02	.02	.06	LIMIT	−.17	−.13**	.05	.05	−.04	−.10**	−.05	−.09**
	(.06)	(.06)	(.13)		(.04)	(.04)	(.04)	(.04)	(.04)	(.05)	(.04)	(.04)
Agesq	.00004	−.0003	−.002		.002**	.002**	−.001**	−.001	.0003	.001	.0004	.001
	(.0001)	(.001)	(.002)		(.001)	(.001)	(.0005)	(.001)	(.001)	(.001)	(.0004)	(.001)
Tenure		−.04*				−.05**		.03*		.003	.02	
		(.02)				(.02)		(.01)		(.02)	(.01)	
Union		−.27				−.21		−.07		.32	.55**	
		(.27)				(.22)		(.18)		(.20)	(.19)	
Female		.33				.21		.33*		−1.13**	−.55**	
		(.28)				(.21)		(.20)		(.24)	(.19)	
Frsize		.0002				−.0004**		−.0002		.0002	.0004	
		(.0001)				(.0001)		(.0001)		(.0001)	(.0001)	
Industry controls		xx				xx		xx		xx	xx	
Occupation controls		xx				xx		xx		xx	xx	
Log:	−269.89	−271.51	−109.79	−401.09	−411.95	−467.62	−470.97	−464.94	−468.19	−530.47	−532.44	
Chi:	3.3	23.1	8.9	21.7	80.7	6.7	30.4	6.5	207.7	3.9	200.9	
	(2)	(14)	(2)	(2)	(14)	(2)	(14)	(2)	(14)	(2)	(14)	

Table 5: CONTINUED

	Weeks Sick (OLS) (7)		*Tired* (8)		*Breath* (9)		*Back* (10)		*Circulation* (11)		*Musc/Skel* (12)		*Nerves* (13)		*Respiratory* (14)	
Age	.27	.24	−.06	−.09**	.01	.01	−.02	−.03	LIMIT	LIMIT	.04	−.01	−.06	LIMIT	LIMIT	LIMIT
	(.27)	(.28)	(.04)	(.04)	(.04)	(.05)	(0.4)	(0.4)			(.11)	(.12)	(.12)			
Agesq	−.004	−.004	.001*	.001**	.0001	.00002	.001	.0004			.00003	.00003	.001			
	(.003)	(.003)	(.001)	(.0001)	(.001)	(.001)	(.001)	(.001)			(.001)	(.001)	(.002)			
Tenure		.05		.01		−.02		.01				.05*				
		(.09)		(.01)		(.02)		(.01)				(.03)				
Union		−.09		.58**		.21		.35**				.11				
		(1.25)		(.18)		(.21)		(.17)				(.49)				
Female		−1.01		.49**		.54**		.51**				−.93				
		(1.32)		(.20)		(.22)		(.18)				(.66)				
Frsize		.001		−.0001		−.0002*		−.0001				−.001				
		(.001)		(.0001)		(.0001)		(.0001)				(.0004)				
Industry controls		xx		xx		xx		xx				xx				
Occupation controls		xx		xx		xx		xx				xx				

Log:			−450.66	−452.43	−382.19	−383.34	−515.18	−515.76	−100.58	−103.91	−77.94
Chi:	(R^2=	(R^2=	3.6	25.3	2.33	30.5	1.2	29.5	6.7	28.3	0.4
	.002)	0.02)	(2)	(14)	(2)	(14)	(2)	(14)	(2)	(14)	(2)

Notes: **$t \geq 1.96$; *$t \geq 1.65$ (<1.96); ( ) standard errors. Since most dependent variables are dichotomous, equations 1–6 and 8–14 are estimated using multinomial Logit. A negative coefficient indicates that the explanatory variable reduces the probability of the outcome in question. "Log" indicates the log likelihood value for all explanatory variables but the constant term being significantly different from zero; the "chi" term is the associated chi square value for this hypothesis test (degrees of freedom are indicated in parentheses). A reported value of "Limit" indicates that the Logit model did not converge because of too few cases in one category of the dependent variable. Since "Weeks Off" is a continuous dependent variable, equation 7 is estimated using linear regression. Here R^2 values are reported in lieu of log values. A notation of "xx" signifies that these variables were also included in the model in question.

Table 6: AGE AND OTHER DETERMINANTS OF JOB SATISFACTION, PRODUCTIVITY, AND HEALTH

	Unsatisfied (1)		*Meaningless* (2)		*Pay Bad* (3)		*Fast Pace* (4)		*Danger* (5)		*Contaminants* (6)	
Age 25	.25	−.05	.82**	LIMIT	.49**	.20	−.03	.04	.21	.47*	[illegible]	.55**
	(.27)	(.30)	(.41)		(.21)	(.23)	(.15)	(.23)	(.20)	(.26)	[illegible]	(.24)
Age 55	−.68	−.56	−6.73		−.16	.09	−.58**	−.71	−.09	−.27	[illegible]	−.37
	(.44)	(.46)	(16.34)		(.28)	(.31)	(.23)	(.24)	(.25)	(.29)	[illegible]	(.27)
Tenure		−.04*				−.05**		.02*		.01	[illegible]	
		(.02)				(.02)		(.01)		(.01)	[illegible]	
Union		−.27				−.24		−.04		.31	[illegible]	
		(.27)				(.22)		(.18)		(.20)	[illegible]	
Female		.34				.21		.32*		−1.12**	[illegible]	
		(.28)				(.21)		(.20)		(.24)	[illegible]	
Frsize		.0002				−.0004**		−.0002**		.0002	[illegible]	
		(.0001)				(.0001)		(.0001)		(.0001)	[illegible]	
Industry controls		xx				xx		xx		xx	xx	
Occupation controls		xx				xx		xx		xx	xx	
Log:	−271.51	−271.51	−114.23	−411.95	−411.95	−470.97	−470.97	−468.19	−468.19	−532.4[illegible]	−532.44
Chi:	4.2	24.5	10.9	6.57	72.6	6.6	28.8	1.5	200.5	1.5	197.8
	(2)	(14)	(2)	(2)	(14)	(2)	(14)	(2)	(14)	(2)	(14)

Table 6: CONTINUED

	Weeks Sick (OLS) (7)		*Tired* (8)		*Breath* (9)		*Back* (10)		*Circulation* (11)		*Musc/Skel* (12)		*Nerves* (13)		*Respiratory* (14)	
Age 25	−1.66	−1.57	.01	.11	−.20	−.23	.04	.09	LIMIT	LIMIT	−.22	.07	.24	LIMIT	LIMIT	LIMIT
	(1.30)	(1.43)	(.21)	(.23)	(.24)	(.27)	(.19)	(.21)			(.65)	(.10)	(.59)			
Age 55	−1.07	−1.48	.31	.26	.15	.15	.17	.04			1.09**	.62	−.75			
	(1.67)	(1.75)	(.24)	(.25)	(.26)	(.28)	(.22)	(.24)			(.48)	(1.19)	(1.05)			
Tenure		.01		.01		−.01		.01				.06*				
		(.09)		(.01)		(.01)		(.01)				(.03)				
Union		−.03		.56**		.19		.34**				.10				
		(1.25)		(.18)		(.21)		(.17)				(.49)				
Female		−.99		.50**		.55**		.51**				−.96				
		(1.32)		(.20)		(.22)		(.18)				(.66)				
Frsize		.001		−.0001		−.0002*		−.0001				−.0006				
		(.001)		(.0001)		(.0001)		(.0001)				(.0004)				
Industry controls		xx		xx		xx		xx				xx				
Occupation controls		xx		xx		xx		xx				xx				
Log:			−452.43	−452.43	−383.34	−383.34	−515.76	−515.76	−103.91	−103.91	−77.70					
Chi:	(R^2= .002)	(R^2= 0.02)	1.6	22.2	1.26	28.4	.57	28.8	5.2	28.5	0.9					
			(2)	(14)	(2)	(14)	(2)	(14)	(2)	(14)	(2)					

Notes: see Table 5.

Table 7: CONTROL VARIABLES EMPLOYED

Variable		Mean or Percentage
Age		
Age	Age in yrs.	36.9 yrs.
Age sq	Age • age	1534.3 yrs.
Age 25	Age less than 25	19 %
Age 55	Age 55 and over	13 %
Other Control Variables		
Tenure	No. of yrs. with present employer	7.16 yrs.
Frsize	No. of employees at firm	548 workers
Union	1 if worker belongs to a union or is covered by a union contract; 0 otherwise	34 %
Female	1 if female; 0 otherwise	39 %
Industry		
Agric/ contruc.	1 if extractive or construction industry; 0 otherwise (reference category)	8 %
Manufacturing	1 if manufacturing industry; 0 otherwise	26 %
Trans/trade	1 if transport, communications, utilities or trade industry; 0 otherwise	26 %
Services	1 if services industry; 0 otherwise	31 %
Public admin.	1 if public administration industry; 0 otherwise	9 %
Occupation		
Professional/ manager	1 if professional, technical, or manager occupation; 0 otherwise (reference category)	28 %
Service	1 if service occupation; 0 otherwise	13 %
Clerical/sales	1 if sales or clerical occupation; 0 otherwise	20 %
Craft/operative	1 if craft or operative occupation; 0 otherwise	34 %
Labor	1 if laborer occupation; 0 otherwise	5 %

1–6 in Tables 5 and 6). When age alone is held constant, neither age nor the age-squared term is individually significant for four of six outcomes, and in the two cases where age is significant it appears to be caused by greater dissatisfaction among the young rather than among the old (see "Fast Pace" and "Pay Bad"). This surmise is confirmed in the "Fast Pace" model, including binary age terms (Table 6), since here the coefficient on the older worker term is statistically negative, indicating fewer instead of more complaints among older employees. In general, then, models which include only age terms tend to cast doubt on the notion that older workers are less satisfied with their jobs.

The overall insignificance of the estimated age effects in the simple models also implies that testing the life cycle and selection hypothesis by including additional controls like tenure and occupation/industry dummies will not provide evidence strongly supportive of either theory. In two cases, adding control variables does remove significance from the age terms, consistent with the life cycle view ("Pay Bad," "Fast Pace"). In two other cases, however, adding control variables increases rather than decreases the statistical significance of the younger worker age effect without altering the insignificant coefficient for the "Age 55+" variable ("Danger" and "Contaminants").[11] Hence there is no evidence that older workers are less satisfied with their jobs after controlling for other factors, contradicting both hypotheses.

Focusing briefly on the statistical significance of the remaining explanatory variables in the job satisfaction equations, it is interesting to note that findings are robust irrespective of the way the age variables are modeled. Greater tenure reduces reports of overall dissatisfaction and dissatisfaction with pay but appears to increase workers' reports of fast-paced work in both Tables 5 and 6. The union effect is surprisingly weak, attaining significance only in a single case ("Contaminants"). Women workers prove rather similar to men insofar as overall job dissatisfaction is concerned, though they do report somewhat more trouble with fast-paced work and less difficulty with contaminants and dangerous jobs in both empirical formulations. Firm size is negatively related to reports of low pay, but to no other variables. Industry and occupation terms are not consistently significant, nor do they display a coherent pattern across models.[12]

D. FINDINGS FOR WORKER PRODUCTIVITY AND HEALTH VARIABLES

Previous studies suggested that older workers are often as productive and are injured less frequently than younger ones, though it has not been determined whether age *per se* is the explanation for the negative age/job risk profile or rather whether the age variable might be reflecting a life cycle phenomenon. We test the hypothesis by controlling for occupation and industry. We also test the exposure hypothesis by controlling for tenure. Results appear in columns 7–14 of Tables 5 and 6.

11. The extended model could not be estimated for one dependent variable, "Meaningless," because there were too few positive responses to the survey question.
12. Coefficient estimates for industry and occupation effects are available from the author on request.

For only one outcome variable the evidence suggests that greater problems reported by older workers may, in fact, be due to lack of controls for other variables: this occurs for the variable "Musc/Skel" indicating the presence of muscular and skeletal problems limiting the worker's job performance. Specifically, the aging effect is statistically insignificant in the extended models of both Tables 5 and 6, whereas older workers had indicated significantly more problems along this dimension in the cross-tabulation of Table 4.

For the remainder of the outcome variables, there is very little evidence in support of a strong link between aging, job performance, and health. In one model of the "Tired" outcome, where age and age-squared are employed, there is no change in statistically significant age coefficients irrespective of whether age effects alone are included or whether the extended model is used (Table 5, column 8). However, this is true only in the first formulation, since age is never significant in the second model. In three cases the extended (and sometimes the simple) models could not be estimated because of insufficient numbers of individuals responding that they had these problems ("Circulation," "Nerves," and "Respiratory"). For the remaining three variables ("Weeks Off," "Breath," and "Back"), the results are similar to those found above: generally, age effects are not statistically significant in either the simple or the extended models. Hence, one cannot conclude that aging has a negative effect on either the most objective measure used here ("Weeks Sick") or on the more subjective reports of health problems and health limitations. Further, the findings also contradict both the life cycle and the exposure hypotheses, since age effects either grow stronger or remain insignificant when other factors are held constant.

Again a brief review of the other control variables is warranted. In contrast to the job satisfaction models, the controls prove to be more statistically significant on the whole. Union workers and those with long tenure have significantly more back problems, irrespective of the way in which age variables are modeled. Interestingly enough, women report more difficulties with being tired, breathing, and back trouble even after holding constant industry and occupation in which they are employed. Employees in larger firms report fewer problems with breathing, though firm size is not significant otherwise.[13]

E. CONCLUSIONS

New empirical evidence on the links between aging, job satisfaction, and job performance using data from a nationally representative

13. A listing of estimated industry and occupation effects is available from the author on request.

survey of workers yields some surprises. Statistical testing of previously reported age effects suggests that aging has only a small impact on overall job satisfaction outcomes. When specific measures of job content are evaluated, where age is significant it appears to be caused by greater dissatisfaction among the young rather than among the old. These results cast doubt on previous reports of more job satisfaction among older workers. Employee reports of problems with job productivity and health limitations are more mixed. In the case of muscular and skeletal problems limiting the worker's job performance, the evidence suggests that greater difficulties reported by older workers in previous studies may be explained by researchers' inability to hold constant other variables. For the remainder of the outcome variables examined here, there is very little support for a link between aging, job performance, and health. Indeed, we find no evidence that aging has a negative effect on either the most "objective" measure used here ("Weeks Sick") or on the more subjective reports of health problems and health limitations.

The purpose of exploring the links between age, job performance, and job satisfaction was to determine how employee productivity and satisfaction changes with age in order to help understand why older workers appear to be retiring earlier over time. The evidence shows that conventional wisdom may be correct: older workers are equally, if not more, healthy, satisfied, and productive employees than their younger counterparts. There is very little support for the contention that earlier retirement is the result of declines in job satisfaction and/or productivity.

It must be emphasized that the empirical research focuses only on workers, like all earlier studies on this topic. If some individuals leave the labor force as a result of workplace problems, the findings may understate older people's limitations on the job. It might be thought that an examination of retirees' health problems could provide an estimate of the extent to which people leave their jobs because of health and/or productivity considerations. However, retirees' reports of health problems probably overstate the actual extent of poor health as a motive for retirement (Anderson and Burkhauser 1985; Burtless 1987; Fields and Mitchell 1984; and Sammartino 1987). As a result, selectivity bias due to workers dropping out of the labor force may not be as significant a problem as might be suspected. The QES survey used here does not permit analysis of this issue; a longitudinal survey following those who leave the labor force would be necessary to determine whether patterns of aging and health-related performance problems of workers on the job look very different from those of workers who leave their jobs.

A final point regarding the role of health and productivity in retirement decisions should be made. There is virtually no evidence that the national trend to early retirement over the last forty years noted at the outset of the paper is attributable to worsening health (Baily 1987). Other explanations must be sought for the increasing prevalence of labor force withdrawal among relatively young workers, those in their late fifties and early sixties. Recent economic research suggests that the growing prevalence and generosity of retirement income programs, both in the form of company pensions and Social Security, may be a more important motivation (Fields and Mitchell 1984; Parsons 1987).

References

Anderson, K., and R. Burkhauser. 1985. "The Retirement-Health Nexus: A New Measure of an Old Puzzle," *Journal of Human Resources* 20: 315–30.

Andrisani, P. 1977. "Effects of Health Problems on the Work Experience of Middle-Aged Workers," *Industrial Gerontology* 4: 97–112.

Aronowitz, S. 1973. *False Promises: The Shaping of American Working Class Consciousness.* New York: McGraw-Hill.

Baily, M. N. 1987. "Aging and the Ability to Work." In *Work, Health and Income among the Elderly,* edited by G. Burtless. Washington, D.C.: Brookings Institution.

Baugher, D. 1978. "Is the Older Worker Inherently Incompetent?" *Aging and Work* 1: 243–50.

Bazzoli, G. 1985. "The Early Retirement Decision: New Empirical Evidence on the Influence of Health," *Journal of Human Resources* 20: 214–34.

Borjas, G. J. 1979. "Job Satisfaction, Wages and Unions," *Journal of Human Resources* 14: 21–40.

Bourne, B. 1982. "Effects of Aging on Work Satisfaction, Performance and Motivation," *Aging and Work* 5: 37–47.

Brousseau, K. 1981. "After Age Forty: Employment Patterns and Practices in the United States." In *After Forty: The Time for Achievement,* edited by C. L. Cooper and D. P. Torrington. Chichester, England: John Wiley and Sons, Ltd.

Burtless, G. 1987. "Occupational Effects on the Health and Work Capacity of Older Men." In *Work, Health and Income among the Elderly,* edited by G. Burtless. Washington, D.C.: Brookings Institution.

Coates, G. D., and R. H. Kirby. 1982. "Organismic Factors and Individual Differences in Human Performance and Productivity." In *Human Performance and Productivity: Stress and Performance Effectiveness,* Vol. 3, edited by E. A. Alluisi and E. A. Fleishman. Hillsdale, N.J.: Lawrence Erlbaum Associates.

Cohn, R. M. 1979. "Age and the Satisfaction from Work," *Journal of Gerontology* 34: 264–72.

Dillingham, A. E. 1979. "The Injury Risk Structure of Occupations and Wages." Ph. D. diss. Cornell University.

———. 1981a. "New Evidence on Age and Workplace Injuries," *Aging and Work* 4: 1–10.

———. 1981b. "Sex Differences in Labor Market Injury Risk," *Industrial Relations* 20: 117–22.
———. 1983. "Demographic and Economic Change and the Costs of Workers' Compensation." In *Safety and the Work Force: Incentives and Disincentives in Workers' Compensation,* edited by J. D. Worrall. Ithaca, N.Y.: ILR Press.
Fields, G. S., and O. S. Mitchell. 1984. *Retirement, Pensions and Social Security.* Cambridge, Mass.: MIT Press.
Fleisher, D., and B. H. Kaplan. 1980. "Characteristics of Older Workers: Implications for Restructuring Work." In *Work and Retirement: Policy Issues,* edited by P. K. Ragan. Los Angeles: University of Southern California Press.
Freeman, R. B., and J. L. Medoff. 1984. *What Do Unions Do?* New York: Basic Books.
Gibson, J. L., and S. M. Klein. 1970. "Employee Attitudes as a Function of Age and Length of Service: A Reconceptualization," *Academy of Management Journal* 13: 411–25.
Gibson, J. L., J. M. Ivancevich, and J. H. Donnelly. 1982. *Organizations: Behavior, Structure, Processes.* 4th ed. Plano, Tex.: Business Publications, Inc.
Giniger, S., A. Dispenzieri, and J. Eisenberg. 1983. "Age, Experience, and Performance on Speed and Skill Jobs in an Applied Setting," *Journal of Applied Psychology* 68: 469–75.
Glenn, N. D., P. A. Taylor, and C. N. Weaver. 1977. "Age and Job Satisfaction among Males and Females: A Multivariate, Multisurvey Study," *Journal of Applied Psychology* 62: 189–93.
Gustman, A. S., and T. L. Steinmeier. 1985. "A Disaggregated, Structural Analysis of Retirement by Race, Difficulty of Work, and Health." NBER Working Paper No. 1585. National Bureau of Economic Research, Cambridge, Mass.
Holley, W. H., H. S. Field, and B. B. Holley. 1978. "Age and Reactions to Jobs: An Empirical Study of Paraprofessional Workers," *Aging and Work* 1: 33–40.
Hulin, C. L., and P. C. Smith. 1965. "A Linear Model of Job Satisfaction," *Journal of Applied Psychology* 49: 209–16.
Hunt, J. W., and P. N. Saul. 1975. "The Relationship of Age, Tenure and Job Satisfaction in Males and Females," *Academy of Management Journal* 18: 690–702.
Hutchens, R. 1986. "Delayed Payment Contracts and Firm's Propensity to Hire Older Workers," *Journal of Labor Economics* 4: 439–57.
Janson, P., and J. K. Martin. 1982. "Job Satisfaction and Age: A Test of Two Views," *Social Forces* 60: 1089–1102.
Kossoris, M. D. 1940. "Relation of Age to Industrial Injuries," *Monthly Labor Review* 4: 789–804.
Lazear, E. 1979. "Why Is There Mandatory Retirement?" *Journal of Political Economy* 87: 1261–84.
Locke, E. A. 1976. "The Nature and Causes of Job Satisfaction." In *Handbook of Industrial and Organizational Psychology,* edited by M. D. Dunnette. Chicago: Rand McNally.

Mitchell, O. S. 1988. "The Relation of Age to Workplace Injury," *Monthly Labor Review* 111: 8–13.

Mitchell, O. S., P. Levine, and S. Pozzebon. 1988. "Retirement Differences by Industry and Occupation," *Gerontologist* 28: 545–51.

Muchinsky, P. M. 1978. "Age and Job Facet Satisfaction: A Conceptual Reconsideration," *Aging and Work* 1: 175–79.

Organ, D. W., and W. C. Hamner. 1982. *Organizational Behavior.* Plano, Tex.: Business Publications, Inc.

Parsons, D. O. 1980. "The Decline in Male Labor Force Participation," *Journal of Political Economy* 70: 117–34.

———. 1982. "The Male Labor Force Participation Decision: Health, Reported Health, and Economic Incentives," *Economica* 49: 81–91.

———. 1987. "Male Retirement Behavior in the US, 1930–1950." Ohio State University Department of Economics working paper. Mimeo.

Phillips, J. S., G. J. Barret, and M. C. Rush. 1978. "Job Structure and Age Satisfaction," *Aging and Work* 1: 109–19.

Quinn, R. P., G. L. Staines, and M. R. McCullough. 1974. *Job Satisfaction: Is There a Trend?* U.S. Department of Labor Manpower Research Monograph 30. Washington, D.C.: U.S. Government Printing Office.

Riley, W. M., and A. Foner, 1968. *Aging and Society,* Vol. 1. New York: Russell Sage Foundation.

Root, N. 1981. "Injuries at Work Are Fewer among Older Employees," *Monthly Labor Review* 104: 30–34.

Sammartino, F. 1987. "The Effect of Health on Retirement," *Social Security Bulletin* 50: 31–47.

Schwab, K. 1974. "Early Labor-Force Withdrawal of Men: Participants and Nonparticipants Aged 58–63," *Social Security Bulletin* 37: 24–38.

Schwab, D. P., and H. G. Heneman. 1977. "Effects of Age and Experience on Productivity," *Industrial Gerontology* 4: 113–17.

Sonnenfeld, J. 1978. "Dealing with the Aging Work Force," *Harvard Business Review* 56: 81–92.

Stagner, R. 1975. "Boredom on the Assembly Line: Age and Personality Variables," *Industrial Gerontology* 2: 23–44.

U.S. Department of Labor, Bureau of Labor Statistics. Current Population Survey data tapes, various years.

———. 1980. *Occupational Injuries and Illnesses in the United States by Industry, 1978.* Bulletin 2078. Washington, D.C.: U.S. Government Printing Office.

———. 1982. *Occupational Injuries and Illnesses in the United States by Industry, 1980.* Bulletin 2130. Washington, D.C.: U.S. Government Printing Office.

———. 1985. *Occupational Injuries and Illnesses in the United States by Industry, 1983.* Bulletin 2236. Washington, D.C.: U.S. Government Printing Office.

Wright, J. D., and R. F. Hamilton. 1978. "Work Satisfaction and Age: Some Evidence for the 'Job Change' Hypothesis," *Social Forces* 56: 1140–58.

Part IV
Productivity, Training, and Retraining

The Aging of Organizations: Strategic Issues

ERNEST J. SAVOIE

Savoie reports a culture change in Ford's human relations approach as the challenges to the viability of the automobile industry escalate. The company had to recognize that retrenchment increased the average age of the work force, with special problems. Key issues include internal cost push (pensions, health care, and vacation pay, for instance); organizational performance; human values; and teamwork. These call for new management systems within the framework of a broad range of adjustments created by current economic challenges. Despite these new demands, it has become evident at Ford, says Savoie, that there are definite advantages to having an older work force, and the employees have responded well to the changed labor relations climate and the transformation within the company.

I. B.

The aging of the U.S. population and the attendant social, political, and labor market implications are well known to human resource professionals and have been extensively documented. The aging individual, too, has long been the subject of thoughtful study, and consequently a fairly large body of knowledge exists. Much less attention, however, has been given to organizations whose people are aging and to the special issues that are associated with this phenomenon.

Many American companies—indeed, many entire industries—are today facing these issues. As competitive pressures grow and as offices and factories are increasingly automated, work forces of numerous organizations are shrinking or, at best, are barely managing to hold their own. Growth prospects are dismal in all too many cases. Year by year, therefore, many organizations see the average age of their work forces increase.

At Ford Motor Company, for example, the average age of the blue-collar work force increased by 7.3 years from 1978 to 1987 (from 37.2 years to 44.5 years). About 16 percent of Ford's worker population is now over 55, compared with 10.4 percent in 1978. The average length of Ford service has increased by 8.3 years, to 18.4.

The same phenomenon is occurring in many firms, divisions, and plants of the so-called mature industries. High age compression—or organizational HAC—is one legacy of the industrial restructuring of the 1980s. Whether this is transitional or a relatively permanent feature of these organizations, it is an aspect of the micro-economy that will have to be managed.

The "aging" of the organization introduces important new strategic issues. Improving organizational effectiveness in the face of these issues is not an easy task. Both human resource managers and strategic planners must re-examine some fundamentals, adjust some management mindsets, and probably plow some new ground. We will review one case study, the Ford experience with an aging work force, and go on to discuss the broader strategic issues inherent in aging organizations. Of necessity, there will be some overlap since the Ford experience is not entirely *sui generis*.

For perspective, consider the age makeup of a work force if a firm had total control of its employment situation. The ideal age and service distribution of a work force presumably would be one which would be sustainable and self-renewing in terms of organizational continuity. A competitive assessment of employment costs and of staffing structure in each geographic, product, technical, and support sub-unit would be made, and market growth or decline, labor market demographics, and the projected nature of the firm internally and versus competition would be taken into account. There would be a dynamic search for a reasonable equilibrium.

In the real world, however, organizations grow or shrink. They are not just designed, though many people would like us to believe that they are, or can be. Organizations respond, among other things, to economic and political forces, consumer tastes, product substitutions, the quality of leadership, the commitments resulting from collective bargaining, and sometimes just plain chance. They expand, shrink, and, these days, are taken over, shaken, absorbed, and sold, as a whole or in chunks. Virtually all organizations, consequently, can experience at least occasional bouts of HAC. And some—those which are consciously downsizing, usually because their markets in one way or another demand it—are in a situation of "chronic HAC." This, of course, is a performance challenge for both an organization and its people and, when they are represented, for collective bargaining.

Ford is currently meeting that challenge, and the Ford experience, a large part of which is the Ford United Auto Workers experience, could be of value to any kind of organization, not just business firms. There may be insights and avenues here for unions, government bodies, educational institutions, and nonprofit organizations.

According to conventional wisdom, when offices and plants are populated by aging employees, it is a sign of impending decay. The organization is on a downhill slide and failure is only a matter of time. But is conventional wisdom correct? Is an older work force really one of nature's organizational calamities, or is this another distortion, perhaps, of our excessive admiration of our youth culture?

The Ford Experience

A CHANGE IN CORPORATE CULTURE

As the 1980s began, the wheels had just about fallen off the U.S. auto industry. It was mired in its worst-ever recession. At Ford, the balance sheet had turned blood red. And it was clear, to Ford management, at least, that this condition was not simply due to the business cycle. The problem was much more complex and far-reaching. Imbedded in it were such factors as the need for improved product quality; an explosive growth in competition on a world-wide basis; a restructuring of the number of locations and of the interrelationships of firms in auto and auto-related industries; an absence of trust in the workplace; ill-defined corporate values; and decades of adversarial labor-management relations.

There was no quick fix, either. And it was not a problem Ford could just wait out. The answer—the only real answer for Ford—was a total transformation of the company. Ford management had to rethink, redefine, redirect, and reshape almost every feature and element of the entire organization. It had to alter everything, from how products looked and worked to the fundamental ways in which the company addressed customers, employees, unions, dealers, and the rest of the world. In effect, although it perhaps didn't quite realize what was happening, Ford began to change the very culture of the company.

In terms of employee relations and labor relations, the cultural change had four key components. First, the company opted for a new, open, problem-centered approach to the way it worked with the UAW. To do that, there had to be changes in thinking and methods of operating. Second, Ford committed itself to extensive, open communications with the employees and, where they were represented, with their union. If an informed citizenry is the bedrock of political vitality, an informed employee body is the source of business performance. Third, the company established employee involvement and other important forms of shared decisionmaking. And fourth, Ford placed a new and creative emphasis on training and education.

But transformation cannot be a one-way street. In the course of this one, Ford made it clear to its employees—both hourly and salaried—that to deal with the powerful new realities, they too would have to make changes. The other side of participation—the other face of employee involvement—is employee responsibility. Thus, employees were asked to give extra effort, to learn new tasks, to accept new responsibilities, to function with less support, to discard some comfortable ways of operating, and generally to contribute more. And they were asked to do all this with a vastly heightened sense of quality performance.

THE AGING PHENOMENON

One thing Ford hadn't considered was the phenomenon of the older work force. When the auto business went into the ditch, Ford was forced to make drastic personnel cuts. The hourly work force, for instance, went from 200,000 to barely 100,000. There also was a proportionate reduction in salaried staffing. To handle these unfortunate dislocations, new approaches were negotiated and applied. Some of these efforts have now been labeled models of joint labor-management action and social responsibility. Still, these were difficult times for those directly affected.

Because of the drastic cuts that had to be made, the average age of Ford U.S. blue-collar and white-collar employees soared. Almost overnight, the company had a work force that averaged 43 years of age, with two-thirds 40 years old or older and only 6 percent under 30. Little was known about older work forces at the time—and Ford's early discoveries weren't very reassuring. It quickly became clear that an older work force is a costly work force. Virtually everyone on the payroll was a long-service employee, at or near the top of the wage or salary scale. There was wage cost escalation without wage increases or, when there were increases, they went beyond the levels of negotiated or stated increases.

Retirement plan obligations went up at the same time that the number of working employees was decreasing. Ford found itself with only 1.6 working employees supporting each retiree and surviving spouse. When this decade began, there were more than three working employees for every retiree and surviving spouse. Twenty-five years ago, the ratio was six to one. Because older employees are more susceptible to serious illness and utilize health care facilities more often, the higher average age of the work force increased disability and medical insurance costs. Other benefit arrangements also cost more. In addition, new job security and retraining approaches were needed.

All these were difficulties that the new competition—the overseas companies and the so-called "transplants"—were not experiencing. They have far younger work forces, in some cases averaging between 27 and 32 years old, with none of Ford's grow-in costs.

There were worries, too, about the long-term effects an aging work force might have on the development of needed technical and managerial skills for future years, and whether it would be possible to hand down valuable accumulated job and organizational knowledge to a new generation. Would there be a critical loss of vigor, resourcefulness, and flexibility? Would the transformation plan succumb to fatigue, obsolescence, and the rigidity of old age? Could an older work force make the company's transformation a reality?

From the beginning, Ford knew the employees' reaction to the transformation efforts was going to be crucial. No matter how sound the plans, the company wasn't going to turn itself into the company it needed to be unless employees and their representatives agreed to help—and did so willingly.

POSITIVE RESPONSES

The employees gave their cooperation for two principal reasons. They recognized that unprecedented world-wide competitive pressures were, in fact, forcing wrenching change in the business. Management was open and candid with them on this score, and the facts were persuasive. It was clear that everyone was in it together. Second, the employees liked the direction the company was taking. The transformation made sense to them. They particularly liked the way the management function was getting a forceful participative twist. The employees saw the logic of the new objectives. They believed these were, in reality, *mutual* goals.

But, of course, commonality of concerns does not in and of itself produce mutual trust or a particular agenda. A heightened awareness of issues, even if widespread, does not translate into consensus. Other companies and unions faced similar challenges, and could not chart successful new directions. Ford agreed not only to reshape its prerogatives but also to share its profits—to put its money where its mouth was—to enlarge the meaning and the consequences of participation. So the employees bought in. Indeed, most of them may have wondered why the company had waited so long.

Most of the UAW's leaders—at both the national and local levels—also came to see the value of the company's transformation efforts. They reacted positively to the new style of labor relations, and added to it—sometimes more than Ford had anticipated. They kept management's feet to the fire. In a great many cases, union leaders proved to be strong, positive forces for constructive change. They understood the link between quality and job security, and through new joint governance processes they would see to it that employee needs were respected—and that Ford would live up to its words.

NEW DIRECTIONS

The result was that, in a remarkably short time, Ford's transformation came to pass. New forms of teamwork were used to redesign and re-engineer entire product lines. Team Taurus is the best known of these efforts, but there were numerous others. The Ford Aero-look became the industry's design standard, and the company won back-to-back *Motor Trend* magazine Car-of-the-Year awards. Some Ford trucks also took honors in the marketplace. The bottom-line result was that the company increased its market share in an intense competitive struggle. As Ford broadened and deepened the employee involvement process, it achieved significantly higher product quality and plant efficiency. For eight years running, Ford has produced the highest-quality domestic car lines in the industry. "Quality is job one" isn't just a marketing theme; it's the reality that gave substance to the theme.

With employee involvement under its belt, Ford negotiated a series of new joint programs with the UAW—all based on sound principles of participation and mutual interest. Joint employee involvement was the first—in 1979. Joint education and training, information-sharing through mutual growth forums, profit sharing, and new forms of job security were all negotiated in 1982. Joint health and safety training, employee assistance plans, and protection against technological displacement followed in 1984. In the 1987 round of bargaining, Ford and the UAW expanded training, established special joint quality committees, agreed to joint efforts to improve business performance, and negotiated job protection against all but market displacement.

As a consequence, labor-management relations took on healthy new overtones of trust, respect, and mutual interest. And employment at Ford now has a wholesome stability. As employees retire, layoff lists have dwindled. All hourly employees are eligible for preferential placement and have had opportunities to relocate. The business success that Ford and the union have mutually earned has generated five consecutive years of profit sharing. In 1988, checks for eligible employees averaged $3,700, and the total profit sharing pool of $635 million is believed to be the largest amount ever paid to employees by any company. *Business Week* magazine called what happened at Ford an "industrial miracle."

ADVANTAGES OF THE OLDER WORK FORCE

Did the older work force present some special problems to the company's revitalization—in addition to the higher costs already mentioned? Yes, of course it did. Some older employees, including many in management, were, in fact, set in their ways, not understanding the need for change. But then youth doesn't guarantee a receptivity to change either. And there can be a number of other difficulties associated with a younger work force. Ford knows about that only too well. It had a relatively high percentage of young workers in its plants during the 1960s and much of the 1970s—and experienced many serious problems as a result.

It's probably safe to conclude that, on balance, when Ford undertook its transformation, an older work force was a good thing to have. Given the challenge and our objectives, it probably was better suited to the task. The know-how the older workers possessed was a valuable asset, especially in terms of the problem-solving process. They had a base of solid experience to work with. You don't brainstorm and produce solutions in the abstract. Ford also found the older workers to be fully as creative as their younger counterparts and much more likely to show up for work every day. In addition, there was no evidence that older employees resisted training and education—far from it.

Since the joint UAW-Ford training program began in 1983, more than 17,000 of Ford's blue-collar employees have taken computer literacy courses on their own time. More than 7,000 workers are enrolled in on-site basic education sessions in 42 locations in 12 states. Tuition plan enrollments have tripled, and employees are now earning associate degrees by attending on-site college classes. Incidentally, to help make all this training and education happen, each major Ford facility is served by a professional full-time life-education advisor, an employee of the University of Michigan, and each facility has its own learning center. In 1987, some 20,000 people, or 20 percent of Ford's blue-collar employees, voluntarily took courses under the UAW-Ford education programs (only 2 percent of the general adult population participates in after-hours education). And this with a Ford average age of 43 years!

There were some other special pluses that Ford derived from an older work force—attitude pluses. Older workers, for example, tended to be more committed to the company and more likely to recognize the severity of the situation it was facing. Older employees also seemed to take more pride in their work and to accept the critical need for product quality. They showed more patience—with their management, with their fellow workers, and probably with their union leadership. They were more forgiving of mistakes and false starts. This can be a very important virtue when you're sailing uncharted waters.

Older workers also wanted the company to succeed in order to leave jobs for their sons and daughters and for their neighbors and communities. Contrary to some news media reports, they weren't ready to shut down plants just because they happened to have vested pension rights and insurance coverage. And older workers, it became clear, were more willing to accept complexity and inconsistencies as features of life that everyone must live with. All these, of course, are attitudes that tend to come with maturity. They were enormously helpful to Ford's transformation. At all levels of the work force the old dogs at this company did indeed learn some nifty new tricks.

In 1988, Ford's work force averaged about 44 years of age. It's still costly—and there is a need to increase the infusion of new blood—but it's a committed and competent work force. In fact, it's probably better now than it was when the company asked it to help with the transformation. It's more knowledgeable about the business, more educated, more committed. It's had the experience of both crisis and success. In a sense, it's as much a product of the transformation as it was the mechanism for that transformation. Today's Ford employees feel the same sense of satisfaction with the transformation that management does. Many blue-collar UAW-Ford joint programs and the companion white-collar policies have led to increased skill and knowledge among employees, even as they elicited commitment and a heightened sense of caring. Everyone has worked hard—and altered institutional thinking—to achieve the transformation. At the same time, Ford's management has learned that, whether employees are old or young, the critical factor is how well management is managing.

The lesson seems clear. An aging work force can be an advantage. Like just about every other complex question, the issue here involves pluses and minuses, and several shades of gray. To make a good strategic review of how work force aging is impacting a particular organization, one must assess and balance all the major factors present in each special fact situation.

Strategic Issues

Lest readers dismiss the Ford experience as unduly specific, what follows is a more general statement of the key factors that loom large in the management of aging organizations. They can be labeled cost push, organizational performance, human values, and the work force of the future. And while this discussion is couched in terms of private sector firms, the same issues arise in public sector, nonprofit, and voluntary organizations and associations because the underlying theme is organizational continuity and effectiveness.

INTERNAL COST PUSH

The first and most apparent strategic issue in an aging organization is an internal cost push on pay and employee benefit structures. Older work forces cost more—sometimes a lot more. This push seems to have a life of its own, often nonsynchronous with the current or future financial needs of the firm and frequently totally independent of competitive developments elsewhere.

As a result of both collectively bargained seniority provisions and the widespread voluntary practice of layoff by low length of service, the average wage or salary becomes skewed at the upper end of compensation ranges, with little likelihood of a return to normalcy from the influx of new, lower-paid entrants. The remaining long-service members, usually the most productive and loyal and with proven track records, may have been accustomed to a pattern of relatively large and frequent pay increases. Their expectations are a fact of life in managing compensation systems or in designing new ones, especially after a crisis period has been weathered. So is the higher wage burden.

Perhaps the most widely publicized cost push factor related to an older work force comes from retirement plan obligations, where fixed or growing costs must be borne by an ever-smaller working group. The so-called "dependency ratio" that we have heard so much about in the various Social Security debates is also very much a reality for private pensions.

Pension plan benefits and costs have been and will continue to be important collective bargaining issues in autos, steel, rubber, copper, and many other sectors. External forces also impact differentially on an aging work force; for example, the taxation of portions of Social Security benefits or the formulas for tax-deferred "salary reduction plans" and IRAs. These can encourage, or discourage, attempts by employees to provide for better retirement through personal effort and savings and increase or decrease the pressure for "more" in the collective bargaining setting.

Insurance costs, too, are not immune from HAC. Health care costs increase because older employees and their spouses are more susceptible to serious illness and utilize health care facilities at higher rates and for longer times than younger employees. Life insurance and disability insurance costs are also pushed upward without any improvement in benefit levels or coverages. Benefit plan specialists and actuaries can show us startling differences in utilization and experience between younger, average, and older work forces.

The cost of health care for retirees also is escalating, and the results of recent litigation suggest that employers may not be permitted to alter retiree health plans once benefits have begun. Among other things, this means that it may not be possible to extend to retirees the cost-containment initiatives designed for active employees. Talk about role reversal! In addition, changes in Medicare and the introduction of state-mandated provisions for health care will increase the cost burdens on employers and on collective bargaining.

In like fashion, job security provisions such as severance pay, long-term income support plans, and preferential placement provisions are skewed toward longer-service employees, and become more costly than originally estimated when younger-service employees drop off the rolls.

Vacation plans also can contribute to attacks of HAC; a higher proportion of employees in the upper vacation brackets can automatically generate additional average work force entitlements, sometimes as much as 20 to 40 or more hours per employee annually, costing millions of unanticipated dollars.

The litany could go on. Each strategic review will uncover its organization's own forms of HAC. The glaring fact is that arrangements which were shaped with perhaps 5–10 percent of a population in mind may now have to handle two, three, and four times that number. No wonder there is wage and benefit reshaping and reassessment. No wonder collective bargaining is under strain. No wonder managers struggle to explain the new realities to employees who believe they've been made implicit promises in the past, and who have their own and varied notions of equity.

The internal, and sometimes external, cost push generated by HAC is exacerbated when a firm must compete with companies that don't have the problem or that, for other reasons, have significantly lower labor and production costs. Here in the United States, Japanese auto plants, for example, enjoy substantially lower costs. Their work forces and worksites are new. They do not experience the normal costs associated with forty years of collective bargaining, and their work forces are at the very low end of the scale for accrual of vacations, pensions, insurance, and job security. They don't suffer from HAC. In addition, they have more flexibility and discretion in work force utilization.

A few years ago, no one would have dared predict it, but it is today a hard fact: some of our toughest cost competition in autos is coming from a nonunion presence in the United States, plus a lower-cost unionized auto sector.

ORGANIZATIONAL PERFORMANCE

The second strategic issue involves organizational performance. Is the HAC-afflicted organization less efficient and less productive? What about its dedication to product quality? How receptive is it to change? Will it be left behind by younger and more innovative rivals?

It is easier to ask the questions than to formulate answers. No single indicator like the fairly measurable relative costs discussed under the cost push issues is available. Judgment, art, and experience are the principal guides in fashioning organization-specific judgments and strategies on the issue of organizational performance.

An aging work force may indeed present a number of performance negatives. It may be inordinately attached to the old systems—systems frequently obtained through difficult bargaining or imposed by management as the correct and only way of doing things. Employees may be less motivated because the expected time return is shorter; if personal and family obligations have been largely met, they may believe that incremental effort is not worth the incremental reward. Work adjustments or flexibility arrangements may be rejected because they appear to benefit future generations more than themselves. The skills of the older workers may be outdated, and "old dogs" may not want to pay the personal price to learn new tricks. There may be insufficient turnover to allow bringing in "new blood," to train the next group, and to pass on inherited wisdom. The current organization may be out of step with future necessities and future business plans.

On the other hand, there can be some positive factors. The mature organization generally exhibits lower overall turnover and has more work force stability. This contributes to lower costs, better product quality, and greater efficiency. Older employees usually have less short-term sporadic absenteeism. They have more experience and more know-how. They can bring more to the problem-solving process. Because of long association, it can be easier to build a more committed and effective work force. There is a greater knowledge of the industry, company, and plant, and a greater stake in the community.

With respect to organizational performance, the impact of HAC must be continually reassessed by management. It is best if this is done consciously, not ignored or responded to by fitful and uncoordinated actions.

HUMAN VALUES

The strategic issue of human values relates to the treatment of older workers in any organization. It involves developing a consciousness of the special situations, problems, and opportunities associated with older workers. It implies an active management stance, not only to meet legal requirements but also to promote a positive environment where personnel decisions are performance-based and are not age-biased.

Managing the older work force in an age-neutral way calls for continuous attention to all personnel programs and policies and to the education and re-education of management. Over and above this, progressive organizations will also look into job sharing, pre-retirement planning, vacation and leave policies, retraining and reassignment, part-time work, post-retirement working, and harnessing of the organizations' retiree contingent. With just a little attention, retirees can be a source of strength for customer identification, good will, community work, and strengthening the social order.

There is a derivative value flowing to organizations which manage their older workers properly. Employees aged 20 to 40 will be older workers (under the definition in the Age Discrimination in Employment Act) by the year 2005. So what management does with respect to managing the older components of the work force will not be lost on the younger group, and will be an important element of future organizational culture and performance, for good or for bad.

It is ironic that just as our society was beginning to make some advances in understanding and appreciation of the special position of the older worker in normal organizations, we were hit by a pronounced bout of HAC in maturing industries and companies. A high age concentration poses additional burdens on managing the human-value aspects of an older work force, but clearly we in management and society must not shortchange the effort. Undeniably, within the aging organization there will continue to be tensions between the need for competitiveness and the need to respect human values. The task is to work hard to accommodate both.

WORK FORCE OF THE FUTURE

Given the attention being focused on the work force of the future, a fourth strategic issue may well be how to lead an aging organization in the face of the emerging work environment. Obviously, a variety of concepts regarding the characteristics of future work organizations could be constructed on the basis of the nature of the industry and the firm, growth or decline, location, type of product or service, personal worker attributes and education, degree and kind of unionization, managerial prowess, and ingenuity in human resources planning.

A common ingredient in virtually all of the new work force directions being discussed appears to be the conscious promotion of various kinds of teamwork. Businesses and organizations are "doing" communities that are also "learning" communities. Daily, participants learn and touch each other, creating powerful group entries that determine the long-term ledger. And indeed, a great deal of "learning" and restructuring may be necessary to create the work force of the future. The most important issue may be the simple question: "Can management meet its obligation to develop and manage tomorrow's work force?"

A "best-in-class" management is needed for a "best-in-class" work force. It must be:

- fully attuned to the technical needs of its business, and growing in its technical capability
- fully aware of advanced human resource management principles and concepts, and committed to introducing those which are right for its business
- fully committed to investing the time and effort needed to foster continuous improvement.

The work force of the future also will have to meet new standards. It will have to be:

- oriented toward problem-solving
- motivated to create opportunity
- team-structured both formally and informally
- dedicated to team success
- communicated with
- recognized and celebrated
- consulted and involved
- encouraged to participate
- prepared to share in some difficult business decisions
- trained and retrained in technical, interpersonal, group, and social skills
- allowed to seek education and assisted in doing so
- afforded organizational structures that are mobile and flexible
- appropriately compensated
- provided as much job security as possible.

When the work force members are represented by a union, management must work toward "best-in-class" labor relations with the employees' chosen representatives.

If these are conscious management goals, the specific methods by which they are carried out will be secondary to the general effort. Structures and systems will be ever-changing, reflecting the broad participation of the work force and addressing the new conditions that inevitably arise as part of human and economic life.

If management's efforts are successful, positive outcomes will flow with respect to product and systems quality, assembly, materials, morale, supplier/customer relationships, efficiency, maintenance, work methods, workplace atmosphere, safety, training, community impact, waste, tools, and other elements that each organizational participant can list. The outcomes that are desired are specific and short-term. But the processes needed to achieve them—participation, openness, respect, and continuous learning—are long-term. The principle is clear: sustained short-term progress is dependent on concentrated long-term effort.

The power of the past, for good or for ill, but probably with a mixture of both, will be a dominating fact in aging organizations that feel a need to reshape their directions and their cultures to meet future competitive needs and address human values. Even more critical than the past, though, will be the determination to create the future. This determination will distinguish the dedicated and the successful from the apathetic and the mediocre.

Conclusion

So where does all this leave organizations? It leaves them with a continuing challenge. An aging work force is only one special case in the broader set of adjustments being required of collective bargaining and of human resource management.

The nation, unfortunately, seems to be in an era of mostly expedient collective bargaining. Patterns are unclear and often unspreadable. The tremendous power of the bargaining process appears capped. Despite more information, and despite the presence of intelligent and highly educated professionals, there often appears to be less social learning. Changes in laws and regulations, even when well-intended, are uncoordinated and frequently made without regard to the country's long-term competitive position in global markets. Economic and political forces tend to dominate, and carry the day.

The imperative for individual organizations is to revamp useful old systems and to create new systems and new approaches. We need to pursue those new approaches with moderate but true hope for the human species. Fortunately, we can continue to influence the future, though we cannot control it.

We should keep in mind that all work forces are a blend of numerous diverse elements. An age factor is only one of the features of the work force. In our republic, it will also contain black and white and in-between; male and female; immigrants and those with deep American roots; craft and noncraft; white-collar, blue-collar, and pink-collar; the educated and the not-so-educated; liberal and conservative; maybe even urban and rural. And within each of these groups we can identify countless other shades of differences. In America, diversity is our heritage. We shouldn't be troubled by it. In fact, this pluralism—properly nurtured and focused—is one of our great strengths.

References

Savoie, Ernest J. 1985. "Current Developments and Future Agenda in Union-Management Cooperation in Training and Retraining of Workers," *Industrial Relations Research Association Spring Proceedings and Labor Law Journal* 36 (August): 535–47.

———. 1986. "Creating the Workforce of the Future: The Ford Focus," statement to President's Advisory Committee on Mediation and Conciliation, September 16.

———. 1988. "Toward the Year 2000: The Ford Direction," testimony before the Congress of the United States, Joint Economic Committee, Subcommittee on Investment, Jobs, and Prices, April 12.

The Effect of Older Work Forces on Individual Firms, Labor Unions, and Industries

FRANK P. DOYLE

Global competition and the aging phenomenon are now important elements in shaping collective bargaining developments, says this General Electric executive. Employers, labor unions, and government can work together to establish training and lifetime learning programs, but income and employment security must rest on the competitiveness of our enterprises and an understanding that there are limits to the obligations of public and private sector policy. However, Doyle is optimistic that we can capitalize on the strengths of our economic and social system and that we will be able to respond to the challenges.

I. B.

My underlying premise is that the issues of concern to our older workers are a product of both the aging phenomenon and the competitive changes sweeping our economy and industries. The reality is that we must not only reposition U.S. companies, industries, and workers to compete in increasingly global markets, but that we must also readjust some of our long-held and most cherished assumptions about employment. That repositioning and readjustment is made even more dramatic—and more imperative—by the shift to an older work force.

The security of an unchanging workplace and employment relationship is no longer available and cannot be artificially sustained. In core manufacturing operations, the growing productivity requirements are speeding the process of change. So the challenge we face is to create a new security by equipping companies and workers alike to deal with—and even gain from—fast-moving and unavoidable change. Our public and private policies should aid businesses and people in taking advantage of new opportunities being created.

So the issue of an older work force is not an independent variable. It is important, not just because the number of older workers is growing but because competitive change has created legitimate security concerns among American workers—concerns most acutely felt by older workers who have the greatest tenure, investment in, and commitment to our industrial enterprises. Their concerns are driving changes in our policies and discussions in collective bargaining. They are the reason why job security is the number one issue in labor talks, the reason why GE has developed a job and income security plan, the reason why the auto industry created the guaranteed employment numbers program.[1] It is the basis for the concerns about rising health care costs and long-term pension funding, and it is reflected in the growth of plan-level programs on wellness, health, nutrition, and pre-retirement planning.

Training—A Key for the Older Work Force

In General Electric—as in other industrial companies—our experienced work force is an older work force. It is also highly productive. Since the early 1980s, we have gone through substantial restructuring in all of our businesses. In the process, the average age of our workers has increased—up from 30 in 1977 to 43 at the end of 1987. While 47 percent of our workers were over age 40 in 1977, 60 percent are over 40 today. We have a career work force, with service averaging 15 years—people who joined us early in their working lives have stayed for 15, 20, and 25 years and want to be with us until retirement. Yet they are retiring earlier. Our average retirement age has dropped by almost two years since 1980, from about 62 years and six months to 60 years and six months, a trend we—and the economy as a whole—may find difficult to sustain. And this change has occurred despite our decision not to use the so-called "early retirement window." Overall, GE's demographics are fairly typical of large industrial employers who led the post-World War II economy.

As this economic metamorphosis continues, I believe that the nucleus of experienced, productive workers *can* make the adjustment to new work and occupations if we help them. In 1986 and 1987, I had

1. The "guaranteed employment numbers" program requires union and management to establish a fixed number as of a given date for active employees in each bargaining unit (separately for skilled and nonskilled employees). Thereafter, that number of employees can only be reduced at half the rate of attrition. Thus, if the guaranteed employment number in a unit (skilled and nonskilled employees separately) is 2,000, and attrition accounts for a work force reduction of 100, management is obligated to fill 50 of the 100 job vacancies. Therefore, the guaranteed employment number will be 1,950.

the privilege of being a member of the Secretary of Labor's task force on economic change and worker displacement. The consensus of the task force was that education and training were the ingredients that made the critical difference in people moving to new work. Training works because it capitalizes on the inherent U.S. work force strengths of flexibility and adaptability. American workers have always been willing to move to new opportunity. Furthermore, as employers, we have made substantial investments in formal and informal training, and the experience of our employees is an asset.

That suggests to me that companies, labor unions, and the government can do the most for long-term job security and mobility through training programs for workers. Obviously, the direct link to a new job within a company provides a powerful incentive to acquire new skills and is the chief reason why in-house training is so successful. But in view of the rapid changes taking place in the economy and labor market, I believe that we must also consider expanding training programs in order to qualify workers for employment outside our firms. Preparing a work force for the benefit of other companies has never had much appeal. Yet company training programs must take into account that, in many industries, individual employment security may rest more on the development of transferrable skills than on long-term service in one company. Training programs and new work patterns which emphasize teamwork and pay-for-knowledge can broaden employee skills and enhance work force mobility both within and outside the firm. Businesses, in re-examining their basic assumptions about lifetime employment, must also be willing to make some investments in future training. It clearly is a critical need for the mid-career work force caught in the transition from the era of "career employment with one firm" to the era of "an employment career with several firms." Lifetime learning is going to be the lubricant for that transition to new employment.

If you will accept my argument that those who age well will be those who train well, then the education system has some adjustments to make. Experienced adults do not train and learn in the same way as teens and young adults. And here I must both challenge and criticize our educational institutions for their inflexibility in responding to the exploding need for continuing education. The experienced worker probably needs two basic types of training: training which connects skills being taught with the real needs of the labor market, not wasted on phantom jobs, and upgrading of basic literacy skills. The fear of résumé preparation and the concerns about inadequacy of expression virtually paralyze people who are back in the job market for the first time in 20 or 25 years. Long-dormant skills must be reconstituted for those older workers facing the reality of competing for new work and opportunity.

My point is that training and learning are transportable, a concept which private firms and public policies have to recognize, as full careers in one firm or industry become increasingly unrealistic. Portability of skills may represent the best form of job security available. It is an issue that must be addressed for the older work force to continue making contributions and ensure its place in our changing economy. Business, labor, and education need to join their efforts on this issue. We must be willing to invest not only in new plants, equipment, and technology but also in updating the skills of our work force.

Benefit Design Driven by the Older Work Force

As our work force has aged, we see the direct connection between competitive change and security concerns. The number one issue at our bargaining tables in the 1980s has been security, both job and income. I expect it to continue to be an issue into the 1990s. The irony is that the pressures for security guarantees come at the same time that our institutions—because of economic forces—are less able to offer ironclad guarantees. The fact is that the only real security is that of competitive enterprises, skilled and productive employees, and a strong economy.

I divide the security issue into two categories: income security and job security. Income security is essentially that provided by our public and private benefits systems. Statutory changes—such as earlier vesting—and bargaining pressures are all emphasizing greater benefit entitlements earlier in the employee's career. From the employer's point of view, these pressures make benefits more transportable—and in the end more expensive. It is also evident that the government is shifting more costs and obligations to the employers—COBRA health benefits extension, Medicare cost-sharing shifts, and proposals regarding mandated benefits all suggest that political leaders know there are limits to the levels of government-provided benefits.

The challenge is how to respond. What are the basic obligations of employers and the government? What should people provide for themselves? What mechanisms are available to ease the burden for all? An important part of the answer to those questions is found in the means provided for people to invest in their own security, mechanisms which have, unfortunately, been eroded by tax reform.

I believe that our system has to equip people to deal with the inevitability of voluntary or involuntary job loss and the transition to retirement or new work. Pensions, Social Security, unemployment compensation, and Medicare are all integral parts of a system of private and statutory benefits which reflect our strong social sense of obligation and responsibility to workers. But there is also an element of personal responsibility that is more important than ever when considering the size of the work force moving into the final half of its work career during the next decade. The government and private employers recognized this change and took major steps in the late 1970s and 1980s through programs such as Individual Retirement Accounts (IRAs), employee thrift plans, 401(K) plans, Employee Stock Ownership Plans (ESOPs), and the like. All provide important incentives for people to save for their future. In view of the need, it is curious that our tax policy has now waffled, restricting IRAs, eliminating payroll ESOPs, and constraining the flexibility of employee thrift plans. Plans that could be used to help people make transitions to new work or retirement have been made less flexible—and less attractive to workers. The perverse logic that imposes tax penalties when these dollars are used for training or living expenses during periods of unemployment discourages workers from making the savings commitment at precisely the time when they need encouragement to set dollars aside.

The other important security item is health benefits. They are threatened by out-of-control costs. There is great need to establish quality care at affordable costs, and the need will increase as this work force ages. It is an enormous concern for individuals and companies, one for which I have no solution to offer, and it will grow in importance over the next decade.

With regard to job security, we face demands to provide greater absolute security through contract language. I know I offer this observation in Detroit at some peril, but a labor contract will not provide security that the marketplace is unwilling to pay for. Successful enterprises which compete in global markets provide job security. I agree with and encourage negotiated or voluntary business-by-business arrangements which provide advance notification and assistance so that people can adjust to economic change. But our focus has to be on easing—not impeding—the impact of necessary economic change. We must assist people in making the transition to new work through training and adjustment programs. But I'm afraid that for most of our enterprises, absolute guarantees of job security are not available without threatening the viability and competitiveness of our business. We can't bargain or create job security; we have to earn it.

Reasons for Optimism

Obviously there are real concerns and issues that are driven by the changes in the economy and the demographics of an older work force. I'm optimistic that our system has the capacity to handle the problems.

Basically, the work force is aging because the population has stopped growing. Yet our economy continues to produce new jobs, some 21 million since 1976. That's the bright side. There is a place and there is work for talented, skilled, and trained workers.

Many of our concerns can be ameliorated by job growth. As jobs grow and population growth declines, the concerns about unemployment will diminish. In the next decade, policymakers face the problems of bridging: bridging people in their thirties and forties and fifties to new work with training, incentives, and investment in these people that the economy will need in the 1990s; and bridging those in their fifties and sixties to retirement through incentives to save and the development of responsible policies on important issues like health care, pensions, and Social Security.

We are a free, open and mobile society; a society which draws and stimulates creative people; a society with the most attractive markets in the world. Our goal must be to capitalize on those strengths by ensuring the continued competitiveness of U.S. businesses in world markets. And the way we do that is by keeping the skills of our workers—young and experienced alike—up to date. Lack of competitiveness is the greatest potential threat to the older work force because the failure to compete will eliminate jobs and diminish our ability to meet the social costs of competitive change.

Perhaps we can learn from the situation created by the trade budget deficits. As our government is fighting to reverse these negative trends, we all see that our economy is weakened. As a result, we are less able to commit public money to the social programs that benefit the aging. The lesson: if we aren't competitive as a nation, those in need will be hurt the most.

I believe that our older workers possess the greatest motivation to be competitive. They know it is the only way they will make it to the promise of a full life after their working years. Our task is to capitalize on their productive capacities. If we don't, those workers and our retirees will be the first victims of the failure to compete. If we do, we assure the rewards which all in our society—young and old—realize from a competitive, vibrant economy.

A Continuing and Important Asset: The Older Employee

ROBERT STEMPEL

In recent years, General Motors and the UAW have moved toward joint action programs to improve human relationships. Examples offered by Stempel are programs aimed at assuring more adequate job security, the Saturn Corporation agreement, training programs for new technology, the Quality of Work Life process, and emphasis on improved product quality. Preretirement counseling programs are also in place, and the UAW and GM are attempting to reduce health care costs without deterioration in quality. Stempel reports a clear recognition on GM's part that the experience, knowledge, and commitment of older employees justify an investment in their welfare, thereby benefiting them, their union, GM, and its customers.

I. B.

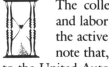

The collective bargaining relationship between management and labor has a need to address the special problems arising as the active work force grows older. It is of particular interest to note that, in the automobile industry—and I refer particularly to the United Auto Workers Union and General Motors Corporation—the labor/management relationship has been moving in new directions which, while comparatively recent, already point to successful constructive joint action.

In the United States, General Motors has about 345,000 hourly employees, and 90 percent of them are UAW-represented. It is no secret that the historical relationship between GM and the UAW was not always a good one. But that started to change about fifteen years ago. That's when GM and the UAW in national contract negotiations agreed to establish the National Committee to Improve the Quality of Work Life (QWL). Its fundamental aim is to improve our human relationships. The QWL process has not eliminated all the disagreements between union and management. It wasn't meant to do that. However, it has given us a different way of resolving many of our differences. And it has also been the basis for some innovative programs.

Employment Security

In the 1984 negotiations, GM and the UAW set up the JOB-S program—the Job Opportunity Bank and Security Program. Essentially, that program protected workers from layoffs in cases of productivity improvements, outsourcing, the introduction of new technology, or plant consolidations. In 1987 contract talks, the UAW and GM were able to develop an even more extensive job security agreement. And we were able to reach that pathbreaking agreement without even setting a strike deadline. Moreover, it was ratified by a better than 80 percent vote.

In 1985, the UAW and GM also developed a novel and innovative agreement for one of GM's subsidiaries, the Saturn Corporation. It's a free-standing agreement. The terms of the national contract do not necessarily apply to Saturn. It also is open-ended—a living document. The union and management can modify it at any time, as they see fit. Job security is an important feature of that agreement. Of major significance, it is an agreement that emphasizes cooperation and consensus in making decisions concerning the enterprise.

These latest labor contracts are leading toward a new concept in work force relations which is proving its value for the employees, the union, the corporation, and, in the final analysis, the customer. A basic premise is that the hourly work force is no longer a purely variable element. It is more like a fixed part of our operations, and that is a fairly new idea for the United States. Some of the European countries have had that social concept for some time, but it came into being legislatively—by government action. The Japanese have talked about "lifetime" employment almost as part of the fabric of their society, although that seems to be changing in some Japanese industries as the growth rate slows and they have had to do some consolidating. Here in the United States, we reached the concept of job security through labor-management negotiations.

The concept of job security has some interesting implications. In order to keep our current work force on the job and bring back some of the 67,000 people currently on layoff, it is likely that new, young people will not be brought into our hourly ranks in large numbers for some time. Our efforts to increase the productivity and efficiency of our operations—to make them more competitive—will only reinforce that trend.

Training for New Technology

Our current work force will provide the vast majority of people working for GM for some time to come. And that means that our work force is—on the average—going to be getting older. Our records already show the population bumps moving through the charts. In 1976, most of our workers were in age groups 25–29 and 30–34. By 1986, the two largest groups were aged 35–39 and 40–44.

While our work force remains relatively stable, the technology involved in manufacturing cars and trucks is changing dramatically. Increasingly, our plants are using robotics, computers, and advanced automation—tools that weren't available when many of the current workers were hired. And that leads to the topic of training people for the new skills they will need in today's highly technological workplace. At many GM facilities, the work force has been with GM for twenty or thirty years. The skills these people have—skills that have served them well throughout their working lives—suddenly may no longer be adequate for the 1980s and 1990s. They know our business. They know our products. They are willing workers. They are motivated. How do we retrain these people for a dynamically changing industry—one where technologies we never even thought about a few years ago are being applied rapidly? It is not just a question of investment, although that is an important decision. It is also a question of effective training for the older worker. Some skills just seem to be easier for younger people to acquire.

On the other hand, we shouldn't downgrade what motivation can do for the older worker. Younger workers may think that books aren't necessary—that they can get what they need from audio or video tapes. They may not understand the need for math skills—they may think that it can all be done on a calculator. Getting an older worker to understand the benefits of new skills may be easier.

At the same time, however, a surprising proportion of the adult American work force is functionally illiterate or is operating with reading and math skills at the elementary school level. Very often training has to start with basic skills and build from there. We literally have to offer reading and arithmetic classes to many of the people in our plants so that they have a base on which to build the necessary technical skills. People often didn't need those skills in the past. It was possible to make a good living based mostly on physical effort. That's changing. It's a change for the good, but it means that we will have to make sure people have the background and skills for the new demands of their jobs. That is one reason why GM is so supportive of the efforts to improve education for American children. The young men and women coming out of our schools need better basic skills that weren't taught—or weren't learned—the first time around. Then we can move on to the training for our new operations.

Our need for training seems to grow geometrically as new technology is installed in our plants. Just one example will provide some notion of the training needs: at our new truck plant in Fort Wayne, Indiana—probably one of the most technologically advanced plants in the auto industry—our work force went through almost 2 million hours of training. In large part, the people at Fort Wayne were not new workers. Most of them came from other GM plants; in fact, many of them were from Janesville, Wisconsin, and had built trucks before. But Fort Wayne is a much different plant—particularly in the technology used to assemble the new pickup trucks. Every employee in that plant—hourly, salaried, production workers, skilled trades—went through an eight-week core training program. Additional training was provided depending on job assignment. Skilled trades people probably had the most extensive training: each one spent 1,000 hours learning about robotics, electronics, and computer programming.

The job of training and retraining the salaried work force can be even more complex. Like the hourly work force, our salaried work force is getting older. In many salaried and managerial jobs a strong performance depends upon judgment. Judgment develops with experience, and experience comes with age. That's why we want to retain those experienced people. It is not easy to come up with training programs that teach people good judgment.

When training needs become so extensive, it is time to re-examine our training methods to see what is most effective for all workers—and particularly older workers—if they are going to comprise the bulk of the work force. Do they respond best to a classroom situation, programmed instruction, or interactive video? And we also need to develop effective ways of reinforcing training once the worker is on the job.

The reason for the emphasis on training needs is that the auto industry, like most industries, requires more and more brain work instead of physical labor, more skill instead of strength, from its workers. For an aging work force, that is a positive development. I want to be very careful about generalizing about "aging" or "older people." If anything, variation among people increases with age. People become less alike as they grow older. But some physiological changes are inevitable. That is not to say that they affect us at the same pace, but we all get there eventually. Our metabolism slows down. As most of us know from experience, it takes fewer calories to sustain our body weight. If we keep eating the way we did when we were younger, we're going to put on weight. Between age 30 and 80, our lungs lose 50 percent of their breathing capacity. Our bone mass peaks in the thirties, and then starts to drop off. And we need less sleep as we age. We won't be as strong or agile as we were in our youth. Our reaction times may become slower. But these physical changes don't necessarily affect our ability to perform our jobs or the other tasks that we face every day.

One of GM's safety engineers, for instance, recently did a study on the older driver. But, before I describe his findings, permit me to put in a plug for seat belts for a moment. It is extremely important that all people, and especially older people, wear their seat belts. Data on fatal injuries indicate that when a car driven by a person over 65 collides with one driven by a person under 20, the older driver is five times as likely to be killed. If the older person survives, it will take him or her longer to recover. Older women are even more vulnerable to fractures in car accidents because they have experienced a significant loss in bone mass. So we have to do a better job of getting older drivers to buckle up. We have to convince them to take full advantage of the safety features designed into their vehicles. If we can get them to let the car, instead of the person, absorb the crash energy, their survival possibilities will be improved and the age difference will be equalized.

To get back to the study by the GM engineer on the older driver, he found that older drivers have a slower eye reaction time, that they are more sensitive to glare, and that they can experience more difficulty picking out pertinent information in traffic. But despite those problems, older drivers are involved in fewer crashes. They bring greater experience to the task of driving. Teenagers think they are invincible—older drivers know better! And older drivers also tend to avoid troublesome situations. Those who are retired, for example, tend to stay away from rush-hour traffic as much as possible.

What that study suggests is that the human mind can overcome the physical shortcomings that may accompany aging. That's just as true in the workplace as it is behind the wheel. Drawing on our collective intelligence, we are also able to change the workplace—make it more accommodating to the needs of the older employee. And the change has been abetted by the new technology coming into automotive manufacturing.

At General Motors, we have devoted a lot of effort to turning physically demanding, boring, repetitive work over to automation. There are a lot of reasons for that transfer. And frankly, I'm not sure that the needs of an aging work force were at the top of the list when we started, but there's no question that older workers benefit from these changes.

There is still much to be done, however. The whole science of ergonomics—suiting the work to the worker—is really still in its infancy, but there are a great many things that can make work less tiring physically. Some of our newer facilities use automated guided vehicles (AGVs) to carry engines or even whole vehicles from work station to work station. These AGVs can be adjusted for height, so that the worker is performing his job at a comfortable level rather than continually reaching up or bending over. Ergonomics is one area where increased worker-management cooperation can really pay off. Who knows the job better than the worker? And who is better equipped to make suggestions on how to make the work easier? I am happy to say that worker involvement is happening at GM. Workers have contributed to the design of their workplaces in many of our plants, creating the climate for enhanced job satisfaction and more efficient operations.

Health Care Costs

One result of the decreasing emphasis on physical labor will be a healthier retiree group. Today's life expectancy is in the seventies, and it's going up. Babies born in the year 2000—just eleven years from now—are expected routinely to live into their nineties. Since 1900, the population of the United States has tripled, but the number of people over 65 living in this country has increased eight times. For most of human history, aging meant an inexorable slide into illness, pain, and immobility. That's not necessarily true any longer. Many older Americans—people in their sixties, seventies, and even eighties and nineties—are free of problems that curb their activities or require special care.

But there is no question that health care needs increase as we grow older. As longevity increases, health care costs are going to be higher and higher. Unlike pensions, health care for retirees is funded through current revenues. Medicare picks up many of the costs, but business is responsible for the "fill" between Medicare benefits and actual costs. And that "fill" is increasing, as every year more and more of the cost is shifted to business.

We are concerned about the costs of health care for our active and retired GM people. The UAW shares that concern. And its leadership has worked actively with us to find ways to reduce the cost of health care—not health care itself, but its costs.

While GM's size hasn't changed much in twenty-five years, our retiree population has: from one retiree for every fourteen active workers to one for every two! Currently 2.1 million people—1 percent of the country's population—depend on General Motors for supplemental pensions and for health care. Some of our competitors (I am speaking of new assembly plants built by foreign-owned companies) will not face the costs of pensions or retiree health care for several years. If we seem to be very preoccupied with keeping General Motors a healthy, profitable corporation, I think that it's understandable. With that kind of responsibility to that many people, we want to be sure that we are well equipped to compete, today and tomorrow. If we are to provide pensions and health care benefits, if we are to invest in training and retraining, then, as a corporation, we must be sure that our total economics are in order. In the long run, we think these investments pay off. Our workers are better employees, better citizens, and better able to continue to contribute to society—to share their knowledge—after they retire.

Pre-Retirement Counseling

The UAW and GM have tried to tackle the whole issue of preparing people for retirement. Joint pre-retirement planning programs were initiated in the mid-1970s at a few GM locations. Today, through the UAW-GM Human Resources Center, we offer a joint pre-retirement program for employees and their spouses throughout the corporation. Almost 10,000 employees and their spouses have participated in this program since it was introduced in November 1986. We "train the trainers" for this program at the UAW-GM Human Resources Center in Auburn Hills, Michigan, and they take the program back to their plant locations. The pre-retirement training is strictly voluntary and delivered at no cost to the employee. All employees and their spouses are eligible to participate, and we strongly recommend that spouses participate. The program lasts six or seven weeks, one session a week, for two and a half hours per session. The objective of the program is to help employees to make informed decisions on retirement and prepare for the transition from work. The changing composition of our work force is causing us to take some innovative approaches in just about everything involving our employees, but that is happening in many other parts of our operations as well.

Accent on Quality

Quality is one area that provides an immediate comparison. Because of the need for improving customer satisfaction, high-quality products are an absolute necessity, and we have devised some innovative approaches to quality—just as we have implemented some new ideas for dealing with the aging work force. We are pleased that the UAW and GM were able to form a Quality Network—a joint process to make sure our products are of the finest quality. The basis for the process is continuous improvement. Every day—no matter how good we are—we expect to get even better tomorrow. We are working to provide our customers with better products and better service. And we depend largely on our aging work force to make improved quality the reality that it is.

Our efforts with our work force have to be based on exactly that same idea—continuous improvement. The mutual commitment to producing quality products, retraining the worker, training for retirement, providing funded pensions, improving health care—those are all part of our effort to make quality of work life and quality of life in general better for all General Motors employees. It is an ongoing joint union-management effort that bodes well for the future welfare of the employees, the company, the union, and, of course, the customers.

Productivity, Age, and Labor Composition Changes in the U.S. Work Force

MARY JABLONSKI,
KENT KUNZE,
AND LARRY ROSENBLUM

Jablonski and her associates present direct evidence (based on U.S. Department of Labor studies of piece-rate workers) that there is only a moderate tendency for productivity to fall with age for older workers. Moreover, they also present an original "labor composition index" for the United States which measures the effect of aging on national productivity. Their index shows that the aging of the American work force has increased the rate of productivity gain, largely because we no longer have to train so many young, inexperienced workers.

J. D. O.

Over the course of a lifetime, an individual worker's productivity varies. A general pattern for this variation is that a worker's productivity rises for many years, after which it will stabilize and then it may decline. Over the course of time, productivity in the economy as a whole also varies. Since a worker's productivity tends to vary with age, one cause of variation in productivity for the economy is fluctuation in the age composition of the work force. Changes in the composition of the work force with respect to educational attainment and sex can also affect productivity, as can other factors such as technological change. In this paper we examine the relationship between productivity and age for both the individual and the work force, using the results of studies that have been conducted by the Bureau of Labor Statistics.

The findings and opinions presented in this paper are strictly those of the authors and should not be attributed to the U.S. Department of Labor, Bureau of Labor Statistics. The authors wish to express their appreciation for the helpful comments and suggestions of Jerome Mark and Edwin Dean.

To start, the results of studies of comparative job performance carried out by the Bureau of Labor Statistics in the 1950s and 1960s are reviewed. These studies are noteworthy because they collected data pertaining to the actual output of individual workers. With the data, the researchers formed indexes of output per hour, which measure worker productivity, and compared the indexes across age groups. The workers in these studies were, in general, paid on a piece-rate basis or were performing highly repetitive tasks, which made it possible to measure their actual contribution to output.

To broaden the scope of this investigation, we turned to data on the earnings of workers in many different jobs because data on actual output are not available for most workers. Using the link between productivity and earnings (the theory of this link also will be discussed), we explore the relationship between earnings and age to find out more about the relationship between productivity and age for individual workers.

We next focus on the work force as a whole. Changes in the composition of the labor force that have taken place in the past forty years are briefly described. The methodology of labor composition measurement is then presented. Labor composition growth is measured to determine the impact of changes in the composition of the work force on productivity change. In this measure of labor composition, age affects labor composition growth indirectly through its effect on work experience.

Finally, empirical results of our research are reported. Results for the individual worker are presented, as are results for the work force in the form of labor composition measures. Those measures are subsequently used to assess the effects of labor composition growth on productivity growth.

Age and Productivity of the Individual Worker

During the 1950s and 1960s, the Bureau of Labor Statistics conducted several studies of comparative job performance by age, under the direction of Jerome Mark.[1] In each study indexes of output per hour were constructed and then compared across age groups. Table 1 reports the major results of each of these studies.

For the first study, data on factory workers in the footwear and furniture industries were collected from plant records. Many of the

1. See U.S. Department of Labor 1956, 1957; Kutscher and Walker 1960; Walker 1964.

Table 1: INDEXES OF OUTPUT PER HOUR FOR WORKERS, SELECTED INDUSTRIES AND OCCUPATIONS (35–44 AGE GROUP = 100)

Industry/ Occupation	Age Group Under 25	25–34	35–44	45–54	55–64	65 +
Footwear						
Men	93.8	100.3	100.0	97.7	92.5	81.1
Coefficient of variation	17.9	16.3	13.8	14.1	14.5	16.6
Women	94.4	102.8	100.0	98.8	94.1	88.0
Coefficient of variation	17.1	17.5	15.2	15.6	13.1	20.7
Household Furniture						
Men	98.5	101.5	100.0	96.1	94.5	93.6
Coefficient of variation	16.3	15.1	11.8	11.0	11.8	11.6
Women	101.4	107.4	100.0	98.7	85.6	—
Coefficient of variation	18.8	19.4	17.8	16.0	18.6	—
Clerical Workers						
All workers	92.4	99.4	100.0	100.1	98.6	101.2
Coefficient of variation	22.3	20.1	18.1	19.4	19.4	20.5

Table 1: CONTINUED

Industry/ Occupation	Age Group								
	Under 25	25–29	30–34	35–39	39–44	45–49	50–54	55–59	60+
Mail Sorters	101.2	100.1	101.3	100.1	99.8	99.5	100.9	99.1	96.2
Coefficient of variation	13.7	13.2	13.0	12.2	12.8	12.6	12.9	15.0	13.7

Sources: U.S. Department of Labor, Bureau of Labor Statistics 1956, 1957; Kutscher and Walker 1960; Walker 1964.

workers in these industries were compensated on a piece-rate basis, which made possible direct comparisons of output per hour.[2] Generally output per hour was measured by the individual's average straight-time hourly piece-rate earnings. The average output per hour for men in each age group in each industry was calculated so that those aged 35–44 were indexed to 100. The same procedure was performed with data on women.

On average, workers in the 25–34 age group were more productive than workers under 25 years of age. There was some decline in output per hour between the ages of 25 and 64. For example, the average index of output per hour for men in the 25–34 age group in the footwear industry was 100.3, while the average index for men in the 55–64 age group was 92.5. More substantial declines in productivity were found among those 65 and over in the footwear industry but not in the furniture industry. Men in the footwear industry aged 65 and over averaged 81.1 on the index of output per hour, while the same age group averaged 93.6 in the furniture industry. However, the study also found that there was much variation in output rates within age groups and that the variability was not closely related to age. In fact, many of the older workers performed better in terms of output per hour than the average for those in the 35–44 age group. For example, among men in the footwear industry, 44 percent of those in the 45–54 age group and 30 percent of those in the 55–64 age group exceeded the average of the 35–44 age group. Therefore, while a decline in average output per hour was associated with age among men over 45 and women over 35, there was much variability about the averages.

In the studies of clerical workers and mail sorters, recorded data on actual output again allowed indexes of output per hour to be computed directly. The clerical workers were employed by the federal government or private industry, and many were paid on an incentive basis. In contrast to factory workers, office workers showed very little decline in output per hour between the ages of 25 and 64—the difference in the average index for those in the 25–34 age group and in the 55–64 age group was less than a percentage point. As in the factory study, workers below the age of 25 were less productive than those between the ages of 25 and 34. Unlike the oldest factory workers, office workers 65 and over had the highest average index of all the age groups. Again, a

2. The measurement of actual job performance is the subject of renewed attention. For example, see Maranto and Rodgers 1984; Horowitz and Sherman 1980; Medoff and Abraham 1980. Unlike the classic BLS studies cited in this paper, these more recent studies use less accurate measures of physical output in more narrowly defined industries and occupations for their analysis.

substantial amount of variation in productivity within age groups was found.

A distinguishing feature of the mail sorters study was that none of the workers were paid on an incentive basis. Measures of individual work performance were based on production records prepared by supervisors. As with the other studies, the output per hour of mail sorters aged 35–44 was indexed to 100. The study indicates that there was not a significant amount of variation in average output per hour among age groups below age 60. The difference between the lowest and the highest average indexes was 2.2 percentage points. Among those aged 60 and over, a small decline was observed. Once again, there was considerable variation in output per hour among individuals within age groups. In each age group the majority of the workers had indexes below 95 or above 105. The average index for all workers was 101.2.

These studies suggest that there was not a large decline in average productivity between the ages of 25 and 64, among the workers covered. The most noteworthy decreases tended to be among those in the oldest age groups (60 or 65 and over, depending on the study). Also, in every study there was generally a large amount of variation in output per hour among workers within age groups.

The job performance studies provide some direct indication of how productivity varies with age. Direct measurement of worker output was possible largely because the studies were confined to a narrow group of workers. In the next section, the analysis is broadened to include most workers in the private economy. However, empirical investigations of broad segments of the work force rely on earnings rather than actual output to measure productivity. Consequently, the job performance studies provide useful guidance on the relationship between age and productivity.

Age, Productivity, and Earnings

In the studies discussed above, measures of output per hour were constructed using observed output or productivity data of individual workers available from employer records. Generally, such data are not available. However, data on wages, which are more widely available, can be analyzed in conjunction with other relevant information so we can learn more about aging and productivity. The link between wages and productivity is based on the assumption of a competitive economy with profit-maximizing firms, which implies that the wage of a group of workers equals the value of their marginal product. Given this type of economy, we can examine the connection between age and a person's wage in order to gain additional insights regarding the connection between age and productivity. We begin this examination by considering how a person's age may affect earnings.

While age is correlated with earnings, it does not directly affect a person's wage. The human capital theory links the two by a string of relationships. Age is related to experience, which is related to on-the-job training, which increases skills and productivity.

Older workers, on average, have more work experience than younger workers because, of course, they have had more time in which to gain experience. While at work, individuals acquire on-the-job training, and we expect that those individuals with more work experience tend to have had more on-the-job training. When workers undergo training, they learn or improve skills, and these new or better skills make them more productive. We expect a worker who becomes more productive to command a higher wage. To summarize, older workers tend to earn more than younger workers because they have had more work experience and, therefore, more on-the-job training, and as a result they tend to be more skilled and hence more productive.[3] This relationship may exist until the latter years of their working lives, when workers may see their hourly earnings level off or possibly drop.[4]

The pattern of real hourly earnings of an individual typically results in a curve that shows earnings rising throughout his working life. Though real hourly earnings generally increase throughout a worker's career, the increase is usually very modest near retirement. However, when the earnings of many different workers at a single point in time are plotted against age, a different curve can be seen. Until some time in their 40s, workers' earnings usually increase with age, with the increase in earnings for each additional year gradually diminishing. However, earnings then peak and may even decline for older workers. The first curve described above follows a cohort across time, while the second curve examines a cross-section of the work force at a point in time. These curves differ, in large part, because cross-sectional studies hold

3. It is assumed that wages equal the value of marginal products in a competitive economy. An exception arises when on-the-job training is specific to the firm, and the firm shares the cost and returns to the investment. In this case, wages are usually less than the value of marginal products for most of the period following the investment. Consequently, wages rise more slowly than marginal products when training is specific to the firm. However, the difference will generally be small whenever workers make most of the investment in training or job turnover occurs with some regularity.

4. See Becker (1975) for a more complete discussion of the human capital theory.

technology constant while cohort studies do not.[5] Since we focus on how age influences productivity through investments in training, we abstract from the issue of technical progress and use cross-sectional studies in this paper.

In his seminal study, Mincer (1974) accounted for the parabolic form of the cross-sectional earnings curve in the following way. During much of their careers, workers devote some portion of their work time to on-the-job training, part of which they pay for by forgoing earnings. In other words, they agree to accept a wage below the maximum that they could earn in order to receive training. The sacrificed earnings are viewed as payment (or investment) for training. Later they receive a return on their investment in the form of higher wages. As the years go by, workers spend a smaller fraction of their time making investments in training because retirement is nearer and the period in which to recoup their investment is shorter. During this period earnings rise not only from the return on the investments in training but also because less of their potential earnings is forgone as payment for new training. Toward the end of their working lives, workers may stop investing altogether. If their skills lose value or erode over time, then an individual worker may find that earnings fall as retirement approaches. So the shape of the age-earnings profile can be explained by three factors: returns on investment in training, declining investment over time, and depreciation of skills.

It should be noted that there are other possible reasons for declining hourly earnings among some individuals who are nearing the end of their working lives. Some workers may change jobs later in life, after being laid off or dismissed. The new job may pay a lower wage than the previous one because a substantial amount of the worker's knowledge and skills may be specific to the old firm and not valuable to the new employer. Also, health problems may lower the average hourly earnings of older workers who are paid in part or whole on the basis of actual output produced. Piece-rate workers, such as those studied in the furniture and footwear industries, or workers earning commissions or bonuses based on sales are among those compensated in this way. Additionally, some workers who choose to retire from a fulltime job subsequently obtain a part-time job. They may find the wage for such a

5. While cross-sectional studies do hold technology fixed, they cannot control for variations in schooling and training quality across generations. See Owen (1986) for a discussion of the difference between cross-sectional and cohort analysis of earnings.

part-time job less than the hourly earnings at the former position.[6] Finally, some older workers may face age discrimination. Their work may be undervalued or they may not be permitted to retain jobs that they are still capable of performing.

Two additional explanations for the shape of the age-earnings profile spring from models of job sorting and implicit contracts. Job sorting refers to the quality of matches that are made between workers and jobs.[7] In such a model, the assessment of the match between a newly hired worker's skills and the requirements of the firm is very imprecise. As the employee gains experience, both the worker and the firm make an increasingly accurate appraisal of the quality of the match. An employee will leave whenever he believes a better match is available elsewhere. Accordingly, a major source of earnings growth is the improvement in job matches that occurs during an individual's career; hence the shape of the age-earnings profile can be explained in part by the increase in the quality of job matches over time, rather than just by investment in training. According to implicit contract models, firms seek to maximize the work effort of their employees by the design of their compensation schedule. Workers are paid less than the value of their marginal product early in their tenure with the firm and subsequently are paid in excess of their marginal product. This arrangement is acceptable to employees because the present discounted value of lifetime earnings is increased. Employees must provide maximum effort or risk losing a job which for most of their career pays more than their marginal product and more than other firms will pay.[8] Such an arrangement can give rise to a positive age-earnings relationship, but without an equivalent rise in worker productivity. Note that neither of the models precludes the validity of the human capital model. Hence all three models could come into play simultaneously.[9]

6. Gustman and Steinmeier 1984; Honig and Hanoch 1985. Both papers found that most partially retired persons have changed employers. Honig and Hanoch found that partial retirement is associated with a reduction in both hours and hourly wage rates, though Gustman and Steinmeier found wage reductions to be more common than declines in hours. In addition, both studies show that health problems increase the likelihood of partial retirement.

7. See Jovanovic (1979a, 1979b) for a discussion of the theory and Abraham and Farber (1987) for empirical estimates of the job matching model.

8. Lazear 1979, 1981; Medoff and Abraham 1980.

9. However, the implicit contract model does suggest that wages rise faster than productivity over a worker's career.

Table 2: MEAN AGE OF CIVILIAN LABOR FORCE AGED 16 OR OLDER, BY SEX, 1948–86

Year	*Mean Age in Years*		
	Women	Men	All Workers
1948	36.6	40.0	39.0
1950	37.5	40.1	39.4
1955	39.0	41.1	40.4
1958	39.6	40.9	40.5
1960	39.8	40.7	40.4
1965	39.5	40.3	40.0
1970	38.4	39.7	39.2
1975	36.8	38.1	37.6
1980	36.3	37.4	36.9
1985	36.5	37.5	37.0
1986	36.6	37.5	37.1

Source: calculated from U.S. Department of Labor, Bureau of Labor Statistics, *Employment and Earnings*, January 1988 and earlier issues.

Labor Composition and Productivity

The typical American worker has changed considerably over the last forty years.[10] Today's average worker is younger, better educated, and more likely to be female. A prolonged period of decline in the average age of the labor force began in the late 1950s (Table 2) and lasted for about two decades. The average age then started to increase slowly. The primary force behind the decline was the entrance into the labor market of members of the baby boom generation (Table 3). From 1960 to 1975, the percentage of the labor force in the 16–24 age group rose from 16.6 to 24.1. It is also evident from Table 3 that the aging of the baby boomers is the primary force behind the rise in the average age of the American worker that is taking place in the 1980s. From 1980 to 1986 the proportion of the labor force between the ages of 35 and 44 jumped from 19.1 percent to 23.1 percent.

Since both the comparative job performance studies and the human capital model indicate that individual differences in productivity can be related to a worker's traits, and the demographic characteristics of the average worker have changed substantially, it is reasonable to suspect that changes in labor composition have had an effect on productivity growth.

The Bureau of Labor Statistics framework for measuring changes in the composition of labor and its effect on productivity

10. See R. Kutscher and H. Fullerton's essay for a description of the changes in the demographics of the work force.

Table 3: PERCENTAGE DISTRIBUTION OF CIVILIAN LABOR FORCE AGED 16 OR OLDER, 1948–86

Year	*Age Group*				
	16–24	25–34	35–44	45–54	55 +
1948	19.51	23.52	22.10	18.00	16.87
1950	18.52	23.50	22.43	18.40	17.15
1955	15.01	23.16	23.68	19.98	18.18
1958	15.57	21.69	23.70	20.96	18.08
1960	16.58	20.66	23.37	21.33	18.07
1965	19.03	19.12	22.62	21.16	18.08
1970	21.56	20.58	19.86	20.48	17.52
1975	24.12	24.38	18.03	18.22	15.25
1980	23.66	27.33	19.14	15.81	14.06
1985	20.46	29.06	22.58	15.00	12.90
1986	19.83	29.36	23.11	15.05	12.65

Source: U.S. Department of Labor, Bureau of Labor Statistics, *Employment and Earnings*, January 1988 and earlier issues.

growth begins with the economic theory of production. In this frame work, it is acknowledged that output per hour varies across workers. Differences in worker productivity result from differences in skills where skills are measured by years of schooling and work experience for each sex.[11] This framework contrasts with studies of productivity growth in which workers are assumed to be homogeneous and labor input is simply measured as total hours of labor.[12] Once workers are recognized to be heterogeneous, it is not possible to directly combine their hours. The present paper is an outgrowth of a major BLS study, not yet completed, in which the hours of each type of labor input are weighted by their contribution to output as measured by their share of labor costs.

The measure of labor composition is based on a Tornqvist index of labor input derived from the growth rates of hours cross-classified by education, work experience, and sex. The Tornqvist index is a weighted average of the growth rates of each type of labor; the weights are each type of labor's share of labor costs.[13] Then the growth rate of the index of labor input ($\dot{L}/L$) equals the weighted average of the growth rates of the appropriately cross-classified hours of labor ($\dot{H}_i/H_i$):[14]

11. Using education, age (or work experience), and sex as sources of productivity differences among workers has a long tradition: see Griliches 1970; Chinloy 1980; Denison 1985; Jorgenson, Gollop, and Fraumeni 1987.
12. For example, see U.S. Department of Labor, Bureau of Labor Statistics 1983.
13. The resultant index does not measure the level of aggregate labor input, only changes in labor input. See Caves, Christensen, and Diewert (1982) for a more complete discussion.
14. The dot notation refers to the change in the variable over time.

(1) $\dot{L}/L = \sum_i w_i \dot{H}_i/H_i$.

The subscript i refers to each particular group defined by the classification of hours by experience, education, and sex. For example, H_i could be the total hours of men with one year of experience and less than five years of education. The weights (w_i) are the two-period averages of the relative cost shares of each labor group:

$w_i = 0.5 * (s_{i,t} + s_{i,t-1})$

where s_i is the cost share of the ith labor group,

$s_i = p_i H_i / \sum_i p_i H_i$,

and p_i is the price of labor for the ith labor group, which is assumed equal to the value of the marginal product of the group.

The growth in labor composition ($\dot{C}/C$) is defined as the difference between the growth rate of labor input ($\dot{L}/L$) and the growth rate of aggregate unweighted hours ($\dot{H}/H$):

(2) $\dot{C}/C = \dot{L}/L - \dot{H}/H$.

Substituting (1) into (2) yields

(3) $\dot{C}/C = \sum_i w_i (\dot{H}_i/H_i - \dot{H}/H)$.

The growth in labor composition is a weighted average of the growth of each group of cross-classified hours relative to the growth in aggregate unweighted hours.

As indicated in the description above, the computation of labor composition growth requires information on the prices and hours of labor cross-classified by experience, education, and sex. While our major data sources for hours, the Annual Demographic File of the Current Population Survey (CPS) and the decennial censuses of 1950 and 1960, supply data regarding the education of workers, they do not contain data on work experience. Because of this, a procedure was developed that allows us to predict the work experience of in-dividuals based on observable characteristics available from the CPS and censuses. Share weights are calculated using labor prices derived from estimated earnings functions. Still another noteworthy feature of the methodology is the construction of the detailed annual hours matrices that are needed for the period of the study, 1948–86. Each of these features—predicted experience, estimated wages, and the construction of the detailed hours matrices—distinguishes the BLS methodology from that of other researchers in this area.[15]

Many researchers have used age or potential experience (the number of years since leaving school) as a proxy for actual experience when estimating earnings functions.[16] We have chosen to use a measure of predicted experience instead, for two important reasons. One reason is that there is a correlation between education and experience. On average, people with more education have more actual work experience at the time they complete school than do those with less education when they complete school. The other reason is that women tend to have interrupted work histories because many spend periods of time out of the labor force bearing and raising children. Neither age nor potential experience reflects these tendencies, and so both proxies can lead to biased estimates when they are included in earnings equations.[17] Our measure of predicted experience avoids these biases by capturing the effects directly.

To derive predicted experience, equations were estimated with data from the 1973 Exact Match File, which linked data from the CPS, Social Security Administration records, and Internal Revenue Service tax returns.[18] The Exact Match File sample was modified to make it more appropriate for the labor composition study. Only paid employees aged 14 or over and currently working in private nonagricultural industries are included. Persons with extensive work experience in jobs not covered by the Social Security program will have their actual work experience under-reported when measured by Social Security records. Their inclusion in the sample would bias downward the coefficients of the experience equation and the measures of predicted experience. Such workers

15. Jorgenson, Gollop, and Fraumeni 1987; Denison 1985; Chinloy 1980; Griliches 1970. Space limitations prevent us from discussing the BLS methodology in detail. See Dean, Kunze, and Rosenblum (1988). A complete discussion of issues and methods will be available in a forthcoming publication of the Office of Productivity and Technology of the Bureau of Labor Statistics.

16. Potential experience is a measure of the duration of time a worker could have spent in the work force if there were no absences except for schooling. One common approximation of potential experience, the one used in this paper, is the worker's age minus years of completed schooling minus six.

17. Wage models which use potential experience can avoid biased estimates if the sample is sufficiently partitioned. However, the sample size will sometimes be too small for reliable estimates.

18. The U.S. Department of Health, Education and Welfare (1979) linked Social Security work histories from 1937 through 1973 to a portion of the 1973 CPS and IRS records. There is also a 1980 Exact Match File, but it is not currently available for use outside of the Census Bureau.

include those in jobs that were not covered by the Social Security program until the early 1950s, such as domestic, agricultural, and railroad workers and employees of welfare and religious organizations. Also, black and Hispanic workers were excluded from the sample, as they were more likely to have been in uncovered employment. (However, black and Hispanic workers are included when earnings functions are estimated and when hours matrices are created.)

The dependent variable in the experience equations is all years of work experience reported to the Social Security Administration, including experience while still in school.[19] For men, the explanatory variables in this equation include potential experience, years of schooling, and interaction terms. In addition to these variables, the women's equation contains variables pertaining to marriage and children. Table 4 displays all of these variables.

As stated, the purpose of the experience equation is to develop a measure more closely related to training than potential experience or age. Predicted work experience, along with years of schooling and other characteristics, is used in a wage model to explain earnings differences across workers.[20] The result of the earnings function is a price for each type of labor, where labor types are defined by the cross-classification of labor by experience, education, and sex.[21]

For the earnings equation, the natural logarithm of hourly earnings is the dependent variable.[22] The variables that appear in the earnings functions are listed in Table 5. Separate functions are estimated for

19. Experimentation with earnings functions indicates that including all experience rather than just experience since leaving school yields the best result. It appears then that experience while in school contributes significantly to future earnings.

20. The functional form of the wage model is based on the work of Mincer (1974). Mincer utilizes an approximation of an infinite series of investments to achieve a log linear estimating form.

21. Since earnings differences by race may be primarily the result of discrimination, the earnings of a specific group are no longer an appropriate measure of their productivity. The combined earnings of blacks and whites will still measure a worker's marginal product provided that white employees rather than employers are the principal beneficiaries of discrimination. It is this assumption which leads to earnings which are not differentiated by race in this study. See Becker (1971) for models of employee and employer discrimination.

22. Our earnings measure does not include fringe benefits because data on such benefits have not been collected for the workers in our sample. It has been suggested that higher-paid workers, such as more educated or experienced workers, receive a higher proportion of their total earnings as fringe benefits because of tax incentives. If this is true, the earnings function underestimates the return to education and experience. The net effect on the labor composition measures is indeterminate.

Table 4: DEPENDENT AND EXPLANATORY VARIABLES FOR PREDICTED EXPERIENCE EQUATIONS

Variable	Definition
Dependent variable	Years of work experience reported to Social Security Administration, 1937–73
Explanatory variables	
POTEXP	Years of potential experience (age–schooling–6)
POTEXPSQ	Years of potential experience squared
S0–4	Dummy variable for those with 0–4 years of completed schooling
S5–8	Dummy variable for those with 5–8 years of completed schooling
S9–11	Dummy variable for those with 9–11 years of completed schooling (omitted variable)
S12	Dummy variable for those with 12 years of completed schooling
S13–15	Dummy variable for those with 13–15 years of completed schooling
S16	Dummy variable for those with 16 years of completed schooling
S17+	Dummy variable for those with 17 or more years of completed schooling
MARRIED	Dummy variable for ever married persons
KID0	Dummy variable for women with no children (omitted)
KID1	Dummy variable for women with 1 child ever born
KID2–3	Dummy variable for women with 2–3 children ever born
KID4UP	Dummy variable for women with 4 or more children ever born
PREVEXP	Years of potential experience prior to 1937
Interaction terms with potential experience	
S0–4 * POTEXP	Interaction of dummy variable for 0–4 years of schooling and potential experience
S5–8 * POTEXP	Interaction of dummy variable for 5–8 years of schooling and potential experience
S9–11 * POTEXP	Interaction of dummy variable for 9–11 years of schooling and potential experience (omitted)
S12 * POTEXP	Interaction of dummy variable for 12 years of schooling and potential experience (omitted)
S13–15 * POTEXP	Interaction of dummy variable for 13–15 years of schooling and potential experience
S16 * POTEXP	Interaction of dummy variable for 16 years of schooling and potential experience

Table 4: CONTINUED

Variable	Definition
17+ * POTEXP	Interaction of dummy variable for 17 or more years of schooling and potential experience
MARRIED * POTEXP	Interaction of dummy variable for ever married women and potential experience
KID0 * POTEXP	Interaction of dummy variable for no children ever born and potential experience (omitted)
KID1 * POTEXP	Interaction of dummy variable for 1 child ever born and potential experience
KID2–3 * POTEXP	Interaction of dummy variable for 2–3 children ever born and potential experience
KID4UP * POTEXP	Interaction of dummy variable for 4 or more children ever born and potential experience
NONPROFIT	Interaction of dummy variable for selected nonprofit industries and years of potential experience

men and women because the pattern of women's earnings was found to differ from that of men.[23]

Prior to the estimation of the wage functions, the samples are adjusted in two ways. First, self-employed workers are excluded because their earnings consist of returns to physical capital as well as labor income. (The hours of the self-employed are included in the hours matrices, as are the hours of unpaid family workers.) Second, measures of labor composition are calculated for the private business sector, which by definition excludes government workers.

The earnings functions are estimated with samples from the 1950 and 1960 Census of Population and with data from the 1968 through 1987 Annual Demographic File of the Current Population Survey. (In each case the estimated parameters are used to compute wages for the year preceding the survey year, since the earnings data amassed by each survey refer to the previous year. For example the 1987 CPS collected information on the amounts that individuals earned in 1986.) While the CPS has been conducted since 1948, data on individual ob-

23. Earnings are also differentiated by sex in other studies of labor composition (Jorgenson, Gollop, and Fraumeni 1987; Denison 1985; Chinloy 1980).

The issue of why women's earnings are lower than men's earnings is not yet resolved. The approach taken in this study is based on a considerable body of literature (Weiss and Gronau 1981; Sandell and Shapiro 1980; Mincer and Ofek 1982) which suggests that the interrupted pattern of work force participation may result in less training and lower earnings for women. If earnings differences are primarily due to sex discrimination, this approach should be modified. See Beller (1982) and Treimann and Hartmann (1981) for an analysis of sex discrimination.

Table 5: VARIABLES IN THE EARNINGS FUNCTIONS

Variable	Definition
Dependent variable	Natural log of hourly wages
Explanatory variables	
S1–4	Dummy variable for those with 1–4 years of completed schooling
S5–8	Dummy variable for those with 5–8 years of completed schooling (omitted variable)
S9–11	Dummy variable for those with 9–11 years of completed schooling
S12	Dummy variable for those with 12 years of completed schooling
S13–15	Dummy variable for those with 13–15 years of completed schooling
S16	Dummy variable for those with 16 years of completed schooling
S17+	Dummy variable for those with more than 16 years of completed schooling
EXPER	Predicted SSA work experience
EXPSQ	Predicted SSA work experience squared
PTIME	Dummy variable for those working part-time (available 1968–87)
VET	Dummy variable for veterans (men only)
NEWENG	Dummy variable for resident of New England Census Division
MIDATL	Dummy variable for resident of Mid-Atlantic Census Division
ENCENT	Dummy variable for resident of East North Central Census Division
WNCENT	Dummy variable for resident of West North Central Census Division
SATL	Dummy variable for resident of South Atlantic Census Division
ESCENT	Dummy variable for resident of East South Central Census Division
WSCENT	Dummy variable for resident of West South Central Census Division
MOUNTAIN	Dummy variable for resident of Mountain Census Division
PACIFIC	Dummy variable for resident of Pacific Census Division (omitted)
CCITY	Dummy variable for resident of central city of SMSA (available 1968–87)
BCITY	Dummy variable for resident of balance of SMSA (available 1968–87)

Table 5: CONTINUED

Variable	Definition
URBAN	Dummy variable for resident of SMSA (available 1950 and 1960)
RURAL	Dummy variable for resident living outside SMSA (omitted)

servations collected before 1968 are not available. For the years for which wage models cannot be estimated, linear interpolation or extrapolation is used to obtain hourly prices of labor.

In the empirical section of this study, measures of labor composition growth are presented along with measures of the individual contributions of experience, education, and sex to labor composition growth.[24]

The prices of labor used in computing the share weights of the Tornqvist index are based on the coefficients of the earnings functions. The estimated prices of labor are computed using only the estimated intercept and coefficients for the experience and schooling terms, since the experience and schooling terms are related to the skills that workers bring to the job and hence to the contribution that they make to productivity.[25]

Detailed matrices of annual hours are required, one for each year from 1948 to 1986. Matrices are created from data taken directly from the decennial censuses of 1950 and 1960 as well as the Annual Demographic File (of the CPS) of 1968–87. For the remaining years, matrices are estimated using the RAS interpolation method.[26] In these matrices hours of work are cross-classified by age, level of schooling, sex, marital status, and number of children ever born. The experience

24. The indexes of the individual contributions to labor composition growth are defined analogously to equation (3). The difference is that instead of using all of the relevant parameters of the wage equation to define the price of labor, p_i, only the parameters of one trait at a time are used. For example, the index of work experience defines a rental price, p_i, from the experience parameters only and sets the remaining parameters to zero. Second-order indexes are defined by using the parameters of two of the three traits.

These indexes should be regarded as approximate because there is no consistent method for dividing the wage into separate payments for education and experience across different types of workers. Another method of decomposing labor composition growth can be found in Chinloy (1981). However, there are other weaknesses in this method which we find unsatisfactory.

25. Prior to share computation, the female intercept is adjusted to take into account regional and locational variations in the female-male wage differential.

26. See Bacharach (1965) for a discussion of biproportional RAS interpolation.

equation is used to condense these detailed matrices into a set of annual hours matrices in which hours of work are cross-classified by work experience, education, and sex; each cell of each matrix contains the total number of hours worked in that year by workers of the same sex and education level who had the same amount of predicted experience. Changes in labor composition are computed with this set of matrices.

Empirical Results for the Individual Worker

The studies of comparative job performance provide one indication of how worker productivity varies by age. However, these studies are limited to a narrow spectrum of the work force. By use of the estimated experience and earnings equations of Tables 4 and 5, differences in worker productivity by age can be measured for nearly all employees in the private sector.

Table 6 contains the estimated experience equations for men and women. Using the coefficients presented in Table 6, a 35-year-old male high school graduate has 17 years of predicted work experience, while a comparable college graduate has 15 years of predicted experience. Similarly, a 35-year-old married woman with two children has 11 years of predicted experience if she is a high school graduate and 9 years if she is a college graduate. Also, a 35-year-old unmarried female high school graduate has 17 years of predicted experience, while a comparable college graduate has 14 years. In this example, it is helpful to recall that, at age 35, a high school graduate has 17 years and a college graduate 13 years of potential experience (defined as age minus years of school minus six). Clearly, marital status and children strongly affect the level of predicted experience for women. In addition, because of experience acquired while still in school, the difference in predicted experience between high school and college graduates is less than the four years suggested by the difference in potential experience.

Tables 7 and 8 display the estimated intercepts and coefficients on the schooling and experience terms of the earnings equations. All of the estimated coefficients on the experience terms are statistically significant and have the expected signs: positive for experience itself and negative for experience squared.

The estimated coefficients on the experience terms are used to calculate the percentage change in the wage due to an additional year of experience. The results for selected years are seen in Table 9. The percentage change measures the difference between the estimated wage of a person with the stated level of experience and the estimated wage of an otherwise identical person with one additional year of experience. We find that the increase in wages from an additional year of experience has risen over time for less experienced workers. Furthermore, as indicated by the average worker, the sensitivity of wages to experience has been increasing over the period. This could be due to increasing returns to training over time or to increases over time in the amount of training per year of experience.

Next we compare the percentage changes in the wage at different levels of experience for a particular year. For men with 5 years of experience, an additional year of experience raised the wage by 6.4 percent in 1986, whereas at 15 years of experience an additional year of experience increased the wage by 3.0 percent. After 35 years of experience, the average wage fell by 3.5 percent per additional year of experience. For women an additional year of experience resulted in a wage that was 4.6 percent higher at 5 years of experience and 0.5 percent higher at 15 years of experience. At 25 years of experience, an additional year of experience led to a decrease in the wage of 3.4 percent.

The estimated experience and wage equations were used to create Figures 1 and 2, which show the relationships between age and hourly earnings in 1986 for high school graduates and college graduates, respectively. For each combination of age, sex, and education level, predicted work experience was calculated with estimates of the parameters of the experience equations. For the women's profiles, marital status and number of children had to be specified, since they enter into the women's experience equation; we specified married with two or three children. Once predicted experience was obtained, we were able to derive estimated hourly earnings by age with the estimated earnings equations for 1986.[27]

Figures 1 and 2 reveal that hourly earnings, for male high school graduates, climb until around age 46 and then begin to drop, while for male college graduates the peak occurs a couple of years later, at approximately age 48. The profiles for women are much flatter than the profiles for men. The estimated hourly earnings of female high school graduates reach the maximum level for women in their late 40s and then remain there. For female college graduates the peak level is attained around age 50, and the wage stays there until their 60s, at which time it begins to decline slowly.

Comparisons can be made between the findings of the studies of comparative job performance and the age-earnings profiles. According to the findings of the performance studies, output per hour is substantially higher for workers aged 25–34 than for younger workers;

27. Since the construction of the profiles involves earnings data for just one year, inflation is not an issue here.

Table 6: ESTIMATED EXPERIENCE EQUATIONS, WOMEN AND MEN, 1973

Variable	Women	Men
Constant	0.72	0.75
	(4.0)	(7.1)
Potential experience	1.04	0.96
	(61)	(84)
POTEXPSQ	−0.009	−0.005
	(24)	(17)
0–4 yr. schooling	−4.87	−4.81
	(2.5)	(5.2)
5–8 yr. schooling	−3.13	−3.29
	(5.0)	(12)
12 yr. schooling	0.81	1.25
	(5.2)	(14)
13–15 yr. schooling	2.02	2.48
	(7.6)	(16)
16 yr. schooling	2.67	3.60
	(6.7)	(18)
17+ yr. schooling	3.97	3.97
	(4.7)	(14)
S0–4 * POTEXP	0.06	−0.02
	(1.2)	(0.6)
S5–8 * POTEXP	0.05	0.04
	(3.0)	(4.6)
S13–15 * POTEXP	−0.10	−0.01
	(8.5)	(1.7)
S16 * POTEXP	−0.14	−0.04
	(6.3)	(4.0)
S17+ * POTEXP	−0.26	−0.11
	(7.4)	(8.2)
MARRIED	0.65	—
	(3.0)	
MARRIED * POTEXP	−0.22	—
	(21)	

Table 6: CONTINUED

Variable	Women	Men
KID1 * POTEXP	−0.07 (11)	—
KID2–3	−0.95 (2.8)	—
KID2–3 * POTEXP	−0.10 (6.9)	—
KID4UP	−1.14 (1.2)	—
KID4UP * POTEXP	−0.18 (4.3)	—
PREVEXP	—	−0.09 (15)
NONPROFIT	−0.06 (11)	−0.08 (15)
Degrees of freedom	8663	17120
R^2	0.608	0.839

Note: *t*-statistics are in parentheses. Experience is measured in years of work experience reported to the Social Security Administration.

Source: U.S. Department of Labor, Bureau of Labor Statistics, Current Population Survey, Administrative Record Exact Match File, 1973.

similarly, estimated hourly earnings are much greater for 30-year-old workers than for recent entrants. In the performance studies the peak level of productivity was generally reached by the time a worker was 35 years of age. In the factory study (footwear and household furniture workers), the measures of the average productivity of men stayed near the peak level until age 45, after which they started to fall. The measures of the average productivity of women in the factory study began to drop after age 35. In the other studies the average productivity of workers remained around the peak level for many years. The average output per hour of the office workers stayed near the peak level until retirement, while a small drop in output per hour was observed among mail sorters who were 60 and over. The peaks of the age-earnings profiles are attained between the ages of 45 and 50. For men, estimated hourly earnings begin to decline after the peak, while for women the peak level is maintained for years.

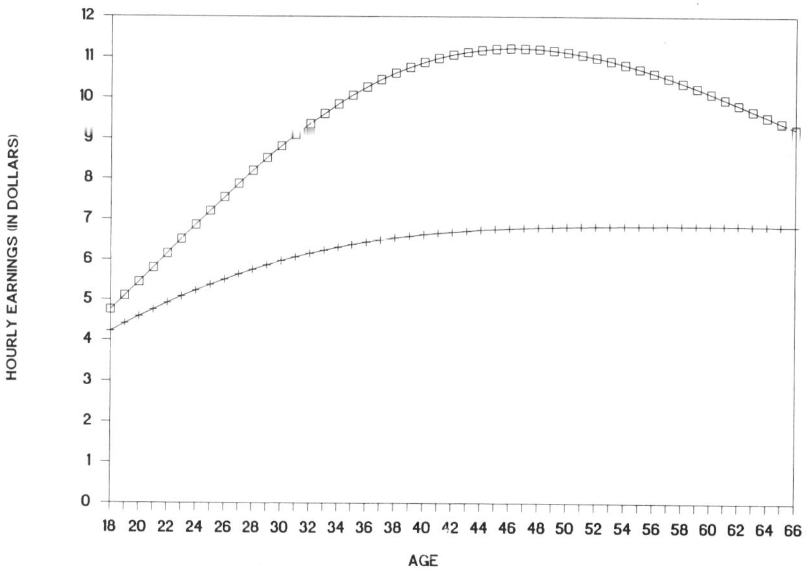

Figure 1. Age and estimated hourly earnings, 12 years of education, 1986. *Key: boxed line,* men; *crossed line,* women. Source: based on coefficients in Tables 6, 7, and 8.

Many other researchers have estimated cross-sectional earnings functions, usually with potential experience (e.g., Oaxaca 1973, Duncan 1976, Rizzuto and Wachtel 1980, Venti 1985, Heywood 1986, and Topel 1986). With their estimates, age at peak earnings can be calculated (in some of the studies the earnings measure was annual or weekly earnings rather than hourly earnings). For male high school graduates, the estimated ages at peak earnings tend to lie in the range of 45 to 50, which places them close to our estimate of 46 years. For female high school graduates, the estimated ages at peak earnings based on other researchers' estimates tend to be in the mid-40s, whereas we found that the peak level was reached in their late 40s.

A few words of caution are necessary because Figures 1 and 2 are based on cross-sectional data. The quality of schooling and the rate of investment in on-the-job training per year of work experience may vary across cohorts. Furthermore, the labor force participation rate for women has increased over time, and the return to experience has also changed over time. Because of such changes, the shapes of the profiles actually realized by following the real hourly earnings of a single cohort of workers across time (even controlling for changes in technical

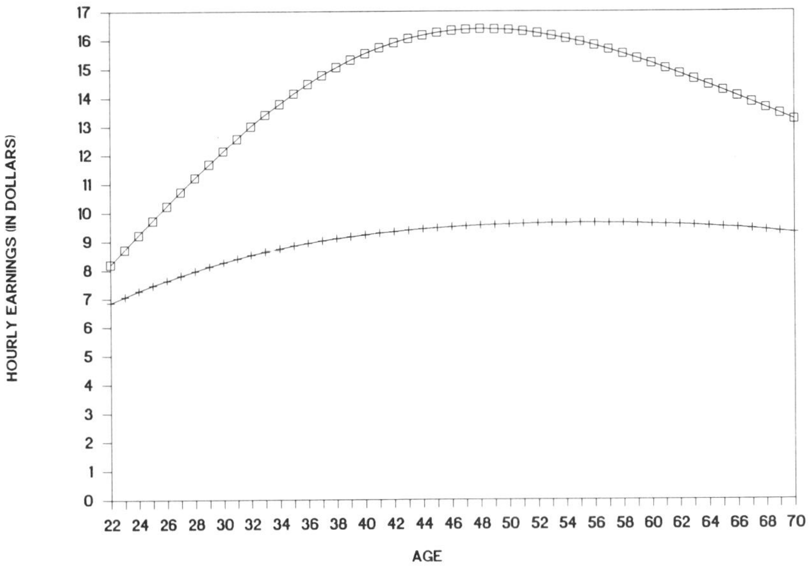

Figure 2. Age and estimated hourly earnings, 16 years of education, 1986. *Key: boxed line,* men; *crossed line,* women. Source: based on coefficients in Tables 6, 7, and 8.

progress) may vary from the shapes of the profiles in the figures. For example, the average female college graduate who was 25 in 1986 will probably have a greater attachment to the work force, make a greater annual investment in skills, and therefore have a profile which more closely resembles the men's earnings profile. That is, they will have a steeper profile which peaks later than the women's profile in Figure 2. Even with these limitations, the profiles in Figures 1 and 2 provide a good indication of the relationship of age to investments in training and real hourly earnings.

Measures of Labor Composition Growth

Between 1948 and 1986 labor composition in the private nonfarm business sector grew at an average annual rate of 0.26 percent. Prior to 1973, labor composition grew 0.24 percent annually. During the 1973–79 period, the annual average growth rate of labor composition was only 0.06 percent. In 1979–86 labor composition growth was faster than in the two previous periods, at 0.51 percent per year. The

Table 7: ESTIMATED EARNINGS FUNCTION COEFFICIENTS, MEN, 1950–87

Survey Year	Int.	Years of education: 1–4	9–11	12	13–15	16	17+	Experience: Linear	Quadratic	R^2
1950	−.354	−.150	.093	.163	.245	.422	.447	.060	−.00 25	.193
	(23)	(12)	(11)	(19)	(19)	(25)	(18)	(48)	(37)	
1960	.133	−.156	.100	.179	.324	.545	.550	.060	−.00 18	.201
	(7.5)	(8.3)	(10)	(18)	(25)	(33)	(24)	(40)	(29)	
1968	.345	−.199	.102	.231	.351	.520	.627	.056	−.00 12	.235
	(16)	(7.7)	(7.9)	(19)	(23)	(29)	(25)	(28)	(21)	
1969	.344	−.132	.112	.242	.364	.531	.638	.060	−.00 28	.232
	(16)	(4.9)	(8.6)	(20)	(24)	(29)	(26)	(31)	(25)	
1970	.508	−.205	.137	.243	.349	.554	.645	.056	−.00 14	.264
	(24)	(7.6)	(10)	(20)	(24)	(32)	(27)	(28)	(22)	
1971	.475	−.194	.112	.241	.395	.572	.553	.060	−.00 31	.267
	(21)	(6.7)	(8.0)	(19)	(25)	(31)	(24)	(30)	(25)	
1972	.425	−.198	.130	.239	.362	.541	.652	.072	−.00 57	.282
	(19)	(6.7)	(9.1)	(18)	(23)	(29)	(27)	(38)	(30)	
1973	.531	−.234	.088	.209	.313	.499	.568	.068	−.00 41	.269
	(23)	(7.5)	(5.8)	(15)	(19)	(26)	(23)	(34)	(27)	
1974	.540	−.237	.155	.250	.326	.485	.615	.072	−.00 54	.275
	(23)	(7.2)	(9.9)	(18)	(20)	(25)	(26)	(36)	(28)	
1975	.671	−.268	.124	.214	.275	.431	.533	.072	−.00 52	.245
	(26)	(7.1)	(7.1)	(13)	(15)	(21)	(21)	(33)	(26)	
1976	.584	−.298	.117	.259	.336	.554	.662	.076	−.00 68	.316
	(27)	(9.1)	(7.8)	(19)	(22)	(32)	(31)	(45)	(36)	

Table 7: CONTINUED

Survey Year	Int.	Years of education 1–4	9–11	12	13–15	16	17+	Experience Linear	Quadratic	R^2
1977	.644	−.158	.117	.275	.337	.562	.686	.076	−.00165	.335
	(33)	(5.2)	(8.6)	(22)	(24)	(36)	(36)	(50)	(39)	
1978	.684	−.208	.154	.305	.376	.571	.695	.080	−.00166	.315
	(34)	(6.7)	(11)	(24)	(26)	(35)	(36)	(49)	(38)	
1979	.805	−.235	.162	.317	.392	.589	.706	.072	−.00149	.295
	(39)	(7.0)	(11)	(23)	(26)	(35)	(36)	(45)	(34)	
1980	.921	−.273	.132	.294	.364	.545	.699	.076	−.00158	.289
	(47)	(8.5)	(8.9)	(22)	(25)	(34)	(38)	(49)	(38)	
1981	1.016	−.204	.142	.293	.351	.547	.704	.076	−.00157	.296
	(51)	(6.3)	(9.4)	(22)	(24)	(34)	(38)	(49)	(38)	
1982	1.038	−.267	.140	.281	.358	.539	.686	.076	−.00155	.275
	(45)	(6.9)	(8.0)	(18)	(21)	(30)	(34)	(44)	(33)	
1983	1.042	−.239	.124	.305	.371	.562	.735	.080	−.00163	.269
	(42)	(5.7)	(6.3)	(17)	(20)	(28)	(34)	(43)	(33)	
1984	1.023	−.183	.138	.294	.379	.598	.782	.080	−.00168	.265
	(40)	(3.9)	(6.8)	(16)	(20)	(29)	(35)	(45)	(34)	
1985	1.079	−.210	.130	.313	.377	.647	.777	.080	−.00162	.305
	(44)	(5.0)	(6.7)	(18)	(20)	(33)	(36)	(45)	(34)	
1986	1.047	−.179	.183	.329	.447	.664	.870	.080	−.00163	.305
	(42)	(4.1)	(9.1)	(18)	(23)	(33)	(39)	(45)	(33)	
1987	1.086	−.215	.143	.318	.421	.697	.865	.080	−.00163	.314
	(44)	(4.9)	(7.2)	(18)	(22)	(35)	(39)	(45)	(33)	

Note: t-statistics are in parentheses. Experience is measured in years of predicted work experience. Earnings functions are estimated on the basis of at least 20,000 observations.

Table 8: ESTIMATED EARNINGS FUNCTION COEFFICIENTS, WOMEN, 1950–87

Survey Year	Int.	*Years of education* 1–4	9–11	12	13–15	16	17+	*Experience* Linear	Quadratic	R^2
1950	−.363	−.015	.072	.145	.247	.297	.313	.030	−.00[illegible]78	.092
	(15)	(0.5)	(5.2)	(12)	(13)	(10)	(7.2)	(13)	(8.7[illegible]	
1960	.048	−.117	.070	.163	.266	.403	.453	.029	−.00[illegible]64	.091
	(1.7)	(2.9)	(4.3)	(11)	(13)	(12)	(8.5)	(11)	(6.5[illegible]	
1968	.087	−.064	.085	.228	.323	.493	.574	.044	−.00[illegible]0	.078
	(2.6)	(1.0)	(3.9)	(12)	(13)	(13)	(9.1)	(14)	(10[illegible]	
1969	.277	−.121	.070	.205	.329	.427	.632	.035	−.00[illegible]6	.076
	(8.5)	(2.1)	(3.2)	(11)	(13)	(12)	(11)	(11)	(7.9[illegible]	
1970	.402	−.099	.049	.170	.302	.380	.376	.033	−.00[illegible]1	.101
	(13)	(1.7)	(2.4)	(9.4)	(13)	(12)	(7.6)	(12)	(8.4[illegible]	
1971	.341	−.108	.102	.252	.390	.504	.359	.041	−.00[illegible]8	.108
	(11)	(1.8)	(4.8)	(13)	(17)	(15)	(7.9)	(14)	(10[illegible]	
1972	.328	−.085	.113	.224	.322	.476	.637	.046	−.00[illegible]3	.113
	(10)	(1.4)	(5.0)	(11)	(13)	(14)	(12)	(15)	(11[illegible]	
1973	.405	−.069	.095	.196	.303	.428	.451	.047	−.00[illegible]1	.105
	(12)	(1.2)	(4.1)	(9.5)	(12)	(13)	(8.9)	(16)	(12[illegible]	
1974	.452	−.063	.100	.192	.340	.416	.532	.048	−.00[illegible]31	.112
	(14)	(1.0)	(4.2)	(8.9)	(14)	(13)	(11)	(16)	(11[illegible]	
1975	.566	.020	.055	.164	.292	.378	.508	.046	−.00[illegible]30	.104
	(17)	(0.3)	(2.2)	(7.3)	(11)	(12)	(11)	(14)	(10[illegible]	
1976	.547	−.081	.052	.216	.331	.402	.462	.051	−.00[illegible]55	.131
	(20)	(1.4)	(2.5)	(12)	(16)	(16)	(13)	(20)	(15[illegible]	

Table 8: CONTINUED

Survey Year	Int.	Years of education 1–4	9–11	12	13–15	16	17+	Experience Linear	Quadratic	R^2
1977	.587	−.061	.067	.214	.326	.456	.576	.056	−.00171	.147
	(24)	(1.2)	(3.7)	(13)	(18)	(20)	(18)	(25)	(19)	
1978	.683	−.049	.094	.245	.360	.487	.659	.049	−.00138	.158
	(30)	(1.0)	(5.2)	(15)	(20)	(23)	(22)	(23)	(16)	
1979	.840	−.018	.042	.216	.316	.404	.552	.042	−.00112	.130
	(35)	(0.3)	(2.1)	(12)	(16)	(18)	(19)	(19)	(12)	
1980	.891	−.070	.093	.230	.340	.507	.609	.049	−.00146	.125
	(37)	(1.3)	(4.8)	(13)	(18)	(23)	(22)	(22)	(16)	
1981	.996	.054	.081	.219	.350	.501	.559	.050	−.00149	.137
	(41)	(1.0)	(4.1)	(12)	(18)	(23)	(20)	(23)	(17)	
1982	1.093	−.175	.036	.200	.343	.453	.619	.046	−.00133	.149
	(43)	(3.1)	(1.7)	(10)	(17)	(20)	(23)	(20)	(14)	
1983	1.008	−.222	.096	.244	.370	.534	.650	.064	−.00208	.154
	(36)	(3.5)	(4.1)	(12)	(16)	(22)	(22)	(26)	(20)	
1984	1.063	−.217	.080	.246	.395	.539	.712	.056	−.00158	.136
	(35)	(3.2)	(3.1)	(11)	(16)	(20)	(23)	(21)	(14)	
1985	1.071	.002	.085	.236	.402	.561	.734	.065	−.00192	.161
	(37)	(0.0)	(3.5)	(11)	(17)	(22)	(25)	(26)	(18)	
1986	1.091	−.120	.112	.258	.410	.617	.768	.054	−.00190	.191
	(38)	(1.7)	(4.6)	(12)	(18)	(25)	(26)	(26)	(18)	
1987	1.064	.015	.063	.250	.404	.624	.806	.067	−.00198	.178
	(35)	(0.2)	(2.4)	(10)	(16)	(24)	(26)	(24)	(17)	

Note: t-statistics are in parentheses. Experience is measured in years of predicted work experience. Earnings functions are estimated on the basis of at least 10,000 observations.

Table 9: PERCENTAGE CHANGE IN WAGE DUE TO AN ADDITIONAL YEAR OF EXPERIENCE, MEN AND WOMEN, 1949–86

Men	*Years of Experience*			Mean
Year	5	15	35	Experience[a]
1949	4.7	2.2	−2.8	1.6
1967	4.7	2.1	−3.0	1.5
1973	5.7	2.5	−3.6	2.0
1979	6.0	2.7	−3.6	2.4
1986	6.4	3.0	−3.5	2.8

Women	*Years of Experience*			Mean
Year	5	15	25	Experience[a]
1949	2.2	0.6	−1.0	1.3
1967	2.5	0.5	−1.4	1.2
1973	3.4	0.7	−1.9	1.9
1979	3.3	0.4	−2.5	1.8
1986	4.6	0.5	−3.4	2.3

[a]The sample mean level of work experience has been fluctuating over the period. For men, the average level of work experience increased from 17.3 years in 1949 to 17.5 years in 1967 and fell to 16.0 years in 1986. For women, the corresponding figures are 10.5 years in 1949, 11.6 years in 1967, and 10.5 years in 1986.

growth rate of the index of labor composition and its components, work experience, education, and sex composition, are presented in Table 10.[28]

Through their influence on the distribution of work experience, changes in the age distribution are an important source of the variation in the growth rate of labor composition. Recalling Table 2, the average age of the civilian labor force peaked around 1958, declined for more than two decades with the most rapid drop after 1965, and since 1980 has once again begun to increase. Despite several important conceptual differences between average age and the index of work experience, Table 11 reveals strikingly similar patterns in the movements of the two. Furthermore, while work experience is one of several influences on the measures of labor composition, periods of rising average age or work experience are associated with substantially faster labor composition growth.

Having developed a measure of labor composition, we can now assess how changes in labor composition contribute to productivity growth. Table 12 presents the growth rates of output per hour and its components for the private nonfarm business sector. The growth rate of

28. The sex construction index measures residual differences between the earnings of men and women which are presumed to reflect skill differences unmeasured by education and experience.

Table 10: AVERAGE ANNUAL GROWTH RATES OF INDEX OF LABOR COMPOSITION AND ITS COMPONENTS, SELECTED PERIODS, 1948–86 (IN PERCENTAGES)

Period	Labor Composition	Work Experience	Education	Sex Composition	Interaction Effects
1948–86	0.26	−0.13	0.39	−0.02	0.02
1948–73	0.24	−0.10	0.35	−0.03	0.02
1973–79	0.06	−0.42	0.47	−0.02	0.03
1979–86	0.51	0.04	0.44	0.01	0.02

Table 11: AVERAGE ANNUAL GROWTH RATES OF AGE OF CIVILIAN LABOR FORCE, INDEXES OF WORK EXPERIENCE, AND LABOR COMPOSITION, SELECTED PERIODS, 1948–86 (IN PERCENTAGES)

Period	Mean Age of Civilian Labor Force	Index of Work Experience[a]	Index of Labor Composition
1948–58	0.38	0.13	0.40
1958–80	−0.42	−0.29	0.13
1980–86	0.09	0.05	0.53

[a]see Work Experience, Table 10.

output per hour is the sum of the contribution of capital intensity (change in the capital-labor ratio), the contribution of labor composition, and multifactor productivity.[29] The contribution of labor composition equals the growth rate of labor composition multiplied by labor's share in current dollar output (which has generally been around 65 percent). From 1948 to 1973 the annual average growth rate of output per hour was 2.5 percent, and then it dropped by two percentage points, to 0.5 percent, in 1973–79. The corresponding drop in the contribution of

29. In previous BLS measures of multifactor productivity (U.S. Department of Labor, Bureau of Labor Statistics 1983, 1987), labor input is measured solely by hours, and multifactor productivity reflects compositional shifts in the work force, among other things. There is a simple relationship between the previous measures of multifactor productivity and the measures in this paper. Using $\dot{A}/A$ as the designation for previous measure of multifactor productivity change and $\dot{B}/B$ as the designation for the measure of multifactor productivity change developed in this paper, the relationship is:

$$\dot{A}/A = \dot{B}/B + s_1 * \dot{C}/C,$$

where s_1 is labor's share of output and $\dot{C}/C$ is the measure of labor composition change.

Table 12: ANNUAL GROWTH RATES OF OUTPUT PER HOUR AND ITS COMPONENTS, ALL WORKERS, PRIVATE NONFARM BUSINESS, SELECTED PERIODS, 1948–86 (IN PERCENTAGES)

Measures	1948–86 (1)	1948–73 (2)	1973–79 (3)	1979–86 (4)	Column (3)−(2)	Column (4)−(3)
Output per hour, all workers	1.9	2.5	0.5	1.2	−2.0	0.7
Contribution of capital intensity[a]	0.8	0.8	0.6	0.9	−0.2	0.3
Contribution of labor composition[b]	0.2	0.2	0.0	0.3	−0.2	0.3
Multifactor productivity[c]	0.9	1.5	−0.1	0.0	−1.6	0.1

[a]Changes in capital services per hour multiplied by capital's share of current dollar output.
[b]Changes in labor composition effects multiplied by labor's share of current dollar output.
[c]Output per unit of combined labor and capital inputs adjusted for labor composition.

labor composition was 0.2 percentage point. So changes in labor composition account for 10 percent of the initial slowdown in the rate of growth of labor productivity.

Between 1979 and 1986 the contribution of labor composition was 0.3 percent, which exceeded the contribution of labor composition in 1948–73. Coincident with the higher labor composition growth rate of recent years, both the average age of the labor force and the index of work experience have been increasing. Hence changes in labor composition of the work force and, in particular, changes in work experience cannot account for the continued, though less severe, slowdown in labor productivity growth witnessed in 1979–86.

Summary and Conclusions

The studies of comparative job performance by age and the age-earnings profiles constructed for this paper indicate that a worker's productivity rises at the beginning of his or her working life. The comparative job performance studies suggest that the peak performance level is generally reached by age 35. In the study of the furniture and footwear industries, average productivity began to decline after age 45 for men and age 35 for women, while in the other studies average productivity stayed near the peak level for decades. According to the cross-sectional age-earnings profiles, hourly earnings tend to peak when workers are in their 40s. Men's earnings begin to drop after the peak, while women's earnings tend to stay level for years after the peak is reached.

According to the studies cited, worker productivity exceeds 90 percent of peak performance (with one exception) for both men and women near age 60 and exceeds 80 percent for those aged 65 or older. The modest decline in productivity for older workers is supported by the earnings equations. The hourly earnings equations also indicate that the hourly earnings of men in their 60s are comparable to those of otherwise identical men aged 30–35, while the earnings of older women are virtually indistinguishable from those of women at the peak earning period.

Better-educated older workers still earn wages above the average for the economy (and have higher than average productivity). This group includes men with at least a high school diploma and women with some college education. (In 1983, these workers comprised 50.3 percent of the 55- to 64-year-old labor force.) When such workers choose to extend their careers rather than retire, the result is that labor composition and productivity growth are higher than if retirement were chosen.

Labor composition grew 0.26 percent annually over the period 1948–86. For shorter periods, labor composition grew 0.24 percent annually in 1948–73, 0.06 percent in 1973–79 and 0.51 percent in 1979–86. An important source of the fluctuations in labor composition growth is change in the level of work experience, which, in turn, is strongly affected by the age distribution of the labor force. The index of work experience over the three shorter periods grew −0.10 percent, −0.42 percent, and 0.04 percent, respectively. While movements in the distribution of work experience are not identical to changes in the age distribution, increases in the average age of the work force contributed (through their effects on work experience) to substantially higher labor composition growth since 1980. The rise in the average age is projected to continue in the near future and is likely to have a positive effect on the growth of labor composition and labor productivity.[30] However, changes in labor composition have contributed little to the productivity slowdown, and labor composition alone should not be expected to return labor productivity growth to its pre-1973 pace.

References

Abraham, K., and H. Farber. 1987. "Job Duration, Seniority, and Earnings," *American Economic Review* 77 (June): 278–97.

30. BLS labor force projections to the year 2000 show a continued increase in the average age of the labor force. See Kutscher 1987; Fullerton 1987.

Bacharach, M. 1965. "Estimating Nonnegative Matrices from Marginal Data," *International Economic Review* 6 (September): 294–310.

Becker, G. 1971. *The Economics of Discrimination*. Chicago: University of Chicago Press.

———. 1975. *Human Capital*. New York: Columbia University Press.

Beller, A. 1982. "Occupational Segregation by Sex: Determinants and Changes," *Journal of Human Resources* 17 (Summer): 371–92.

Caves, D., L. Christensen, and E. Diewert. 1982. "The Economic Theory of Index Numbers and the Measurement of Input, Output, and Productivity," *Econometrica* 50 (November): 1393–1414.

Chinloy, P. 1980. "Sources of Quality Change in Labor Input," *American Economic Review* 70 (March): 108–19.

———. 1981. *Labor Productivity*. Cambridge, Mass.: Abt Books.

Corcoran, M., and G. Duncan. 1979. "Work History, Labor Force Attachment and Earnings Differences between the Races and Sexes," *Journal of Human Resources* 14 (Winter): 3–20.

Dean, E., K. Kunze, and L. Rosenblum. 1988. "Productivity Change and the Measurement of Heterogeneous Labor Inputs." Presented at the U.S. Department of Agriculture Conference on New Measurement Procedures for U.S. Agricultural Productivity, Washington, D.C.

Denison, E. 1985. *Trends in American Economic Growth: 1929–1982*. Washington, D.C.: Brookings Institution.

Duncan, G. 1976. "Earnings Functions and Nonpecuniary Benefits," *Journal of Human Resources* 11 (Fall): 462–83.

Fullerton, H., Jr. 1987. "Labor Force Projections: 1986 to 2000," *Monthly Labor Review* 110 (September): 19–29.

Griliches, Z. 1970. "Notes on the Role of Education in Production Functions and Growth Accounting." In *Education, Income and Human Capital*, edited by W. L. Hansen. New York: Columbia University Press.

Gustman, A., and T. Steinmeier. 1984. "Partial Retirement and the Analysis of Retirement Behavior," *Industrial and Labor Relations Review* 37 (April): 403–15.

Heywood, J. 1986. "Labor Quality and the Concentration-Earnings Hypothesis," *Review of Economics and Statistics* 68 (May): 342–46.

Honig, M., and G. Hanoch. 1985. "Partial Retirement as a Separate Mode of Retirement Behavior," *Journal of Human Resources* 20 (Winter): 21–46.

Horowitz, S., and A. Sherman. 1980. "A Direct Measure of the Relationship between Human Capital and Productivity," *Journal of Human Resources* 15 (Winter): 67–76.

Jorgenson, D., F. Gollop, and B. Fraumeni. 1987. *Productivity and U.S. Economic Growth*. Cambridge, Mass.: Harvard University Press.

Jovanovic, B. 1979a. "Job Matching and the Theory of Turnover," *Journal of Political Economy* 87 (October): 972–90.

———. 1979b. "Firm Specific Capital and Turnover," *Journal of Political Economy* 87 (December): 1246–60.

Kutscher, R. E. 1987. "Overview and Implications of the Projections to 2000," *Monthly Labor Review* 110 (September): 3–9.

Kutscher, R. E., and J. F. Walker, 1960. "Comparative Job Performance of Office Workers by Age," *Monthly Labor Review* 83 (January): 39–43.

Lazear, E. 1979. "Why Is There Mandatory Retirement?" *Journal of Political Economy* 87 (December): 1261–84.

———. 1981. "Agency, Earnings Profiles and Productivity," *American Economic Review* 71 (September): 606–20.

Maranto, C., and R. Rodgers. 1984. "Does Work Experience Increase Productivity? A Test of the On-the-Job Training Hypothesis," *Journal of Human Resources* 19 (Fall): 341–57.

Medoff, J., and K. Abraham. 1980. "Experience, Performance and Earnings," *Quarterly Journal of Economics* 95 (December): 703–36.

Mincer, J. 1974. *Schooling, Experience and Earnings*. New York: Columbia University Press.

Mincer, J., and H. Ofek. 1982. "Interrupted Work Careers: Depreciation and Restoration of Human Capital," *Journal of Human Resources* 17 (Winter): 3–24.

Oaxaca, R. 1973. "Male-Female Wage Differentials in Urban Labor Markets," *International Economic Review* 14 (October): 693–709.

Owen, J. 1986. *Working Lives*. Lexington, Mass.: D. C. Heath–Lexington Books.

Rizzuto, R., and P. Wachtel. 1980. "Further Evidence on the Returns to School Quality," *Journal of Human Resources* 15 (Spring): 240–54.

Sandell, S., and D. Shapiro. 1980. "Work Expectations, Human Capital Accumulation, and the Wages of Young Women," *Journal of Human Resources* 15 (Summer): 335–53.

Topel, R. 1986. "Local Labor Markets," *Journal of Political Economy* 94 (June): S111–43.

Treimann, D., and H. Hartmann. 1981. *Women, Work and Wages: Equal Pay for Jobs of Equal Value*. Washington, D.C.: National Academy Press.

U.S. Department of Commerce, Bureau of the Census. 1975. *Census of Population, 1950: Public Use Micro Data Sample Technical Documentation* (1 in 100 samples). Washington, D.C.: U.S. Government Printing Office.

———. 1984. *A Public Use Sample of Basic Records in the 1960 Census, Description and Technical Documentation* (1 in 1,000 samples). Washington, D.C.: U.S. Government Printing Office.

U.S. Department of Health, Education and Welfare, Social Security Administration. 1979. "Studies in Interagency Data Linkages: Administrative Record Exact Match File Codebook." Item Pub. No. (SSA) 79-11750. Washington, D.C.: U.S. Government Printing Office.

U.S. Department of Labor, Bureau of Labor Statistics. 1956. *Job Performance and Age: A Study in Measurement*. Bulletin 1203. Washington, D.C.: U.S. Government Printing Office.

———. 1957. *Comparative Job Performance by Age: Large Plants in the Men's Footwear and Household Furniture Industries*. Bulletin 1223. Washington, D.C.: U.S. Government Printing Office.

———. 1968–87. Current Population Survey, Annual Demographic File (machine readable data file).

———. 1983. *Trends in Multifactor Productivity, 1948–81*. Bulletin 2178. Washington, D.C.: U.S. Government Printing Office.

———. 1987. "Multifactor Productivity Measures, 1986." USDL 87-436. Washington, D.C.: U.S. Department of Labor.

Venti, S. 1985. "Wages in the Federal and Private Sectors." NBER Working Paper 1641. Cambridge, Mass.: National Bureau of Economic Research.

Waldorf, W., K. Kunze, L. Rosenblum, and M. Tannen. 1986. "New Measures of the Contribution of Education and Experience to U.S. Productivity Growth." Presented at the annual meeting of the American Economic Association, New Orleans, La.

Walker, J. 1964. "The Job Performance of Federal Mail Sorters by Age," *Monthly Labor Review* 87 (March): 296–300.

Weiss, Y., and R. Gronau. 1981. "Expected Interruptions in Labor Force Participation and Sex Related Differences in Earnings Growth." NBER Working Paper 667. Cambridge, Mass.: National Bureau of Economic Research.

Part V
Promotion Opportunities, Discrimination, Marginalization

Managing a Changing Work Force

DAVID N. GAMSE

Employment practices that discriminate against older workers continue to be a widespread concern of members of the American Association of Retired Persons (AARP). Gamse, director of the AARP Worker Equity Department, describes hiring, training, and retirement practices that are often associated with downsizing. Because AARP believes that exemplary models are the most persuasive approach, the group maintains a computerized database of company and union programs that are doing good things for older workers, several of which are described here.

R. J. V. M.

Age discrimination in employment is on the rise. Each year, older workers are filing more complaints with the U.S. Equal Employment Opportunity Commission. Although many employers, organized labor leaders, and researchers believe that "ability is ageless" and that older workers can be productive workers, there are many others who don't agree.

The American Association of Retired Persons (AARP) hears a lot from its members about their age discrimination problems. Not only is AARP the nation's largest membership organization of retirees, but it is the nation's largest organization of older workers as well. One-third of AARP's 29 million members work fulltime or part-time. About one-fifth of the membership has been affiliated with organized labor.

Last year, AARP's Worker Equity Department received more than 26,000 letters from members and other older persons. Many who wrote said that their union or employer had failed to help them make proper retirement planning decisions. Others said they were confronting discriminatory workplace policies in hiring, firing, training, and promotion. And still more told us that despite rhetoric to the contrary, they could not find a single agency in their community that was skilled in placing older workers or providing them career guidance.

The focus group research that AARP conducts and the opinion poll data that we gather confirm how widespread and critical are our members' concerns. On behalf of members and others who are facing age discrimination in employment, AARP has filed suits against Du Pont and Farmer's Insurance Group. We have also filed nearly two dozen *amicus curiae* briefs against union and employer programs that treat older workers unfairly.

The "Bad Guys"

Through AARP's focus group and other research, and through our meetings with employer and union representatives, AARP has developed images of the "good guy" employer and the "bad guy" employer. The "bad guys" are familiar to most of us through newspaper and television stories. Many have sound older worker personnel policies on the books, yet front-line supervisors and managers who make hire/fire decisions lack knowledge of older workers' capabilities and sensitivities. They state they are uncomfortable in supervising someone who looks like "grandma" or "grandpa." Many talk a lot about "overqualified" employees.

In AARP's view, "overqualified" is the way a hiring manager says a worker has too many years of experience under the belt. We believe that a worker is either qualified to do the job or simply unqualified for it.

"Bad guy" training programs are available almost exclusively to young, new entrants in the work force. The practices that Ford, Chrysler, GM, and other employers have shared in this volume are atypical of the employer population.

In 1985–86, AARP commissioned the Yankelovich Group to conduct a major survey of U.S. employers, statistically representative of all American companies. In that survey, most employers said older workers contributed to the corporation's bottom-line profitability, and a majority said that training could help older people to become even better employees. Yet 70 percent of all U.S. employers provide no training for their older employees. Similarly, apprenticeship programs rarely allow older persons to participate, despite the fact that an older apprentice may be willing and able to work for a decade or more.

Deficient and sometimes illegal recruitment practices are another hallmark of the "bad guys." You'll find "bad guys" recruiting exclusively on college campuses where older people are rarely found. But you won't find them using strategies that many employers find successful in recruiting older workers: advertising job opportunities for *experienced* workers, contacting older worker placement agencies such as Over Forty Counseling and Employment and Operation ABLE, and using the services of the Department of Labor's Title V and Job Training Partnership Act programs.

Downsizing is yet another means by which some employers practice age discrimination. While I understand the need of some employers to downsize, I do not understand why older workers need to bear the brunt of a downsizing program.

One needn't be an attorney to know how wrong it would be to offer cash incentives or other enticements to blacks, women, or Hispanics who are "willing to get out of the work force, and stay out." Indeed, people cannot legally be separated into a particular gender, race, or age class and told, because they are members of that class, "We don't want you." Yet many employers interpret the monetary incentive in an early retirement exit incentive scheme as not only legitimate and legal but one that should be welcome to all or most older people.

Many workers say they welcome and benefit from early retirement. Others do not. Given short early retirement windows, many older workers who are faced with an early retirement decision and many older workers' families cannot get the information they need to formulate realistic plans. AARP has found that many older adults spend more time planning a two-week vacation than in planning for retirement that could last a third of a lifetime. Poor planners discover too late that the early retirement "bonus" isn't enough to carry them the rest of their lives.

Some older people decide to retire early on the false assumption that if retirement doesn't work out, they can always return to work. Yet when they try to do so, they may face age discrimination all over again. Indeed, unemployed older persons may face even more severe age discrimination than do employed older persons seeking a different kind of work.

There will be many more news stories about the plight of older persons who are denied equal employment opportunity. We are going to see more court cases and more expensive settlements. Today's older population is healthier, better educated, and living longer and more active lives than older persons have ever lived in our nation's history. This vocal older group is unwilling to let itself be thrown on the employment scrap heap.

The "Good Guys"

The "good guys" may be harder to locate because they may be less newsworthy; they certainly don't find their way into the courtrooms as often as do the "bad guys." Yet AARP believes that more pervasive change in employment practice can be achieved by offering good examples than by offering bad ones. For that reason, AARP has computerized a database of "good guy" company programs. This database is called the National Older Workers Information System (NOWIS).

NOWIS was started by the University of Michigan under a grant from the U.S. Administration on Aging. It has found a permanent home at AARP. NOWIS is like a computerized Rolodex. It lists about 100 company programs that are doing good things for older workers in terms of recruitment, training, job design, and retirement. The system provides a brief description of the company program and the names and telephone numbers of program administrators within the company. Interested employers can contact that person and learn how the program works and what the potential problems might be.

Among the many program descriptions that NOWIS contains is that of Travelers Insurance Company. Travelers has organized its retirees into a ready and available pool of temporary workers. The company no longer needs to rely exclusively upon the use of more expensive employment agencies to acquire part-time help. Instead, the company can bring back its own people who know the workplace. Thus, downtime caused by bringing in new and inexperienced employees has largely been eliminated.

NOWIS also lists programs by Wells Fargo, Xerox, Polaroid, and other companies that grant innovative forms of release time to older workers and other persons who want to do community service, try out retirement, or experiment with new careers. Many of the innovative programs NOWIS contains are described in a brochure called "Using the Experience of a Lifetime." Single copies are available free from the AARP Worker Equity Department, Washington, D.C. 20049.

Older people are an active and viable force. They are not going to let age discrimination, in either a subtle or not so subtle form, roll over them. They turn to AARP and their other membership organizations to defend their rights. Yet an individual's access to equal employment opportunity needn't be the result of a battle. Employers and unions can voluntarily implement programs and policies, many at little or no cost, that ensure equal employment opportunity while preserving the corporation's bottom-line profitability. That's what AARP and many older workers seek: no special concessions—simply an age-neutral work environment in America's fast-aging and changing workplace.

Labor Market Opportunities for Middle-Aged and Older Workers

SHELBY STEWMAN

This writer sees a silver lining in the early retirement pattern discussed by a number of contributors. Early retirements mean increased opportunities for younger people, as they create openings which are typically not filled by new entrants but by middle-aged employees. The movement thus created leaves a vacancy for a younger employee, and creates yet another opening for someone still more junior, in a snowball effect. Stewman presents empirical estimates of these multiple opportunities.

Data on the job mobility rates of middle-aged and older workers presented here reveal little difference between older and prime-age workers. However, Stewman finds relatively high mobility rates for middle-aged and older workers within the U.S. Civil Service. His partial explanation is the better promotional opportunities available to those who have already worked their way up through a large organizational hierarchy.

J. D. O.

There are at least four distinct population processes underlying an aging work force: entrances into the labor market, exits from the labor market, aging of workers within the labor market, and mobility of workers between jobs. Currently, due to the baby bust, there is a decreasing number of eligible entrants. However, this shortage has been partially offset by the continued increase in the labor force participation rates of women.

This research was supported in part by a grant from the National Institute of Aging (1R01 AG04139-01). I wish to thank the Personnel Systems and Oversight Group of the U.S. Government Office of Personnel Management for their assistance regarding the organizational database. Also, I owe special thanks to Bing Wang of Carnegie Mellon University for his assistance on this research.

The declines at the younger end of the age distribution are also concomitant with the second major process: the increase in retirement rates of older workers and the shift to part-time work by more older workers. As in the entry process for younger workers, some of the decline in numbers of older workers is offset by a countervailing process: the fact that for some older workers, retirement is not a permanent decision, and they return to work. Nevertheless, overall, there are decreases in the relative number of workers on both ends of the age distribution.

The third process at work is the future aging of the work force due to the aging of the unusually large cohorts born between 1945 and 1960—the baby boomers. The oldest of this group will become 40–54 years old around the turn of the century, 2000–2005, a little more than 10 years from now, so that there will be a large increment in the 55–64 age group around 2015–20. Thus, while both entrance and exit processes are important, the aging of the baby boom cohorts will be quite pertinent over the next thirty to forty years. The labor market impacts of the baby boom cohorts, the group aged 25–39 in 1985, has just begun.

All three of the above population processes point to the importance of increasing productivity and increasing use of those middle-aged and older workers who remain in the labor market. It is here that the fourth population process, the mobility of workers between jobs, becomes a potentially integral component, since it pertains to the flexibility and rate of adaptation of a labor market. Furthermore, it should be noted that the United States is not alone in projecting an aging work force. Other major industrialized nations, particularly West Germany and Japan, are also experiencing such population dynamics. Hence the question of the labor market opportunities of middle-aged and older workers and the dynamics of our labor market takes on increased significance.

Methods and Focus

It is not simply the population of workers that is changing over time, but also the population of jobs. Just as populations of workers experience entrances, exits, aging, and mobility, the population of jobs also undergoes massive changes: new job creations, job abolishments, and changing distributions of jobs (e.g., industrial and occupational distributions). For instance, in 1900 the national labor market had the following composition: 38 percent in farming, 37 percent in blue-collar jobs, 9 percent in service jobs, and 18 percent in white-collar jobs. By 1980, in contrast, farming represented but 3 percent, blue-collar 32 percent, service 13 percent, and white-collar 52 percent. With such shifts, some workers are displaced, while others' opportunities improve. The modeling and analyses which can best address such mechanisms must therefore contain both populations and their dynamics. We refer to such modeling and analyses as two-population demography. Moreover, the link which we will use to couple the two populations is that of managerial or employer decisionmaking in creating and abolishing jobs and in selecting individuals to fill jobs. For instance, consider the following questions: who gets the jobs by age and what was the origin of the job opportunities that generated the moves by current workers and new entrants to the labor market? Employer staffing and hiring decisions provide the link between the two populations of persons and jobs. New developments in two-population demography discussed in this paper provide the tools for answering these types of questions.

Presently, there are two basic levels of analysis in two-population demography: organizational and national. The former pertains to the demographic processes of both populations of workers and jobs within organizations. Attention has focused not only on promotion but also on job and occupational mobility within an organization. Such organizational analyses permit investigation of personnel policies bearing on different issues—retirement, affirmative action, career development, and organizational restructuring, for example. One may look at the initial events which create job vacancies. There are two basic types of such triggering events: exits by workers and new job creations by employers. Furthermore, if the employer selections for filling these initial vacancies are internal, then a chain reaction of job opportunities is set off; that is, if the first selection is internal, then this opens an additional vacancy, and so on, setting off a chain reaction of job opportunities within the organization. These chain reactions produce important and generally unforeseen results. In fact, analysis of such demographic processes within organizations have yielded unexpected findings regarding job opportunities for middle-aged and older workers, as well as new insights into the dynamics of the organizations.

The endings of the vacancy chain reactions are also of considerable interest. There are two basic ways in which they end: by selecting a new recruit from outside the organization or by abolishing the job. The incorporation of the creation of new jobs and the abolishment of old jobs by employers enable the analysis of downsizing, as well as growth, either of which may result in new organizational structures. It is, of course, the linkage of the initial triggering events with the internal job opportunities and, finally, with the ending events that may produce new insights which had not been obtained by focusing on each basic process: turnover (exits), internal mobility (e.g., promotion), growth, cutbacks, or recruitment. Within two-population demography, all are joined into an ongoing, overall, interdependent process which is generally beyond the purview of a single worker or manager but which may now be systematically investigated.

In contrast to intraorganizational processes, data regarding national labor markets primarily record moves between organizations. For the most part, national-level analyses involve interorganizational dynamics and are complementary to the intraorganizational work. Analyses at this level may also examine initial triggering events which open job vacancies, such as retirements or new job creations. The latter may stem from technological innovations or changing market demand, resulting in new distributions of jobs (e.g., by occupation and industry). The consequent chain reactions of job opportunities between organizations stemming from the initial triggering events are also of considerable importance, as are the ending events, because job opportunities within the chain reactions involve moves between organizations, and opportunities at the end of the chain reactions involve entry from outside the work force. Job abolishments, of course, are also occurring, including entire plant shutdowns, firms going out of business, and the phasing out of governmental programs due to shifts in policy or in the national administration.

Two overarching questions will guide the discussion: how dynamic are our labor markets, and what are the labor market opportunities for middle-aged and older workers? Both questions will be pursued at each level of analysis.

National Labor Markets

THE POPULATION OF JOBS

On the job side of the labor market, Bluestone (1982) has estimated that in order for the private sector of the U.S. economy to grow by 12 million jobs between 1969 and 1976, 61 million new jobs had to be created because an estimated 49 million jobs were abolished during this brief period. Thus, 80 percent of the new jobs created were "replacements." Job growth in the national labor market is by no means just a process of adding jobs. Rather, it is the result of the dynamics of job birth and death processes. That the abolishment side of the process is such a large fraction of total job creations is quite surprising.

This process is occurring in the fast-growing regions of the South and West, as well as in the Midwest and Northeast (Birch 1979). What differentiates these regions is not the rate of job abolishment (estimated at 8 percent per year in all regions) but the rate of job creations, with the South and West having higher job creation rates. Thus, Greene (1982) uses Birch's job abolishment parameter of 8 percent per year to provide an illuminating example for the city of Phoenix, Arizona. In 1980, nonagricultural employment in Phoenix grew by 2.9 percent, from 613,000 to 631,000 workers, or 18,000 jobs. To accomplish such growth, Greene estimated that it was necessary to create 67,000 jobs because 49,000 had been eliminated. Hence, even in Phoenix, almost 75 percent of the newly created jobs were replacements.

It is clear from such examples that the labor market is a highly volatile and dynamic one in terms of the population of jobs. It is significant not only because of its massive size but also because of its implications for labor market theory. That is, the area of the labor market process in which there are substantial disequilibria is in the population of jobs, and modeling of labor supply-side processes using cross-sectional data, as if the job dynamics were in equilibrium, has serious theoretical and empirical problems. Greater insight into the forces which are driving the labor market chances of workers should be obtained by examining jobs and job dynamics, including the behavior of job vacancies. In fact, one of the tactics which has been useful in beginning to unravel the job side of the story has been the modeling of job vacancies. Within these highly dynamic job populations there are underlying vacancy processes which have substantial stability and which are keyed to employer staffing and hiring behavior. The instability of the job populations further underscores the importance of a flexible work force which can accommodate these rapid changes. This flexibility, of course, applies to middle-aged and older workers as much as to the young.

THE POPULATION OF WORKERS

Given the sheer magnitude of the job dynamics depicted above, what are the implications for workers, in terms of job mobility, and what are the job opportunity linkages between those who are retiring and those who are entering the labor market? Over a five-year period (1965–70), Sommers and Eck (1977) found that twice as many workers changed occupation as left the labor market. Moreover, in the national-level data, most workers who changed occupations also changed organizations (Byrne's [1975] analysis for 1972 indicates that the percentage is 90 percent). Therefore, what is viewed as organizational turnover consists of two processes: leaving the labor market and changing firms, with the latter twice as common as the former. This helps to explain why turnover generally dominates growth in most organizations as far as generation of job opportunities is concerned. If for each exit from the labor market there are two internal moves, generally between organizations (employers), then there are national chain reactions of job opportunities linking organizations into a national opportunity structure. What are some of the implications from such chain reactions and who benefits from these job opportunities? Are they primarily for the young? How often are middle-aged and older workers involved?

To size up the implications of these chain reactions, let us use a measure of labor market change which takes into account both job vacancy and worker behavior. We define the Employee-Job Renewal Rate (ERR) of a labor market as the proportion of the total jobs which have new incumbents. There are three types of moves for new incumbents: (1) the movement from one type of occupation to another; (2) the movement from one organization to another, changing jobs but not occupations;[1] and (3) the entry into a job of a person not holding a job previously (unemployed or not in the labor force). All three types of movement are important in generating a set of workers who are new to their job. The ERR reflects the ratio of this set to the total set of all jobholders. What is the percentage of all jobs that have new incumbents? Of interest to this discussion is the magnitude of the ERR in the country's national labor market. Reinterpreting Byrne's (1975) national-level data, the U.S. annual ERR is at least 25 percent per year; that is, 25 percent of all the jobs in the United States have new incumbents each year. Reinterpreting Sommers and Eck's (1977) data, the five-year ERR in the United States is over 50 percent;[2] that is, at the end of a five-year period over 50 percent of all jobs in the United States had new incumbents!

These results indicate that work force mobility is quite massive. The mechanisms behind such behavior include not only the job dynamics described earlier but, even more important, the job vacancy chain reactions occurring within the labor market. These chain reactions are initially triggered by new job creations or exits from the labor market, indicating an integral connection between the dynamics of both populations of jobs and workers.

ERRS BY AGE AND GENDER

If the five-year national labor market ERR is over 50 percent, to what extent are job opportunities available for middle-aged and older

1. This is referred to as a job (employer) change by the BLS. The first type of move (change in occupation) may also include an employer change, but as defined here the three types are mutually exclusive as follows: (1) occupational change (with and without change of employer); (2) no occupational change, but employer change; and (3) entry from either the unemployed or from outside the labor force.
2. Byrne's (1975) data were for 1972 and included all three types of movement; Sommers and Eck's (1977) data were for 1965–70 and included only moves of types (1) and (3) but did not include moves between employers of workers who remained in the same occupational category.

Table 1: FIVE-YEAR NATIONAL LABOR MARKET ERRs BY GENDER AND AGE, 1965–70

Age (1970)	A Same Detailed Occupation[a]	B Different Detailed Occupation[a] (percentages)	C Outside Hire	D ERRs (B+C)
		Females		
20–24	10	19	71	90
25–34	30	27	44	70
35–44	38	25	37	62
45–54	47	28	25	53
55–64	54	28	18	46
65+	50	28	22	50
Σ	38	26	37	62
		Males		
20–24	10	29	60	90
25–34	35	43	22	66
35–44	56	37	7	45
45–54	61	33	6	39
55–64	63	31	6	37
65+	56	31	13	44
Σ	49	36	16	51
		Males and Females		
Σ	45	32	24	55

[a]Detailed occupation means the 441 distinct occupations used in the U.S. census for 1970.
Source: for columns A–C, see Sommers and Eck 1977.

workers? We now need data on ERRs per age group, disaggregating the national ERR rates into age cohort distributions. For example, out of all the jobs held by workers aged 50–59, how many had new incumbents? We will also inquire as to whether the new incumbent came from another job within the labor market or from the outside.

Table 1 provides the five-year ERRs by gender and age. For female workers, the overall ERR is over 60 percent. Moreover, all middle-aged and older female cohorts have ERRs of approximately 50 percent. This means, for example, that of all women aged 45–54 who held jobs in 1970, 53 percent had moved into the job in the five-year period between 1965 and 1970. The ERRs for age cohorts 55–64 and 65+ are 46 percent and 50 percent, respectively. These data provide strong evidence that there are indeed job opportunities for middle-aged and older women.

In each of the three older cohorts of women in Table 1, between 50 and 60 percent of the job opportunities were filled by women already working in the labor market (e.g. 28/50 = .56 for women aged 65 or over). Obviously, there are not only job opportunities available for middle-aged and older women who do not currently hold a job but also alternative job opportunities for those who are currently working.

Does the same story hold for middle-aged and older men? For these cohorts of men, the ERRs are about 40 percent. More specifically, of all men aged 45–54 holding jobs in 1970, 39 percent had moved into the job within the past five years. For the oldest cohort, ERRs were even higher, 44 percent. Thus, while the ERRs are a little lower for middle-aged and older cohorts of men than for women, the size of these ERRs is great in both cases.

In brief, over 50 percent—in fact, 55 percent (see Table 1 *bottom)*—of all jobs held in 1970 were filled by persons who had moved to the job in the last five years. More important, around 40 to 50 percent of all jobs held by workers aged 45 or above are also held by new incumbents, a statistic that comes as a major surprise to most of us. It is clear that the U.S. labor market is not only quite dynamic but offers massive job opportunities for middle-aged and older workers.

In the group of middle-aged and older female workers, almost 40 percent of the job opportunities were filled by women who were not working.[3] For men the figures are below 20 percent for age cohorts 45–54 and 55–64. For the older male cohort (65 +), the percentage is 30 percent (13/44). Overall, about 60 percent of the ERRs involve moves by workers within the labor market, and 40 percent involve moves by individuals not holding jobs (Table 1 *bottom:* 32/55 and 24/55, respectively).

Perhaps as important as the massive nature of job dynamics, indicated by the size of the ERRs, is the following observation: out of the current population of workers there are very few differences in relative job opportunities between those middle-aged and older workers who remain in the labor market and younger cohorts of workers. For example, approximately 25–30 percent of all age cohorts of women in the labor market changed occupations between 1965 and 1970 (Table 1, column B). This proportion is remarkably stable. For males, the proportion changing occupations is approximately 30–35 percent for all but one cohort (Table 1, column B).[4]

We hypothesize that given the decreasing labor force participation rates by age, the stability of these data indicate self-selection of two

3. Table 1, columns C and D (for the female cohort aged 55–64, 18/46 = 39 percent).

4. This exception is for the cohort aged 25–34.

kinds. Some proportion of middle-aged and older workers leave the labor market for varying reasons, including health and disability (cf. Stewman 1986b), discouragement and/or inflexibility (Pampel and Weiss 1983), and by choice. Of those who remain, however, it is remarkable, given current perceptions of aging and productivity or flexibility, that the proportions that change occupations are so stable across age groups. Perhaps these perceptions are simply inaccurate—this would certainly appear to be the case for the middle-aged and older cohorts of workers who remain in the labor market. In terms of changing occupations, there is virtually no difference by age in the figures for changing jobs among the populations who continue to work!

In contrast, for both female and male age cohorts, the proportion of workers who enter from the outside (Table 1, column C) decreases monotonically by age, with the exception of the oldest cohorts (aged 65 +). This outcome is due, in part, to the older cohort's higher exit rates,[5] which decrease the denominator so that equivalent entrances have higher impacts (see Stewman 1986b). Nevertheless, it further underscores a point made earlier that retirement need not be permanent for older workers. Thus the process that produces higher exit rates at age 60 and older also produces higher relative entrance rates for this age cohort of workers.

To provide some indication of the relative nature of the job change taking place, ERRs have been computed using only major occupational changes for moves within the labor market. The ten major job groups used here are professional/technical, managerial, sales, clerical, crafts, non-transportation operatives, transportation operatives, laborers, farm workers, and service/private household. A major occupational move means that a worker changes major occupational group (e.g., from sales to managerial, or operative to craft). Table 2 provides the five-year ERR estimates for the U.S. labor market based on major occupational changes and external hires.

For female workers, the overall ERR is 49 percent. That is, out of all jobs held by women in 1970, 49 percent were held by new incumbents who had either made a major occupational change since 1965 or did not have a job in 1965. Both middle-aged and older cohorts of women had ERRs of 30 percent, taking into account only major occupational change for workers within the labor market. For males, the comparable overall ERR is almost 40 percent. The ERRs for the males and for the total population (male and female) of middle-aged and older workers range from 20 to 30 percent.

5. For exiting, one must use the 1965 age, which becomes 60 + for this group.

Table 2: FIVE-YEAR NATIONAL LABOR MARKET ERRs BASED ON MAJOR OCCUPATIONAL CHANGE AND EXTERNAL HIRES, BY GENDER AND AGE, 1965–70

Age (1970)	A Same Major Occupation	B Different Major Occupation (percentages)	C Outside Hire	D ERRs (B+C)
		Females		
20–34	31	11	58	69
35–49	55	11	33	45
50–64	70	10	20	30
65+	68	10	22	32
Σ	51	11	38	49
		Males		
20–34	38	25	37	62
35–49	73	20	8	27
50–64	78	16	7	22
65+	71	16	13	29
Σ	62	20	18	38
		Males and Females		
20–34	35	20	45	65
35–49	66	17	17	34
50–64	75	14	12	25
65+				
Σ	58	17	26	42

Source: U.S. Bureau of the Census 1973.

Data from Tables 1 and 2 provide a clearer picture of the nature of the labor market dynamics. Although the age groupings are not strictly comparable, the internal mobility rates are sufficiently stable across age cohorts to give good approximations for the breakdown into the following kinds of labor market behavior: major occupational change, minor occupational change (i.e., moves between occupations within each major occupational group), and outside hire. The breakdowns show that approximately 10 percent of female workers made major occupational changes, that 15 percent made minor occupational changes, and that 35 percent of those taking jobs did not hold a job in 1965. For middle-aged and older women, these figures are approximately 10 percent, 20 percent, and 20 percent, respectively.

Overall, for the male segment of the labor market, the five-year ERRs break down approximately as follows: 15 percent made major occupational changes, 18 percent made minor occupational changes, and

16 percent took a job from outside.[6] For the middle-aged and older workers, the breakdowns are approximately 15 percent, 15 percent, and 10 percent, respectively. Thus, while about 30 percent of both middle-aged and older male and female workers changed occupations, the nature of these moves differs: females made about twice as many minor occupational moves as major ones, while males made minor and major occupational moves in about equal proportions. The higher overall ERRs for female middle-aged and older workers is due to a difference in labor market entrance rates: middle-aged and older male cohorts have about a 10 percent entrance rate; comparable female cohorts have about a 20 percent entrance rate, thus accounting for the ERR differences of approximately 40 and 50 percent, respectively, for these age ranges.

In sum, we see not only a massive number of occupational moves by the U.S. work force in a short period of time but also a large number of labor market opportunities available for middle-aged and older workers—and these are not hypothetical job opportunities. The data reflect job offers which were actually accepted by this older group.

Organizational Labor Markets

THE POPULATION OF JOBS

While there has been some work on the creation and abolishment of jobs at this level of analysis (Stewman and Konda 1981, 1983; Rosenbaum 1984; Stewman 1988a, 1988b), the more insightful analyses of intraorganizational job opportunities for middle-aged and older workers have focused on job distributions in organizations. At least three important lines of research are ongoing in this regard, one addressing the hierarchical distribution of jobs, another addressing the segmentation or independence of job opportunities by type of occupation, and the third dealing with segregation by gender.

Hierarchical Distribution Organizational hierarchies are often pyramidal in terms of job distributions, particularly the managerial segments. Two partially overlapping streams of research have probed into promotions in pyramidal organizations, with particular attention to management. In Rosenbaum's (1984) tournament model, an organizational career is treated as a sequence of competitions in a hierarchical tournament. Each competition results in a selection of winners and losers. The winners continue to compete at higher levels, with a progressive winnowing process as one rises higher. While losers, according to Rosen-

6. For convenience, the "outside" category includes the unemployed, military personnel, and those not in the labor market.

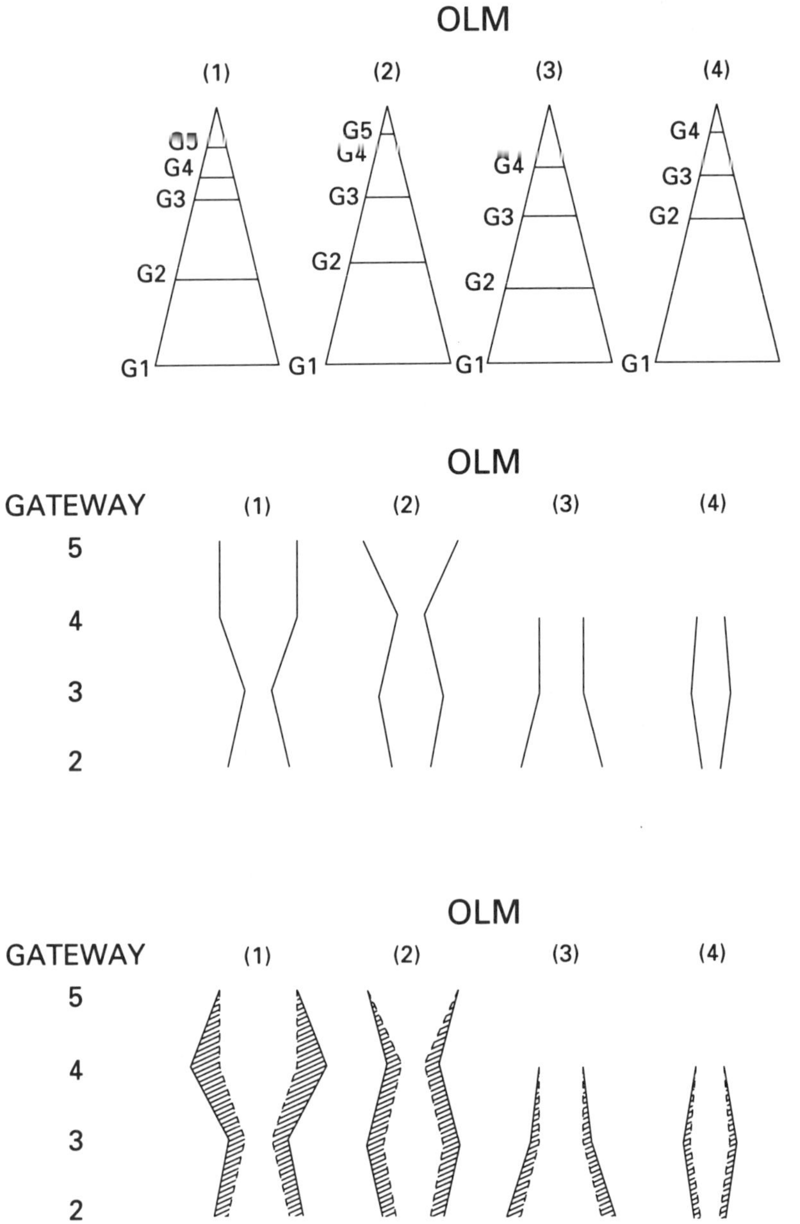

Figure 1. Organizational labor market (OLM) profiles, showing organizational pyramids at top and the associated Venturi tubes at middle and bottom.

Figure 1 (cont') *Top,* percentage distribution per grade; *middle,* grade ratios at each gateway; *bottom,* multiple grade ratios at each gateway created by the chain reaction. (The *hatched area* indicates the impact of higher-level vacancies beyond the adjacent grade.) The relative career chances at each grade are indicated by the width of the tube (as measured by the *outer solid lines*) at each gateway, as shown at the bottom of this figure. Source: S. Stewman and S. L. Konda, "Careers and Organizational Labor Markets: Demographic Models of Organizational Behavior," *American Journal of Sociology* 88:637–85; © 1983 by the University of Chicago.

baum, are not eliminated, they are relegated to minor tournaments. Rosenbaum's model appears to imply pyramidal chances overall, but allows for an elite or cohort of "stars" to continue to have differential success.

Stewman and Konda (1983) demonstrated that the usual perceptions of organizations as hierarchical pyramids do not provide the best view of one's career prospects. Other features of organizational structure or process provide better clues. Thus, for instance, in managerial pyramids, an individual's chances may *not* be declining the higher he or she rises in the hierarchy. Instead, at various promotion gateways they may improve.

To better grasp one of the central organizational features bringing this about, see Figure 1. At the top of this figure are four organizational pyramids depicting the managerial hierarchies in four different organizations. Since the four organizational labor markets are of different sizes, percentages have been used to denote the relative size of each grade in the management hierarchy. Clearly, all four are pyramidal. It is not the percentage per grade, however, but the ratios between grades which are important for promotion chances. The grade ratios are indicated in the middle of the figure. From these grade ratios, we can observe a Venturi tube indicating different contracting and expanding points within the hierarchy of each organization.

From this vantage point, one can now more readily perceive how career chances change and are not steadily declining as one moves up in a firm. If we also take into account the internal chain reaction of the opportunities which result from internal selections, then a more complete image of one's relative career chances is obtained, as shown at the bottom of the figure. Recall that if the initial selection in filling a vacancy is internal, this then opens another vacancy, and so on, setting off a chain reaction of job opportunities within the organization. These chain reactions end when a new recruit is hired from the outside or the vacant job is abolished. The chain reaction effect is shown as the hatched area at the bottom of the figure. Thus the single grade ratios in the middle of the figure are transformed into multiple grade ratios by the chain reactions, which not only link adjacent grades, but also other higher grades in the hierarchy. Since multiple grades are being linked, the best indication of career chances is indicated by the set of multiple grade ratios.[7]

In the four organizations shown in the figure, only organization (3), a military hierarchy, has pyramidal promotion chances. In the other three, including a multinational private firm, career chances change, including dramatic improvements at higher hierarchical levels in some cases. For instance, in organization (1), chances are best at upper middle management levels, whereas in organization (2), upper middle management offers the least chances; once there, however, the chances for then moving into top management are substantially better.

In sum, in the four pyramidal managerial hierarchies depicted here, only one (the military) had declining career chances the higher the level. If we add a fifth organization (Rosenbaum's private firm), as indicated by Stewman (1988b), then only one in five had such declining career chances. Neither of the two private corporations had declining career opportunities.

The Venturi model initially predicted the relative career chances in seven out of eight comparisons (Stewman and Konda 1983). Adding Rosenbaum's data to the four organizational labor markets shown in the figure, its predictions are accurate in nine out of ten promotion gateways (cf. Stewman 1988b). The model also takes into account career acceleration and deceleration, as well as the "stardom" effects postulated by Rosenbaum.

Both the Venturi and the tournament models indicate the potential of continued career acceleration throughout the career for certain cohorts and "stars." The Venturi model, however, indicates something additional in terms of aging and productivity: since pyramidal hierarchies often do not have pyramidal promotion chances, productivity may, in fact, increase for some individuals as they age because of organizationally induced accelerations in promotion. That is, if, in pyramidal organizations, the opportunity structures often expand in the middle or at the top (cf. Stewman and Konda 1983; Stewman 1986b), then many individuals will experience acceleration and deceleration at different levels, depending on the location of the narrow

7. The depiction of the entire set of multiple grade ratios into a "tube" structure, as in Figure 1, is referred to as a Venturi tube. The Venturi model of Stewman and Konda has roots in White's (1970) vacancy chain model, Bartholomew's (1973) renewal model, and demographic modeling by Keyfitz (1973).

and expanded gateways in the organizational Venturi tubes. Productivity for some might be increasing with age at certain points in the worklife or might iteratively accelerate and decelerate in accordance with the organization's opportunity structure. Both of these ideas—nonpyramidal promotion chances in pyramidal hierarchies and associated accelerated productivity at different ages (neither monotonically declining nor constant)—are counter-intuitive and point to the need for more careful examination of the implications of organizational structures and demography.

Segmentation by Occupation In studying career ladders and the segmentation of an organizational work force into distinct internal labor markets, Doeringer and Piore (1971) postulated that organizational job opportunities are often shielded from external competition. Thus these opportunity structures are organizationally administered or internal labor markets (ILMs). Doeringer and Piore depict an ILM as an isolated "mobility cluster" (the set of jobs within which an individual is usually promoted, demoted, or transferred once he or she has entered one of its ports of entry from outside the organization). Furthermore, they specifically discuss managerial, professional, technical, clerical, and blue-collar ILMs. Internal career ladders, with only a limited port of entry from the outside and at the bottom of the ladder, were noted as primary features of enterprise ILMs.

Doeringer and Piore's work is particularly important here because it stresses the significance of looking within organizations for labor market behavior. It stresses the importance of actual employer decisionmaking with respect to staffing and hiring and also jobs. More recent work by Osterman (1984) and Stewman (1988a) suggests that the initial assumptions of ILM theory as to the degree to which internal "mobility clusters" are isolated may in many cases be incorrect. There appears to be substantially more fluidity and crossover between occupational "mobility clusters" than is generally perceived. Conventional measures of segmentation at 80–95 percent, for instance, may be very misleading (Stewman 1988a). It has been shown that professional ILMs which appeared to be 90 percent segmented[8] had about 20 percent of their outside hires elsewhere (e.g., management, technical, clerical, or blue-collar jobs). For technical ILMs, which initially appeared to be 80 percent segmented, around 40 percent of the initial vacancies beginning in technical jobs ended in outside hires elsewhere. For managerial ILMs,

8. The segmentation measure used was the percentage of all staffing and hiring selections made from within the occupational group and the percentage made directly from outside.

which appeared to be 80 percent segmented, 50 percent of the initial vacancies ended in hires elsewhere (e.g., professional, technical, clerical, blue-collar).

The basis for the misperception as to the degree of isolation, using conventional measures of segmentation, is the tacit assumption that staffing and hiring decisions are independent. Stewman's (1988a) model incorporated the interdependence of the staffing and hiring decisions, central to the ILM theory postulate that internal job opportunities are shielded from external competition. More specifically, as noted earlier, if an initial vacancy[9] is filled from within, this creates another vacancy, and so on, until someone is hired from the outside. This internal chain reaction is, of course, an outcome of a set of interdependent staffing decisions. Thus the initial set of vacancies which begin in a specific occupational ILM is by no means equal to the number of external hires which will subsequently take place there, as indicated by the fact that 50 percent of managerial vacancies end in outside hires elsewhere (Stewman 1988a). These types of job opportunity transformations are quite important and may be particularly crucial for middle-aged and older workers applying for jobs in an organization.

Stewman (1988c) has also used the model discussed above to examine who gets the jobs generated by retirement. Because of the internal chain reaction of job opportunities, almost three job opportunities were generated for every initial vacancy opened by retirement in the U.S. Civil Service.[10] Thus, on average, there were two internal job opportunities, as well as the subsequent outside hire, generated by each retirement. Over a 15-year period 214,000 retirements generated over 630,000 job opportunities. The significance of the ILM postulate regarding internal staffing behavior should now be clear. Obviously, such internal job opportunities are quite important for the middle-aged and older workers within that organization. Taking into account both the internal staffing decisions and the external hires, Stewman (1988c) found slightly more job openings filled by workers aged 40 and above than by workers less than age 30. These surprising results are based on analysis of internal as well as external job opportunities. In organizations such as this, to miss the internal labor market opportunities is to miss almost two-thirds of the behavior. Such job opportunities are significant for middle-aged and older workers and are generally overlooked by labor market analysts.

9. Whether generated by a new job creation or an exit.

10. The data covered a fifteen-year period (1962–76) and were based on a continuous 10-percent sample of all white-collar workers over the period. The model used was an extension of the initial Venturi model (cf. Stewman and Konda 1983; Stewman 1986a).

Segregation by Gender Segregation by gender results in different job opportunities for middle-aged and older men and women. One of the most thorough reviews of this subject was written under the direction of the National Research Council's Committee on Women's Employment and Related Social Issues (Reskin and Hartmann 1986). Bielby and Baron (1986) have analyzed statistical discrimination at the firm level and found very high sex segregation. Using detailed job titles, they found almost 60 percent of firms to be totally sex-segregated and 80 percent of firms to have 90 percent or more of jobs in one category to be held by one sex. The type of sex segregation found by Bielby and Baron was first discovered by Blau (1977) in a study of white-collar labor markets in three cities. She pointed out that occupational analyses of sex segregation could be underestimating its actual occurrence due to a process at the organizational level—selection into firms. She suggested that part of the wage differentials by gender were the result of the point of entry within the stratification of firms. High-wage firms hired men and lower-wage firms hired women for the same type of job, so that within each group of firms a very high degree of sex segregation was found. Of significance to this discussion is the degree to which such sex segregation is constant over time or is decreasing. If the latter, at what rate is it decreasing? How much of the process is determined at the point of hire? Certainly ILM analyses such as those discussed above with respect to interdependence (Stewman 1988a, 1988c) are pertinent. Simple analyses of occupational distributions tell us little about rates and mechanisms of change. We may further inquire as to how middle-aged and older women are faring at the external ports and with respect to internal job opportunities. Since there is substantial evidence that opportunities affect motivation and aspiration, it would appear that employers have a major untapped resource for improving productivity, and that it is based on the distribution and allocation of jobs.

THE POPULATION OF WORKERS

While the discussion thus far has focused on the job population, here we will stress the worker population. The Venturi model specifies both the relative squeeze points and expansion points, in terms of career advancement, throughout the full set of hierarchical levels of an organizational labor market. Stewman and Konda (1983) found that relative career opportunities increase, as well as decrease, at middle and upper managerial levels. The relative increases were the unexpected element. Even at the squeeze points, however, Stewman and Konda found that for about one-half of the careers, the individual's career acceleration continued; that is, the individual's waiting time before promotion was less than at the prior promotion gateway. The key to the continued acceleration lies in the managerial selection preferences.

Using selections by seniority in grade, Konda and Stewman had earlier (1980) found an acceleration mechanism. It was discovered that the higher one rises in the hierarchy, the earlier are his/her best selection chances. In one organization, Stewman and Konda (1983) then joined these selection acceleration processes to the Venturi job structures to find out what happened when the two basic forces opposed one another. They found that about one-half the careers decelerated at the squeeze point and one-half continued to accelerate due to the employer staffing/selection effect. Both the Venturi or job structure and the employer staffing or choice structure had very strong effects on a worker's chances. Earlier movement at the gateway prior to the squeeze point was also found to increase one's chances; that is, a significant amount of leverage for promotion from grade three (middle management) to grade four (upper middle management)—the toughest passage in the hierarchy—was gained by those preparing and moving earlier, at the grade two (lower management) to grade three gateway. Finally, Stewman and Konda found that individuals who are members of small entering cohorts are not only advantaged at the initial promotion gateways but throughout their work life. Thus the relative internal chances of middle-aged and older workers depend on their entering cohort size, on their rate of movement at earlier grades, and on the joint effects of the job structures and managerial selection behavior. For the last two factors, the relative squeeze points and the time in grade at each level are significant arbiters.

In terms of mobility between jobs and occupations, Stewman (1988a) has found that the organization ERRs were greater than both the promotion and turnover rates combined. Thus, while the latter types of rates have been the more commonly studied organizational behavior, a major gap appears to exist in terms of our knowledge of the internal job opportunities for workers. More specifically, there are many more job opportunities, and our organizations are much more dynamic, than is apparent from the study of promotion alone, or even of promotion and turnover. For white-collar federal civil servants, Stewman found the annual renewal rate to be about one-third; that is, approximately one-third of all the organization's white-collar workers were new to their job each year. Promotion rates were about 15 percent and turnover rates approximately 9 percent per year.

Thus, just as in the case of the national labor market analysis, here we find very dynamic organizational labor markets. Of central concern, then, given such internal dynamics, is the extent to which these job opportunities are available for middle-aged and older workers. As in the

Table 3: RELATIVE SHARE OF VARIOUS TRIGGERING EVENTS BY OCCUPATION OF ORIGIN, FEDERAL CIVIL SERVICE, 1962–76

	Triggering Effect			
Occupation When Chain Reaction Began	A % Distribution Overall Exit Rate	B % Distribution New Job Creation Rate	C % Distribution Overall Activation Rate (B+C)[a]	D % Distribution Retirement Rate
Professional	.11	.20	.13	.15
Managerial	.10	.43	.17	.28
Technical	.26	.30	.26	.24
Clerical	.50	.07	.41	.27
Other white-collar	.05	0	.04	.06

[a]Weighted.

national-level analysis, to examine this issue, we will look deeper into the ERRs by age and gender.

EMPLOYEE-JOB RENEWAL RATES (ERRS) BY AGE AND GENDER

Answers to the question of who gets the jobs generated by retirement (Stewman 1988c) may differ from answers to the question of who gets the jobs generated by all exits and by new job creations. First, the distribution of the overall events triggering the job vacancy chain reactions may differ from that based only on retirement. The overall exit rates will probably differ, and new job creation distributions will almost certainly differ. Second, the behavior of the internal chain reactions (e.g., the routes and sequences of job opportunities opened) depends on the occupation at which the chain reaction originates. The differential weighting or relative share of the activations by type of triggering event and occupation in federal Civil Service white-collar jobs is shown in Table 3. Indeed, the overall activation distribution differs substantially from activations due solely to retirement. Here our interest is in the overall activation rates and the total job opportunities generated for the organization's white-collar ILMs. Additionally, we wish to know the ERRs by both age and gender. Table 4 provides the data on overall annual ERRs, disaggregated by age cohort for each type of ILM.

Again, what we find is a remarkable stability across age cohorts for the proportion of the ILM which makes internal moves. This holds for all white-collar ILMs: professional, managerial, technical, clerical, and "other." Of all professional jobs, 17 to 20 percent have a new incumbent per year moving in from within the organization. For technical

Table 4: OVERALL ANNUAL ERRS, BY AGE COHORT AND LOCATION OF MOVE, WHITE-COLLAR ILMS, FEDERAL CIVIL SERVICE, 1962–76

ILM	Location of Move	*Age* <30	30–39	40–49	50–59	60+	Σ
Professional	Internal[a]	.168	.189	.175	.199	.192	.182
	External[b]	.201	.066	.038	.029	.032	.083
	Total[c]	.369	.255	.213	.228	.224	.265
Managerial	Internal	.177	.211	.207	.269	.256	.218
	External	.183	.057	.034	.024	.023	.060
	Total	.360	.269	.241	.293	.279	.278
Technical	Internal	.201	.184	.174	.210	.215	.190
	External	.323	.079	.049	.034	.034	.117
	Total	.524	.262	.223	.244	.249	.307
Clerical	Internal	.308	.304	.256	.263	.242	.286
	External	.280	.136	.093	.061	.038	.167
	Total	.588	.440	.348	.324	.280	.453
Other white-collar	Internal	.151	.124	.131	.186	.159	.146
	External	.324	.085	.054	.033	.047	.118
	Total	.475	.210	.184	.219	.206	.264
All white-collar	Internal	.244	.222	.203	.238	.226	.225
	External	.267	.088	.056	.039	.033	.117
	Total	.511	.310	.260	.277	.259	.342

[a]Includes (1) job change (same detailed occupation but different job, e.g., change in agency, geography, or reassignment); (2) minor occupation change (move to a different detailed occupation within the major occupational group); and (3) major occupation change (move between major occupational groups, e.g., technical to managerial).

[b]External hire.

[c]Total ERR within an age cohort=Internal+External.

jobs, the figure is 18 to 21 percent; for clerical jobs, 25 to 32 percent; for other white-collar jobs, 13 to 19 percent. The greatest range of variation is for managerial jobs: 18 to 27 percent. For the entire set of white-collar jobs, the range is from 21 to 25 percent. In brief, middle-aged and older workers are moving internally at the same rate as younger workers. This holds for workers aged 50 to 59 as well as for those aged 60 and above. In fact, for all but the clerical ILM, the internal mobility rate for these older workers is slightly higher than for workers in their 40s, their 30s, or below age 30.

Overall, the striking feature here is the stability or constancy across age cohorts, which was not anticipated, perhaps because of the general assumption that job activity decreases with age. What differs here is that the ERR pertains to those who remain in or enter the labor market. It is a measure of labor market behavior, applying to current workers. For projecting the labor market forward in time, one must take account of exits and new jobs, both of which activate the chain reactions of job opportunities. New entrants and job abolishments are events which end the chain reactions.

Normally, analysts take the population of workers at time *t* and follow them forward in time, treating those who remain in the labor market and those who leave it. But the labor market contains stayers, leavers, and entrants. What the ERR measure captures pertains to the set of all currently occupied jobs in the labor market: what proportion of these jobholders are new incumbents? Measures which deal with workers at time *t* who remain or exit have lost important segments of the ongoing job population by not taking into account new jobs (growth) and the entrants who replace the leavers or are at least on the end of the chain reactions initiated by the leavers. Thus measurements pertaining solely to cohorts of workers at time *t* and thereafter have labor market selectivity biases, based on the differences in exit-entrance distributions and on a truncation bias stemming from the omission of entrance cohorts. If we are looking at the ongoing labor market populations of workers and jobs, the ERRs provide a measure of the behavior of these joint populations.

The findings of no age cohort effects are thus, in part, a reframing of the measures pertaining to labor market behavior that more closely captures the ongoing process. From the perspective of cohorts of workers at time *t*, the ERR is in part a conditional probability, which applies to the proportion of stayers and deletes the proportion of leavers. It also, however, adds cohorts who enter, all of whom are new incumbents, thus changing the base in a second way. Both of these changes are necessary to obtain labor market behavior at any point in time.

In terms of labor market dynamics, we again postulate that exits result from selection processes dominated by self-selections for a variety of reasons—health, adaptation/flexibility, family, and leisure, for example. The stayers also represent a set of self-selection processes, but of a different kind. Moreover, it is these stayers, with the additional population of entrance cohorts, for whom the invariance by age holds. Perhaps we have too often been looking at the process from the wrong angle to notice such stability.

As for the external entrance part of the ERRs in Table 4, we observe, in general, a monotonic decline with age.[11] The range of differences by age are as follows: professional, 2 to 20 percent; managerial, 2 to 18 percent; technical, 3 to 32 percent; clerical, 4 to 28 percent; and other white-collar, 3 to 27 percent. Overall, the differences by age in the proportion of jobs which are held by a new entrant range from 3 to 27 percent of each cohort. This range is much greater than that observed for the internal job opportunities.

The overall ERR for the entire set of white-collar ILMs is 34 percent. (.342; see Table 4, last row, last column); that is, on average, over one-third of all white-collar ILMs are filled annually by a new incumbent. The highest ERRs are in the clerical ILM, with 45 percent. Otherwise, for professional, managerial, technical and other white-collar ILMs, it is around 30 percent (27, 28, 31, and 26 percent, respectively). It is also noteworthy that with the exception of the clerical ILM, the overall range of age differences in ERRs for cohorts of workers above age 30 are quite small (professional, 22–26 percent; managerial, 24–29 percent; technical, 22–26 percent; other, 18–22 percent). Of course, given the relative size of the group of entrants over age 30, most of this effect is due to stability of the internal movement, which held across age cohorts.

Table 5 provides the data on annual ERRs by age and gender for each white-collar ILM. The earlier observation regarding the stability of internal movement rates by age holds for both genders. Of all the professional jobs held by women, 16–20 percent have a new incumbent who moved there from a different job within the organization. For technical jobs held by women, the figure is 18–24 percent; for clerical jobs, 26–32 percent. Managerial and other white-collar jobs show slightly more variation, 21–33 percent and 11–22 percent, respectively. For jobs held by male age cohorts, very similar rates hold: for professionals, it is 16–21 percent; for technical jobs, 17–22 percent; and for other white-collar jobs, 12–19 percent. For both managerial and clerical jobs, males have slightly lower internal in-movement rates than females. For all ILMs combined, a similar observation holds: women have somewhat higher overall internal mobility rates than men, but this finding is largely the result of the higher mobility rates in clerical ILMs and of the large share of the total female work force (68 percent) within this ILM. The proportion of all male workers in this organization holding clerical jobs is 10 percent. Thus the primary basis for the aggregated gender differences is job allocation.

11. The two exceptions are for professional and other white-collar ILMs, both of which show slight increases at age 60. The same logic used in the national labor market section holds for these cases.

Table 5: ANNUAL ERRs BY GENDER, AGE COHORT, AND LOCATION OF MOVE, WHITE-COLLAR ILMs, FEDERAL CIVIL SERVICE, 1962–76

		Female Age Cohorts						*Male Age Cohorts*					
Occupational ILM	Location of Move	<30	30–39	40–49	50–59	60+	Σ	<30	30–39	40–49	50–59	60+	Σ
Professional	Internal	.191	.201	.155	.166	.165	.179	.163	.187	.178	.205	.212	.183
	External	.271	.133	.080	.050	.050	.144	.185	.058	.032	.025	.029	.072
	Total	.462	.334	.235	.216	.215	.323	.348	.245	.210	.230	.241	.255
Managerial	Internal	.246	.254	.211	.265	.332	.244	.151	.203	.206	.257	.246	.210
	External	.191	.058	.032	.023	.025	.068	.173	.056	.034	.023	.022	.056
	Total	.437	.312	.243	.288	.357	.312	.324	.259	.240	.280	.268	.266
Technical	Internal	.213	.198	.184	.214	.240	.202	.193	.178	.169	.208	.216	.184
	External	.278	.107	.063	.038	.026	.119	.329	.065	.042	.029	.037	.109
	Total	.491	.305	.247	.252	.266	.321	.522	.243	.211	.237	.253	.293
Clerical	Internal	.321	.319	.266	.266	.261	.298	.262	.251	.226	.257	.227	.248
	External	.272	.144	.096	.063	.034	.168	.359	.100	.074	.048	.048	.167
	Total	.593	.463	.362	.329	.295	.466	.621	.351	.300	.305	.275	.415
Other white-collar	Internal	.211	.220	.154	.215	.114	.198	.145	.121	.131	.185	.167	.144
	External	.499	.122	.087	.069	.040	.290	.303	.083	.052	.031	.047	.108
	Total	.710	.342	.241	.284	.154	.488	.448	.204	.183	.216	.214	.252
All white-collar	Internal	.297	.283	.236	.249	.256	.270	.184	.190	.185	.227	.221	.195
	External	.270	.128	.082	.052	.033	.150	.260	.064	.040	.028	.032	.090
	Total	.567	.411	.318	.301	.289	.420	.444	.254	.225	.255	.253	.285

Note: see notes to Table 4.

Within each type of white-collar ILM the relative internal in-mobility rate for both genders is virtually identical. This is a very important finding, underscoring job access and job allocation. Not only are the internal rates quite stable across age cohorts but also by gender, once the ILM is taken into account.

While the in-mobility rates across age cohorts are within a very limited range, it is worth noting that in several cases middle-aged and older workers have slightly higher rates. This is true for women in managerial and technical ILMs and for men in professional, managerial, technical, and other white-collar ILMS. Not only are internal job opportunities distributed quite equally by age within this organization's white-collar ILMs but, in several cases where there are small differences, the selections slightly favor middle-aged and older workers.

As for the external component of the ERRs, a general monotonic decrease with age is the more general pattern, with one exception: in the male cohorts and in two of the female cohorts, there is either no difference or a slight increase from the 50–59 age cohorts to the 60+ age cohorts. As noted earlier, this pattern is due to the higher exit rates in these age ranges, which lower the relative denominators more in the oldest age cohorts and thereby increase their relative entrance rates.

Overall, the ERRs of women are over 40 percent; that is, over 40 percent of women in this organization hold a new job each year. The rate for men is almost 30 percent (.285). For women aged 40 and above, the ERRs are approximately 30 percent per year; for men they are about 25 percent. In short, these data provide strong evidence of a substantial number of internal labor market opportunities for men and women middle-aged and older.

In terms of job opportunities, there appear to be many, and once the leavers are gone, the middle-aged and older stayers appear to be much more flexible and adaptive, as evidenced in the ERRs, than one might expect. In terms of productivity, there are two important features here. First, organizations must continually change, and one of the ways in which this can be done is by shifting of jobs and job assignments. In this regard, these data indicate no differences by age cohort or gender once the leavers are self-selected out. Second, research by Katz (1982a, 1982b) indicates that, for research and development groups, job and group assignment longevity is important for performance. Groups with very short (less than 1.5 years) and "long" (over 5 years) longevity on a job assignment were less productive. Thus group renewal, via incorporating "new blood," and individual renewal, via a new assignment or new work associates, appear to be important organizational regenerative processes. Moreover, as found here, over two-thirds of such renewals involve moves within the organization. It appears that in this regard one of the avenues for maintaining continued productivity with age is via job change, and that middle-aged and older cohorts of men and women are "holding up their share of the sky," as a Chinese adage expresses it.

Summary

The findings for both the national and organizational labor markets discussed here have, for the most part, not been anticipated. The massive size of the labor market opportunities is not generally known. In the U.S. national labor market, for instance, we found that at least 25 percent of jobs were held by new incumbents each year and that in a five-year period the rate is over 50 percent. There are a large number of labor market opportunities for middle-aged and older workers.

In terms of the proportion of jobs which have new incumbents in a five-year period, there were basically no differences by age cohort for those who change jobs within the labor market. For women, the percentage of labor market jobholders moving within the labor market (generally changing firms) was 25–30 percent, and this proportion held for middle-aged and older women as much as for younger women. For men the figure was about 30–35 percent. It is only for the 25–34 age cohorts of males that the internal rate is over 40 percent. In brief, the basic finding here indicates stability across age and substantial labor market opportunities for those middle-aged and older workers who remain in the labor market.

In terms of organizational labor market behavior, again very large proportions of jobs were held by new incumbents each year (34 percent). This rate varied by type of internal labor market. For managerial, professional, and technical ILMs, the ERR rate was generally between 25 and 30 percent. For clerical ILMs, it was over 40 percent, with almost two-thirds involving moves within the organization. In fact, in general, there were two internal moves for every external hire in all of the major white-collar ILMs.

Not only the massive nature of internal labor market dynamics but also the allocation of these internal job opportunities by age and gender has been unknown for the most part. The initial differential allocation of jobs by gender—that is, at the point of hire—is not a particularly new observation. However, here we found few differences by gender in internal mobility rates once the initial job allocation by occupational ILM was taken into account. The productivity issue is therefore one of initial access.

Perhaps most important, the internal rate of mobility was quite stable across age cohorts for both men and women. For current jobholders per ILM, the rate of movement into those jobs did not vary by age or gender for individuals who were already inside the organization. For managerial, professional, and technical ILMs, the rates were between 18 and 24 percent. For clerical ILMs, the rates were somewhat higher, 25 to 30 percent. In almost all cases, however, the internal rates for both male and female middle-aged and older workers were as high as, if not higher than, for younger workers.

The two levels of analysis conducted here are complementary, with the internal national-level data generally referring to movement between employers and the internal organizational analysis, of course, referring to moves within organizations. However, the same bottom line holds at both levels. In addressing the initial primary questions, we can now assert with some degree of confidence that both national and organizational labor markets are much more dynamic than generally thought. In part, these dynamics pertain to the regenerative nature of our organizations and our economy. The role of middle-aged and older workers is not minor in any sense of the word. At both the organizational and the national level there are substantial labor market opportunities for such workers.

It is clear that this story needs much more fleshing out so that the basic processes at work are more fully understood. Also, both positive and negative outcomes for individual workers must be investigated in more detail. The self-selection processes operative among middle-aged and older workers who leave the labor market should also be examined. Such analyses would have to take into account the perceived versus actual decreases in labor market opportunities and the internal demographic composition of firms, as well as changing retirement incentives of firms.

Another area for further research is the nature of the internal moves taking place, at both levels of analysis. In particular, to what extent are moves of middle-aged and older workers upward, downward, or lateral? In Japan, for instance, Tsuda (1974) pointed to the movement of retirees at age 55 (now somewhat later) from large firms to smaller ones, and Yoshio (1980) noted the re-employment of older workers in jobs with less status and pay. Much more information of this sort is needed for the U.S. labor market.

Movement between fulltime and part-time jobs would also appear to be increasingly important. Here, for instance, older workers might be involved at either end of a chain reaction pertaining to part-time work.[12] Of course, part of the story may just as well involve upward or lateral moves, either of which might be involved in increased productivity, the first due to hierarchical responsibility, the second to more flexibility. There will surely be many more surprises as additional data are analyzed. Such investigations are significant not only for the human side of the story of opportunities for older men and women but also for the economy in general, in terms of the regenerative nature of labor markets.[13]

References

Bartholomew, D. J. 1973 *Stochastic Models for Social Processes.* New York: John Wiley & Sons.

Bielby, W. T., and J. N. Baron. 1986. "Men and Women at Work: Sex Segregation and Statistical Discrimination," *American Journal of Sociology* 91: 759–99.

Birch, D. 1979. "The Job Generation Process." Unpublished manuscript. Program on Neighborhood and Regional Change, Massachusetts Institute of Technology.

Blau, A. C. 1977. *Equal Pay in the Office.* Lexington, Mass.: D. C. Heath-Lexington Books.

Bluestone, B. 1982. "Deindustrialization and the Abandonment of Community." In *Community and Capital in Conflict: Plant Closings and Job Loss,* edited by J. C. Raines, L. E. Berson, and D. McI. Gracie, pp. 38–61. Philadelphia: Temple University Press.

Brittain, J. W., and J. H. Freeman. 1980. "Organizational Proliferation and Density Dependent Selection: Organizational Evolution in the Semiconductor Industry." In *The Organizational Life Cycle,* edited by J. R. Kimberly, R. H. Miles, et al., pp. 291–338. San Francisco: Jossey-Bass.

Byrne, J. J. 1975. "Occupational Mobility of Workers," *Monthly Labor Review* 98: 52–59.

Doeringer, P. B., and M. J. Piore. 1971. *Internal Labor Markets and Manpower Analysis.* Lexington, Mass.: D. C. Heath-Lexington Books.

Green, R. 1982. "Tracking Job Growth in Private Industry," *Monthly Labor Review* 105: 3–9.

12. For instance, the creation of a new part-time job, to which a fulltime older worker wishes to move, may open a fulltime vacancy for another worker; or, at the end of a chain reaction, a fulltime vacancy may become two part-time jobs for older workers who wish to re-enter the labor market.

13. The latter, of course, also pertains to the regenerative nature of organizations (a demographic story) and of the populations of organizations (cf. ecological theory for the latter—e.g., Hannan and Freeman 1977). The story also illuminates the interface of demography and ecology as new firms are created (cf. Brittain and Freeman 1980).

Hannan, M. T., and J. Freeman. 1977 "The Population Ecology of Organizations," *American Journal of Sociology* 82: 929–64.

Katz, R. 1982a. "The Effects of Group Longevity on Project Communication and Performance," *Administrative Science Quarterly* 27: 81–104.

———. 1982b. "Managing Careers: The Influence of Job and Group Longevities." In *Career Issues in Human Resource Management*, edited by R. Katz. Englewood Cliffs, N.J.: Prentice-Hall.

Keyfitz, N. 1973. "Individual Mobility in a Stationary Population," *Population Studies* 27: 335–52.

Konda, S. L., and S. Stewman. 1980. "An Opportunity Labor Demand Model and Markovian Labor Supply Models: Comparative Tests in an Organization," *American Sociological Review* 45: 276–301.

Osterman, P. 1984. "White-Collar Internal Labor Markets." In *Internal Labor Markets,* edited by P. Osterman, pp. 163–89. Cambridge, Mass.: MIT Press.

Pampel, F. C., and J. A. Weiss. 1983. "Economic Development, Pension Policies, and the Labor Force Participation of Aged Males: A Cross-Sectional, Longitudinal Approach," *American Journal of Sociology* 89: 350–72.

Reskin, B. F., and H. I. Hartmann, editors. 1986. *Women's Work, Men's Work: Sex Segregation on the Job.* Washington, D.C.: National Academy Press.

Rosenbaum, J. E. 1984. *Career Mobility in a Corporate Hierarchy.* New York: Academic Press.

Sommers, D., and A. Eck. 1977. "Occupational Mobility in the American Labor Force," *Monthly Labor Review* 199: 3–19.

Stewman, S. 1988a. "Interdependent Managerial Decisions and the Opportunity Structures of White-Collar Internal Labor Markets." Unpublished paper.

———. 1988b. "Organizational Demography," *Annual Review of Sociology* 14: 173–202.

———. 1988c. "Who Gets the Jobs That Are Generated by Retirement? A Demographic Analysis of Organizational Behavior." Unpublished paper.

———. 1986a. "Demographic Models of Internal Labor Markets," *Administrative Science Quarterly* 31: 212–47.

———. 1986b. "Labor Markets, Aging, and Health." In *Age, Health and Employment,* edited by J. E. Birren, P. K. Robinson, and J. E. Livingston. Englewood Cliffs, N.J.: Prentice-Hall.

Stewman, S., and S. L. Konda. 1983. "Careers and Organizational Labor Markets: Demographic Models of Organizational Behavior," *American Journal of Sociology* 88: 637–85.

———. 1981. "Demographic Models of Labor Squeezes and Cutbacks." Paper presented at the annual meeting of the Operations Research Society of America and the Institute of Management Science, Houston, Tex., October.

Tsuda, M. 1974. "Personnel Administration at the Industrial Plant Level." In *Workers and Employees in Japan: The Japanese Employment Relations System,* edited by K. Okochi, B. Karsh, and S. B. Levin, pp. 399–440. Englewood Cliffs, N.J.: Prentice-Hall.

U.S. Bureau of the Census. 1973. *1970 Census of Population: Occupation and Residence in 1965*. Washington, D.C.: U.S. Government Printing Office.

White, H. C. 1970. *Chains of Opportunity: System Models of Mobility in Organizations*. Cambridge, Mass.: Harvard University Press.

Yoshio, K. 1980. "The Future of the Fixed Age Retirement System." In *The Labor Market in Japan*, edited by S. Nishikawa. Tokyo: Japan Foundation.

Social Insecurity: The Economic Marginalization of Older Women Workers

KAREN NUSSBAUM

For older women, the economic strains that have surfaced to turn American workers' dreams of retirement into nightmares have been exacerbated by discrimination that makes them the greatest of victims. Nussbaum reports that older women in the work force include large numbers who work out of economic need but earn little pay compared to men. Older women are also disproportionately hurt by layoffs, and those women who manage to stay in the work force until retirement can look forward to an average pension income that is only 58 percent of that received by men.

R. J. V. M.

The focus of this chapter is on older women. It's a particularly important focus because the numbers of women will roughly equal those of men in the work force soon after the turn of the century.[1]

When 9 to 5, the National Association of Working Women, was created fifteen years ago as a membership group of working women, many of the founders were young. Even then, however, we had an understanding of the problems we would face as older workers. In fact, the first issue of our newsletter carried a letter from a Boston secretary who prophesied that we "will be called 'girls' until the day we retire without pensions."

The stories we heard from working women in the early days all pointed in the same direction: "People say that life begins at forty," one woman told us, "but for working women, this saying is far from the truth. Older women who have put in years of dedicated service to the companies they work for get passed up for promotions and raises, train

1. Howard Fullerton, "Labor Force Projections: 1986–2000," *Monthly Labor Review* 110 (September 1987): 20.

younger men to do more highly paid jobs, and retire with a tiny pension—or no pension at all—to live out their remaining years in poverty."

A secretary in Cleveland said, "No one will hire you when you are 53, even with 12 good years ahead of you. They want young women. If you don't have a hold on a good job by the time you are 40, you might as well forget it." And an insurance worker lamented, "You would think that 20 years of doing this work would count for *something*. But they started me at an entry-level salary, and now I'm making only 10 cents an hour more than kids just coming in."

While very little is different for working women, the economy has changed. The underlying economic strains have surfaced and are turning American workers' dreams of retirement into nightmares. Discrimination against women exacerbates these problems, making older women even greater victims. In this chapter, trends for older workers will be discussed with attention given to how these trends affect women—first, when they work; second, when they are laid off; and third, when they retire.

Women Who Work

In 9 to 5's recent report (September 1987), "Social Insecurity: The Economic Marginalization of Older Workers," we found that older workers bear a disproportionate burden of the current era of restructuring. In effect, they are the "shock absorbers" of the changing economy, an economy characterized by more marginal working conditions. The "contingent work force" is growing, with a full 28 percent of the work force now working as part-time, temporary, contracted-out, or home-based workers.[2] Contingent workers typically have low pay, few benefits, and no job security, and they are being used to replace fulltime jobs. Older workers are a growing part of the marginal work force.

The number of women 45 years of age and over who are working part-time involuntarily has been increasing steadily—by 51 percent over the last seven years.[3] Yet growing numbers of older women need to work. Work force participation rates for older men are declining

2. Hilda Kahne, "Part-Time Work: A Positive Case," paper presented at the annual meeting of the American Economic Association, New York, December 1986.
3. U.S. Department of Labor, Bureau of Labor Statistics, *Employment and Earnings*, January 1987.

sharply, but women's rates are constant. Women are staying on the job, in many cases, out of economic need.

But despite their financial need, women work for relatively little pay compared to men. The pay gap between men and women workers widens with age. For all workers, a woman makes 68 cents to a man's dollar; the paycheck shrinks to 61 cents to the dollar for women over 45, while a woman over 65 years of age and older earns only 57 cents to a man's dollar.[4]

Women Who Are Laid Off

Older workers are disproportionately hurt by layoffs, which are used by a growing number of companies as a short-term strategy to cut costs. The effect is that older workers are being pushed out of the work force through displacement into longer durations of unemployment. What follows is either early retirement or re-employment at lower pay.[5]

Older women with substantial job tenure suffer the greatest loss of earnings after displacement—higher than younger women, even higher than displaced older men in blue-collar jobs.[6] This fact is not in keeping with common expectations. When we think of displacement, we think, first, of the older man laid off from a steel mill, unable to find another job. But the facts are otherwise: when women are laid off, they are out longer; over the term of their displacement they suffer a greater loss in pay; and, although more men than women are displaced (two out of three displaced workers are men), women tend to have a higher likelihood of being pushed out of the labor force entirely.[7]

4. U.S. Bureau of the Census, *Money Income and Poverty Status of Families and Persons in the United States: 1986*, Current Population Reports, Series P-60, No. 157 (Washington, D.C.: U.S. Government Printing Office, 1987).

5. Steven H. Sandell and David Shapiro, "Economic Conditions, Job Loss and Induced Retirement," unpublished paper; National Commission for Employment Policy, *Older Worker Employment Comes of Age* (Washington, D.C.: National Commission for Employment Policy, 1985), pp. 21–22.

6. Michael Podgursky and Paul Swaim, "Labor Market Adjustment and Job Displacement: Evidence from the January 1984 Displaced Worker Survey," Final Report, Bureau of International Affairs, U.S. Department of Labor, January 1986.

7. Paul Flame and Ellen Sehgal, "Displaced Workers of 1979–1983: How Well They Fared," *Monthly Labor Review* 108 (June 1985).

Women Who Retire

If a woman manages to stay in the work force until retirement age, she faces another set of problems—getting access to retirement benefits and maintaining her income. Today, retired workers in several industries are being recruited to come back to their old companies or to work for new ones. Their years of experience, however, are being rewarded with entry-level pay and no benefits. Most manage to live on these low wages only because of their pension or Social Security benefits. An increasing number of older workers who return to work after retirement find themselves subsidizing their own employment.

Early retirement schemes are increasing in popularity among employers: 40 percent of Fortune 500 companies have used them to cut staff.[8] The schemes that are more lucrative to the workers, however, tend to be offered to men and higher-level employees. Women tend to work in lower-paying jobs and are not typically offered "golden handshakes." As a 9 to 5 member from Los Angeles remarked, "I've never heard of inducements to go. Clericals have enough trouble getting inducements to stay."

Pension coverage for women (and low-wage workers in general) is still rare. Despite the fact that 42 percent of all workers participate in pension plans, only 20 percent of women, compared to 43 percent of men, receive pension benefits at retirement.[9] And when a women does receive a pension, it usually does not amount to much. Average pension income for women is only 58 percent of the level received by men.[10] And to make matters worse, only 2 percent of widows ever collect spousal benefits after their husband's death.[11]

Poverty

Together these trends—discrimination during employment years, greater trauma as a result of displacement, and fewer retirement benefits—lead to poverty for women. Older women are more likely to live in poverty. Half of all women 65 and older living alone live in

8. Elizabeth M. Fowler, "The Early Retirement Schemes," *New York Times*, April 25, 1984.
9. Gregory Stricharchuk, "Retirement Prospects Grow Bleaker for Many as Job Scene Changes," *Wall Street Journal*, August 26, 1987; Older Women's League, *The Status of Midlife and Older Women in America* (Washington, D.C.: OWL, 1986).
10. 9 to 5, National Association of Working Women, *Vanished Dreams: Age Discrimination and the Older Woman Worker* (Cleveland: 9 to 5, 1980).
11. Ibid.

poverty.[12] This rate is twice that for older men. Almost 20 percent of all women over 85 years of age live in poverty, and 72 percent of the elderly poor are women.[13] In four different ways, these numbers and facts show that many older women are poor.

12. Villers Foundation, *On the Other Side of Easy Street* (Washington, D.C.: Villers Foundation, 1987).

13. Ibid.

Investing in Experience: Job Barriers to Older Workers in Michigan

OLIVIA P. MAYNARD

In 1986 the Michigan Governor's Task Force on Employment Opportunities for Older Citizens, chaired by Maynard, issued a report that emphasized the need to invest in older workers. Evidence of legal and illegal discrimination against older workers is presented here, and Maynard calls for new strategies for economic development and training of older workers that address the varied composition of this work force: displaced homemakers, persistently marginal workers, dislocated workers, individuals working to supplement Social Security, and those who work for social reasons. The feminization of poverty evident among the young is likely to be replicated among older women, who will continue to comprise the largest portion of the aging population, and Maynard emphasizes the need to confront the inequities that women face in the marketplace.

R. J. V. M.

According to legend, when someone in China wants to curse you, he says, "May you live in interesting times." The number of people aged sixty-five living today is one-half the total number of sixty-five-year-olds who have ever lived on the earth. Add to this rather startling statement the demographers' projection that, by the year 2025, the 64-and-over population in the United States will go from 28.6 million to 58.8 million, while the 15- to 50-year-old group will increase only a nominal 7 million, and we can see that we do indeed live in an interesting time.

We can look around us for collective wisdom to guide our public policy and private research, even if we cannot look behind us for ancestral wisdom. This volume is part of the process of developing that collective wisdom, as well as renewing our commitment to build an America that will benefit from and reward an aging work force.

Three years ago Governor James Blanchard of Michigan created a task force on Employment Opportunities for Older Citizens, with members drawn from public agencies, trade unions, the business community, and human resource advocacy groups. I served as the chair of that task force, which was to make comprehensive recommendations for program development and legislative policy changes to encourage job development, training, and opportunities for Michigan's older citizens. Governor Blanchard's charge included:

- Identification of the characteristics of the population 55 and older and determination of their economic and employment needs.
- Evaluation of current public and private sector economic and employment policies, focusing on the maintenance of Michigan's economic prosperity, and recommending options for new employment and retirement arrangements.
- Review of existing job programs for older adults and the role of education and training programs in educational institutions.
- Review of existing job programs to determine whether additional policies are needed to improve and coordinate these services.
- Collection of information and advice from all sectors of the aging network: business, labor, academia, the general public, members of the legislature, and local, state, and national agencies and officials.

In 1986 the task force issued its report, entitled *Investing in Experience,* a title that sounds a persistent theme of the Blanchard administration and serves as a pragmatic reminder that economic opportunity, as well as revitalization, does not arise without investment. The report's recommendations fall under four main headings:

changing attitudes and eliminating barriers;
employment and economic development strategies;
education and training initiatives;
new work and retirement arrangements.

Eliminating Ageism

The first thrust of the task force was to speak out against ageism in the workplace by advocating a change in attitudes toward older citizens and the elimination of barriers to employing older workers.

Lest you think that age discrimination is dead, consider the following: in 1981 a national poll conducted for the National Council on Aging by Louis Harris and Associates found that 70 percent of all adults agree with the statement, "Most employers discriminate against older people and make it hard for them to do a good job." A Michigan Office of Services to the Aging 1985 Needs Survey of the population 60 years of age and older in the state found that 76.9 percent of older adults think age hurts their chances of getting a job and that 63.9 percent think employers discriminate against older people in the workplace (Dluhy 1987). Last year a federal jury in western Michigan found that the Clark Equipment Company illegally discriminated against older workers when it closed its plant in Berrien County specifically to get rid of older workers in favor of younger workers located at a Clark facility in North Carolina. Age discrimination complaints are still not a top priority among civil rights regulatory agencies. This January the Equal Employment Opportunity Commission (EEOC) took no action at all in over 900 cases of age discrimination before procedural deadlines had passed, thereby nullifying the complaints.

But illegal age discrimination is not the only barrier to retaining and retraining older workers. Ageism has its licit side as well. Up until last year, mandatory retirement policies both in the public and the private sector were the most common and acceptable form of age discrimination. Tenured faculty today do not enjoy the protection of Claude Pepper's recent amendment to the 1967 Federal Age in Discrimination Employment Act (1986) that outlawed mandatory retirement based upon age for almost all public and private employees in this country. This change in federal law was a bold declaration that age was no longer to be considered a valid criterion for measuring an individual's capacity to perform in the workplace. It was consistent with the task force's recommendation that mandatory retirement be eliminated in Michigan: a recommendation that Governor Blanchard made the keystone of his address to the 1986 Governor's Conference on Aging. With mandatory retirement now illegal for most employees, the war against ageism can claim a significant victory.

Corporate policymakers and trade union leaders must reconsider early retirement plans as options that benefit the worker who exercises them and, in the long run, the company who offers them. Early retirement incentives can sometimes be nothing more than age discrimination wearing a happy face, as the following evidence suggests. National unemployment figures show that the unemployment rate among persons 50 and over is about half the rate of unemployment of all workers (National Commission for Employment Policy 1987). On the surface, this statistic should be good news. When considered more critically, however, a more alarming statistic emerges. Unemployment rates for older workers are distorted by classifying as "retired" many older workers pushed out of the labor force who would otherwise be classified as "discouraged" or "unemployed." When they do get laid off, older workers experience significantly greater periods of unemployment before returning to work.

"Early retirement" is too often either a severance mechanism of the employer or a response of the worker to continued inability to re-enter the work force. A Bureau of Labor Statistics survey found that 18 percent of the workers displaced nationally between 1979 and 1983 were 55 or older, although workers of that age represent only 13 percent of the labor force (U.S. Department of Labor 1984). And while 65 percent of displaced workers under 65 had found jobs by January 1984, only 37 percent of those 55 and over had done so. Even among older workers who did find work, the unemployment period was 29 percent longer than for others. Among all dislocated workers, less than 14 percent dropped out of the labor force; among dislocated workers over 55, over 25 percent failed to re-enter the work force.

These data suggest that retirement has become synonymous with unemployment for all but those few privileged older adults whose incomes from a number of sources permit them to live comfortably without employment. The stereotype of the happily retired couple, golfing away their days and dancing away their nights in Sun City, Arizona, must be dismissed if we are going to bring our collective wisdom to bear on the rather serious problems facing an aging work force.

Variation in the Older Work Force

The task force's employment and economic development strategies and its support for training and educating older workers presuppose an understanding of the aging work force and the problems endemic to it. Since this volume is attempting to identify problems of this sort and pose constructive solutions that enhance employment opportunities for older adults, let me share my view of another problem we face. In addition to the problem of ageism, public policymakers, academics, and the shapers of the marketplace of human capital must not lose sight of the variability of an aging work force. It may be useful to identify clusters of characteristics that warrant special attention. The older work force tends to fall into five general categories. Let us consider these groups and their problems briefly.

DISPLACED HOMEMAKERS

Women who have met their social responsibilities and now find that the rules have changed are displaced homemakers. Increasingly, the duties performed by a homemaker—raising the children, caring for the elderly, providing food and domestic services to maintain the household—are now carried out by persons outside the family, by either private or public providers. These jobs are still largely performed by women; however, those women who performed these services without wages, on the understanding that they would be taken care of in their old age, are now, through death of or divorce from the wage earner, left without support. Like the skilled machinist of the auto industry, whose job is now performed by a computer-driven robot, these skilled domestic workers have been displaced by new technology and outsourcing in the household economy.

In the state of Michigan, there are 160,000 women between the ages of 55 and 64 working, and another 10,000 looking for work. Among women over the age of 55 working or looking for work, activity is most likely to be concentrated in the low-wage sectors of the economy. The loss of higher-wage jobs and the lack of skills or experience among these women only add to their difficulty. Older women are three times more likely to be working in the technical and sales area than men and only one-tenth as likely to be working in areas of precision production, crafts, and repair. Nearly 40 percent of women aged 45–64 and 25 percent of those 65 and older are working in clerical positions, and nearly 10 percent of women 65 and older are classified as private household workers. Women who are self-employed, those who work for a nonprofit organization, and those who are in the service industry and have held a job for over 10 years are the most likely to continue working after retirement (Social Security Administration 1986).

PERSISTENTLY MARGINAL WORKERS

An older worker may fall into this category because of many factors, ranging from physical or mental disability to illiteracy, problems with alcohol or drugs, or a criminal record. Some careers just never take off; there may be patterns of job-hopping or persistent conflicts with employers. Both can result in a lack of marketable skills or stable employment, despite years in the work force. Race and sex correlate very strongly with membership in the marginal labor force, as past practices that kept women and minorities out of the stable, well-paying jobs continue to show their effects.

Other long-term problems continue to show concentrated effects in the older work force. Nearly 17 percent of older workers in Michigan have less than an eighth-grade education, seriously affecting their ability to retain a job or retrain for a new job in our changing economy (U.S. Bureau of the Census 1980).

DISLOCATED WORKERS

"Dislocated workers" is a phrase currently in use to describe workers who formerly were working but are now without jobs due to changes in the workplace. For an industrial state like Michigan, the contraction in the auto, steel, and mining industries has been particularly severe, not only for blue-collar workers but, more recently, for white-collar workers as well. Decisions by service-sector employers in grocery, retailing, and banking to close or relocate major facilities in the state have dislocated additional thousands of workers. The dislocated industrial workers are often losing high-seniority, high-wage jobs with good benefits and pension plans and must re-enter the job market with old, often obsolete skills and, frequently, a low level of formal education.

INDIVIDUALS WORKING TO SUPPLEMENT SOCIAL SECURITY

When we look at the characteristics of those who continue to work while receiving Social Security benefits, we see (predictably enough) that the major factors are sex, income, and marital status. The worker least likely to continue working after retirement is a married woman. The worker most likely to continue working—more likely than married or unmarried men—is an unmarried woman, particularly if she is in good health, with no pension, and a lifetime of low earnings (Social Security Administration 1982).

SOCIAL WORKERS

There is a category of older workers, widely known anecdotally but difficult to quantify, who continue to work not for income but, essentially, for social reasons. These reasons may include personal beliefs about the importance of work as a means of socialization, the desire to remain mentally alert, or an abiding interest in or commitment to the work group, company, or service delivered. Other older workers use "retirement" as a chance to change careers and undertake something new or of particular interest to them. Such workers are often in high demand because of their experience, commitment to their work, flexibility, and general indifference to conditions of work such as wages or benefits that often constrain other employees.

Each of these sets of older workers creates it own rewards and problems. The Michigan Task Force developed recommendations for responding to these problems through both individual and systematic solutions.

Recommendations for Change

Training or retraining represents one area of response from both the public and private sectors to the problems associated with displaced workers or marginally employable workers. The Job Training Partnership Act (JTPA) requires a 3 percent setaside of federal funds to train persons 55 or over (PL 97-300, 1982). Title V of the Older Americans Act (PL 89-73, 1965) creates a community service employment program for persons 55 and over. The latter program serves both as an employment and training program and as a program subsidizing workers for senior and community services. Under the provisions of Title V, seniors can work for 20 hours a week for a nonprofit community service agency if their income is below 125 percent of the poverty level. In fiscal year 1985, this program provided 62,000 slots nationally and served 98,000 participants; however, 1980 data indicate that only 7 percent of the persons eligible for this program actually participate.

While there are other programs intended to assist older citizens, especially the displaced, dislocated, and poor older adults, the sad fact is that older workers are under-represented in our training and retraining programs. It appears that ageism, as well as economics, is partly responsible.

Most older workers do not participate in retraining programs. Often, both potential participants and program operators feel that older persons with labor market problems cannot successfully re-enter a classroom setting due to their lower educational levels and the long period since they were last in school. Further, because they have fewer years to use the skills they will learn, some administrators, and some older workers themselves, feel that an investment in training is not warranted. Many displaced workers hope to be recalled to jobs in which they can use the skills they possess or in which they have seniority. They are reluctant to enter a training program that may interfere with finding employment in their former occupation or that offers jobs that pay considerably less and are, perhaps, less secure. As a result of these factors, government retraining programs have included only a small percentage of older workers. In the year ending June 1985, only 2 percent of the trainees under the JTPA in Michigan were 55 or older (Michigan Department of Labor 1985).

The cultural bias that suggests that older workers should retire and give way to younger employees also seems to be a factor in the failure of training programs to accommodate the older worker. Therefore, the task force and aging advocates have called for the creation of new jobs as a more direct and effective way to address the problem.

Along with job development, the task force recommended a series of changes in work arrangements, including phased retirement, leaves and sabbaticals, volunteer time, job sharing, flextime, and rehiring work options. These systematic changes could be implemented either through corporate policy changes or collective bargaining agreements that accommodate an aging work force's needs.

Inequities for Women

Before concluding, I want to stress that, as a society, we must confront the inequities that women face with a more equitable and just marketplace of human capital, as well as a full investment of civil liberties for all citizens regardless of age or sex or race. A female work force is emerging that will need employment to survive in our world. Of all women 55 and older, 50 percent are single today, primarily because of widowhood or divorce (U.S. Department of Labor 1984). Many of these women must work to live. The stark truth about the older workers, who do not enjoy the option of retiring to Sun City or West Palm Beach, is that they are females or minorities or poorly educated persons who have been out of the marketplace for most of their lives but now find they must enter the work force or perish.

The feminization of poverty evident among young, single-mother heads of households is often replicated among older women who lose their economic resources through widowhood or divorce or who have had only spotty involvement with the labor market throughout their younger years. These individuals often have no pension rights or benefits attached to their work and, certainly, none to their retirement. Even if they are eligible for Social Security, they have to live on Social Security benefits alone, placing them barely above the poverty level.

Our population, as it ages, becomes increasingly female. If we are to truly venerate and serve the dignity of our elderly citizens, then we must begin in the marketplace of human capital by bringing equity to occupations, transcending a reward system based on age or sex or race. In the marketplace of human capital, black older women should not be favored more than young, white, Anglo-Saxon males, but they should and must have their equal chance to compete in the global economy.

The Policymaker's Challenge

In Michigan as well as in other industrial states, labor relations policy develops at the collective bargaining table much more rapidly than through public mandates from federal, state, or local governments. Indeed, in this era of deregulation and entrepreneurial spirit, which rewards risk unfettered by government interference, it is unrealistic to expect public policy to dictate employer-employee relations policy too dramatically. For example, the Michigan legislature has before it a bill that would mandate parental leave to employees with either children or parents who depend upon them for care. This legislation, which our office supports, has been branded "Public Enemy No. 1" by the State Chamber of Commerce, and small businesses have uniformly opposed it, for many of the reasons that they oppose mandated health insurance for their employees.

In this essay I have attempted to address public policy considerations for an aging work force. I am reminded of the apocryphal story of a state senator years ago who, when asked what public policy was, said, "Public policy is 56 votes in the State House, 20 in the State Senate, and the Governor's blessing. Everything else is just a good idea." While we may be short on public policies for an aging work force by this definition, we are not short of good ideas. We know our challenge. We are, indeed, creatures of an interesting time. We have the tools and the wisdom to change the curse into a blessing, and leave our children and their children a place where social justice and economic justice are here in reality.

References

Dluhy, Milan J. 1987. *Michigan Needs Assessment of the 60 and Over Population.* Lansing: Office of Services to the Aging.

Governor's Task Force on Employment Opportunities for Older Workers. 1986. "Investing in Experience." A report to the Governor of Michigan. Lansing, Michigan.

Louis Harris and Associates. 1981. "Aging in the 80's: America in Transition," national poll conducted for the National Council on Aging, Inc., Washington, D.C.

Meier, Elizabeth L. 1986. "Early Retirement Incentive Programs: Trends and Implications," report for the American Association of Retired Persons Public Policy Institute, Washington, D.C.

Michigan Department of Labor, Bureau of Employment and Training. 1985. "Michigan Statewide Evaluation System. Summary of Participant Characteristics," unpublished paper.

National Commission for Employment Policy. 1987. *Labor Market Problems of Older Workers.* Washington, D.C.: National Commission for Employment Policy.

Social Security Administration. 1982. New Beneficiary Survey No. 10, "Employment of Retired Women," cited in *Social Security Bulletin* 49 (March 1986): 5–10.

U.S. Bureau of the Census. 1980. *Detailed Population Characteristics: Michigan,* Table 239. Washington, D.C.: U.S. Government Printing Office.

U.S. Department of Labor, Bureau of Labor Statistics. 1984. Displaced Workers Survey (unpublished), cited in National Commission for Employment Policy, *Labor Market Problems of Older Workers.*

Part VI
Meeting the Challenge of the Future

Labor Looks at the Aging Work Force

BERT SEIDMAN

Fewer than one-half of employees in the United States have private pension plan coverage, and with deindustrialization even that number is declining. Moreover, reconsideration should be given to the legislation which will change in the year 2002 the age at which employees will be eligible for full Social Security benefits to 67. The problem, moreover, is exacerbated by managements which, increasingly, are shifting from defined benefit *plans to* defined contribution *plans. Similarly, health care issues loom large under the current system of private insurance, Medicare, and Medicaid. Collective bargaining will continue to grapple with the problems of retirement income and health care protection, but, at the same time, unions will continue to seek solutions through the legislative process. This representative of the AFL-CIO describes a nationwide study by the AFL-CIO which reviewed problems of older and retired union members and presents the retired worker program recently adopted by the AFL-CIO Executive Council.*

I. B.

This paper will focus on three major issues as they affect the aging work force: income security, health care, and dependent care. Of course, there are many other issues to which our society will have to respond, but these three must attract priority attention.

Income Security

It goes without saying that as long as workers remain in the work force, wages are their main source of income. Older workers, like younger workers, are therefore principally concerned with wages, benefits, and other terms and conditions of employment. However, because they are close to retirement, their emphasis is also on post-retirement income. As we are all well aware, in the United States the main sources of post-retirement income for the vast majority of people are Social Security benefits and pensions. It is somewhat paradoxical that of these two sources of income, Social Security is the more secure; pensions have become doubtful for many workers. The *Wall Street Journal* made this point in an item published on August 26, 1987: "Major corporate overhauls, job-hopping and family breakups are making retirement benefits less secure." This is particularly true of private pensions.

Fewer than half of current workers have pension coverage, and the percentage is not increasing. In 1950, only 22 percent of the then currently employed had pension coverage. By 1981, this figure had increased to 45 percent. But by 1985, according to a report by the Employment Benefit Research Institute, the figure had slipped back to 43 percent. This slippage can be explained in the same way as the slippage in health care coverage. Jobs for which pension plans are provided are declining in number as deindustrialization and employment retrenchment occur. As a result, large numbers of those who had been protected by a pension plan are no longer covered.

Unlike the private pension plan system, the Social Security system is fiscally sound. Moreover, it provides inflation-resistant benefits. One of the major problems in the years ahead is the scheduled transition, beginning in the year 2002, to 67 as the minimum age at which a retiree can receive full Social Security benefits. This legislated transition is intended to extend the age for retirement. For many, however, it could simple mean a reduction in the Social Security benefit. We still have time between now and the year 2002 to determine whether, in fact, the suppositions which were accepted (in my opinion, far too readily) as the basis for extending the age for receipt of full benefits should be reconsidered. Such reconsideration should also, of course, include the planned reduction of the 80-percent benefit at age 62 to 70 percent, as scheduled in present law. One thing is certain, however: the Social Security system is sound, and workers, upon retirement, will indeed receive their Social Security benefits.

Private pension benefits, however, are considerably more vulnerable to national and international economic developments, and vulnerable as well to the sheer greed of employers. Many workers are finding that their pension security has evaporated because the employer has violated, whether legally or illegally, basic fiduciary principles, including the arbitrary arrogation of pension funds. The increasing shift from a defined benefit plan to a defined contribution plan also exacerbates the lack of security of workers' pensions. Workers in defined contribution plans not only cannot be assured of receiving real benefits in terms of purchasing power; they cannot even be sure that they will receive the same dollar value of their pension. Early retirees are in particular danger as the security of their pension benefit diminishes or evaporates, for they are not yet eligible for Social Security benefits.

Health Care

The second major issue affecting the aging work force is health care. Of the total number of people in our country—old and young, black, white, Hispanic, rural and urban—37 million today have no health care coverage whatsoever, and that number is increasing. Anywhere from two-thirds to three-fourths of those people are in the labor force, many with families. Among them are older workers who have been forced to shift out of jobs where they had decent health care protection, either into unemployment, with no protection at all, or into jobs where there is no health care protection provided or where it is inadequate. Still other workers receive coverage but are victimized by employer takeaways, which narrow their health care protection.

When workers retire, they depend upon Medicare and supplemental health care benefits to meet their health care needs. For many employees, these supplemental health care benefits are provided by the employer, usually with varying degrees of employee cost-sharing. The cost of premiums is often part of a negotiated package and thus is, in reality, borne by the employees, since the amount of money negotiated for this purpose out of the total money package could well have been incorporated as a wage increase or some other benefit of equivalent cost.

A major gap in Medicare is its failure to cover long-term care, either in the home or in nursing homes. It does not cover prescription drugs, hearing aids, eyeglasses, and dental care—all essential for the health care of the elderly. Some or all of these items are included in most employment-based or other supplemental plans. Early retirees (that is, those under age 65) are ineligible for Medicare coverage and must therefore depend entirely on employment-based protection, if available. This is all the more important because the number of early retirees, both voluntary and involuntary, is increasing.

It is evident that deficiencies in employment-based plans are important and must be addressed. The most crucial problem is that they are not funded; moreover, instead of seeking out viable funding mechanisms, many employers simply try to divest themselves of their health care commitments to their retirees. Unless and until the United States adopts a universal health care program, as have all other industrialized countries (with the exception of South Africa), these deficiencies will no doubt swell the ranks of the current one-sixth of the population with no health care coverage.

As is the case with Medicare, employment-based plans do not cover long-term care. It has been suggested that private insurance may fill this gap, but as yet there is little indication that the insurance industry will provide genuine long-term care with all the essential options at an affordable cost. It would be unconscionable to continue to depend on Medicaid as our principal long-term-care program. Medicaid is a welfare program intended only for the poor, and does not represent a viable answer to the problem of long-term care for the entire population.

A recent Brookings Institution report pointed to the fact that while some of the nation's health care problems may appear to be intractable, this is not true of long-term care if we approach it with commitment, in a rational way, and with adequate resources. One thing is quite clear: if we depend upon the private insurance industry to provide it, long-term care for the people who need it will not become a reality soon. Therefore, major reliance will have to be placed on public programs, perhaps supplemented by private insurance for those who can afford it.

Dependent Care

Care of dependents is an intergenerational problem. Increasingly, it embraces not just child care but elder care—often both in the same family. People who are themselves middle-aged or older may be providing care for their older relatives. And both the care-givers and the elders who receive care are likely to be women. The proportion of the national population requiring elder care, especially the "old-old" (those over the age of 80), is growing rapidly and will increase even more rapidly in the future. Unfortunately, community resources to help manage this problem are meager, and employment-based financing of such services is almost nonexistent.

The lack of essential services for the elderly and of assistance for care-givers gives rise to increased absenteeism and tardiness, a lack of concentration at work, emotional stress, and low morale. Some workers faced with the insuperable burden of providing care for older relatives while continuing to work fulltime drop out of employment altogether. And very few employers provide even unpaid, much less paid, leave for care-givers who are caught in this dilemma. It should be noted that such unpaid leave would be required if the Family and Medical Leave Bill were to be passed by the Congress. Here, again, the United States has not yet caught up with other advanced countries, which do have laws covering this subject.

The Union Role: Bargaining for Benefits

Unions will seek in the future, as they have in the past, to negotiate new benefits and to protect existing ones. They will strive to preserve for their members the retirement income and health care commitments they have achieved through collective bargaining. They will insist that employers not walk away from their obligations to their older workers and retirees. Unions will negotiate for employer-funded programs to fill current major gaps in coverage. They will direct increased attention to the issues of long-term care and dependent care, including elder care. The UAW, in its last negotiations with the major automobile companies, succeeded in obtaining an agreement to establish a pilot program for long-term care. This is one of the first programs of its kind negotiated with an employer.

Collective bargaining will be grappling with the growing use of retired workers in part-time work. More and more older workers will retire into part-time work. We can anticipate that more and more retirees will re-enter the labor force as part-time employees—especially as, in the years ahead, there may be a shortage of younger people to fill the jobs that will be available. We can anticipate also that some pension plans will increasingly afford potential retirees numerous options such as phased retirement. Such a development will have a more neutral impact upon a worker's decision to retire. It seems more likely that this greater flexibility of options will be more typical of public employment and expanding industries than of industries hard hit by foreign imports, restructuring, and high unemployment.

LEGISLATIVE CHANGE

The role of the union is, of course, not confined to collective bargaining, and unions will continue to be active on the legislative front. The legislative goals of the labor movement will no doubt include:

- Reconsideration of the requirement, effective in 2002, that Social Security eligibility for full benefits be raised to age 67. If this change cannot be set aside, unions may work toward setting a lower retirement age for certain industries or occupations involving arduous labor and debilitating working conditions, as has been done in several other countries.
- Setting restrictions on the termination of pension funds in cases in which there is no economic duress and on employer appropriation of the assets of pension funds.
- Expansion of government-sponsored health care programs with the ultimate goal of establishing a universal compre-

hensive national health program. On the road to that goal, legislative effort will be directed toward requiring employers to provide basic health care benefits for their employees and their dependents and including long-term care—both home health and nursing home care—as Medicare benefits.

- Establishment of programs of dependent care, including hospice care.

AFL-CIO PROGRAM FOR RETIREES

The AFL-CIO has enjoyed a long association with the National Council of Senior Citizens, whose members include large numbers of retired union members. The AFL-CIO itself has established a Committee on Older and Retired Union Members. Its past chair was Douglas Fraser, former president of the United Auto Workers; its current chair is William Winpisinger, president of the International Association of Machinists. This committee studies and reviews problems related to older and retired union members and submits policy and action recommendations for adoption by the Executive Council of the AFL-CIO.

Under auspices of the AFL-CIO and fourteen international unions, the National Institute for Work and Learning has recently concluded a major three-part study which includes an elaborate questionnaire survey of retired members of the unions which sponsored the study, as well as a sample of retired members of other AFL-CIO affiliates. The study also included a telephone survey of activities undertaken by local unions related to concerns of older and retired members. The third part of the report comprises the findings from field studies in five metropolitan communities. The detailed questionnaire was mailed to 11,417 retirees throughout the country and received a phenomenal 62 percent response, particularly impressive as it required from one to two hours to complete. Moreover, many of the respondents added explanatory comments.

Based on the findings of this study, on August 22, 1988, the AFL-CIO Executive Council adopted a statement that retired union members are valuable resources for organized labor and the nation as a whole and that it is the responsibility of the AFL-CIO and its affiliated unions to develop policies and programs to keep retirees in the union family. It pledged to involve retirees in educational programs, organizing drives, legislative initiatives, and various community activities. The National Council of Senior Citizens will be an essential partner in this important endeavor. The Executive Council urged its affiliated international and local unions as well as state and local central bodies, within the limits of their resources, to consider implementing a series of recommendations drawn up by its Committee on Older and Retired Union

Members. These recommendations were addressed, respectively, to national and international unions, state and local central bodies, and the AFL-CIO.

National and international unions were urged to:

- establish an internal structure for developing policies and programs concerning retirees;
- ensure that retirees are accepted as part of the union family, with various forms of continued membership suggested;
- maintain contact with retired union activists who could be called upon to organize retirees for political campaigns, organizing drives, legislative initiatives, and labor education efforts;
- develop pre-retirement programs;
- work with employers to develop voluntary, mutually acceptable flexible work schedules for retirees where such schedules are appropriate; and
- assist local unions in establishing retiree clubs, with such activities and programs as planning pre-retirement programs, negotiating post-retirement health insurance, publicizing names of doctors who accept Medicare assignment, and maintaining job banks for members interested in post-retirement work.

State and local central bodies were urged to:

- support the development of retiree clubs by local unions or, when appropriate, by regional and district bodies;
- facilitate education programs;
- encourage local colleges and universities to offer special programs for seniors;
- negotiate discounts for retirees with utility companies, local merchants, transit systems, and theaters and other entertainment centers;
- publish, if possible, a periodic retiree newsletter; and
- stimulate AFL-CIO Community Services representatives and labor agencies to develop programs aimed at and served by retirees.

Finally, the AFL-CIO itself pledged to:

- establish an advisory committee to its Committee on Older and Retired Union Members, composed of retired union members and AFL-CIO and international union staff members responsible for retiree issues;

- work with the Committee on Older and Retired Union Members to improve services to retirees and coordinate and promote retirement activities within the Federation.
- assist international and local unions in developing their preretirement and retiree programs; and
- work with state and local central bodies in developing their retiree activities.

The goals are to involve more unions, affiliate more retirees, develop more and better programs and services for retirees, and to do all this in close coordination with the National Council of Senior Citizens. The measure of success of this enhanced program will be the extent to which it enriches the lives and enhances the contribution of union retirees in the years to come.

Extending Working Life

JEROME M. ROSOW

Today there are incentives to retire early and incentives to prolong working life. Rosow's data indicate that a large minority of older workers prefer employment to retirement. Redesign of work schedules and of jobs, reassignment and relocation opportunities, education and retraining programs, part-time work, and phased retirement are some strategies suggested here to accommodate this preference, which, he notes, is also in the national interest. Rosow points out that changes in public policy as well as private behavior are required in this effort, and that employers and labor unions must work with government toward this goal.

I. B.

The aging of the work force in the United States has made the extension of working life an urgent policy issue. This, therefore, is the focus of this paper.

In section I we examine the Forces Restraining the Extension of Working Life, and in Section II we examine the Forces Prolonging Working Life. The third section highlights some of the issues relating to national employment policy changes which would be necessary to extend working life, and the most extensive discussions are in the fourth section, Options for Extending Working Life. These include: 1) Redesign of Work Schedules; 2) Redesign of Jobs; 3) Transfer and Reassignment; 4) Reassignment with Lesser Responsibilities; 5) Work-Education Combinations; 6) Part-Time Work; 7) Phased Retirement; 8) Recall of Annuitants; 9) Second Careers and Small Business Opportunities; and

Much of the research reported here is based upon an updating of a policy study published in 1982, carried out by the Work in America Institute, entitled *The Future of Older Workers in America*, and its companion casebook, *Young Programs for Older Workers*.

10) Outplacement. Finally, the paper presents some concluding observations with regard to the future.

I. Forces Restraining the Extension of Working Life

Early retirement. Corporate restructuring, "downsizing," mergers, and acquisitions have accelerated massive personnel cuts, with early retirement the most popular method of achieving this goal. The labor force participation rate of men 55–64 has dropped sharply, from 80.47 percent in 1972 to 67.3 percent in 1986 and projected to drop to 63 percent by the year 2000.

Hiring practices. Custom and practice continue to discriminate against older workers, particularly in the hiring of people over 50.

Youth culture. Our society assumes that young people are the primary source of the vitality, dynamism, and up-to-the-minute knowledge needed to run a successful enterprise.

Economy and labor market. Millions of older Americans who would like to enter or re-enter the work force cannot work because the slow-growth economy creates too few jobs, the minimum is too low, and labor exchanges are inadequate.

Labor cost control. Pressure to cut labor costs leads employers to reduce the number of older workers first because, age group for age group, they cost more than younger workers.

Labor union policy. Labor union policy is pointed toward better and earlier pensions. Unions also view early retirement as a means of work-sharing.

Negative stereotypes. Stereotyped ideas about the health, vigor, competence, productivity, and ambition of older workers often become self-fulfilling prophecies.

National policies. The lack of training programs, the failure to allocate resources, and the absence of a coordinated employment policy reduce the employment of older workers. Social Security law contains disincentives to work, especially for those in the 65–69 age group. In addition, the cost of working (transportation, meals, clothes, etc.) reduces net take-home pay.

II. Forces Prolonging Working Life

National policy. Current law, giving due regard to the rapidly rising cost of Social Security because of increasing benefits and greater longevity has, effective in the year 2022, increased to age 67 eligibility for the full Social Security benefit.

Human resource policy. Changes in the Social Security and tax laws, elimination of the mandatory retirement age, pension indexing, and the demographic shift increase the need to retain older workers and in the long term may deter employers from encouraging early retirement.

Economic necessity. Inflation, which erodes pensions, may induce employees to continue working. The elimination of the mandatory retirement age enables them to do so.

Psychosocial needs. Improvements in health, vigor, and longevity encourage older workers to continue their attachment to the world of work.

Better jobs. In the years ahead the higher educational levels of older workers mean that a higher proportion will hold better jobs and therefore will have a stronger desire to remain at work.

Better balance between work, family, and leisure. Expanding use of flextime and part-time work will allow a better balance among competing needs and changing life styles.

III. The Role of National Employment Policy

For each dollar of earned income over the minimum amount, those 63 to 69 years of age lose fifty cents in Social Security benefits; when earnings rise high enough, the entire benefit is cancelled. One of the principal obstacles to older workers remaining actively in the work force, fulltime or part-time, is these earnings caps and tax penalties. They create a strong disincentive to re-enter the labor force and tend to disrupt or limit the duration and continuity of the work pattern. The penalty restricts or precludes the most flexible and promising employment opportunities, namely, part-time work and temporary work over the course of an entire year.

In November 1987, Health and Human Services Secretary Otis Bowen advised the White House that the repeal of the earnings limitation for people over 65 would represent a relatively minor increase in Social Security outlays. In a program aggregating $240 billion a year, this $7.5 billion in benefits that otherwise would not have been paid could be spread over five years. After deducting administrative costs of $200 million annually to enforce the earnings limitation, which would no longer be incurred in Bowen's plan, the net cost would be $6.5 billion, or about $1.3 billion per year—about one-half of 1 percent of the current annual outlay.

The General Accounting Office reviewed trends and costs of early retirement in 1974, 1979, and 1984. Its analysis revealed that:

1. pension receipts increased more rapidly for those under age 65 than for those over age 65;
2. labor force participation was lower for persons with employer-sponsored pensions than for nonrecipients;
3. most retired voluntarily, but a significant number below age 62 retired due to poor health or disability;
4. some 11 percent of men and 8 percent of women recipients aged 55–61 were unable to find employment;
5. early retirement represented a significant loss in federal revenues: for example, if 10 to 25 percent of voluntary retirees (aged 50–64) returned to the labor force, tax revenues could increase anywhere from $550 million to $1.4 billion.

The current Social Security law limits the amount of work per year, restricts jobs choice, and is especially harsh on the more skilled and educated people, who have higher earning potential. The law is designed to reduce employment of older people, while U.S. demographics point to increased need for their services. Elimination of the earnings limitation would remove an existing disincentive to continue working.

Social Security lifetime benefits at present peak in value at age 64 and decline thereafter. Thus the 65- to 69-year-olds are penalized in two ways: by working at all and by continuing to pay Social Security tax while they do work.

When we consider the low and declining participation rates of workers over 65, we realize the size and variety of personnel in the labor pool. Even assuming that only a portion of these people prefer work to full retirement, the potential numbers remain quite high. A 1985 survey by Gallup for the American Association of Retired Persons (AARP) shows that almost 30 percent of their registered members would prefer some paid employment; after adjusting for health problems and age, about 15 percent are reported as able and ready to work. With the amendment of Social Security to remove existing disincentives, that proportion would increase significantly.

There are other advantages to the nation:

- active employment tends to promote a healthy, useful old age;
- improved health among the employed moderates the financial burden on the health services industry and the Medicare program;

- annuitants become active workers and contribute directly to GNP growth as producers;
- older workers enjoy increased income, a higher standard of living and self-esteem, and contribute to GNP growth as consumers;
- the need to join the underground economy is reduced, and a higher proportion of all earnings produces a tax revenue;
- the sidetracked talent pool of skilled and experienced older (aged 50–64) workers would be mainlined into the labor force to offset some of the serious demographic shortages in the decade ahead.

Recent legal improvements include:

- elimination of mandatory retirement at age 70, which removes a legal distinction and creates an open-ended option for extended working life, limited only by health, opportunity, and choice;
- continuation of pension accrual for employees who work after reaching age 65 (or the firm's normal retirement age), which provides equity and the incentive to work longer;
- stricter regulations on integrating Social Security and pension benefits, so that retired employees must receive at least half of the accrued employer benefits, to be consistent with the tax imposed upon employer and worker;
- two shortened vesting period choices, the five-year "cliff" or the three- to seven-year "graded" plan (20 percent after three years with 20 percent increments per year) (effective 1989, some union contracts to 1991), which will provide better pension coverage and could provide the building blocks for portable pensions.

These positive reforms have limited effect on the early retirement trends, however, nor do they address the problems of re-entry into the labor force.

IV. Options for Extending Working Life

REDESIGN OF WORK SCHEDULES

The Bureau of Labor Statistics survey of work schedules of May 1985 presents the most representative and valid information of flexible work schedules for fulltime wage and salary workers in the United States. According to the report, about 12 percent of all workers were on flexible work schedules. This is a considerable improvement from the conditions two decades ago, when flexible work schedules were virtually unknown. In an analysis of occupational characteristics, the data reveal that managerial and professional occupations were almost twice as likely as others to have flexible work schedules, with about 22 percent of these occupations enjoying this type of flexibility.

It is interesting to note that about 17 percent of all men aged 65 or older are on flexible schedules, substantially above the national average. This is a low-cost strategy with great appeal to older workers and an excellent potential payout to the employer. The Gallup survey for AARP in 1985 noted that flextime ranked first among all incentives that might keep people working past retirement age: 50 percent of women and 39 percent of men cited this factor.

Fortunately, work schedules in America have been responding to changes in the labor force, the feminization of the work force, and work/family stresses. A study by the Administrative Management Society of 500 large companies found that flextime scheduling has doubled in the past ten years, rising from 15 percent to 30 percent. While these data are more typical of large firms with advanced personnel policies than of medium-sized and small companies, they do represent an encouraging shift in the proper direction.

Since these schedules allow the individual some latitude in deciding which hours or days to work, and since the employer provides greater choice, they fit older workers with reduced home responsibilities. They can work earlier, later, evening shifts, or overtime, in time periods which are more difficult for younger people with family responsibilities.

The Gallup poll also reflected substantial interest (33–40 percent of women and about 30 percent of men) in job sharing, the compressed work week, and phased retirement. Employers will tend to respond to these preferences not for societal reasons but because of a tightening labor market.

REDESIGN OF JOBS

Changing technology, along with the demographically induced need to retain and make better use of older workers, will motivate employers to redesign jobs. Jobs should be redesigned to reduce undue stress, whether physical or mental, which often impairs the performance of older workers. The firm which ignores such stress may be losing many of its best employees prematurely, incurring excessive costs for workers' compensation, or risking lowered performance.

The rationale for redesigning jobs to increase productivity, reduce job monotony, eliminate waste, improve quality, and increase worker motivation applies as much to younger as to older workers. Multi-skilling and flexibility are critical factors in cost-effectiveness. Some older workers may learn a bit more slowly, but they retain the new knowledge as well as younger people.

Another goal should be to mix younger and older workers more fruitfully within each work unit in order to produce a better interchange of training and skills. As the demand for older workers increases during the next twenty years, and as more displaced homemakers enter or reenter the work force, job duties and schedules will have to be adapted to the needs of these workers.

Hitherto, experimentation with redesign has been directed mainly to blue-collar and junior office jobs, with outstanding results when programs are well planned and well executed. Much less attention has been paid to redesign of managerial, professional, and technical positions, reflecting the lower relative numbers of these jobs, the difficulty of defining their content, and the variety and subtlety of the skills they involve. More attention should be focused on middle-management, professional, and technical jobs, many of which are poorly designed. Planning, coordination, and facilitating duties should receive greater emphasis; less demanding tasks and decisions should be assigned to lower levels. Redesign is particularly important when senior people occupy these jobs.

The need for job redesign is intensified by widespread corporate reorganizations. Although these radical shifts in corporate structure and demassing have affected older workers disproportionately, they also mandate the urgency of radical job redesign to accommodate to lean staffing and new forms of decisionmaking. The Gallup survey of 1985 reflected high interest in working beyond retirement age in a redesigned job; over one-third reported job redesign as an incentive to stay on the job. This could include reduced responsibility, reduced hours, and reduced compensation.

Redesign should open many options for improved organizational relationships and provide an additional escape valve for pent-up job pressures.

TRANSFER AND REASSIGNMENT

What accounts for these movements? According to David L. Birch, in a study entitled *The Job Generation Process,* branching is the main form of corporate expansion:.

> Virtually no firms migrate from one area to another in the sense of hiring a moving van and relocating their operations. The oft-cited move of textiles and shoes from New England to the South represented a rare fluke in the 1950s, not an example of a significant process today.

> The rate of job loss . . . is about the same everywhere and is quite high—8 percent each year. Northern cities are not losing jobs faster than southern ones, nor are cities losing jobs particularly faster than suburbs.

Often a shift coincides with the closure of an old plant, with the result that a significant proportion of middle-aged and older workers have to choose between losing jobs and accepting a transfer or reassignment to a new location. It has generally been assumed that older workers are less willing to relocate than younger ones. In fact, readiness may depend more on occupational status or family situation than on age. With the exception of executive ranks, the job mobility of the average American worker has not been very high, and even among managers some observers have noted increasing disinclination to accept transfer and reassignments. People whose children attend school in the local community are generally least mobile.

Many older workers whose children are in postsecondary schools or have already entered the work force may be willing to move to the Sun Belt, with a view to finding a more desirable climate for eventual retirement. In many locations, particularly within the Sun Belt, employers find older workers to be a significant proportion of potential hires. Older people are a principal human resource in Florida, where the population now includes about two million retirees.

When employers are hiring for a new site, they should seek a balance between older and younger employees. Older employees are demonstrably more stable, and a leavening of them will offset the tendency of younger people to change jobs.

Management should also adopt the policy of reassignment of older workers to different duties. This policy can raise their productivity and give them a new lease on life by utilizing their long experience more fully and enabling them to make a more valued contribution. In many projects designed to improve the quality of work life in recent years, companies have made good use of senior workers on problem-solving teams, quality-review teams, projects to improve productivity, and other tasks where they can apply knowledge and wisdom to problems which have important long-range implications for the firm. These workers can be freed from the day-to-day responsibilities which confine their skills, experience, knowledge, and common sense to a narrowly focused area.

Japanese companies have been especially daring in this respect. During business recessions, for example, senior workers in some firms are assigned to serve as paraconsultants on quality-control problems, changes in work methods or processes, and studies of customer relations. The fact that these workers have job security until retirement compels employers to view them as long-term investments which must be managed for the highest long-term return.

In the United States, General Motors is one of a number of companies experimenting with mixed teams of people drawn from different specialties, both in autonomous work teams and in special problem-solving groups. The problem-solvers are given company facilities and a budget and meet once a week to develop new ideas about how the business ought to be run. According to the company, a great many challenging proposals have emerged, of which some are already being applied successfully.

Reassignment of jobs in lieu of retirement was favored by about 30 percent of the respondents in the Gallup survey cited above.

REASSIGNMENT WITH LESSER RESPONSIBILITIES

When Danish managers were asked in a 1978 survey whether they preferred demotion to early reitrement, a resounding 70 percent opted for demotion. The survey, conducted by the Danish Institute for Personnel Management, asked 1,285 managers in 154 of Denmark's largest companies how they would react to the prospect of being replaced by a younger executive, provided that there were no changes in job title or reductions in salary. Nearly three-quarters of the managers over the age of 54 and 46 percent of those between 40 and 54 indicated that they would accept the change in jobs. Only 8 percent of executives under the age of 40 agreed.

When the question was reframed to include downgrading in title as well as responsibility and a 10 percent reduction in salary, 28 percent of the managers over 55 years old still said that they would prefer this type of demotion to early retirement. Another 28 percent would accept if the change also entailed reduced work effort.

In the United States a few companies have experimented with demotion. Maremont Corporation has had ten years of experience with what it describes as "down placement." At the Kellogg Company in Battle Creek, Michigan, where most of the company's 8,000 workers are employed, the firm has experimented successfully on a small scale with offering lower-level positions as an alternative to termination or reassignment.

The Danish experience with demotion suggests that employers should consider allowing workers to take a voluntary reduction of responsibility and pay provided that the negative connotations of demotions can be avoided. A reassignment should decrease the difficulty and responsibility of the job without implying that the change was either punitive or the individual's fault. Because American society has tended to worship promotion for its own sake, even when it leads to work assignments which are too onerous, too stressful, or unsuited to the talents of the individual, the very word "demotion" sounds punitive and deprecatory.

Work organizations might therefore investigate the attitudes of their long-service employees toward voluntary reduction of responsibilities. Whenever these reassignments occur, the firm should be sensitive to the need for saving face. In some cases, pay may remain the same or be protected for a specified time. Status symbols, job title, size of office, continued supervisory responsibility, or access to line management are also important.

We may need to invent a new language for reduction of responsibilities. There are a great many cases in which an employee considers it socially respectable to retire early, to accept a transfer, or to move to a less lucrative occupation or job. If a similar rationale can be applied to voluntary reassignments, they need not be seen as humiliating, and early retirement will not be the first option in so many cases.

WORK-EDUCATION COMBINATIONS

Employers should develop arrangements whereby employees can gain further education or training while still keeping their status with the firm. The outstanding issue in expanding these arrangements, however, is how to finance fulltime training or education for people who have substantial financial responsibilities. A number of alternative schemes is possible.

Since it is uncommon to find a middle-aged or older person who can afford to go to school fulltime without help or an employer who will pay for support of dependents, a number of alternative financing schemes may be developed. In some multiple-worker families, a combination of savings and company loans might suffice. Loans could be drawn against a company thrift and savings plan, at either no or low interest, to allow employees to attend an educational institution fulltime and then return to the firm. Arrangements for part-time work in the company might also be feasible.

Another means of financing might be a temporary lien against the employee's pension. The worker could borrow against future pension benefits and repay by payroll deductions over a number of years after returning to work. The company might forgive all or part of the repayment after the education had been successfully completed or after a certain period of demonstrated work performance back on the job. Indeed, the firm could, as a training bonus, forgive part or all of a loan in return for several years of good performance in a more demanding or higher-skilled job than the one held before the educational furlough.

These work-education combinations differ fundamentally from the usual tuition-refund plans. Actual separation of the employee from the firm in order to be retrained or to continue education on a fulltime basis, with re-employment rights, is much more effective than attending night school or taking one or two courses per year.

Another financing method might be through unemployment insurance benefits. Present regulations in most states allow a person to draw these benefits only when out of the labor force and available for gainful employment. An individual attending school fulltime is considered unavailable for work. State law could be amended to allow persons pursuing education as an interval from work to qualify for unemployment insurance benefits.

PART-TIME WORK

According to the Bureau of Labor Statistics annual survey for 1985, an average of 18 million Americans—one out of every six workers—worked part-time. The part-time work force has grown considerably but relatively slowly, according to the BLS. In 1968, 14 percent of the work force was working part-time; in 1988 the proportion is almost 18 percent.

Part-time work is one of the strongest incentives cited in the 1985 Gallup survey for choosing to work past retirement: 47 percent of women and 38 percent of men indicated this as a preferred option. The National Older Workers Information System (NOWIS) has a database for 1982–83 personnel practices which includes information on 180 companies representing 369 programs and practices. These data indicate that 50 percent of the companies surveyed hired older workers for part-time or temporary employment. Using pools of retirees to meet ongoing temporary and part-time employment needs has been a growing phenomenon, as is the recall of specialists and experts to meet short-term requirements.

The increased use of temporary help and the growing reliance upon firms such as Manpower and Kelly Services have fostered a new industry to fill the vacuum which exists in the current labor market exchange systems. There are many reasons for the use of these services, related to flexibility, cost, and greater sensitivity to fluctuating work loads. There is every indication that the use of temporary employees will continue to increase, especially in the light of corporate "demassing" and the increased reliance on more flexible staffing. There is also a strong motivation for employers to use the temporary help industry as a means of avoiding an employment contract and the responsibility for benefit costs (although part of the benefit cost saving is passed through in the fee structure).

However, despite the growth of this industry and the prospects for continued expansion, it has been slow to respond to services for blue-collar workers and, especially, for managerial, technical, and professional personnel. Agencies will ultimately enter this market because of high compensation levels and the rise in demand as American industry restructures. However, they are not the most cost-effective or efficient means of serving older workers. The nation needs new, vigorous employment services in all major metropolitan areas.

The older men and women with managerial, technical, and professional experience over their life career represent a talent supply which is largely disconnected from employer demands, nor are older workers trained to locate employment. They lack job search skills and are at a marked disadvantage in the competitive marketplace. Yet these people present a significant pool of talent which needs to be exploited.

Part-time work, whether temporary or permanent, will be increasingly the most favored method for retraining and hiring older workers. They are ready to slow the work pace; they need partial income; they do not want to lose the rhythm of work; and they want to continue the social, psychological, and professional benefits of work. Part-time is usually a happy compromise between retirement and full-time work or a means of continuing productive activity while phasing into a new career or job.

Part-time work can be infinitely varied in scope, comprising not only a specified number of hours per week but also alternating weeks, alternating months, and seasonal or periodic work. While part-time jobs have increased at more than double the rate of full-time jobs in both the private and public sectors, they are still more apt to be found in sales and clerical areas or in laboring than in professional or managerial positions. The BLS states, "The higher the job skills and the degree of supervisory responsibilities, the less likely is the worker to be employed on a part-time basis." However, the massive corporate restructuring of the past few years has stripped away many older, expert people, creating unmet needs. An effective response would be the part-time employment of older persons with the experience and knowledge.

Currently there are many more people desirous of working part-time than there are part-time jobs. In these circumstances, employers feel no need to offer attractive benefits to part-timers. The number of part-time jobs is also depressed by the Employee Retirement Income Security Act's requirement that benefit coverage be provided for any employee who works more than 1,000 hours annually.

We recommend that employers make part-time work more attractive by prorating employee benefits in proportion to fulltime work. Fulltime and part-time workers have usually been regarded as separate and distinct species, so that fulltime workers who move to part-time often lose their benefit protection. The goal should be benefits that meet management's reasonable cost objectives and at the same time give part-time workers fair treatment. If a union is present, these part-time arrangements will be bargained collectively. In the absence of a union, companies should still take soundings among employees to ensure that the formula is acceptable and that costs are kept in line.

We predict that part-time jobs will gradually lose their image of second-class employment, not only because they are growing steadily but also because they meet an important need, particularly among older workers, and most of all in times of high inflation. In many work organizations, such as large retail stores, part-time employees are already a primary part of the labor force. When employers do decide that it makes sense to hire people part-time, they develop effective ways to work out the benefit arrangements.

To give two examples, Toro, a fast-growth Minneapolis company, has 65 of its 4,200 employees on part-time, on either a permanent or overload basis. Permanent part-timers work between 20 and 40 hours a week. They are eligible for profit sharing if they put in at least 1,000 hours a year, and they receive five days of paid vacation for each 1,000 hours worked. A few older employees work three days a week. To make part-time work more attractive, the company is considering adding medical and life insurance benefits.

In Kansas, the Wichita Board of Education accepts teacher-initiated job-sharing arrangements, in which each member receives half of the base pay and half of the benefits and teaching credits. In addition, 1978 state law allows board employees to retire at 60, receive their pensions, and be rehired into any job for which they are qualified. The new law is expected to give a big boost to job sharing, making possible many fruitful combinations of older and younger teachers.

Employers who need more part-time workers and cannot offer an attractive total benefits package can expect higher turnover, lower motivation and productivity, and greater difficulty in hiring qualified people.

Numerous advantages of part-time employment have been cited by both public and private employers: increased flexibility in managing heavy workloads or in scheduling personnel for peak hours, reduced absenteeism and turnover, retention of skilled and experienced employees who want to reduce their hours, extension of service hours to the public, and recruitment of people with specialized skills who may not be available for fulltime work.

On the other hand, there may be real negatives: a bigger management load, the employment of more people, more instability in the work force because part-time workers sometimes feel less committed to employment than fulltime workers, more variations in part-time work styles, and the potential for lower morale if fulltime workers resent the flexibility afforded to part-time employees. Other disadvantages mentioned by employers are increased administrative costs for training, supervision, paperwork, and office needs; possible increased costs of fringe benefits; and possible reduction of authorized positions when part-time people replace fulltime employees. These adverse factors apply more to irregular and temporary part-time than to permanent part-time employment.

The major obstacle to expanding permanent part-time opportunities may be the belief, shared by managers and supervisors, that part-time employees are not really committed to the job, despite many examples to the contrary. Permanent or regular part-time jobs, which enable older people to work on a less demanding schedule and yet retain certain benefit arrangements, give the employer the best four or five hours of that person's day. The most desirable situation for an older worker is to work part-time with the organization that previously employed him or her fulltime. Wider use of shared jobs may be the key to these arrangements.

PHASED RETIREMENT

Phased retirement is a concept which has benefits for both career employees and the employer. It provides a planned mechanism for reducing either the responsibilities or, more typically, the amount of time at work over an extended period of one or more years. As a transition process, it provides an opportunity for the individual to experience reduced work and reduced income and to gradually change from fulltime employment to fulltime leisure. These programs depend to a high degree on planning within the organization, with a strong element of choice, and are geared into phased retirement planning. If extended, they would reduce the suddenness and the irreversible nature of full retirement. The expanded use of early retirement programs and the generous application of special incentive programs to encourage early retirement probably have aborted the development and expansion of phased retirement practices in many cases.

However, in the Work in America study in 1980, we did develop information with regard to these practices which is worth repeating here as models for the future.

In a study of retirement by the Conference Board, "Retirement: Reward or Rejection," 21 companies—only 2 percent of the sample—were found to have experimented with phased (also called "gliding" or "gradual") retirement. This is the practice of allowing employees to reduce their hours of work as they near retirement. Of the 21 companies, 7 were insurance firms, whose high proportion of office and white-collar workers may lend itself more easily to gradual retirement.

Employers should provide options for phased retirement as a means of giving employees a chance to sample the leisure and the new activities of retired life before actually taking the plunge. This offers a reasonable transition from fulltime work to retirement.

Two distinct approaches were evident among the 21 firms surveyed. Phased retirement before the normal retirement age was allowed by 16 companies. These companies, which regarded the plan as an integral part of the benefits package, paid the employee for the time off. The other five provided phased retirement after the normal retirement age and did not pay for time off. In some cases, the plan was compulsory; in others, the time off was meant to induce the employee to continue working part-time during a period of semi-retirement. For example:

—At Wrigley Company, employees approaching normal retirement age could taper off over a three-year period, starting at age 62. They could take one month off (without pay) in the first year; two months in the second; three months in the third. Subsequent pension benefits increased by 8 percent per month to compensate in part for the lost wages.

—Towle Silver Company granted workers 40 paid days off over the four months before retirement: one day per week during the first month, two days per week during the second, and so on.

—New England Mutual Life Insurance Company's plan allowed extra paid vacation time after age 62: two weeks the first year, three weeks the second year, and so on.

Employee reactions to phased retirement plans are varied. Both the Wrigley and Towle plans have been functioning for many years, however, which indicates that they respond to a felt need.

RECALL OF ANNUITANTS

Callback of annuitants from retirement has proved cost-effective, especially in high-technology and financial firms, where older workers' skills are scarce or hard to replace. Aerospace Corporation hired annuitants as short-term consultants for up to 20 working days a year. Of 100 consultants at the company in 1970, 40 were annuitants. A few were employed for longer periods, on special contracts.

—Lockheed Corporation in 1978 hired 12 annuitants for a wide variety of jobs.

—Northrop Corporation had an on-call force of annuitants who were allowed to work up to 60 days at a stretch but then had to take 30 days off. They received pension payments and an hourly wage and could rejoin the savings plan.

—General Electric Aircraft Engine Group had 25 to 30 annuitants on annual retainer, based on 50 to 100 days of work a year.

Sun Company announced that it wanted annuitants for 200 temporary jobs and received 600 applications—10 percent of all its annuitants. Most of those hired worked full eight-hour days.

—Bankers Life & Casualty Company had a pool of 35 annuitants on temporary or part-time basis, mainly doing clerical work.

—Each year, Morgan Guaranty Trust Company of New York, which retired about 70 employees, hired about 50 annuitants to handle proxies and coupon bonds during peak periods and to fill in during summer vacation. For performing these services, they received hourly wages and their pension payments, plus a few small benefits.

Companies should provide the flexibility for managers to recall annuitants on a consulting basis. For many seasonal demands—preparing annual reports or budgets, peak sales loads, inventory taking, production peaks—it makes sense to use annuitants who know the ropes rather than to look outside. The policy obviously has to be moderated by the existing labor force situation: if middle-aged employees have few chances to advance, calling annuitants back for anything other than short-term noncompetitive assignments would arouse hostility.

When annuitants are recalled, new pension arrangements or credits may have to be worked out. Normally, the annuitant will accrue additional pension rights for fulltime employment, although other arrangements may be acceptable. Full benefits coverage should be given while the annuitant is actively employed. It may also be feasible to recall annuitants without changing their pension status, particularly if they are used as part-time consultants for a short period of time.

A Work in America study offered another example of part-time arrangements. Sundstrand Data Control, Inc., in the state of Washington, had a shortage of engineers and technicians. Although the work force was young, with only 30 annuitants in 1979, 6 of them (5 engineers, 1 technician) had returned to work, some as temporary employees (paid hourly while continuing to draw a pension), others fulltime (with salary plus fringes, with no pension payments, but with credits accruing toward a second pension).

If and when the amount of Social Security earnings is not reduced by an earned income test, phased retirement and callback from retirement will be even more attractive to retirees. At the same time, we can anticipate that the callback of annuitants from retirement will increase in the short term over the next few years, since many companies have elected early retirement programs as the preferred instrument for massive staff cutbacks. Those programs are all largely voluntary and have been very penetrating, and they have inevitably led to the loss of high-talent, highly productive people who have special skills and knowledge that are not readily replaced. Rather than recruit, train, and develop new and younger people for these critical needs, companies will find it more cost-effective to recall some of these annuitants, many of whom are relatively young and all of whom can adapt to the task at hand with virtually no start-up time.

SECOND CAREERS AND SMALL BUSINESS OPPORTUNITIES

There is a certain romantic notion that employees long to become entrepreneurs. Many companies have flirted with the idea of separating the older worker by early retirement and encouraging himor her to embark on a new career as a self-employed business person. The effectiveness of self-employment is a function of the age and vigor of the individual, the capital resources available, and, just as important as these two factors, the effectiveness of the market research with regard to the opportunities and competition in the enterprise being considered.

Further, the person starting a small business is often baffled, if not defeated, by the need for technical and professional advice on legal, financial, and marketing matters. There is little evidence to suggest that the small business opportunity is the long-term answer to second careers for older workers in any large numbers. However, it does represent an attractive and different option with higher risks and more exciting challenges for those individuals who have the drive, talent, and staying power to make such a transition.

Employers should assist employees who want to start a second career of their own business. In many cases, it may be cheaper—and better for morale—for the firm to provide such assistance than to continue paying the salary of an employee who wants to leave. In addition, large companies may find that former employees can become useful subcontractors and vendors.

OUTPLACEMENT

In dealing with surplus personnel, especially older workers, more use should be made of outplacement—assisting these people to find suitable jobs with other employers. This is a successful and growing technique for recycling talent. The same techniques are applicable and useful for all occupational groups, since there is no inherent reason why the company owes more loyalty to one group than to another. Outplacement may also make it easier to terminate a failing work relationship and may thus remove one major source of anxiety when older workers are hired.

The process, carried out sometimes by in-house staff, but perhaps more often by outside consultants, usually has two stages. First, a pre-termination interview allows the employee to vent shock, anger, and frustration and then is directed toward more rational consideration of alternative goals and aspirations. In the second stage, which continues until placement, the employee gets down to cases. Daily counseling sessions cover testing, the development of goals and résumé, listing of contracts, practice interviews, and analysis of actual interviews.

Many outplacements find new jobs that pay more than the ones they left. Two-thirds of placements are in jobs that did not exist before (which bears out the assertion that 80 to 90 percent of employment opportunities are never publicized). Employees over age 55, because of their high pay and status, are the hardest to place, which brings us back to the starting point, hiring.

The majority of retired older workers have had limited experience in job search. In addition, they have a sense that age discrimination prevails in employer practice (which may be exaggerated), which acts as a psychological barrier to re-employment. Because they have no training in considering the various options that exist, they have difficulty connecting with effective community resources. When they do, job search programs which exist in the community are inadequate to the needs of society and especially inadequate to the needs of these workers.

Displaced workers can be relocated in part-time or fulltime employment with firms in the industries in which they have been working. If they downscale their search to medium and small companies that would benefit greatly from their experience, their chances are increased significantly. The growing shortage of young people in the labor force from now to 1995 opens a window of opportunity for older workers, since many firms will continue to experience labor shortages. The predominance of small and medium-sized firms in the United States underlines the diversity of opportunities to redeploy older workers (caught by early retirement programs) from larger firms to new jobs in a smaller setting. Such workers bring valuable, sophisticated experience to bear at low cost with high payouts to the employer.

Conclusion and Recommendations

The goal of extending working life in a manner consistent with demographic and gerontological trends remains out of reach. The favorable forces are blocked by custom, practice, and lack of infrastructure. The nation has yet to provide a true measure of equal employment opportunity for workers over age 50.

National employment policies have not faced up to the complex issues presented by the unprecedented effects of longevity and the need to retain older Americans in the work force in the coming decades. In 1986 there were about 10.4 million men aged 55–64 in the civilian population, but only 67 percent of these men participated in the labor force; about 3.4 million men were out of the labor force. Projecting to the year 2000, of 11 million men in this age group, only 63 percent will participate in the labor force, while 4 million men will be out, many of whom are willing and able to work. The economic and social consequences of these wasted resources are enormous and require action now.

The enriched incentives for those in well-funded private pensions to retire early have lowered the retirement age to 50 in many cases, as these one-time special incentives have been too tempting to refuse. These programs have been accelerated in the past few years as corporations reduce and downsize their work forces. Although socially preferable to dismissal, forced early retirements have relegated relatively young people in the prime of their careers with major financial commitments to the ranks of the unemployed. Many of them are forced to withdraw from the labor force permanently, yet they have 20 to 25 years of productive energy remaining in their lifespan.

The current Social Security law continues to impose an unrealistic earnings test which penalizes workers aged 65 to 69. Repeal would make Social Security more of an annuity program. Unless, and until, this penalty is removed, the incentives to work are limited. In fact, the law at the present time induces people to draw benefits and enter the underground economy and/or limit their earnings to the earnings test ceiling. The initial costs of this reform would be modest and would ultimately be offset by increased tax revenues.

A variety of options for the extension of working life are available to employers who are progressive enough to engage the services of older workers in a cost-effective manner, including redesign of schedules; redesign of jobs; transfer and reassignment; reassignment with lesser responsibilities; work-education combination; part-time work; phased retirement; recall of annuitants; second careers and small business opportunities; and outplacement.

Legal remedies to reduce discrimination are significant and valuable. However, they are not addressed to the re-employment of older workers who have been displaced from their careers. The critical area for attention is the recycling and re-entry of workers aged 50–54 for extended career employment.

Labor market exchange systems are very limited and inadequate to the needs of society, especially for workers over age 50. Federal, state, and local government policies should interface with employers and their organizations to create an effective exchange system in major labor markets which would attract an active supply of older workers and match them up with the demands of employers.

Private and public employment policies require the combined efforts of employers, labor unions, and government. A coordinated and forward-looking national policy should address the needs of older workers in terms of retraining, labor market services, incentives to work, and demographic factors.

References

Birch, David L. 1979. *The Job Generation Process*. Cambridge, Mass.: MIT Program on Neighborhood and Regional Change.

"Danish Survey Suggests Demotion for 'Obsolete' Managers; Finds Execs Prefer Lesser Jobs to Retirement," *World of Work Report*, November 1978, p. 92.

Gallup Organization. 1985. *American Association of Retired Persons—Older Worker Study*.

General Accounting Office. 1984. *Report on Early Retirement*. Washington, D.C.: General Accounting Office.

Horvath, Francis W. 1987. "The Pulse of Economic Change: Displaced Workers of 1981–1985," *Monthly Labor Review*, June, pp. 3–12.

Jacobson, Beverly. 1980. *Young Programs for Older Workers: Case Studies in Progressive Personnel Policies*. New York: Van Nostrand Reinhold Company/Work in America.

"National Older Workers Information System," *Working Age*, January/February 1988.

O'Meara, J. Roger. 1977. "Retirement: Reward or Rejection." The Conference Board, New York.

Work in America Institute. 1980. *The Future of Older Workers in America: New Options for an Extended Working Life*. New York: Work in America Institute, Inc.

Afterword

The aging of the U.S. population will continue to have a major impact on all aspects of American society. Over two decades ago, the passage of the Older Americans Act and the creation of Medicare as an addition to the Social Security program publicly recognized the special needs of this rapidly increasing group. Since that time, the proportion of the population over 65—in particular, the "old-old," those over 85—has continued to grow at an unprecedented rate. The older population is no longer a small minority within the larger population, and income security, adequate health care, and the productive employment of older persons must now be the concerns of society as a whole.

The contributions to this volume testify to the many manifestations of this new demographic phenomenon in the workplace and the wide range of strategies that have been implemented in response. Yet the issues are complex, and the solutions not always clear. Our writers from the academic community, business, labor, and government have outlined for us the facts of the new situation and have indicated the ways in which such issues as pensions, health care, and continuity of employment have been experienced by individual companies and labor organizations. Despite the diversity of the contributors' viewpoints, we can identify several common themes in these essays.

There seems to be agreement that past public and private policies operated to encourage or force retirement at ever younger ages, and that there are now good grounds for questioning their appropriateness and desirability. Whether for reasons of age discrimination or of sound fiscal management, the retirement age must be re-examined. Along with the notion of "retirement age" itself, however, we are told that assumptions about the skills and abilities of older workers, their productivity, and their ability to benefit from training and retraining must be questioned. We are told, in fact, that retirement, in the form in which we think of it today, will itself become a variable rather than a constant in the demographic equation, and that a variety of forms of partial retirement and part-time employment of those at retirement age, described by many contributors, must be scrutinized.

A second theme that emerges is that of income security. As the years of life after retirement are extended for greater numbers of workers, income security in the last years of life becomes a very serious matter. Pension plans and programs that were designed within the context of the Social Security program of earlier decades may not adequately meet the needs of future retirees. Again, both public and private pension policies beg for re-examination.

Health care and health insurance are also major concerns in these essays. The growing cost of care, in combination with the increase in the numbers of those who use the greatest amount of it, has placed health insurance at the top of many observers' lists of concerns. Guaranteed delivery of adequate health care at a reasonable cost has become an item for the labor-management bargaining agenda all over the country and has prompted a variety of changes in company policies and practices, as well as research efforts by all parties.

Finally, and probably most important, our contributors all stress the need for an attack on these societal problems on many fronts. Income security, adequate health care, and productive employment of our older citizens will not be accomplished by industry, organized labor, or government acting alone. For an older society to be fair, responsive, and equitable to its members, cooperation and creativity are required from *all* partners in this new American enterprise.

Index

The book was designed by James Billingsly. The typeface for the text and the display face is Galliard. The book is printed on 50-lb. Glatfelter paper and is bound in Holliston Mills Roxite B grade cloth.

Manufactured in the United States of America.